Hegel's Philosophy of Freedom

Hegel's Philosophy of Freedom

Paul Franco

Yale University Press

New Haven and London

Published with assistance from the Ernst Cassirer Publication Fund.

Printed in the United States of America.

Library of Congress Cataloging-in-Publication Data

Franco, Paul, 1956–
Hegel's philosophy of freedom / Paul Franco.
p.   cm.
Includes bibliographical references and index.
ISBN 0-300-07832-3 (cloth : alk. paper)
ISBN 0-300-09322-5 (pbk. : alk. paper)
1. Hegel, Georg Wilhelm Friedrich, 1770–1831—Contributions in political science.   2. Hegel, Georg Wilhelm Friedrich, 1770–1831—Contributions in the concept of liberty.   I. Title.
JC233.H46F73   1999
320'.092—dc21   99-22437
                          CIP

A catalogue record for this book is available from the British Library.

The paper in this book meets the guidelines for permanence and durability of the Committee on Production Guidelines for Book Longevity of the Council on Library Resources.

10 9 8 7 6 5 4 3 2

for Jill, Clare, and Sam

Contents

Preface

For the past thirty years or so, there has been a tremendous revival of interest in Hegel's social and political philosophy. At first largely motivated by the quest for the origins of Marx's project, this revival of interest has begun to focus on Hegel as a thinker in his own right, and one with perhaps something more profound to offer than Marx. The trend has been to see Hegel as a thinker who, without abandoning many of the principles associated with liberalism, provides a penetrating critique of some of its key assumptions deriving from the Enlightenment—for example, its atomistic conception of the self, its negative conception of liberty, its rationalistic and ahistorical conception of society, and its impoverished conception of community and the social good. For so-called communitarian writers—Charles Taylor most prominent among them—Hegel's political philosophy has thus come to represent an important alternative, or at least the seed of an alternative, to current utilitarian and Kant-inspired versions of liberalism.

Although there is much that is exaggerated or problematic in the communitarian interpretation of Hegel, it does begin to touch on the real significance of Hegel for us at the end of the twentieth century.

For me this lies in his providing a powerful interpretation of freedom and reformulation of liberalism that does not rest on the questionable assumptions mentioned above. Hegel offers us a way out of the atomism and narrow self-interest of traditional liberal theory. And he offers us a conception of the social good that is more inspiring than that of mere security of life and property. Moreover, he does all this without sacrificing the individual rights and liberties that constitute the central political ideals of liberalism. To characterize Hegel's political philosophy thus perhaps risks making it sound too good to be true. But the study that follows, without denying that there are difficulties, will try to demonstrate that Hegel is largely successful in defending the modern, liberal social order on a basis that goes beyond liberalism and does not fall prey to its debilitating individualism.

The thread that runs through my interpretation of Hegel's political philosophy is Hegel's idea of freedom. To focus on Hegel's idea of freedom is not, of course, to pick out a merely incidental aspect of his philosophy. Human freedom is the first, last, and in many respects *only* theme of Hegel's political philosophy. It is, of course, also the central theme of liberal political thought and of modern political philosophy in general. But the freedom that the Hegelian state ultimately realizes is not simply the "negative" freedom to pursue one's empirical desires in an unobstructed fashion that is found in Hobbes and Locke and all of their liberal progeny. Rather, it is the "positive" freedom that springs from the will's being determined by nothing outside itself, or merely given, but only by what accords with its free and rational nature; it is freedom understood in terms of rational self-determination, radical self-dependence, autonomy. This positive idea of freedom as rational self-determination or autonomy was introduced into modern political philosophy by Rousseau, and it was systematically developed by Kant and Fichte. Much of this study is devoted to bringing out Hegel's relation to this tradition of reflection on human autonomy, indicating how he appropriates it and just where he modifies it. Indeed, I will argue that Hegel's political philosophy represents the high-water mark of this idealist tradition of thought, which itself constitutes the most profound modern European reflection on freedom.

Where does my interpretation fit in the general drift of recent scholarship on Hegel's political philosophy? Early on in the recent Hegel revival, the focus was mainly on vindicating Hegel of the charge (made by Karl Popper, among others) of fascism and totalitarianism. Z. A. Pelczynski and Shlomo Avineri led the way in this apologetic effort. But while their work served as a useful corrective to the Hegel-as-totalitarian myth, it also tended to drain Hegel's political philosophy of its radical implications by focusing on his conventional political opinions instead of on his more original philosophical reasons. This conventional liberal picture of Hegel was significantly altered in the "communitarian" interpretation of Hegel (best exemplified by Charles Taylor's *Hegel*), which reclaimed Hegel as a critic of liberalism, stressing his divergence from the individualism, rationalism, and universalism of Enlightenment modernity. Although this communitarian approach begins to recapture the originality and relevance of Hegel's political philosophy, it also understates Hegel's link to Enlightenment modernity, especially in its Kantian guise, and exaggerates Hegel's affiliation with certain romantic themes such as organic unity, wholeness, overcoming alienation, and so forth. This distortion has begun to be redressed, notably in Allen Wood's *Hegel's Ethical Thought* and the work of Robert Pippin.[1] Wood's book has become the standard for current work on Hegel's ethical and political thought, though his approach differs from mine in its "analytic" and vaguely "left Hegelian" orientation as well as in its jettisoning of Hegel's logic and metaphysics (in this Wood follows Taylor). Pippin's work is of special interest to me because it brings out Hegel's significant affinities with the modern project of autonomy as it unfolds from Rousseau through Kant. I, too, am particularly concerned with establishing Hegel's relationship to this modern, liberationist tradition of thought, bringing out the originality of his solutions to certain problems arising within it, but without seeing him as presenting a communitarian, romantic, or nostalgic alternative to it.

So much for the larger themes of the book. I proceed by carefully explicating and interpreting Hegel's texts, primarily the *Philosophy of Right*. The *Philosophy of Right* is, of course, the definitive statement of Hegel's mature political philosophy. It also belongs to that select group of masterpieces in the literature of political philosophy that includes Plato's *Republic*, Aristotle's *Politics*, Hobbes's *Leviathan*, and Rousseau's *Social Contract*. Unlike these books, however, the *Philosophy of Right* presents immediate challenges of access to even the most equipped and persevering of readers. My experience in studying and teaching the book does not confirm Alan Ryan's assertion that "Hegel's *Philosophy of Right* is not in the least difficult."[2] In chapters 4–8, therefore, I provide a detailed commentary on the *Philosophy of Right,* bringing out the underlying coherence of the argument and relating it to Hegel's other writings, especially his unpublished lectures on the philosophy of right. My aim is not only to demonstrate the larger philosophical themes mentioned above but also to illuminate the details of Hegel's dense masterpiece and make it more accessible to the general student and teacher of political philosophy.

The full meaning of the *Philosophy of Right,* however, does not disclose itself within the boundaries of its two covers. It is a text which emphatically requires a context within which to understand it; and this I provide in chapters 1–4. In chapter 1, I sketch the essential philosophical background—the tradition of reflection on autonomy and politics that runs from Rousseau through Kant and Fichte—against which I intend to view Hegel's political philosophy. In chapter 2, I provide an overview of Hegel's early political philosophical development up to 1806. Here I have sought to contain my consideration of Hegel's early writings so that it does not overwhelm the central focus of this study, namely, Hegel's mature political philosophy as it is articulated in the *Philosophy of Right.* Nevertheless, these early writings are vitally important for understanding some basic concerns and themes that run through Hegel's political philosophy. In chapter 3, I treat the moral and political ideas of the *Phenomenology of Spirit.* This most fascinating and obscure of Hegel's works marks the end of the intellectual development considered in chapter 2, and it lays out the view of European history that underpins the whole of Hegel's mature political philosophy. Finally, in chapter 4, I give a brief account of Hegel's logic in connection with his idea of philosophical method. The argument of the *Philosophy of Right* is incomprehensible without some acquaintance with Hegel's logic; and a serious defense of Hegel's political philosophy cannot avoid addressing the issues raised by it. Here again, though, I have tried to prevent my consideration of Hegel's logic from overwhelming the focus on the political philosophy or expanding this study to unmanageable proportions.

In the Epilogue, I offer a critical assessment of Hegel's political philosophy, indicating its practical relevance to the understanding of liberal democracy at the end of the twentieth century. Recognizing that not every aspect of the Hegelian state is applicable to contemporary social and political reality—for example, its patriarchal conception of the family, its quasi-medieval division of society into sharply defined estates and corporations, and its limitations on democracy—I nevertheless argue that the general framework it embodies remains one from which we may continue to learn. From its emphasis on the family, religion, and the mediating institutions of civil society, to its concern with curbing the subjectivism of romantic culture, the individualism of economic activity, and the atomism of mass democracy, the Hegelian state continues to offer one of the most compelling solutions to the problems posed by modern liberal democracy. Admittedly, Hegel's rather grandiose vision of the state as the realization of rational freedom does not fit well with the skeptical temper of our times. But I argue that contemporary skeptical or nonmetaphysical accounts of liberalism may err on the side of the too little, neither fully capturing the liberating vision of liberalism nor containing the necessary moral resources to sustain it.

The writing of this book has been generously supported by grants from several institutions, including the National Endowment for the Humanities, the Olin Foundation, the Earhart Foundation, and Bowdoin College. The students in my Kant-Hegel seminar at Bowdoin have contributed enormously to my understanding of what is dark and requires explanation in Hegel's political philosophy. Paul Stern has carefully read and helpfully commented on portions of the manuscript. Even more important, his friendship and encouragement, along with that of my colleague Jean Yarbrough, have sustained me over the years of writing it. Finally, thanks to my wife, Jill, and children, Clare and Sam—the invisible (but not inaudible) basis of my existence to which habit may sometimes blind me but a moment's reflection leads me constantly to bless.

Abbreviations

References to Hegel's works appear in the text with the following abbreviations. I have generally relied on the English translations, though in a number of instances I have modified the translation slightly; some of the older translations I have altered more radically. Reference to the English pagination is followed by the German, separated by a slash (/). In works cited by paragraph (§), R stands for Remark and A for Addition.

Werke   *Werke in zwanzig Bänden.* Edited by E. Moldenhauer and K. Michel. Frankfurt: Suhrkamp, 1971. Cited by volume and page number.

A   *Aesthetics: Lectures on Fine Art.* Translated by T. M. Knox. 2 vols. Oxford: Clarendon Press, 1975. Cited by volume and page number. *Werke* 13–16.

"BF"   "Berne Fragments." In *Three Essays, 1793–95.* Translated by Peter Fuss and John Dobbins. Notre Dame: University of Notre Dame Press, 1984. *Werke* 1:47–101.

BP   *The Berlin Phenomenology.* Translated by M. J. Petry. Dordrecht, Holland: D. Reidel, 1981. German facing.

"DFS"   *The Difference Between Fichte's and Schelling's System of Philosophy.*
Translated by H. S. Harris and W. Cerf. Albany: SUNY Press,
1977. *Werke* 2:8–138.

EL   *The Encyclopedia Logic.* Translated by T. F. Geraets, W. A. Sucht-
ing, and H. S. Harris. Indianapolis: Hackett, 1991. Cited by paragraph (§). *Werke* 8.

EPS   *The Encyclopedia Philosophy of Spirit.* Translated by William Wallace and A. V. Miller as *Hegel's Philosophy of Mind.* Oxford: Clarendon Press, 1971. Cited by paragraph (§). *Werke* 10.

"ERB"   "The English Reform Bill." In *Hegel's Political Writings.* Translated
by T. M. Knox. Oxford: Clarendon Press, 1964. *Werke* 11:83–128.

FK   *Faith and Knowledge.* Translated by W. Cerf and H. S. Harris.
Albany: SUNY Press, 1977. *Werke* 2:287–433.

FPS   *First Philosophy of Spirit.* Translated by H. S. Harris. Albany:
SUNY Press, 1979.
1803–4 *Philosophie des Geistes. Gesammelte Werke.* Edited by Rhein-
isch-Westfälischen Akademie der Wissenschaften. Hamburg: Felix
Meiner, 1968– . 6:265–326.

GC   *The German Constitution.* In *Hegel's Political Writings.* Translated
by T. M. Knox. Oxford: Clarendon Press, 1964. *Werke* 1:449–581.

HHS   *Hegel and the Human Spirit: The Jena Lectures on the Philosophy of
Spirit of 1805–6.* Translated by Leo Rauch. Detroit: Wayne State
University Press, 1983.
1805–6 *Philosophie des Geistes. Gesammelte Werke.* Edited by Rhein-
isch-Westfälischen Akademie der Wissenschaften. Hamburg: Felix
Meiner, 1968– . 8:185–288.

HP   *Lectures on the History of Philosophy.* Translated by E. S. Haldane
and F. H. Simson. 3 vols. London: K. Paul, Trench & Trübner,
1892–96. Cited by volume and page number. *Werke* 18–20.

IPH   *Introduction to the Philosophy of History.* Translated by Leo Rauch.
Indianapolis: Hackett, 1988. *Werke* 12:11–141.

L   *Hegel: The Letters.* Translated by Clark Butler and Christiane Seiler.
Bloomington: Indiana University Press, 1984.
Hegels Briefe. Edited by Johannes Hoffmeister and Friedhelm
Nicolin. 4 vols. Hamburg: Felix Meiner, 1981. Cited by volume and
page number.

"LJ"   "The Life of Jesus." In *Three Essays, 1793–95.* Translated by Peter
            Fuss and John Dobbins. Notre Dame: University of Notre Dame
            Press, 1984.
            Das Leben Jesu. In *Hegels theologische Jugendschriften.* Edited by
            Hermann Nohl. Tübingen: Mohr, 1907. Pp. 75–136.

LNR   *Lectures on Natural Right and Political Science.* Translated by J.
            Michael Stewart and Peter C. Hodgson. Berkeley: University of
            California Press, 1995. Cited by paragraph (§).
            Vorlesungen über Naturrecht and Staatswissenschaft. Edited by the
            Staff of the Hegel Archives. Hamburg: Felix Meiner, 1983.

LPHI   *Lectures on the Philosophy of World History: Introduction.* Translated
            by H. B. Nisbet. Cambridge: Cambridge University Press, 1975.
            *Vorlesungen über die Philosophie der Weltgeschichte: Band 1: Die
            Vernunft in der Geschichte.* Edited by Johannes Hoffmeister. Ham-
            burg: Felix Meiner, 1955.

NL   *Natural Law: The Scientific Ways of Treating Natural Law, Its Place
            in Moral Philosophy, and Its Relation to the Positive Science of Law.*
            Translated by T. M. Knox. Philadelphia: University of Pennsylva-
            nia Press, 1975. *Werke* 2:434–530.

"PC"   "The Positivity of the Christian Religion." In *Early Theological
            Writings.* Translated by T. M. Knox. Chicago: University of Chi-
            cago Press, 1948. *Werke* 1:104–229.

"PEAW"   "Proceedings of the Estates Assembly in the Kingdom of Württem-
            berg." In *Hegel's Political Writings.* Translated by T. M. Knox.
            Oxford: Clarendon Press, 1964. *Werke* 4:462–597.

PH   *The Philosophy of History.* Translated by J. Sibree. New York:
            Dover, 1956. *Werke* 12.

PP   *The Philosophical Propaedeutic.* Translated by A. V. Miller. Oxford:
            Basil Blackwell, 1986. *Werke* 4:7–301.

PR   *Elements of the Philosophy of Right.* Edited by Allen Wood. Trans-
            lated by H. B. Nisbet. Cambridge: Cambridge University Press,
            1991. Cited by paragraph (§), except for Preface, which is cited by
            page number. *Werke* 7.

PS   *Phenomenology of Spirit.* Translated by A. V. Miller. Oxford:
            Clarendon Press, 1977. *Werke* 3.

R   *Lectures on the Philosophy of Religion.* Translated by R. F. Brown,
            P. C. Hodgson, and J. M. Stewart. 3 vols. Berkeley: University of

California Press, 1984–87. Cited by volume and page number. *Werke* 16–17.

"RDA"   "On the Recent Domestic Affairs in Württemberg." In *Hegel's Political Writings*. Translated by T. M. Knox. Oxford: Clarendon Press, 1964. *Werke* 1:268–73.

"SC"   "The Spirit of Christianity and Its Fate." In *Early Theological Writings*. Translated by T. M. Knox. Chicago: University of Chicago Press, 1948. *Werke* 1:274–418.

SEL   *System of Ethical Life*. Translated by H. S. Harris and T. M. Knox. Albany: SUNY Press, 1979.
System der Sittlichkeit. Edited by Georg Lasson. Hamburg: Felix Meiner, 1967.

SL   *Science of Logic*. Translated by A. V. Miller. London: George Allen & Unwin, 1969. Cited by volume and page number. *Werke* 5–6.

"TE"   "The Tübingen Essay." Translated by H. S. Harris. In *Hegel's Development: Toward the Sunlight, 1770–1801*. Oxford: Clarendon Press, 1972. Pp. 481–507. *Werke* 1:9–44.

VPR   *Vorlesungen über Rechtsphilosophie (1818–31)*. Edited by K.-H. Ilting. 4 vols. Stuttgart: Fromann, 1974. Cited by volume and page number.

VPR19   *Philosophie des Rechts: Die Vorlesung von 1819/20*. Edited by Dieter Henrich. Frankfurt: Suhrkamp, 1983.

Chapter 1 Autonomy and Politics: Rousseau, Kant, and Fichte

It is a reliable, if not altogether surprising, principle of interpretation that in order to understand a political philosopher one must understand him in his context. But what constitutes the appropriate context in which to consider any particular political philosopher? In the case of a minor or second-rank thinker, of course, the appropriate context may consist of the particular historical or political circumstances in which that thinker's thought takes shape. But in the case of a truly great or first-rank political philosopher—and to this select class Hegel surely belongs—such a narrow construction of the interpretive context will fail to grasp what is most distinctive and important in his political philosophy. In the case of the great political philosopher, nothing less than the whole history of political philosophy can serve as the appropriate context in which to understand his thought and against which to measure his achievement. This is the context in which I view Hegel's political philosophy in this book. Hegel's *Philosophy of Right* belongs to that select group of masterpieces in the literature of political philosophy that includes Plato's *Republic*, Aristotle's *Politics*, Hobbes's *Le-*

viathan, and Rousseau's *Social Contract*; and it is in the context of these masterpieces that it deserves to be read.[1]

The history of political philosophy as it stretches from Plato to Hegel is not, of course, a homogeneous continuum. It can be divided into a variety of more specific traditions; and it is within one of these more specific traditions that Hegel's political philosophy must be situated. The most fundamental divide in the history of political philosophy is that between ancient and modern political philosophy. There are, no doubt, a number of different ways in which this fundamental division between ancient and modern political philosophy might be characterized, but perhaps the most decisive contrast—and certainly the one most relevant to my purposes in this book—concerns the place of freedom. Whereas modern political philosophy begins, ends, and is animated throughout by the idea of freedom, ancient political philosophy takes its bearings from the idea of a natural order discernible by reason to which human beings ought to conform. As M. B. Foster puts it in his insightful book comparing the political philosophies of Plato and Hegel:

> Modern political theories differ from ancient principally in making freedom the ground, end, and limit of the state; however much modern theories may differ from one another, according to the variety of meanings which freedom may bear, these differences sink into relative insignificance when they are seen to be differences only in the interpretation of a principle which all have in common and in virtue of which they may all be contrasted with the ancient theories that the state is natural.[2]

Regardless of the significant modifications he wreaks upon it, Hegel develops his political philosophy wholly within the framework of the modern standpoint of freedom.

Though the modern tradition of political philosophy is characterized by near unanimity on the question of the centrality of freedom in understanding political life, there are significant differences in the way in which this central principle has been interpreted. Again simplifying somewhat, two main outlooks may be distinguished in modern reflection on freedom. The first, shared by such otherwise different thinkers as Hobbes, Locke, Hume, Bentham, and Mill, conceives of liberty largely in terms of the ability to pursue our wants and desires without obstruction or interference. This is what Isaiah Berlin has denominated the "negative" conception of liberty,[3] and it receives its most succinct expression in Hobbes's famous definition of freedom as the "absence of external impediments."[4] Beginning with Rousseau, however, another, more "positive" conception of freedom enters the bloodstream of modern political philosophy. This conception may be understood as a radicalization of the idea of self-determination that belongs to the earlier, negative conception of freedom. But self-determination now no longer means simply the unfettered pursuit of one's empirical desires, whatever they happen to be; rather, it means being determined by those desires or impulses that reflect one's own most authentic or spiritual nature; it means radical self-dependence or (to use the Kantian term) autonomy. This idea of freedom as radical self-determination, self-dependence, or autonomy was, of course, taken over from Rousseau by Kant and Fichte and significantly developed by them.[5]

It is in the context of this tradition of reflection on freedom that runs from Rousseau through Kant and Fichte that Hegel's political philosophy ultimately must be seen. Indeed, it is the contention of this book that Hegel's political philosophy constitutes the high-water mark of this particular tradition, providing the most profound and compelling application of the idea of freedom as radical self-determination or autonomy to the realm of politics. The demonstration of this contention, however, must await the full elaboration of Hegel's political philosophy in the following chapters. This chapter will be concerned only with giving a somewhat fuller account of the tradition of political philosophy that runs from Rousseau through Kant and Fichte, indicating just how Hegel's political philosophy develops out of it, and briefly sketching at the end just how his political philosophy modifies and ultimately contributes to this tradition.

ROUSSEAU

In seeing Rousseau as the crucial turning point in the tradition of modern political philosophy, I am doing no more than following Hegel himself. "[I]t was the achievement of Rousseau," Hegel writes, in a passage that recurs throughout this book, "to put forward the *will* as the principle of the state, a principle which has *thought* not only as its form (as with social instinct, for example, or divine authority) but also as its content, and which is in fact *thinking* itself" (*PR*, §258R). It might seem that the innovation Hegel here ascribes to Rousseau, namely, making will the basis of the state, could just as easily be ascribed to Hobbes or to any of the other early modern thinkers who sought to ground political authority in individual consent. But such a supposition mistakes the exact nature of the innovation Hegel is attributing to Rousseau. It is true that in the modern natural right teachings of Hobbes and Locke "right and ethical life came to be looked upon as having their foundation in the present will of men," instead of in the external commands of God or the purely positive rights found in "old parchments" (*PH*, 440/522). In this regard, Hegel sees Hobbes as the pivotal figure. Before Hobbes, "ideals were set before us, or Holy Scripture or positive law was quoted as authoritative. Hobbes on the contrary sought to derive the bond which holds the state together and the nature of state-power from principles which lie within us and which we recognize as our own" (*HP,* III, 316/226). But this alone does not quite reach to Rousseau's theoretical achievement. Though Hobbes and Locke undoubtedly make free will the basis of the state in a certain sense, they do so only with respect to the genesis or form of the state and not with respect to its content. The latter remains grounded in the natural or empirical desires of self-preservation or property protection. It is only with Rousseau, Hegel argues, that free will is made both the form and content of the state. It is only with Rousseau that freedom was recognized as "the distinguishing feature of man" and that there came "into consciousness as content the sense that man has liberty in his spirit as the altogether absolute, that free will is the notion of man" (*HP,* III, 401–2/306–7).

What Hegel is driving at here needs to be fleshed out by glancing at some of Rousseau's major writings on politics and connecting them with the idea of radical self-determination or self-dependence alluded to above. The place to begin is with the *Discourse on the Origins of Inequality,* for it is here that Rousseau presents his most scathing indictment of the sort of civilized man that forms the basis of the political theories of Hobbes and Locke, what Rousseau sometimes refers to as the "bourgeois."[6] While the Lockean bourgeois may indeed enjoy the security of life and property in civil society, he is otherwise a slave, according to Rousseau, dependent on others, on opinions, on technology, and on wealth. In the *Second Discourse,* Rousseau brings out the unfreedom and radical dependence of civilized man by constantly contrasting it with the freedom, independence, and self-sufficiency of the natural man. Of the latter, he writes:

> [W]andering in the forests, without industry, without speech, without dwelling, without war, without relationships, with no need for his fellow men, and correspondingly with no desire to do them harm, perhaps never even recognizing any of them individually, savage man, subject to few passions and self-sufficient, had only the sentiments and enlightenment appropriate to that state; he felt only his true needs, took notice of only what he believed he had an interest in seeing; and his intelligence made no more progress than his vanity.[7]

Civilized man, on the other hand, as a result of the division of labor and the emergence of private property, is subject, by virtue of a multitude of fresh needs, to all of nature and particularly to his fellowmen, whose slave in a sense he becomes even in becoming their master; rich, he needs their services; poor, he needs their help; and being midway between wealth and poverty does not put him in a position to get along without them. It is therefore necessary for him to seek incessantly to interest them in his fate and to make them find their own profit, in fact or in appearance, in working for his. . . . [C]onsuming ambition, the zeal for raising the relative level of his fortune, less out of real need than in order to put himself above others, inspires in all men a wicked tendency to harm one another, a secret jealousy all the more dangerous because, in order to strike its blow in greater safety, it often wears the mask of benevolence; in short, competition and rivalry on the one hand, opposition of interest on the other, and always the hidden desire to profit at the expense of someone else.[8]

Rousseau concisely sums up the difference between the natural man and the civilized bourgeois in the penultimate paragraph of the *Second Discourse:*

Savage man breathes only tranquility and liberty; he wants simply to live and rest easy; and not even the unperturbed tranquility of the Stoic approaches his profound indifference for any other objects. On the other hand, the citizen is always active and in a sweat, always agitated, and unceasingly tormenting himself in order to seek still more laborious occupations. . . . Such, in fact, is the true cause of all these differences: the savage lives in himself; the man accustomed to the ways of society is always outside himself and knows how to live only in the opinion of others. And it is, as it were, from their judgment alone that he draws the sentiment of his own existence.[9]

The *Second Discourse* graphically shows that Hobbes's and Locke's solution to the problem of civil society is no solution. The security of life and property provided for by classical liberalism are purchased at the price of human dignity and freedom. Bourgeois civil society is simply the war of all against all carried on by other, more hypocritical means. This does not mean that we must return to the state of nature. As every careful reader of Rousseau knows, he does not think it is either possible or desirable for human beings to return to the original state of nature.[10] The state of nature merely serves to illuminate the essence of human nature, the essential freedom and independence that originally characterized human beings, and to measure how far modern society has fallen away from this essence. The fundamental problem of civil society is to establish conditions in which the essential freedom and independence of human beings is preserved while they coexist and cooperate with one another. Rousseau proposes two different, though not unrelated, solutions to this problem in the two major works he published in 1762, the *Emile* and the *Social Contract.*

In the *Emile,* Rousseau sets himself the task of overcoming the dividedness and hypocrisy of the bourgeois by educating the individual to be a natural man. Such a natural man, however, is not to be confused with the savage in the state of nature; he is not a solitary but will ultimately take his place among others in civil society. "There is a great deal of difference," Rousseau writes, "between the natural man living in the state of nature and the natural man living in the state of society."[11] Nevertheless, Rousseau hopes to produce in the natural man living in the state of society the essential qualities of freedom, independence, and self-sufficiency that characterized man in the state of nature. The whole thrust of the elaborate education Rousseau gives to Emile is to insure that the latter's desires, fueled by imagination, do not outstrip his ability to satisfy them; only in this way can Emile avoid an enslaving dependence on others. The latter is the great evil to be averted. "The only one who does his own will," Rousseau writes, "is he who, in order to do it, has no need to put another's arms at the end of his own . . . The truly free man wants only what he can do and does what he pleases."[12]

The freedom and independence Rousseau speaks of here is threatened from the moment the child is born and, crying out, seeks to manipulate those around him to satisfy his whims and desires. With the infant's tears begins the fateful cycle of domination and servitude that continues into civil society.[13] The greatest challenge to the freedom and self-mastery of the individual, however, comes from the awakening of sexual desire. Rousseau treats this challenge at some length in Books IV–V of the *Emile,* showing how, in paradoxical fashion, imagination and the sentiment of love can be used to regulate the passions and render Emile moderate.[14] The final outcome of Emile's education is that he is made into a virtuous individual. Anticipating Kant, who was, of course, greatly influenced by the *Emile* early in his career,[15] Rousseau equates the virtuous man's mastery of his passions with true freedom. The virtuous man, he writes, "is he who knows how to conquer his affections; for then he follows his reason and his conscience; he does his duty; he keeps himself in order, and nothing can make him deviate from it. Up to now you were only apparently free. You had only the precarious freedom of a slave to whom nothing has been commanded. Now be really free. Learn to become your own master."[16] The natural man Rousseau forms in the *Emile* is ultimately the morally autonomous man.

In the *Social Contract,* Rousseau presents a different solution to the problem of human freedom or self-determination in civil society. In the *Emile,* the natural man Rousseau forms remains somewhat aloof from civil society. Although he must eventually take his place in civil society, he never really fully engages with it. His freedom consists mainly in independence and self-sufficiency.[17] In the *Social Contract,* on the other hand, Rousseau seems to have a different image of human freedom or self-determination in mind: that of the republican citizen who actively participates in politics and in doing so genuinely governs himself. Rousseau gives some indication of the radical difference between these two solutions toward the beginning of the *Emile,* when he argues that, in educating the individual, "one must choose between making a man or a citizen, for one cannot make both at the same time." The natural man and the citizen are two distinct human types, each free and self-determining in its own way:

> Natural man is entirely for himself. He is a numerical unity, the absolute whole which is relative only to itself or its kind. Civil man is only a fractional unity dependent on the denominator; his value is determined by his relation to the whole, which is the social body. Good social institutions are those that best know how to denature man, to take his absolute existence from him in order to give him a relative one and transport the *I* into the common unity, with the result that each individual believes himself no longer one but a part of the unity and no longer feels except within the whole.[18]

Freedom or wholeness is to be found either in cultivating the individual's natural dispositions or in completely denaturing the individual. To look for a compromise between these two alternatives and try to accommodate the natural passions within civil society—Hobbes's and Locke's solution—leads only to the self-division and hypocrisy of the bourgeois, who is "always in contradiction with himself, always floating between his inclinations and his duties."[19]

In the *Social Contract,* then, Rousseau explores the conditions of human freedom or self-determination in terms of the ideal of republican citizenship which he associates with Rome and Sparta. The freedom to pursue one's private desires—and especially to acquire property—that the Hobbesian and Lockean state secures is not what genuine freedom consists in for Rousseau. Rather, genuine freedom consists in active participation in the public business and in obedience to laws that one has given oneself.[20] Of course, to achieve this ideal of republican freedom requires that the state not be too large.[21] In large commercial states, of the sort Montesquieu celebrated in his treatment of England,[22] it is not possible for all the people to assemble and legislate, and therefore resort must be made to the device of representation. To this device, however, Rousseau is implacably opposed. The general will of the people, he insists, cannot be represented. "In a truly free state the citizens do everything with their own hands"; "the moment a people gives itself representatives, it is no longer free; it no longer exists." For this reason, he argues that the English are not really free except during elections. Once they have elected their representatives to Parliament, "the populace is enslaved; it is nothing."[23]

Republicanism or democratic sovereignty is not, of course, the only idea in the *Social Contract*. The will of the people is ultimately subordinate to something else, namely, the general will. These two wills do not always coincide. As Rousseau tells us, the general will cannot simply be equated with the will of all.[24] The general will is not merely the sum of the private wills of individuals; rather, it is the common interest that underlies them: "what makes the will general is not so much the number of votes as the common interest that unites them."[25] The ultimate political problem—and one to which Rousseau shows himself to be acutely sensitive in the *Social Contract*—is how to get the democratic will of all or even of the majority to be a reliable vehicle for the general will. Sometimes Rousseau suggests a mechanical solution to this problem—as when he argues that the general will results when the "pluses and minuses" of private wills cancel each other out.[26] But his most considered reflections point to the necessity of forming the character and mores of the people. The *Social Contract*, like the *Emile*, ultimately turns into an educational project; and the figure who is responsible for shaping the people so that they reliably express the general will is the legislator. It is the legislator who carries out the "denaturing" that we saw Rousseau speak of above in the *Emile*:

> He who dares to undertake the establishment of a people should feel that he is, so to speak, in a position to change human nature, to transform each individual (who by himself is a perfect and solitary whole), into a part of a larger whole from which this individual receives, in a sense, his life and his being; to alter man's constitution in order to strengthen it; to substitute a partial and moral existence for the physical and independent existence we have all received from nature. In a word, he must deny man his own forces in order to give him forces that are alien to him and that he cannot make use of without the help of others. The more these natural forces are dead and obliterated, and the greater and more durable are the acquired forces, the more too is the institution solid and perfect.[27]

Rousseau's idea of the legislator, of course, raises as many questions as it answers, and the concept of the general will is notoriously ambiguous; but this is not the place to go into such difficulties. Following Hegel, our concern has been to show how Rousseau marks a crucial turning point in modern European reflection on freedom and its relation to the state. Hegel characterizes Rousseau's innovation vis-à-vis his predecessors Hobbes and Locke in terms of his making free will not only the form but also the content of the state; and the truth of this *aperçu* has been borne out by our brief analysis of the *Social Contract*. For Rousseau, the content of the state, its purpose, is not mere security of life or property, as in Hobbes and Locke, but freedom itself. What the social contract brings into effect is not simply peace but the self-government of individuals who act not on their private wills but on the general will that has the common good for its object. As virtuous republican citizens, these individuals are truly masters of themselves and truly free; for, as Rousseau writes, again anticipating Kant, "to be driven by appetite alone is slavery, and obedience to the law one has prescribed for oneself is liberty."[28]

Hegel's characterization of Rousseau's achievement in the tradition of modern political philosophy is, then, well considered. What is more puzzling, on the other hand, is the criticism with which he follows this insightful characterization of Rousseau's achievement. After crediting Rousseau with having "put forward the *will* as the principle of the state," Hegel goes on to write:

> But Rousseau considered the will only in the determinate form of the *individual* will (as Fichte subsequently also did) and regarded the general will not as the will's rationality in and for itself, but only as the *common element* arising out of this individual will *as a conscious will*. The union of individuals within the state thus becomes a *contract*, which is accordingly based on their arbitrary will and opinions, and on their express consent given at their own discretion. (*PR*, §258R)[29]

This seems to be a one-sidedly individualistic interpretation of Rousseau's teaching about the general will. It seems to ignore Rousseau's distinction between the general will and the will of all, and it completely overlooks the educative function of the legislator with respect to the arbitrary wills of individuals. Contrary to Hegel's assessment, Rousseau's whole project in the *Social Contract* seems to be to subordinate the private will to the general will, or (as he puts it in the *Emile*) to "transport the *I* into the common unity."[30] Hegel provides a more judicious assessment of Rousseau's notion of the general will in the *Encyclopedia Logic*, where he states that the distinction "between what is merely held in common and the genuine universal is strikingly expressed in Rousseau's well-known *Contrat Social*, when he says that the laws of a state must emerge from the general will (*volonté générale*), but that they do not at all need on that account to be the will *of all* (*volonté de tous*)." But even here he criticizes Rousseau for only inconsistently maintaining this important distinction: "With regard to the theory of the state, Rousseau would have achieved something sounder if he had kept this distinction in mind all the time" (*EL*, §163A1).

What are we to make of Hegel's criticism of Rousseau? Although it is difficult to credit the criticism in the exact way that Hegel formulates it, it would be a mistake to simply dismiss it. There is something in Rousseau's notion of the general will that renders it problematic from a Hegelian perspective and that differentiates it sharply from Hegel's own notion of the rational will. Though Rousseau certainly distinguishes between the general will and the will of all, the success of his social contract to a large extent depends on the characteristics of the former being found in the latter. Rousseau's republican ideal presupposes a certain identity between the will of the individual and the general will, albeit (contrary to Hegel's suggestion) this identity rests on purging the individual will of its particularity and arbitrariness. It is this radically democratic demand for direct identity between the will of the individual and the general will that Hegel finds so dangerous, especially in the context of the modern, differentiated state. He articulates this concern most persuasively in his analysis of "absolute freedom" and the French Revolution in the *Phenomenology of Spirit*. There the idea of the general will is interpreted as implying that "each, undivided from the whole, always does everything, and what appears as done by the whole is the direct and conscious deed of each." But such a notion of absolute freedom ultimately proves incapable of dealing with the meaningful differentiation, social and political, which characterizes the modern state. As a result, it can only vent itself in "negative action" and the "fury of destruction" (*PS*, 357–59/432–36).

What, in the end, Hegel rejects in Rousseau is the ancient republican ideal of patriotic citizens actively engaged in politics, completely consumed by the public business, and directly deliberating on the totality of public affairs. Such an ideal cannot be made to fit with the complex reality of the modern European state. And when the attempt is made to realize this ideal in the modern world, the result is the sort of violence and destruction seen in the French Revolution. Of course, as we will see in greater detail in the next chapter, Hegel himself was smitten by a version of this ancient republican ideal early in his career. But by the time he publishes the *Phenomenology* in 1807, he has long since abandoned it. Indeed, as early as the *German Constitution,* which was written sporadically between 1799–1802, Hegel already begins to show some realization of how anachronistic his Hellenic ideal is with respect to the modern European state.

Hegel's rejection of Rousseau's republicanism, however, should not blind us to the important commonality between these two thinkers. Hegel's political philosophy clearly reflects that he has learned much from Rousseau's critique of the bourgeois and his call for a restoration of dignity and moral freedom to modern politics. Indeed, Hegel's political philosophy can in one sense be viewed as an attempt to defend and reinterpret the institutions of the modern state, including modern bourgeois society, in the light of Rousseau's critique and call.[31] This is reflected not only in his sharp distinction between bourgeois civil society and the state but also, as we shall see later, in his interpretation of the former as being not simply a realm of selfish individualism but also a school that educates the individual to the universality that is characteristic of the state. In his political philosophy, Hegel is engaged in a profound dialogue, both explicit and implicit, with Rousseau's political philosophy—more so in many respects than with the more conventionally liberal and individualistic political philosophies of his great German predecessors, Kant and Fichte. This dialogue continues to this day to frame the essential alternatives of our modern world.

KANT

The idea of freedom as radical self-determination or self-dependence introduced by Rousseau is worked out much more fully and consistently in the moral philosophy of Kant. Like Rousseau, Kant rejects the naturalistic understanding of freedom exemplified by Hobbes that sees it as the unimpeded pursuit of one's empirically given desires. In giving into natural desire or inclination, the will is determined by something other than itself and its own rationality. The will is truly free or autonomous only when it gives itself the law instead of being subjected to the natural mechanism of desire and inclination. This it does by obeying the moral law or categorical imperative. Only by fulfilling the categorical imperative does the will live up to its own rationality and escape the determinism of nature. Only by doing its duty for the sake of duty does the will become truly self-legislative. Through his notion of moral autonomy, Kant, thus, like Rousseau, restores the link between morality and freedom that had been destroyed by Hobbes and his naturalistic followers.[32] Morality is no longer seen as a restriction (albeit a necessary one) on human freedom but as a fulfillment of it. Moral duty does not limit but liberates.

This, of course, is but the barest of sketches of Kant's powerful and highly nuanced moral teaching. I do not intend, however, to fill it out much more, since the focus of this chapter is on the political philosophy of Hegel's predecessors rather than on their moral theory per se. Not that the two can really be separated; but our interest here is less with Kant's moral theory on its own than with its relation to his political theory. In later chapters, I will take up Kant's ethical doctrine in connection with Hegel's famous critique of it. But here I confine myself to the question of how, if at all, this ethical doctrine and the idea of freedom or autonomy it embodies is reflected in Kant's political philosophy.

An initial glance reveals that the relationship of Kant's idea of moral autonomy to his political philosophy is quite oblique. Unlike Rousseau, Kant sharply distinguishes between morality (and the freedom that belongs to it) and politics, or, as he tends to put it, between morality and legality. The laws that relate to ethical laws are not simply restricted to external actions but also include the subjective ground or incentive of the action. Juridical laws, on the other hand, because they involve coercion, cannot legislate with respect to the subjective ground or incentive of an action. They must confine themselves to external actions, leaving the incentive free. A juridical law demands that a citizen simply conform his action to the law, regardless of whether he does so out of fear of punishment or a sense of moral duty.[33] The greatest damage that a political or legal system can do is to compel its citizens to be moral, that is, to interfere directly in the moral lives of its citizens by legislating not only their external actions but also the incentives or motives with which they perform those actions. As Kant writes in *Religion Within the Limits of Reason,* "[W]oe to the legislator who wishes to establish through force a polity directed to ethical ends! For in doing so he would not merely achieve the very opposite of an ethical polity but also undermine his political state and make it insecure."[34]

Because he makes such a sharp distinction between morality and legality, Kant's political philosophy can sometimes appear to be not that dissimilar from the individualistic political philosophies of Hobbes and Locke. Like the political philosophies of these latter thinkers, Kant's political philosophy seems to restrict itself to securing the negative freedom of individuals, leaving the achievement of positive freedom or autonomy to the realm of morality.[35] Thus, in his "Theory and Practice" essay, Kant defines right (*Recht*) as "the restriction of each individual's freedom so that it harmonizes with the freedom of everyone else in so far as this is possible within the terms of a general law."[36] He formulates this essentially liberal principle in the *Rechtslehre* (or *Doctrine of Right*) in the following way: "so act externally that the free use of your will (*Willkür*) can coexist with the freedom of everyone in accordance with a universal law."[37] The conception of freedom that is being invoked in these definitions of right is essentially the negative conception found in Hobbes and Locke or even Mill; the conception of freedom according to which "each may seek his happiness in whatever way he sees fit, so long as he does not infringe upon the freedom of others to pursue a similar end which can be reconciled with the freedom of everyone else within a general workable law."[38]

The most graphic example of the Hobbesian strand in Kant's political philosophy comes, of course, in "Perpetual Peace," where Kant famously asserts that "as hard as it may sound, the problem of setting up a state can be solved even by a nation of devils (so long as they possess understanding)." In tones that recall, if not Hobbes, at least Madison, Kant argues that the task of creating a good organization of the state only involves arranging the state in such a way that the "self-seeking energies [of men] are opposed to one another, each thereby neutralizing or eliminating the destructive effects of the rest. And as far as reason is concerned, the result is the same as if man's selfish tendencies were nonexistent, so that man, even if he is not morally good in himself, is nevertheless compelled to be a good citizen." The task of setting up a state, thus, "does not involve the moral improvement of man; it only means finding out how the mechanism of nature can be applied to men in such a manner that the antagonism of their hostile attitudes will make them compel one another to submit to coercive laws, thereby producing a condition of peace within which the laws can be enforced."[39]

For all the liberating promise of his moral philosophy, then, Kant's political philosophy appears to provide us with nothing more than the *modus vivendi* model of politics familiar from Hobbes and a good deal of the liberal tradition. As Charles Taylor has put it: "Thus although Kant starts with a radically new conception of morality, his political theory is disappointingly familiar. It does not take us very far beyond utilitarianism, in that its main problem remains that of harmonizing individual wills."[40] This seems to be Hegel's judgment of Kant's political philosophy as well. In the early *Natural Law* essay, for example, he complains that, although the unity of right and duty, on the one hand, and the thinking and willing subject, on the other, constitutes "the great element in the philosophy of Kant and Fichte," this unity is confined to morality, leaving the sphere of right to be governed by mere externality and compulsion (*NL*, 83–85/469–71). In the *Lectures on the Philosophy of History*, he pays Kant the same compliment we see him pay Rousseau above, stating that "Kant began to ground right upon freedom," but he goes on to criticize Kant in the same way he criticized Rousseau for taking "freedom in the form of the isolated individual" (*PH*, III, 503/413). Hegel develops this comparison between Kant and Rousseau most fully in the *Philosophy of Right*. There he quotes (more or less) Kant's definition of right as "the *limitation* of my freedom or *arbitrary will* [*Willkür*] in such a way that it may coexist with the arbitrary will of everyone else in accordance with a universal law" and comments critically:

On the one hand, this definition contains only a *negative* determination—that of limitation; and on the other hand, the positive [element]—the universal law or so-called "law of reason," the consonance of the arbitrary will of one individual with that of the other—amounts simply to the familiar [principle of] formal identity and the law of contradiction. The definition of right in question embodies the view, especially prevalent since Rousseau, according to which the substantial basis and primary factor is supposed to be not the will as rational will which has being in and for itself or the spirit as *true* spirit, but will and spirit as the *particular* individual, as the will of the single person in his distinctive arbitrariness. (*PR*, §29R)

Again, the individualistic interpretation of Rousseau's political philosophy contained in this passage does not entirely do that political philosophy justice. Can the same can be said for Hegel's interpretation of Kant's political philosophy? I shall be arguing shortly that the charge of individualism Hegel levels in this passage is in many respects more applicable to Kant's political philosophy than to Rousseau's. But before we can arrive at such a conclusion, we must first deepen our understanding of the relationship between morality and politics in Kant's philosophy; for the view we have so far of Kant as some sort of Hobbesian is altogether too simple to capture the important way in which his political philosophy is grounded in his moral philosophy. Though Kant maintains that the problem of setting up a state can be solved by a nation of intelligent devils, he also says that "a true system of politics cannot take a single step without first paying tribute to morality."[41] We must now investigate how Kant's system of politics pays tribute to his moral philosophy and especially to his idea of moral autonomy.[42]

The best place to begin is with Kant's contention that it is a moral duty to enter the state. Membership in the state is not simply a matter of arbitrary choice or prudential calculation; nor is it contingent on the consent of individuals. Rather, it is an obligation laid upon individuals by reason. Kant writes: "it can be said of a *rightful* condition that all men who could (even involuntarily) come into relations of rights with one another *ought* to enter this condition."[43] Though Hegel generally tries to link Kant with the individualistic social contract tradition (see *PR*, §§29R, 258R), it is clear that Kant, no less than Hegel himself, rejects the idea that the state is merely a contract based on the arbitrary wills of individuals. Indeed, Kant would probably agree with Hegel, against the social contract tradition, that "it is the rational destiny of human beings to live within a state, and even if no state is yet present, reason requires that one be established" (*PR*, §75A). Kant's departure from the social contract teachings of Hobbes and Locke in this regard, his contention that entrance into civil society is not simply a matter of empirical or prudential calculation but of a priori moral obligation, is captured in the following passage from the *Rechtslehre:*

> It is not experience from which we learn of men's maxim of violence and of their malevolent tendency to attack one another before external legislation endowed with power appears. It is therefore not some fact that makes coercion through public law necessary. On the contrary, however well disposed and law-abiding men might be, it still lies a priori in the rational Idea of such a condition (one that is not rightful) that before a public lawful condition is established, individual men, peoples, and states can never be secure against violence from one another, since each has its own right to do *what seems right and good to it* and not to be dependent upon another's opinion about this. So, unless the individual wants to renounce all concepts of right, the first thing he has to resolve upon is the principle that he must leave the state of nature, in which each follows his own judgment, unite himself with all others (with whom he cannot avoid interacting), subject himself to a public lawful external coercion, and so enter into a condition in which what is recognized as belonging to each person is determined by *law* and is allotted to it by adequate *power* (not its own but an external power); that is to say, he ought above all else to enter a civil condition.[44]

Of course, Kant does not entirely reject the notion of the social contract in his political philosophy; but in his hands the social contract loses the merely empirical, discretionary, and individualistic character it possesses in Hobbes and Locke. Thus, he writes that "the contract establishing a *civil constitution* is of an exceptional nature." Whereas in other social contracts, "we find a union of many individuals for some common end which they all *share*," in the contract establishing a civil state we find "a union as an end in itself which they all *ought to share* and which is thus an absolute and primary duty in all external relationships whatsoever among human beings (who cannot avoid mutually influencing one another)."[45] Nor does Kant accept the conventional, Hobbesian-Lockean understanding of the social contract as a kind of trade-off with respect to human freedom, the idea that in entering the social contract an individual gives up a part of his freedom in order to enjoy the rest. Echoing Rousseau, Kant sees the passage from the state of nature to the civil state as involving a total gain, the surrender of one kind of freedom for another, more valuable kind of freedom. Through the "original contract," he writes, everyone

> gives up his external freedom in order to take it up immediately as a member of a commonwealth . . . And one cannot say that man within a state has sacrificed a *part* of his innate outer freedom for the sake of an end, but rather, he has relinquished entirely his wild and lawless freedom in order to find his freedom as such un-

diminished, in a dependence upon laws, that is, in a rightful condition, since this dependence arises from his own lawgiving will.[46]

So far we have concerned ourselves mainly with Kant's claim that we have a moral duty to join the state. But why? How exactly does our living in the rightful condition of the state and abiding by its laws connect with morality and the ultimate end of moral autonomy? Kant gives two different answers. Frst, he argues that the civil condition or state is instrumental to morality. While the state cannot directly promote morality in individuals, having to confine itself to the legality of their external actions, it can create conditions which make it more likely for genuine moral action and motivation to result. "[B]y putting an end to outbreaks of lawless proclivities," Kant writes, coercive civil law

> genuinely makes it much easier for the moral capacities of men to develop into an immediate respect for right. For each individual believes of himself that he would by all means maintain the sanctity of the concept of right and obey it faithfully, if only he could be certain that all the others would do likewise, and the government in part guarantees this for him; thus a great step is taken *towards* morality (although this is still not the same as a moral step), towards a state where the concept of duty is recognized for its own sake, irrespective of any possible gain in return.[47]

The other reason why Kant believes we have a moral duty to join the state or bring about the rightful condition has to do with the categorical imperative. It is, of course, a matter of some dispute just how our political duties—and in the first instance, our duty to enter the civil condition—can be derived from the categorical imperative.[48] Without pretending to resolve this difficult issue, let me simply assert that the most straightforward way of deriving our political duties from the categorical imperative seems to be through the second formulation of the latter: "Act so that you treat humanity, whether in your own person or in that of another, always as an end and never as a means only."[49] Treating others as ends means treating them as rational agents who set their own ends, both with respect to happiness and moral perfection. Treating others as ends therefore demands that we respect the freedom of others to set their own ends. When we infringe on the freedom or property of another, the end of our action cannot possibly be one that is shared by or contained in that other. In that way, we treat the other person merely as a means to our own end. As Kant writes: "[I]t is clear that he who transgresses the rights of men intends to make use of the persons of others merely as a means, without considering that, as rational beings, they must always be esteemed at the same time as ends, i.e., only as beings who must be able to contain in themselves the end of the very same action."[50] In the civil condition, where everyone's freedom is respected so long as it does not infringe on the freedom of others, the injunction to treat humanity as an end and never merely as a means governs the external actions of individuals. Though coercive civil law can never insure that this injunction is made the incentive of individuals' actions, by guaranteeing that it governs their external behavior, it once again proves to be an important step toward morality.

The injunction to treat others as ends and never merely as means not only serves to ground our bare duty to belong to the state—or the corresponding negative duty not to rebel against it;[51] it also generates many of the specific features of the Kantian republic. Kant's vehement opposition to any sort of paternalism in the state, for example, follows directly from his principle that human beings must be treated as ends, that is, as rational beings who set their own ends and pursue their own goals and happiness in their own way. One of the a priori principles of the rightful state, Kant tells us, is the "*freedom* of every member of society as a *human being*." Above all, this freedom consists in the fact that "no one can compel me to be happy in accordance with his conception of the welfare of others, for each may seek his happiness in whatever way he sees fit, so long as he does not infringe upon the freedom of others to pursue a similar end which can be reconciled with the freedom of everyone else with a workable general law." A paternal government fails to respect this fundamental freedom of human beings. It treats its subjects as "immature children" who are incapable of setting their own ends or pursuing their own conceptions of happiness and thereby treats them as mere means.[52] Earlier I quoted from this passage to show that Kant's conception of freedom in the state is essentially the negative conception found in Hobbes, Locke, Bentham, and Mill. But it is clear that Kant defends this negative notion of freedom not on the basis of some sort of empirical impulse-satisfaction but on the basis of his moral conception of the person as an end in himself.

The categorical imperative to treat human beings as ends in themselves also underpins Kant's conception of the political role of citizens in civil legislation. As ends in themselves, citizens have a right not to be subjected to laws to which they have not in some sense consented. In "Theory and Practice," Kant considers this right under the rubric of the a priori principle of the "independence" of citizens, that is, their quality of not being dependent on the will of another. Public laws, he argues, require the consent of everyone, "for only towards oneself can one never act unjustly," whereas "the will of another person cannot decide anything for someone without injustice."[53] In other places, Kant treats this right of self-legislation under the rubric of the a priori principle or rightful

attribute of freedom. Thus, in "Perpetual Peace," he defines the rightful freedom of citizens as "a warrant to obey no external laws except those to which I
have been able to give my own consent."[54] And in the *Rechtslehre*, he maintains
that one of the rightful attributes that every citizen possesses is the "lawful
freedom to obey no law other than that to which he has given his consent."[55] It
is in the *Rechtslehre*, too, that Kant makes explicit the connection between the
categorical imperative to treat human beings as ends in themselves and the right
of citizens to legislate for themselves. Arguing against the notion that a monarch may send his subjects to war without their consent, Kant writes that
citizens "must always be regarded as co-legislating members of a state (not
merely as means, but also as ends in themselves)."[56]

There is in Kant's emphasis on the self-legislative character of citizens, of
course, more than an echo of Rousseau. But Kant's republicanism is ultimately
very different from the ancient civic republican ideal which Rousseau harks back
to. Leaving aside Kant's undemocratic strictures on who qualifies as a voting
citizen,[57] it never seems that the active participation of citizens in political life
that Rousseau celebrated was ever central to Kant's republican vision. This is
perhaps most pronounced in "Theory and Practice," where Kant interprets the
general will in such a way that it requires only the possible, and not even the
actual, consent of all citizens. The general will embodied in the original contract,
Kant argues, is "merely an *idea* of reason" that obliges "every legislator to frame
his laws in such a way that they could have been produced by the united will of a
whole nation, and to regard each subject, in so far as he can claim citizenship, as if
he consented within the general will." In other words, the original contract
merely serves as a "test of the rightfulness of every public law," so that, "if it is at
least *possible* that a people could agree to it, it is our duty to consider the law as
just, even if the people is at present in such a position or attitude of mind that it
would probably refuse its consent if it were consulted."[58]

In general, though, Kant's republicanism, like Madison's, takes the form of a
representative—not purely democratic—system of government: "Any true
republic . . . is and cannot be anything other than a *representative system* of the
people whereby the people's rights are looked after on their behalf by the
deputies who represent the united will of the citizens."[59] But even here Kant's
view is tempered by a realism which accepts that such a representative system of
government may not be possible in the political circumstances of his time, a
realism which therefore must content itself with something less than the actual
consent of the people. It is our duty to enter into a republican constitution
based on a representative system of government, Kant writes, but

in the meantime, since it will be a considerable time before this takes place, it is the duty of monarchs to govern in a *republican* (not a democratic) manner, even although they may rule *autocratically*. In other words, they should treat the people in accordance with principles akin in spirit to the laws of freedom which a people of mature rational powers would prescribe for itself, even if the people is not literally asked for its consent.[60]

Let us now return to the original question from which this excursus into the relation between Kant's moral philosophy and his political philosophy began. Is there any foundation to Hegel's charge that Kant's political philosophy is thoroughly individualistic in that it bases itself not on the rational will but on the "will of the individual in his distinctive arbitrariness" (*PR*, §29R)? Put another way, is Hegel correct in suggesting that Kant's political philosophy fails to incorporate into its understanding of right the momentous idea of freedom as radical self-determination or autonomy, basing itself instead on the more familiar, negative notion of freedom found in the individualistic and empirical political philosophies of Hobbes and Locke? We have shown that the crude formulation of this criticism, presupposing a complete rift between Kant's political philosophy and the idea of autonomy in his moral philosophy, cannot be sustained. Kant's political philosophy is not identical to that of Hobbes or Locke; it is connected to his moral philosophy and the idea of moral autonomy in deep and complex ways. Nevertheless, posed more subtly, the question still lingers whether there isn't something to Hegel's criticism after all. At the very least, does the criticism point to an important difference between Kant's and Hegel's respective understandings of the relationship between freedom and the state?

The answer to the last question is definitely yes. Despite the important ways in which Kant links politics to morality and the idea of moral autonomy, it remains the case that his conception of politics is still largely instrumental. The state establishes conditions of negative freedom that are instrumental to the moral autonomy and positive freedom of individuals, but the state itself is not seen as the embodiment or realization of freedom in the truest sense. The locus of autonomy and positive freedom remains the moral life of the individual understood as separate from, albeit protected and supported by, the state. Though Kant adds to the liberal, individualistic understanding of the state a more exalted moral purpose—the state does not merely protect life, liberty, and property but enables the moral autonomy of individuals—his conception of the state remains for the most part liberal, instrumental, and individualistic.

A completely different spirit animates Hegel's political philosophy. The state is not merely instrumental to the self-determination and positive freedom of individuals; it is the embodiment or realization of such self-determination and freedom. In the paragraph of the *Philosophy of Right* in which he criticizes Kant's individualistic definition of right, Hegel is defending the proposition that "*right* is any existence in general which is the *existence* of the *free will*. Right is therefore in general freedom, as Idea" (*PR*, §29). Right is not merely instrumental to freedom but is the very existence of freedom; nor is this freedom to be understood negatively in terms of the arbitrary will but positively in terms of the rational will, the free will which wills itself, the radically self-determining will. Another way of putting this difference between Hegel and Kant is that Hegel rejects Kant's distinction between legality and morality. Hegel does not, of course, deny that legal coercion cannot apply to the inner disposition or moral motivation of individuals (see *PR*, §§94A, 213). But he does reject the idea that acting legally and acting morally are essentially different; that right and morality are fundamentally distinguishable, with the former being subordinate and at best instrumental to the latter. This is the main significance of Hegel's characterization of the state in terms of the notion of *Sittlichkeit* or "ethical life." Such a characterization conveys that the moral or the ethical is not to be found anywhere beyond the state but precisely in it. "The state embodies what is truly ethical."[61]

In this respect, Hegel's political philosophy ultimately has more in common with Rousseau's political philosophy than it does with Kant's. For Rousseau, too, the state is more than a merely external arrangement designed to promote the private freedom—however understood—of individuals. It is through participation in the public life of the state, Rousseau argues, that the individual attains true freedom and autonomy. The state does not merely enable the moral freedom of the individual but in an important way embodies it. Radical self-determination is to be found not in the private moral sphere opened up by the liberal state but in the life of the public-spirited citizen. Hegel, of course, does not subscribe to Rousseau's civic republicanism. But he does share with Rousseau the idea that the state is more than an instrument to individual freedom; the idea that, in an important way, the state actualizes the freedom of individuals, that it is through identification with the universal interest of the state that the individual becomes truly free. Kant is not willing to accord the state or political life in general this much importance. In this regard, his liberal vision remains equally far from the more communitarian outlooks of both his most important predecessor and his greatest successor.

FICHTE

In Fichte, we find the idea of autonomy and radical self-determination that we have been tracing developed to its highest pitch. Fichte's whole system is an attempt to purge the world of its brute externality and reveal it to be the product of the free act of the self.[62] In a letter written in 1795, he compares the liberating effect of his philosophy to the liberating effect of the French Revolution: "Mine will be the first system of liberty. Just as [France] delivers mankind from its material chains, my system will deliver it from the yoke of the thing in itself; its first principles make man into an autonomous being."[63] According to the famous first principle of the *Wissenschaftslehre* of 1794, I=I, there is in every empirical state of consciousness an implicit awareness of the self or I, an awareness that it is I who am experiencing this or that. This I, which is not itself the object of experience but posited prior to it, serves to ground and unify empirical experience in much the same way as Kant's transcendental unity of apperception. It constitutes, for Fichte, "the genuinely spiritual element in man" and leads him to define the "ultimate characteristic feature of all rational beings" as being "absolute unity, constant self-identity, complete agreement with oneself."[64] The task or vocation of human beings is to develop the unity and self-identity implicit in all experience into the explicit principle and goal of action, that is, to modify those things which are external to the I in such a way as "to bring them into harmony with the pure form of the I."[65]

It is in connection with this conception of the essential vocation of human beings that Fichte's most extravagant claims for the radical self-determination and self-dependence of human beings appear. In the *Lectures Concerning the Vocation of the Scholar,* for example, he states that "man's highest drive is the drive toward identity, toward complete harmony with himself, and—as a means for staying constantly in harmony with himself—toward the harmony of all external things with his necessary concepts of them."[66] And in the *Sittenlehre* (or *Doctrine of Ethics*) of 1798, he refers throughout to the self's "absolute tendency to self-activity,"[67] which he also describes in terms of the will's "*absolute tendency to the absolute;* its absolute undeterminability through anything outside of itself; its tendency to determine itself absolutely without any external impulses."[68] In all of this, one can already begin to discern the tones of Hegel's own large claims on behalf of the radical self-determination and self-dependence of human beings, his holding out the possibility of a radical freedom that consists in being "purely at home with oneself [*bei sich selbst*] . . . depending upon oneself, and being one's own determinant" (*EL,* §24A2).[69]

Unlike Hegel, however, and very much like Kant, Fichte identifies human autonomy and self-determination with the realm of morality. And like Kant again, he conceives the moral life largely in terms of the struggle between duty and inclination, or, as he characterizes it in the *Sittenlehre*, between the "natural impulse" that craves only the satisfaction of our natural desires and the "pure impulse" that "craves absolute independence of the active as such from natural impulse, or craves freedom simply for the sake of freedom."[70] Fichte, no less than Kant, sees the moral life as a ceaseless effort to elevate oneself above and emancipate oneself from merely natural or empirical desire. Therein lies the essential dignity and autonomy of human beings. As he writes in the *Sittenlehre:*

> [I]n its relation to the inclination which would drag me down into the series of natural causality, the higher impulse manifests itself as an impulse which claims my respect, arouses me to respect myself, and invests me with a dignity superior to all nature. It never has enjoyment for its object and, on the contrary, despises enjoyment. The higher impulse makes enjoyment for mere enjoyment's sake contemptible. It has for its object solely the maintenance of my dignity, which consists in absolute independence and self-sufficiency.[71]

Fichte does not, however, view the moral life as primarily a solitary or purely private affair. To the contrary, his understanding of morality has a substantial communitarian twist. Taking off from the Kantian notion of a kingdom of ends or ethical commonwealth,[72] Fichte argues that human beings can only fulfill their moral end if they live in a community in which they try to perfect one another by sharing their moral convictions and mutually influencing one another so that they eventually arrive at complete unity and unanimity. Thus, he writes in the *Vocation of the Scholar* that "it is man's *destiny* to live in society; he *ought to* live in society. One who lives in isolation is not a complete human being. He contradicts his own self."[73] And in the *Sittenlehre,* he asserts the imperative that "each one *shall* live in a community, for otherwise he cannot produce harmony with himself, as is absolutely commanded. Whosoever separates himself from mankind, renounces his final end and aim, and holds the extension of morality to be utterly indifferent."[74] Every human being must strive for the moral perfection of others as well as of himself; otherwise he cannot achieve that harmony with others that is the precondition of harmony with himself. At the end of such striving, Fichte envisages a time—though it may take "millions or trillions of years"—when humanity will be united in an ethical commonwealth governed entirely by the good wills of its members, "a time when my heart will be joined with yours by the loveliest bond of all—the bond of free, mutual give and take."[75]

Fichte insists, however, that such an ethical commonwealth must not be confused with the juridical state. The latter, since it operates through compulsion, cannot secure the good will and moral conviction upon which any ethical commonwealth is based. For this reason, Fichte asserts that "life in the state is not one of man's absolute aims. The state is, instead, only a *means for establishing a perfect society,* a means which exists only under specific circumstances. Like all those human institutions which are mere means, the state aims at abolishing itself. *The goal of all government is to make government superfluous.*"[76] Fichte seems to conceive the state as instrumental to morality in much the same way as Kant. In an ethical commonwealth, human beings try to influence and persuade one another with the goal of achieving complete agreement. But as a precondition of this moral activity, human beings must first agree on "how each one may influence the other," that is, they must come to agreement about their "common rights." The community that embodies this original agreement is the state, whose task it is to enforce it.[77] Fichte sometimes gives the impression, as in the passage above, that he thinks the state will eventually wither away: "there will certainly be a point in the a priori foreordained career of the human species when all civic bonds will become superfluous."[78] In the *Sittenlehre* he makes a similar point: once "all have the same convictions, and the conviction of each is the conviction of all," then the "state falls away as a *legislating and compulsory* power."[79] But in that same passage, Fichte goes on to say that such a moral end is "unattainable." And in a note to a later edition of the *Vocation of the Scholar,* he indicates that insofar as human beings are fallible, "the state is completely necessary and can never cease to exist."[80]

Though political right can ultimately be understood as being instrumental to morality, Fichte nevertheless sharply distinguishes between them—even more so than Kant. In the *Foundations of Natural Right,* the first part of which was actually published one year before Kant's *Rechtslehre,* in 1796, Fichte deduces the concept of right (*Recht*) entirely independently of morality. The fundamental principle of right, which Fichte defines largely along the lines Kant did—"each individual must restrict his [external] freedom through the conception of the possibility of the freedom of the other"[81]—is said to have "nothing to do with the ethical law and is deduced without it." Whereas morality is concerned exclusively with the good will of the individual, "in the sphere of natural right the good will counts for nothing. Right must be allowed to impose itself, even if no man has a good will; and it is the very business and object of the science of right to establish such an order of things."[82] Like Kant, but in an even more rigorous and uncompromising manner, Fichte shows that the problem of setting up a rightful state is capable of being solved even by a nation of intelligent devils.

Even from this sketch of Fichte's project in the *Foundations of Natural Right*, it is not difficult to guess the direction from which Hegel's criticisms will come. For the most part, Hegel's criticisms of Fichte's political philosophy are the same as his criticisms of Kant's. Indeed, Hegel tends to focus more on Fichte's political philosophy than on Kant's precisely because he sees it as expressing more purely and consistently the essentially individualistic and negative standpoint common to both. The hallmark of the Fichtean state, according to Hegel, is its external and coercive character. In Fichte's political philosophy, there is no real unity or identity between the individual and the state, the sort of unity that Hegel expresses in terms of his notions of ethical life and "spirit" (*Geist*). The Fichtean state is unspiritual, a "machine state," devoid of ethical unity. This negative and atomistic character of Fichte's political philosophy is epitomized in his distinction between right and morality. In the sphere of right, all is negative, external, based on compulsion. It is only in morality that genuine freedom and identity are to be found.[83]

To fully grasp Hegel's criticisms, however, we must develop Fichte's argument in the *Foundations of Natural Right* in more detail.[84] We have seen that Fichte does not intend to deduce right from morality. Instead, he deduces right as a transcendental condition of the self-consciousness of a rational being. Such self-consciousness presupposes in the first place that the rational being ascribe to itself free causality or efficacy. But the rational being cannot ascribe free causality to itself without at the same time positing something outside of and opposed to itself upon which to direct its causality. But to posit something as other than and opposed to the self already seems to presuppose precisely the self-consciousness that Fichte is trying to explain. Another ground for the possibility of self-consciousness must be sought, and Fichte finds it in the rational being's assumption that there are other rational beings outside of itself. Thus begins Fichte's tortuous argument leading to the conclusion that mutual recognition is the basis of right. Because this argument, as Fichte himself tells us, forms "the basis of [his] whole theory of right,"[85] but also because it proved to be enormously influential for Hegel's own, more famous account of recognition, we must examine it more closely.

For Fichte, the rational being does not become aware of its free causality simply by exerting itself against dead nature. Rather, it can only come by this awareness by encountering its free causality outside of itself as object. "I must *find* myself free," Fichte writes in the *Sittenlehre,* "I must be given to myself as free, curious as this may appear at first."[86] The subject finds itself as free, finds its free causality given to it as object, Fichte goes on to argue, only on the presupposition that a "demand" or "request" (*Aufforderung*) is addressed to the subject to determine itself or "resolve on manifesting its causality."[87] The subject may act on this demand or resist it—it cannot be compelled to comply, for this could never give rise to the awareness of freedom—but either way the subject will have grasped the concept of its causality. Whence comes this demand for the subject to manifest its causality? Since the demand presupposes that the subject addressed can understand and freely respond to it, the source of the demand must itself have a conception of reason and freedom in advance. It must, therefore, be a free and rational being as well.[88] In this way, Fichte establishes that the rational being cannot ascribe free causality to itself—which is an essential condition of self-consciousness—without at the same time assuming free and rational beings outside of it. "Man becomes man only amongst men," he writes. And if we understand the demand addressed to the rational being to manifest its free causality as "education" (*Erziehung*), we can conclude that "all individuals must be educated to be men; otherwise, they would not be men."[89]

How do we get from here to mutual recognition and right? Fichte argues that individuation is also an essential condition of the rational being's conception of its own causality and hence self-consciousness. The rational being must differentiate itself from the rational being it assumes outside of itself. It must, therefore, posit its own exclusive sphere of action in which to manifest its free causality. In positing such an exclusive sphere, however, it must also posit the other rational being as an individual with its own determinate sphere of action. To be a free individual necessarily involves the positing of another free individual against which to define itself. The concept of individuality is, thus, a "reciprocal concept" (*Wechselbegriff*); it rests on a "community of consciousness," a "common conception in which two consciousnesses are united into one." Another way of putting this is that free individuality rests on the mutual "recognition" (*Anerkennung*) of rational beings. From the necessity of such mutual recognition, Fichte deduces that rational beings must be governed by the "relation of right" (*Rechtsverhältnis*), that is, "each individual must restrict his freedom through the conception of the freedom of the other."[90]

This completes Fichte's deduction of right as a condition of self-consciousness: self-consciousness postulates individuality, which postulates the mutual recognition of individuals, which ultimately postulates the relation of right. Fichte next deduces the concrete rights and political arrangements that follow from his general concept of right as the restriction of each individual's external freedom so that it can coexist with the freedom of others. Like earlier liberal theorists, he begins with the natural rights or "original rights" (*Urrechte*) of human beings. These rights essentially articulate the conditions of free personality.[91] It should be pointed out that the freedom of personality to which Fichte draws our attention here is what he elsewhere refers to as "formal freedom," the freedom to act in accordance with our conceptions of things and thus independently of causal or natural mechanism. Such formal freedom belongs to all human conduct insofar as it is human; and it is to be distinguished from the more exalted "material freedom" or substantive self-direction that Fichte associates with morality.[92] There are two principal original rights that Fichte identifies: the "right to the continuance of the absolute freedom and inviolability of the body"; and the "right to the continuance of our free influence upon the whole sensible world."[93] Under the latter right he comprehends the right of property.

What impels human beings into political society is that no one can be sure that their original rights will be respected by others. Here Fichte's political philosophy takes a distinctly Hobbesian turn. Because of his distinction between right and morality, Fichte cannot assume that individuals are characterized by a good will or a moral disposition. As he writes in one place: "constancy and faith [*Treue und Glauben*] are qualities never to be presupposed in legal relations."[94] Therefore, in the absence of faith and constancy, a law of compulsion (*Zwangsrecht*) is needed to insure that individuals do not infringe on one another's rights. Furthermore, since this law of compulsion cannot serve as an adequate guarantee of individuals' rights if the individuals in question themselves apply it, there must be a third party, stronger than the other parties, to execute it. A compulsory power is needed to resolve disputes and punish those who violate the rights of others. "Hence, an application of the law of compulsion is not possible except in a commonwealth."[95]

The same assumption of distrust among human beings by which Fichte explains the necessity of the state also informs his account of the constitution of the state. "The state," he writes, "is the very result of distrust; nay, it is even the *object* of distrust, as is shown by the whole constitution."[96] The state comes into existence in order to adjudicate disputes between and protect the rights of individuals. But how can it be guaranteed that the state will not itself become an arbitrary power, that it will rule in accordance with law or the general will of the people? Like Kant, Fichte rejects democracy as a solution to this problem. In a democracy, the people are both judges and parties in the administration of law, and this poses the greatest danger to the rights of individuals and the rule of law. The only legitimate form of government is a representative government, though Fichte allows that such a government may consist of one representative, as in a monarchy, or of many representatives, as in a republic. Unlike Kant, however, Fichte does not see the division of legislative and executive powers as an effective guarantee against despotism. All legislation is, in effect, an exercise of executive power insofar as it is merely an interpretation and application of the one fundamental law that government was originally instituted to administer. Nevertheless, there must be a constitutional check on the executive-legislative power, and Fichte finds such a check in the "ephorate," a body of elected officials who oversee the conduct of government and have the power to suspend the government if it believes it has violated the rights of the people. This is the sole extent of the ephorate's power. Once the government has been suspended, a convention of the people is called into being to judge whether a violation of right has indeed occurred.[97]

From this summary of the argument of the *Foundations of Natural Right*, it would seem that Fichte's political philosophy is largely animated by the typical liberal concerns with the preservation of the negative liberty and natural rights of the individual and the prevention of arbitrary rule on the part of the government. And, indeed, Fichte's political philosophy does constitute one of the most thoroughgoing and uncompromising attempts in European political thought to deduce the political arrangements that correspond to the modern experience of individuality.[98] Nevertheless, the arrangements Fichte defends are not always the typical liberal ones. For instance, with respect to political economy, he is quite hostile to the free market and defends instead substantial governmental regulation of economic activity. This follows, in large part, from his belief that the free efficacy of the individual with respect to the sensible world depends on everything in that world remaining constant and subject to calculation.[99] A similar concern with certainty and calculability informs Fichte's reflections on police-power, giving rise to the notion of the Fichtean "police-state." It is the task of the police, Fichte argues, not only to detect and punish crimes but to prevent them. To this end, he advocates that citizens be required to carry identity-cards at all times, and he enunciates the ominous-sounding principle that "in a state such as we have described, each citizen has his fixed position; and the police know pretty well where each citizen is, and what he does at every hour of the day."[100]

It is this intrusive and potentially oppressive aspect of the Fichtean state that Hegel fixes on in his earliest criticisms of the *Foundations of Natural Right*. In *The Difference Between Fichte's and Schelling's System of Philosophy* (1801), for example, he cites Fichte's comment about the police knowing where every citizen is at every hour of the day as an illustration of how the Fichtean state can come to dominate every aspect of society at the expense of all "stirrings of life" (*DFS*, 146–47/83–85). By subjecting everything to the supervision of the police, the Fichtean state becomes nothing more than a "machine-state" in which everything is regulated from the top down by the intellect. Fichte's *Foundations of Natural Right,* Hegel argues,

> offers us a picture of the complete lordship of the intellect and the complete bondage of the living being. It is an edifice in which reason has no part and which it therefore repudiates. For reason is bound to find itself most explicitly in its self-shaping as a people (*Volk*), which is the most perfect organization it can give itself. But the state as conceived by the intellect is not an organization at all, but a machine; and the people is not an organic body of a communal and rich life, but an atomistic, life-impoverished multitude. . . . *Fiat justitia, pereat mundus* is the law, and not even in the sense Kant gave it: "let right be done though all the scoundrels in the world perish." But rather in this sense: right must be done, even though for its sake, all trust, all joy and love, all the potencies of a genuinely ethical [*sittlichen*] identity, must be eradicated root and branch. (*DFS*, 148–49/87)[101]

This passage suggests that it is not only excessive police-power that constitutes the defect of the Fichtean state. The "totalitarian" character of the Fichtean state is itself only the consequence of the wholly external and coercive character of Fichte's conception of right. This aspect of Fichte's political philosophy Hegel criticizes in his *Natural Law* essay (1802–3), tracing it back to Fichte's sharp distinction between morality and right. Whereas morality is concerned with the internal motives and intentions in which true freedom or autonomy is to be found, right is concerned with external actions—injuries to human bodies and property—which it regulates by means of compulsion (*NL*, 83–85/469–71). On Fichte's view, the state does not represent the realization of true freedom but only restricts each individual's external freedom so that it can coexist with the external freedom of others. In other words, Fichte's political philosophy ultimately partakes of the same individualism that Hegel attributes to the political philosophies of Rousseau and Kant. Hegel brings out the individualistic, negative, and external character of Fichte's political philosophy, at the same time linking him to Rousseau and Kant, in an important passage from the *Lectures on the History of Philosophy*. The organization of the state described in Fichte's *Foundations of Natural Right*, he writes, is completely "spiritless" (*Geistlos*), consisting merely of

> a formal, external uniting and connecting, in which individuals as such are held to be absolute, or in which right is the highest principle. The universal is not the spirit, the substance of the whole, but an external, negative power of the finite understanding directed against individuals. The state is not apprehended in its essence, but only as a condition of right [*Rechtzustand*], i.e. as an external relation of finite to finite. . . . Kant began to ground right on freedom, and Fichte likewise makes freedom the principle of natural right; but, as was the case with Rousseau, it is freedom in the form of the isolated individual. This is a great beginning, but in order to arrive at the particular, they have to make or accept certain assumptions. There are various individuals; the whole construction of the state has as its main determination that the freedom of individuals must be limited by the freedom of the whole. The individuals always remain hard and negative with respect to one another. The confinement, the bonds, always become greater, instead of the state being grasped as the realization of freedom. (*HP,* III, 503–4/412–13)

We have seen that Hegel's interpretations of Kant and especially Rousseau cannot be accepted as simply true; and we might ask whether this is also the case with his interpretation of Fichte. The answer, I think, is that the individualism Hegel attributes to Fichte largely fits. It is true that Fichte can sometimes describe the relationship between individual and state in more "organic" terms, emphasizing unity and identity. In one place, for example, he states that, by virtue of the social contract, "each single person becomes part of an organized whole and melts into one with it."[102] But he quickly goes on to demarcate the freedom that the individual retains independently of the state, the value of which is seen to lie in its being instrumental to the achievement of true freedom or autonomy in the realm of morality:

> That which the individual does not contribute to the end of the state is completely his own. In this respect he is not interwoven with the whole of the body of the state, but remains individual, a free, independent person; and it is this very freedom which the state has secured to him and for which alone he entered the contract. Man separates himself from his citizenship in order to elevate himself with absolute freedom to morality; but in order to be able to do so he goes through the state.[103]

Here Fichte articulates essentially the same instrumental conception of the state that we found in Kant. It is a conception that, as noted in connection with Kant, sharply contrasts with Hegel's own conception of the state as the realization or fulfillment of freedom. This is not to diminish the important ground that Hegel shares with Fichte. In his account of recognition and his treatment of abstract right, Hegel draws heavily from Fichte. But abstract right, for Hegel, constitutes only one, abstract aspect of the ethical life of the state, one that needs to be supplemented by the internality or subjectivity of morality. Insofar as Fichte identifies the state with what Hegel refers to as abstract right, his political philosophy remains stuck in the individualistic and external standpoint which Hegel seeks to overcome.

HEGEL

In this chapter, we have traced the development of the tradition of political philosophy that takes its bearings from the idea of freedom understood in terms of radical self-determination, self-dependence, or autonomy—a tradition that receives its decisive impetus from Rousseau and is most profoundly explored by Kant and Fichte. It remains now only to indicate more pointedly Hegel's relationship to this tradition of moral and political thought.

The key change Hegel effects on the tradition of political philosophy that runs from Rousseau through Kant and Fichte has to do with the way in which he conceives the relationship between freedom understood as radical self-determination or autonomy and politics. In Kant and Fichte, the link between human autonomy and politics remains largely indirect. For them, true freedom, autonomy, self-identity can be found only in the realm of morality, in which the good wills of individuals, their subjective motives and convictions, count for everything. The realm of legal right, on the other hand, because it is based on compulsion or coercion, can only reach to the external actions of individuals. It can secure the negative or formal freedom of individuals, but it cannot directly promote their positive freedom or autonomy, which resides in their uncoercible good wills. While Kant and Fichte concede that politics or the state can play an indirect role in moralizing human beings and enabling them to become autonomous or self-determining, in the end they envisage political life as at best establishing the external conditions for the individual's quest for autonomy through morality. Legal or political institutions are at best auxiliary to this quest; they hinder hindrances, but they do not directly promote or constitute the liberation or autonomy of individuals. In this respect, Kant's and Fichte's political philosophies do not take us very far beyond the individualistic and instrumental conception of the state that belongs to traditional liberalism. While they certainly attribute a loftier end or purpose to the state than earlier liberalism—

no longer mere security of life or property but the moral autonomy of individuals—they nevertheless see the state as a mere means to this end.

Hegel rejects the Kantian-Fichtean division of politics and morality and their identification of true freedom or autonomy with the latter. This may constitute his most important contribution to the political philosophy of German idealism. The state, for Hegel, is not a mere means to human freedom or autonomy; rather, it is the very realization and embodiment of such freedom or autonomy. The unity and self-identity that Kant and Fichte ascribe to morality Hegel locates squarely in the political realm. And the coerciveness and externality that loom so large in Kant's and Fichte's conceptions of right recede in Hegel's political philosophy, to be replaced by a conception of the state as the "being with oneself in the other" which he identifies with true freedom. By grasping the state as the realization or fulfillment of human freedom, Hegel overcomes the individualism that still adheres to the political philosophies of Kant and Fichte. At one and the same time, he redresses the negative, external, and coercive character of Kantian-Fichtean right; and he also redresses the emptiness of Kantian-Fichtean morality. Against the sharp distinction between right and morality, Hegel offers his doctrine of the ethical state as a synthesis of both.

Of course, it might be objected that Hegel's claims on behalf of the state are hopelessly extravagant and utopian; that by identifying the state with human autonomy or self-determination he burdens the state with a task it can never fulfill; that, in fact, Kant's and Fichte's distinction between right and morality and their refusal to see the former as anything more than instrumental to moral autonomy represents a much more sensible and realistic understanding of the relationship between politics and human freedom than the one Hegel adopts. This raises a rather large issue, one that cannot be definitively resolved in this chapter. What can be said is that it is probably a mistake to view Hegel's political philosophy as being fundamentally animated by a utopian impulse. Hegel's location of human freedom or autonomy in the political sphere and his ethical conception of the state seem to be motivated more by a concern to chasten and discipline the subjectivism unleashed by the Kantian-Fichtean conception of morality than by a desire to raise the stakes of politics. During his school days, Hegel's nickname was "the old man," suggesting that even then, in the heady aftermath of the French Revolution, his outlook on the world was not wild-eyed or devoid of healthy skepticism.[104] This sober and realistic outlook on politics deepened as Hegel grew older. This is not to suggest that Hegel's political philosophy is somehow complacent or characterized by "resignation to the limitations of human freedom" in the practical world,[105] only that it is not usefully seen as utopian in character.

But what of Hegel's relationship to Rousseau? Despite Hegel's interpretation of him, Rousseau cannot simply be reduced to the same liberal-individualist model of politics that is found in Kant and Fichte. Nor does Rousseau subscribe to the Kantian-Fichtean division between morality and politics or between autonomy and politics. In his civic republican guise, Rousseau places much more importance than either Kant or Fichte do on the role of politics in liberating individuals to be self-directing and autonomous beings. In this respect, he intimates the Hegelian view of the state as the realization or fulfillment of human freedom. Rousseau differs from Hegel in that his civic republicanism is heavily influenced by the model of classical democracy and fails to take adequate account of modern individuality, the institutions of modern bourgeois society, and the circumstances of the modern state. Rousseau restores the unity to politics, morality, and human autonomy only by appealing to the model of antiquity, whereas Hegel effects this unity on the plane of the modern state and modern civil society.

All of this suggests that Hegel's political philosophy is to be seen as a culmination of the tradition of reflection on freedom and politics that begins with Rousseau and runs through Kant and Fichte; that it represents the most powerful and philosophically satisfying expression of this tradition, preserving the insights of Hegel's predecessors while at the same time correcting their deficiencies. That, indeed, is the point of view of this book. But up to this point, I have provided only the bare statement of this point of view. The chapters that follow must elaborate its meaning and establish its truth. For this purpose a thorough analysis of Hegel's mature political philosophy in the *Philosophy of Right* is absolutely crucial. But before we can approach this work, and especially in order to see it in the context of Hegel's engagement with his philosophical predecessors, an overview of his early development is necessary.

Chapter 2 Hegel's
Development to 1806

In this chapter, I do not provide a detailed analysis of Hegel's early development up to the *Phenomenology of Spirit*, to which a number of books have been devoted already;[1] rather, I give a broad overview designed to bring out the concerns which bear on, if only to be transmuted in, Hegel's mature political philosophical outlook. The focus of this book is Hegel's mature political philosophy as it is most coherently and comprehensively presented in the *Philosophy of Right*, and I do not wish the earlier, immature writings to obscure this focus.[2] I am sensitive to Stanley Rosen's concern about basing "the study of a philosopher's ripe teaching on impressions garnered from the study of fragments composed by a boy scarcely out of his teens."[3] Nevertheless, these early writings, when properly circumscribed, can be quite helpful in gaining a purchase on the meaning of Hegel's later philosophy and its animating concerns.

The writings examined in this chapter are largely fragmentary, sometimes barely intelligible, and they do not form a settled doctrine. Nevertheless, they do contain certain recurrent themes that bear importantly on Hegel's later political philosophy. The first theme has to do with Hegel's relation to his philosophical predecessors and contemporaries, especially Kant and Fichte. Hegel's earliest philosophical efforts show themselves to be heavily influenced by Kant and his idea of freedom as autonomy. "From the Kantian system and its highest completion," he writes to his friend Schelling in 1795, "I expect a revolution in Germany."

> The consequences that will result from it will astonish many a gentleman. Heads will be reeling at this summit of all philosophy by which man is being so greatly exalted. Yet why have we been so late in recognizing man's capacity for freedom, placing him in the same rank with all spirits? I believe there is no better sign of the times than this, that mankind is being presented as so worthy of respect in itself. . . . The philosophers are proving the dignity of man. The peoples will learn to feel it. Not only will they demand their rights, which have been trampled in the dust, they will take them back themselves, they will appropriate them. (*L*, 35/1:23–24)

Toward the end of the 1790s, however, Hegel's attitude toward Kant begins to change. Here we find the first formulations of Hegel's famous critique of Kantian morality, which remains a constant feature of his moral and political thought throughout his career. Shortly thereafter, Hegel extends this critique to the political application of the Kantian moral outlook that he identifies with the political philosophy of Fichte.

This leads to the second principal theme with which we will be concerned in this chapter, namely, the theme of *Sittlichkeit* or ethical life. This idea, of course, plays an enormous role in Hegel's mature political philosophical outlook. Appearing for the first time in *Faith and Knowledge* (1802–3), the idea of *Sittlichkeit* develops directly out of Hegel's critique of the emptiness and formalism of Kantian-Fichtean morality. Against Kant's and Fichte's identification of morality with subjective reflection, Hegel argues that our ethical duties derive from the concrete customs and political institutions of a people. This, in turn, suggests that the Kantian-Fichtean distinction between morality and legality discussed in the previous chapter cannot be maintained. The moral life of the individual and the legal-political life of the community are inseparable. That is what the idea of *Sittlichkeit* is chiefly meant to express.

A third theme concerns the tension between what might be called Hegel's "Hellenic" and "modern" conceptions of politics. This theme is connected with the theme of *Sittlichkeit* insofar as Hegel tends to conceive the latter largely in terms of the Greek polis in his early writings. But the hold of the classical polis on Hegel's imagination antedates his formulation of the idea of *Sittlichkeit,* going all the way back to his earliest writings on religion and politics. A

typical way of viewing Hegel's early political philosophical development is that
he begins by romantically invoking the model of the Greek polis, but that this
Hellenic ideal gradually gives way to a more sober appreciation of the differences between ancient and modern moral and political circumstances. Although there is a certain amount of truth to this view, the relationship between
Hegel's "Hellenism" and his "modernism" is more complex, less linear, than it
suggests. Hegel's appreciation for modern individuality appears long before he
has given up on his Hellenic ideal; and it never completely displaces what the
latter was meant to represent and what Hegel continued to refer to under the
rubric of *Sittlichkeit.*

There is one other conventional opinion about Hegel's intellectual development that I will at least implicitly challenge here. Hegel's career is frequently
divided into a youthful, romantic period, in which the alienating divisions of
modern life are dissolved in the wholeness and harmony of the Greek polis, and
a mature, realistic, conservative period—dating from the *Phenomenology* and
culminating in the *Philosophy of Right*—in which Hegel largely acquiesces in
and even defends these alienating divisions.[4] Here again, though, the reality is
more complicated, less tidy. The degree to which Hegel's mature political
philosophy does not fit this conservative, not to say complacent, image will
have to await our discussion in later chapters. In this chapter, though, we will
find that the picture of the young Hegel as a wide-eyed idealist and romantic
utopian seriously distorts his basic cast of mind. I have already alluded to the
fact that Hegel's nickname in his school days was "the old man." And in his
early writings, perhaps most notably *The German Constitution* (1799–1802),
there is ample evidence of a sober and realistic sense of contemporary social and
political realities. This sense does of course deepen as Hegel matures—as for
whom does it not?—but it does not simply supervene on a youthful disposition
characterized chiefly by romantic enthusiasm.[5]

EARLY THEOLOGICAL WRITINGS OF THE 1790s

Hegel's so-called early theological writings consist of fragments written between 1793 and 1800 and devoted to historico-philosophical reflection on
religion. In these writings, Hegel is not so much interested in religion for its
own sake but, rather, as the most important means to the education and
moralization of humanity.[6] His understanding of the exact role of religion in
this larger moral and political project, however, changes in the course of these
writings. The earliest writings, from the "Tübingen Essay" of 1793 to "The

Positivity of the Christian Religion" (1795–96), are heavily influenced by Kant, especially by his *Religion Within the Limits of Reason*. In these writings, religion is viewed mainly as a means to morality. As Hegel puts it succinctly in one of them: "the aim and essence of all true religion, our religion included, is human morality" ("PC," 68/105). With "The Spirit of Christianity and Its Fate" (1798–99), an important shift takes place. In this essay, we find Hegel's first attempt at a critique of Kantian morality. Correlative with this critique, religion is no longer viewed as a means, but rather as an alternative, to morality. It is in this essay, too, that we catch our first glimpse of the distinctively Hegelian concern with overcoming all dualism. In what follows, we will be particularly interested in this shift in Hegel's attitude toward Kantian morality, since it is a theme that will figure largely in Hegel's mature moral and political philosophy.

The "Tübingen Essay" of 1793 lays down the main outlines of Hegel's earliest understanding of religion and its relation to morality. In this essay, religion is viewed as a means to the moralization and education of human beings. Pure morality, Hegel argues, while certainly the rational end of humanity, is by itself incapable of determining the wills of most human beings; their sensibility, hearts, and imaginations must be engaged. This is the task of religion. Religion works through the sensibility to draw the individual toward morality; it provides sensible motives for moral action. Religion "is a concern of the heart, it has an influence on our feelings . . . [it] gives to morality and its motive powers a new and more exalted light, it furnishes a new and more solid barrier against the might of sensual impulses" ("TE," 482–83/11–12).

Although Hegel's emphasis on the role of sensibility and imagination here in many ways marks a divergence from Kant, it would be a mistake to exaggerate the difference. The difference comes more at the level of means than of ends. Hegel agrees with Kant that "pure morality must in the abstract be sharply distinguished from sensibility in a system of morals." But he also believes that "in dealing with human nature and human life in general we must take particular account of man's sensibility, his dependence on external and internal nature" ("TE," 482/11). As he says elsewhere in the essay, while it is true that moral principles cannot be grounded in empirical nature, "when we are discussing how to influence men, we must take them as they are, and seek out all the good impulses and sentiments through which their nature can be ennobled" ("TE," 496–97/30).

Hegel's modification of Kant's moral teaching here in many respects resembles Schiller's. Schiller, too, while accepting the basic principles of Kant's moral philosophy, believed that sensibility had to be engaged in leading human beings to rational or moral freedom. Schiller, however, looked to art, not religion, to mediate thus between duty and inclination, reason and sense.[7] In emphasizing the role of sensibility and imagination in moral education in this way, Hegel and Schiller may both be said to be disciples of Rousseau. Rousseau considered it "one of the great errors of our age" that reason is used in "too unadorned a form, as if men were all mind," and "the language of signs that speak to the imagination" is completely neglected. In contrast to this modern rationalism, the ancients "acted much more by persuasion and by the affections of the soul because they did not neglect the language of signs." Rousseau sums up his teaching on the role of sensibility and imagination in moral education in this way:

> Never reason in a dry manner with youth. Clothe reason in a body if you want to make youth able to grasp it. Make the language of the mind pass through the heart, so that it may make itself understood. I repeat, cold arguments can determine our opinions, but not our actions. They make us believe and not act. They demonstrate what must be thought but not what must be done. If that is true for all men, it is a fortiori true for young people, who are still enveloped in their senses and think only insofar as they imagine.[8]

The question with which Hegel is mainly concerned in the "Tübingen Essay" is how to make religion—specifically a "public" or "folk" religion, a religion designed to influence the thoughts and actions of a people—effective toward the end of moral education. In this connection, he distinguishes between "objective" religion, which is a matter of the understanding and expresses itself in a theology, and "subjective" religion, which is a "matter of the heart" and "expresses itself only in feelings and actions" ("TE," 484/13–14, 487/17). It is, of course, the latter that Hegel is interested in. Objective religion, insofar as it operates through the understanding, is totally incapable of determining moral actions or inspiring noble emotions. Hegel's scathing critique of the understanding here, and of the Enlightenment, which is defined as "the intent to work through the understanding," is once again full of Rousseauan overtones. "Religion," he writes, "gains very little from the understanding, whose operations, whose doubts, are on the contrary more apt to numb the heart than to warm it." And: "Enlightenment of the understanding makes us cleverer certainly, but not better" ("TE," 488–94/19–27).

Hegel's task in the "Tübingen Essay" thus resolves itself into finding out how to make religion subjective, how to ensure that a folk religion "enter the web of human feelings, become associated with human impulses to action, and prove living and active in them" ("TE," 486/16). Here again he lays the greatest stress on a folk religion's appealing to the imagination, heart, and sensibility: "In a folk-religion . . . it is of the greatest moment that heart and fancy should be fulfilled with great and pure images, and that the more beneficent feelings should be aroused in the heart" ("TE," 497/30–31). This emphasis on the role of imagination, heart, and sensibility in an effective folk religion recurs throughout Hegel's early theological writings, accompanied increasingly by the critical observation of how impoverished Christianity is in this regard as compared with the Greeks or ancient Germans. Thus, in the "Berne Fragments" of 1793–94 he writes: "So long as no provision is made for the imagination (contrary to the Greek practice), the Christian religion remains a dreary and melancholy affair—something oriental, neither grown in our own soil nor readily assimilable" ("BF," 80/72). And in "The Positivity of the Christian Religion," there appears the famous passage that begins, "Every nation has its own imagery," and continues "Christianity has emptied Valhalla, felled the sacred groves, extirpated the national imagery as shameful superstition, as a devilish poison, and given us instead the imagery of a nation whose climate, laws, and interests are strange to us and whose history has no connection whatever with our own" ("PC," 145–46/197).

Here again, though, we must be careful not to exaggerate what might seem to be a romantic emphasis on imagination and national culture in Hegel's early thought. For he goes on to stipulate that, in addition to accommodating fancy, heart, and sensibility, an effective folk religion must ground its doctrines on "universal Reason." If it does not, its doctrines, besides becoming the object of controversy and critical attack, will lose "the significance in our feelings of a pure and authentic practical moment that has direct bearing upon morality" ("TE," 499–500/33–34). This condition reveals that, despite his criticisms of the Enlightenment and his seemingly romantic invocation of folk culture, Hegel continues to operate largely with the Enlightenment ideal of religion within the bounds of reason most radically expressed by Kant and his disciple (at least in this regard) Fichte.

It is this Kantian ideal of religion within the bounds of reason, of religion as the counterpart to rational morality, that dominates Hegel's outlook at Berne in the "Berne Fragments," "The Life of Jesus" (1795), and "The Positivity of the Christian Religion." The contrast that runs through these writings is between "positive" religion, on the one hand—religion based solely on external authority—and moral religion, on the other—religion whose laws emanate from the free reason of individuals. Adopting the typical and simplistic Enlightenment attitude toward Judaism found in Kant and stretching all the way back to Spinoza, Hegel sees Judaism at the time of Jesus' coming as an example of a legalistic positive religion.[9] Characterized throughout by statutory commands covering every aspect of life, the Jewish religion had reduced virtue to mechanical and spiritless obedience to the external letter of the law. Jesus came to overthrow this mechanical and slavish ethic ("LJ," 111/82–83, 118/89, 127/98; "PC," 68–71/105–8). "He undertook . . . to restore to morality the freedom which is its essence" ("PC," 69/106). He taught human beings to follow the reason residing within themselves in the form of conscience. It is only in such self-legislation that the dignity of human beings lies. At his most Kantian, Hegel has Jesus preach the categorical imperative: "To act only on principles that you can will to become universal laws among men, no less binding on you than on them—this is the fundamental law of morality" ("LJ," 115–16/87).

Hegel is concerned not only to bring out the purely moral character of Jesus' original teaching but also to inquire how this purely moral teaching came to be perverted into a positive religion. He stresses first the limitations of the Jewish audience to whom Jesus' teaching was addressed. Because the Jews were incapable of adhering to anything not based on authority, Jesus was forced to couch his moral teaching in authoritarian terms, appealing to his divine personality. This same circumstance also led to the placing of an inordinate emphasis on miracles, directly contravening the "dignity of morality, which is independent, spurns any foundation outside itself, and insists on being self-sufficient and self-grounded." Nor did Jesus' disciples, who were responsible for disseminating his teaching, altogether escape their Jewish inheritance; Hegel contrasts their dependence and narrowness with the independence of Socrates' followers in several places. Finally, a significant positive element was introduced into Christianity when small Christian sects grew into large states. The moral and religious prescriptions that had previously been a matter of voluntary subscription now became a matter of legal and coercive command ("BF," 61–65/50–54, 90–92/84–87; "PC," 71–87/108–25).

The last point raises the general issue of the young Hegel's understanding of the relationship between religion and politics, church and state. His views on this subject during the 1790s are not easy to sort out. In "The Positivity of the Christian Religion" and some of his other Berne writings, he draws the line between church and state quite sharply, relying heavily on the Kantian distinction between legality and morality. The former, insofar as it is a sphere of coercion, must not be allowed to infringe on the freedom that is the essence of the latter. Thus, Hegel argues that "the institutions and laws of a small society (whose every citizen retains the freedom to be or not to be a member), when expanded to encompass civil society at large, are no longer appropriate and cannot coexist with civil liberty" ("BF," 74–75/66).[10] Moral and religious prescriptions cannot be made into civil obligations. It is true that at one point Hegel insists that the state must take on the great task of making objective religion subjective. But even here he goes on to say that "to this end [the state's] institutions must be compatible with freedom of conviction; they must not violate conscience and liberty, but exert only an indirect influence on the motives of the will." And in the same fragment he reiterates that "civil legislation has legality rather than morality as its objective" ("BF," 78/70, 79/71).

In many of his Berne writings, then, Hegel seems to adopt a fairly conventional liberal attitude toward church-state relations. But another, more integrated view of the relationship between religion and political life can be discerned in some of Hegel's other writings from the 1790s, beginning with the "Tübingen Essay" of 1793. In that essay, Hegel states that the third requirement for an effective folk religion—besides the fact that it must be grounded in universal reason and appeal to "fancy, heart, and sensibility"—is that it "must be so constituted that all the needs of life, including the public affairs of the State, are tied in with it." And he goes on to hold up as a model the Greek polis, in which religion and politics were completely intertwined, against the unworldly and nonpolitical character of Christianity.[11] Nor is this ideal of a folk religion in which state and religion are unified something Hegel simply abandons shortly after leaving Tübingen; for it pops up once again, after he †leaves Berne, in his writings at Frankfurt.

How can these seemingly divergent positions on religion and politics, church and state, be reconciled? The answer lies in Hegel's distinction between a "folk" or "public" religion and a "private" religion. A folk religion, according to Hegel, is concerned "to form the spirit of the people (*Geist des Volks*)." Its doctrines consist of simple, uncontroversial truths bearing on people's living together—akin to Rousseau's "sentiments of sociability without which it is impossible to be a good citizen or a faithful subject."[12] Such a religion presents no problems for the autonomy of individual conscience when united with the state. A private religion, on the other hand, is concerned "to form the character of individual men." Its doctrines are much more specific, controversial, and dogmatic, and they presume to affect the individual in his innermost conscience. It is when this moralistic private religion becomes united with the public authority or state that problems arise ("TE," 505/42; also 500–2/34–

37).[13] This is what Hegel sees as having happened with Christianity, which he regards as essentially a private religion:

> Little by little this arrogant practice of prying into a person's innards, of judging and punishing his conscience, began insinuating itself [in Christian society], and did so without much difficulty, since the germ of this presumptuous attitude—its tendency falsely to extend what is appropriate only in the context of the immediate family to civil society as a whole—lay within Christianity from its very inception. . . . [T]he reformers, intent upon patterning their principles of conduct on the maxims of the New Testament and meaning to reproduce—by setting up Christian magistracies (ecclesiastical police)—the unity and uniformity of the earliest church, were misled into losing sight of the difference between measures requisite for a folk religion to gain ascendancy and the sort of regulations appropriate only for an exclusive group or private organization. ("BF," 72/62–63)

It is thus to a private religion such as Christianity, and not to a properly constituted folk religion, that Hegel's strictures on the separation of church and state apply.

The hostility to Christianity and corresponding idolization of Greek religion that characterizes Hegel's reflections on church and state receives its supreme expression in the section of "The Positivity of the Christian Religion" entitled "Difference Between the Imaginative Religion of the Greeks and the Positive Religion of the Christians." Hegel is concerned here to explain the appeal of Christianity in the ancient world, how it could have conquered paganism. His explanation ultimately focuses on the very different political spirits underlying the two religions. The religion of the Greeks and Romans was a religion for free, republican peoples, peoples who "obeyed laws laid down by themselves" and who were animated by the transindividual idea of their country or state. But republicanism eventually gave way to aristocracy and despotism, and the "picture of the state as a product of his own energies disappeared from the citizen's soul." In place of civic virtue and the "freedom to obey self-given laws" appeared individualism and the "right to the security of property." To this unfree condition corresponded Christianity, a religion in which the "right of legislation was ceded to God" and every good impulse was regarded "as the work of a being outside us in whom we have no part, a being foreign to us with whom we have nothing in common" ("PC," 151–65/202–14).[14]

This section is notable for a number of reasons. Hegel's analysis of the positive and "alienated" character of Christianity anticipates the religion-critiques of later thinkers such as Feuerbach and Marx; although it is equally important to point out that the connection he draws between Christianity and despotism looks back to thinkers such as Machiavelli and Rousseau.[15] Most importantly, though, this passage gives the clearest evidence of the young Hegel's civic republicanism and, connected with it, his Hellenic ideal. It is the Greek citizen's participation in and identification with the polis, an idea before which "his own individuality vanished," that Hegel admires, in contrast with the individualism and concern for the right to the security of private property that have characterized Europe since late Roman times.

With respect to this individualism, Hegel seems to sense another historic shift taking place in his own time, signaled perhaps by the French Revolution or, as is more likely, by the Kantian moral revolution.[16] In a Berne fragment that in many respects parallels the section of "Positivity" under consideration, he writes that humanity has begun to emerge from its "centuries-long preoc-cupation with the individual in his particularity." The "comforts and adorn-ments" of private existence have begun to "sink in value"; and "constitutions that merely guarantee life and property are no longer regarded as the best." Under this new moral and political dispensation, "the whole timorous contriv-ance" of Christianity, "this artificial system of drives and means of consolation under which so many thousand weak souls have found comfort, is becoming more and more superfluous" ("BF," 102–3/100–1).

Hegel's Hellenic ideal in "The Positivity of the Christian Religion" should not be seen as detracting from the overall Kantian character of the essay. In "Positivity," as in the writings that precede it, Hellenic ideas mix freely with Kantian ideas, sometimes complementing them, sometimes modifying them, but never wholly displacing them. The Kantian influence remains dominant. This changes, however, in the series of studies that make up "The Spirit of Christianity and Its Fate" (1798–99), written after Hegel moved from Berne to Frankfurt. Here Hegel criticizes Kantian morality, attributing to it the pos-itivity he has hitherto identified with Judaism. This marks an important devel-opment in Hegel's outlook, although the gulf between this essay and the writings that precede it has sometimes been exaggerated.

The essay begins, paradoxically, not with the spirit of Christianity, but with the spirit of Judaism. Indeed, the latter plays such an enormous role in the fate of the former that the essay could easily have been called, as one commentator has suggested, "The Spirit of Judaism and Its Fate."[17] Hegel's attitude toward Judaism here is, if anything, even more hostile than it was in his earlier writings. He characterizes Judaism chiefly in terms of opposition: in the first instance, opposition to nature, which is seen as the infinite and hostile other to be mastered; opposition to communal bonds and love, over against which loveless independence is prized; finally, the projection of this opposition into the relationship of God to nature and human beings. With respect to the latter, Hegel attributes to Judaism the same slavish and passive relationship to God that he attributed to Christianity in the "Positivity" essay. God is seen as an utterly transcendent, alien, and masterful being; there is no interpenetration of divine and human, infinite and finite. To all this Hegel contrasts the harmoniousness, freedom, and "beauty" of the Greeks. The Greeks exemplify the "beautiful" overcoming and reconciliation of the oppositions—between human beings and nature, individual and community, the divine and the human, the infinite and the finite—which characterize the spirit of Judaism ("SC," 182–205/274–97).

From this general evocation of the spirit of Judaism, Hegel goes on to consider Mosaic law and Jesus' overturning of it in his moral teaching. As in his earlier writings, Hegel here characterizes Jewish morality as thoroughly positive, consisting in slavish obedience to the external letter of the law. Against the positivity and objective commands of Mosaic law, he contends, Jesus set the "subjective in general." Here, however, the similarity to Hegel's earlier outlook ends. For, in appealing to the "subjective in general," Hegel no longer has in mind the Kantian aim of grounding moral commands in reason and the autonomy of the human will. This Kantian aim only partially removes positivity:

> [B]etween the Shaman of the Tungus, and the European prelate who rules church and state, the Voguls, and the Puritans, on the one hand, and the man who listens to his own command of duty, on the other, the difference is not that the former make themselves slaves, while the latter is free, but that the former have their lord outside themselves, while the latter carries his lord in himself, yet at the same time is his own slave. ("SC," 205–11/317–23)

Kantian ethics retain an element of positivity in the form of the dualism of duty and inclination, mastering reason and enslaved desire. Hegel finds in Jesus' moral teaching an alternative to this dualism. "To complete subjection under the law of an alien Lord, Jesus opposed not a partial subjection under a law of one's own, the self-coercion of Kantian virtue, but virtues without lordship and without submission, i.e., virtues as modifications of love" ("SC," 244/359–60). It is love that Hegel opposes to Kantian duty and bloodless respect for the law. Love—also "life"—is Hegel's formula for the unification of duty and inclination effected by Jesus, a unification in which the Kantian "ought" is replaced by "is." This "is" represents not only the synthesis of duty and inclination but also of subject and object, universal and particular, concept and intuition ("SC," 212–15/324–27). Already Hegel's speculative project of overcoming all dualism is on the horizon.

What exactly has changed in Hegel's outlook here? As far back as the "Tübingen Essay" of 1793 there is evidence of Hegel's dissatisfaction with the rigid Kantian dichotomy between duty and inclination. In that essay Hegel even speaks of love as an aspect of our empirical character which, while still pathological, nevertheless "has something analogous to Reason in it," and which therefore should be appealed to in leading human beings to full moral autonomy ("TE," 496/30). But this is not exactly Hegel's view in "The Spirit of Christianity." Whereas in the "Tübingen Essay" love—and religion in general—is conceived as a means to (Kantian) morality, in "The Spirit of Christianity" love—and again religion—is seen as something altogether different from and superior to morality. In "The Spirit of Christianity" Hegel seems finally to have realized that the synthesis between duty and inclination he has been after represents not just a modification of Kantian moral doctrine but a practical ideal of a different sort. With this realization comes a deeper appreciation of religion and its irreducibility (contra Kant) to morality.[18]

One other aspect of Hegel's critique of Kantian ethics here needs to be noticed, since it plays an important role in Hegel's later formulations of that critique. One of the most serious defects of the Kantian approach to ethics, according to Hegel, is its tendency to promote and inability to resolve conflicts of duty. "If the virtues had to be regarded otherwise than as modifications of one living spirit, if every virtue were an absolute virtue, the result would be insoluble conflicts arising from the plurality of absolutes." The universality of Kantian virtue is always purchased at the expense of particularity. A Kantian virtue or principle is always restricted to a specific, determinate, and simple circumstance. In any concrete and complex situation, therefore, a multiplicity of such virtues may be relevant, and there is no way to establish a hierarchy among them. As a result, "nothing remains save despair of virtue and trespass of virtue itself." It is otherwise when virtue is regarded as a modification of one living spirit and action is guided by a unitary disposition and not the reflective application of abstract principles. Here virtue is not "divided by the manifold character of the situation; . . . the many-sidedness of the situation remains, though the mass of absolute and incompatible virtues vanishes." Hegel sums up his difference with Kant on the nature of virtue in the following way:

A living bond of the virtues, a living unity, is quite different from the unity of the concept; it does not set up a determinate virtue for determinate circumstances, but appears, even in the most variegated mixture of relations, untorn and unitary. Its external shape may be modified in infinite ways; it will never have the same shape twice. Its expression will never be able to afford a rule, since it never has the force of a universal opposed to a particular. ("SC," 244–46/359–62)[19]

From Jesus' moral teaching, Hegel goes on to consider his specifically religious teaching, his understanding of the relationship of God to human beings. The effort here is again to see how Jesus overcame the dualisms inherent in Judaism. Thus, contrary to the Jewish idea of God as master, remote from and utterly alien to his slavish subjects, Jesus saw the relationship between God and human beings as that of a father to his children. Hegel stresses the mutuality and commonality of nature such a relationship implies ("SC," 253–67/370–82). This mutuality and commonality receives its highest expression in the idea of the "Kingdom of God," the "living harmony of men" in love, "their fellowship in God." "Is there an idea more beautiful than that of a nation of men related to one another by love?" Hegel asks. Or, was "there still to be an incompleteness in this idea . . . which would give fate a power over it" ("SC,"277–78/393–94)? It is to this question of the fate of Jesus and his church that Hegel turns in the final section of "The Spirit of Christianity."

The question of the aftermath of Jesus' moral and religious teaching in the early church is one that Hegel had grappled with before in "The Positivity of the Christian Religion," but his treatment of it here is very different. Instead of focusing on the perversion of Jesus' original message of moral autonomy through the positive emphasis on miracles and so forth, Hegel concentrates, in keeping with the general theme of "The Spirit of Christianity," on the opposition between God and the world, God and human beings, that developed in Christianity—on the failure of Christianity to fulfill its original promise of overcoming the dualisms of Jewish life. For this failure Jesus was partly to blame. Embittered by the indifference and hatred with which his teaching was met by the Jews, Jesus fled the world and all living relations and found freedom "only in the void." This opposition to the world and dread of contact with it Jesus passed on to his followers, and their spirit thereby "remained as poor as the Jewish spirit," incapable of attaining "beauty." Of course, the members of the early Christian community remained united in love, but this love proved incapable of translating itself into a living religion. Love alone, Hegel writes, in an analysis which prefigures his critique of the "beautiful soul" in the *Phenomenology*, "still falls short of religion. To become religion, it must manifest itself in an objective form." The difficulty with Christianity lay in the fact that it sought this objectification of its love in the man Jesus, who died, and who, even in resurrected form, retained an indestructible element of evanescent and unattainable individuality. "By conjoining the man Jesus with the glorified and deified Jesus," the early Christians' urge for religion was "turned into an endless, unquenchable, and unappeased longing." Christianity is ultimately unable, Hegel concludes, "to find peace in a nonpersonal living beauty. And it is its fate that church and state, worship and life, piety and virtue, spiritual and worldly action, can never dissolve into one" ("SC," 281–301/397–418).

The implicit contrast to the dualism and oppositionalism of Christianity in these last few lines of "The Spirit of Christianity"—and, indeed, throughout the entire final section—is once again with the Greeks. Contrary to what some commentators have argued,[20] the image of the social and religious integrity of ancient Greece seems to have maintained or, if anything, intensified its hold on Hegel's imagination toward the end of the 1790s. The final sentence of "The Spirit of Christianity" also suggests that, contrary to what appeared to be the case in "Positivity," Hegel has not abandoned the essentially Hellenic understanding of the relationship between church and state that he first articulated in the "Tübingen Essay." This impression is confirmed by a contemporary fragment, in which Hegel writes that "if the principle of the state is a complete whole, then church and state cannot possibly be distinct. . . . The whole of the church is thus only a fragment if men are totally smashed into particular statemen and particular church-men" (*Werke* 1:444). All of which raises the vital question of the impact of the young Hegel's Hellenic ideal on his understanding of modern politics. It is a question which must await being answered until we have considered Hegel's first substantial piece of writing on contemporary politics, *The German Constitution,* an essay which, in its defense of the minimal state, at first seems to heighten our puzzlement regarding the role of Hegel's Hellenic ideal in his understanding of modern politics.

THE GERMAN CONSTITUTION

The earliest substantial piece of writing on modern politics of Hegel's that we have is *The German Constitution.*[21] Begun at Frankfurt in 1799, the work was not completed until the end of 1802, almost two years after Hegel had moved to Jena.[22] The composition of the essay thus straddles the period of Hegel's life treated in the previous section and the Jena period to be treated in the following two. Its approach and subject-matter also do not coincide with either the "theological" framework of the earlier writings or the systematically philosophical framework of the Jena writings, although connections can (and will) be drawn to both. For these reasons, and because *The German Constitution* contains the clearest indication so far of Hegel's thinking about the actual politics of his time, I have chosen to treat it separately.

What is, of course, most striking about *The German Constitution*, especially when viewed against the background of Hegel's earlier writings, is how modern and realistic it is. The minimal, seemingly classical liberal definition of the state that lies at its center seems a far cry from the Hellenic ideal of the earlier writings, an ideal that seemed to be growing more, not less, intense for Hegel toward the end of the 1790s. For this reason scholars have had great difficulty in accounting for this essay, generally regarding it as an anomaly in Hegel's political philosophical development.[23] I argue, however, that *The German Constitution* is not an anomaly. It contains definite affinities with Hegel's earlier writings, as well as with the later Jena writings, in which the image of the Greek polis once again figures prominently. It does not represent a radical departure from Hegel's earlier Hellenic ideal but rather suggests the figurative way in which that ideal has been operating in Hegel's thought all along. Hegel's Hellenic ideal—and this expression is itself partly to blame for the misunderstanding—never functioned as a blueprint for society but rather "as a counterimage to present day reality,"[24] an alternative way of thinking about the realities of modern politics.

The German Constitution begins with the memorable line, "Germany is a state no longer." By this Hegel means that Germany, whose political identity had been maintained for centuries through the multifarious institutions of the Holy Roman Empire, is no longer a political whole united under a single, common authority but only a mass of independent and essentially sovereign principalities and city-states. Though the unifying power of the Holy Roman Empire had been on the wane throughout the eighteenth century, as states such as Prussia and Austria consolidated their administrative authority, its utter impotence had become manifest in Germany's recent defeats at the hands of the French Republic.[25] "The health of a state," Hegel comments, "is generally revealed not so much in the calm of peace as in the stir of war . . . in war the power of the association of all with the whole is in evidence" (*GC*, 143–44/461–62).

Hegel, however, does not regard the recent collapse of the Empire and the dissolution of Germany as a sudden event coming from the outside. Rather, he sees it as rooted in Germany's historic particularism—that combination of arbitrary will, independence, and stubbornness which has come to be known as

"German freedom." It is this "free," particularistic disposition of Germans, Hegel argues, which has prevented them from "being subdued to the point where the individual parts [of Germany] would have sacrificed their particular [interests] to society, united themselves together into a universal whole, and found freedom in a common, free subjection to a supreme public authority" (*GC*, 146–52/464–70). Already we can see how the simplistic individualistic interpretations of *The German Constitution* fall short. Hegel's notion of genuine freedom here, versus the particularistic German variety, retains a strong resemblance to the civic republican notion found in his earlier essays.

Hegel directs his point that Germany is no longer a state against those theorists who continue to talk about Germany as if the concept of the state were still relevant to it. This he sees as part of the general propensity of Germans—of which Marx was later to make much—to occupy themselves with concepts that no longer bear any relation to reality. It is in this context that he makes the much-commented upon methodological remark:

> The thoughts contained in this essay can have no other aim or effect, when published, save that of promoting the understanding of what is, and therefore a calmer outlook and a moderately tolerant attitude alike in words and in actual contact [with affairs]. For it is not what is that makes us irascible and resentful, but the fact that it is not as it ought to be. But if we recognize that it is as it must be, i.e. that it is not arbitrariness and chance that make it what it is, then we also recognize that it is as it ought to be. (*GC*, 145/463)

This remark has generally been seen as signaling a fundamental shift in the focus of Hegel's practical philosophy from socio-religious reform to philosophical comprehension; also as anticipating the views later expressed in the preface to the *Philosophy of Right* concerning the rationality of and the importance of comprehending and becoming reconciled to the actual.[26] Although it is difficult not to see glimmerings of Hegel's later, reconciliationist view of philosophy in this passage, it would be a mistake to see it as signaling a complete abandonment of his earlier concern with social and political reform. The context of the passage, indeed the whole argument of *The German Constitution,* suggests that we are not to understand what is in order to acquiesce in or become reconciled to it but rather in order to transform it; understanding is preliminary to reform.[27] A passage from an essay written shortly before *The German Constitution* was begun expresses Hegel's practical concern here well:

> General and deep is the feeling that the fabric of the state in its present condition is untenable. . . . Should men not wish to abandon the untenable fabric themselves

and examine with a calm eye what is really untenable in it? For judging that matter, justice is the sole criterion. The courage to do justice is the one power which can completely, honourably, and peaceably remove the tottering edifice and produce something safe in its place. How blind they are who may hope that institutions, constitutions, laws which no longer correspond to human manners, needs, and opinions, and from which the spirit has flown, can subsist any longer; or that forms in which intellect and feeling now take no interest are powerful enough to be any longer the bond of a nation! ("RDA," 244/269)

Historical comprehension of what is serves here—as in many of Hegel's early writings[28]—less as a conservative justification of the status quo than as a means of accepting the necessity of the status quo's going under.

Having argued that Germany is no longer a state, Hegel goes on to lay out what is necessary to be considered a state: "A multitude of human beings can only call itself a state if it be united for the common defence of the entirety of its property" (*GC,* 153/472). At first this definition of the state seems to jar with Hegel's disdain in his earlier writings for the notion of the state as a guarantor of the individual's right to property. Upon closer inspection, though, we notice that Hegel does not refer to the individual's property but rather to the state's. In keeping with his earlier attack on German particularism, the emphasis is on the defense of what is common and universal, not on the protection of what is private and particular.[29]

From this minimal, though not particularistic, definition of the state, Hegel goes on to recommend that the government confine itself to what is necessary to secure this minimum, leaving broad scope to the "living freedom and the individual will of the citizen." "[T]he public authority, concentrated necessarily at the centre, in the government, is regarded by the individuals at the periphery with a less jaundiced eye when it demands what it regards as necessary and what everyone can see *is* indispensable for the whole." Of particular interest in this connection is what Hegel regards as merely accidental, nonessential, to the state: not only the form of government, the type of administration, and the mode of taxation but also common language, manners, education, and religion. With respect to the cultural factors, Hegel makes an important distinction between the ancient polis and the modern state: whereas the identity of the former depended on a certain homogeneity of manners, education, and so forth, the identity of the latter does not. Indeed, Hegel argues here, as he will later on in the *Philosophy of Right,* that a good deal of the stability of modern states derives from their diversity of manners and culture. This is the first unambiguous evidence of Hegel's recognition of the fundamental difference between ancient and modern conditions. The Greek polis cannot simply be transplanted to the modern world (*GC*, 154–59/473–79).[30] The passage also points up that Hegel's political outlook in *The German Constitution* has nothing to do with modern theories of ethnic nationalism.[31]

One of the most interesting sections of *The German Constitution* is that in which Hegel contrasts his conception of the minimal state with recent theories, the central presupposition of which is that "a state is a machine with a single spring which imparts movement to all the rest of the infinite wheelwork, and that all institutions implicit in the nature of a society should proceed from the supreme public authority and be regulated, commanded, overseen, and conducted by it" (*GC*, 161/481). Hegel identifies this notion of a centralized administrative state, or "machine state," with Fichte, on the one hand, and with Jacobin France and Frederician Prussia, on the other. And to it he opposes something like Tocqueville's notion of "administrative decentralization": the central government should concern itself only with what is absolutely necessary to the state, leaving to individual citizens and smaller associations the bulk of administrative tasks and the management of local affairs. Hegel also gives rather Tocquevillean reasons for such administrative decentralization. Not only does it protect the freedom of citizens, which is "inherently sacrosanct," but it also makes for a more spirited, vital, and virtuous citizen-body. "How dull and spiritless a life is engendered in a modern state where everything is regulated from the top downwards, where nothing with any general implications is left to the management and execution of interested parties of the people." And: "A mechanical hierarchy . . . evinces no confidence whatever in its citizens and can thus expect nothing from them" (*GC*, 161–64/482–85).[32] In all this can be discerned some of Hegel's earlier civic republicanism. And it is worth noting that, for Hegel, as for Tocqueville, such civic republicanism is compatible with, indeed in the modern world inseparable from, a minimal, nonpaternalist conception of the state.

In addition to considering the essential function and scope of the modern state, Hegel offers some remarks on its political constitution. And here he shows the same appreciation for the differences between ancient and modern conditions noted above. Ancient republicanism, in which every citizen had a share in the deliberation of public affairs, is no longer a possibility for the modern state. The modern state has become too large to realize such democracy; national affairs have grown too complex for the intelligence of the average individual; and finally, in there has arisen a large class of individuals, the bourgeoisie, who are preoccupied with their own necessities and private affairs. For these reasons, direct democracy has come to be replaced in the modern world by what Hegel calls "the system of representation," consisting of a monarch ruling in conjunction with a representative assembly composed of nobility, clergy, and the third estate. If Hegel sounded like Tocqueville before, he now sounds (less anachronistically) like Montesquieu or Burke in his celebration of the system of representation, which he identifies with the feudal constitution. And like Burke, he laments the destruction of this feudal system of representation by the French Revolution, with its "blind clamour for freedom," its radical egalitarianism, and its erosion of differences and distinctions, especially between the nobility and the bourgeoisie (*GC*, 160/479–80, 202–6/532–37, 217/550–51, 234/571–72, 237/575, 241/580).

Hegel concludes *The German Constitution* by returning to Germany's plight—its radical particularism, its failure to unite under a common public authority—and he details what Germany must do to unify itself into a state. This concluding section resembles nothing more than the final chapter of *The Prince,* where Machiavelli exhorts the prince to unify Italy and liberate her from foreign domination. And this, of course, is no accident. Hegel believes that Germany confronts essentially the same anarchic situation that Italy confronted in Machiavelli's time; and he admires Machiavelli for having had the courage and insight to prescribe the drastic measures necessary to overcome this situation. "Gangrenous limbs cannot be cured with lavender water." Like Machiavelli, Hegel believes force will be necessary to make Germany into a single state; and he calls for a new Theseus to accomplish this violent deed of unification (*GC*, 217–23/551–58, 238–41/577–80). Insight and thinking are no longer enough; for

> [o]nce man's social instincts are distorted and he is compelled to throw himself into interests peculiarly his own, his nature becomes so deeply perverted that it now spends its strength on variance from others, and in the course of maintaining its separation it sinks into madness, for madness is simply the complete separation of the individual from his kind. The German people may not be capable of intensifying its obstinate adherence to particularism to that point of madness reached by the Jewish people—a people incapable of uniting in a common social life with any other. . . . Nevertheless, particularism has prerogative and precedence in Germany, and it is something so intimately personal that thinking and an insight into necessity are far too weak in themselves to become effective in action. Thought and judgement carry with them so much self-mistrust that they have to be validated by force, and only then does man submit to them. (*GC*, 242/580–81)

This final passage on German particularism brings out the connection, not always evident in the rest of the essay, between *The German Constitution* and some of Hegel's earlier (and later) writings. The reference to the particularism of the Jewish people recalls "The Spirit of Christianity" and points up the common concern that links that essay with *The German Constitution:* the concern with overcoming particularism and finding a way for human beings to unite in a common universal life. It is in the context of this concern that the concept of the minimal state in *The German Constitution* must be viewed. This concept has been so difficult to square with some of Hegel's other views, especially his Hellenic ideal, because it seems implicated in the assumptions of liberal individualism. But this is not the way Hegel sees it. For Hegel, the concept of the minimal state emerges precisely from a critique of German particularism and negative freedom; it suggests a way of realizing the unity and universality Hegel associates with the Greek polis in circumstances that are otherwise quite different from those surrounding Greek political life.[33]

When viewed in this way, Hegel's concept of the minimal state in *The German Constitution* no longer appears incompatible with the Hellenic ideal of his earlier and contemporary writings. This suggests something else: that what has been called Hegel's Hellenic ideal functions in a way that is more complex than is commonly supposed. It is not some rigid blueprint for society, an ahistorical attempt to revive the Greek polis in the modern world, but rather something more fluid and capable of being adapted to modern circumstances. It is only if we grasp Hegel's Hellenic ideal in this nonliteral way that we can make sense of Hegel's overall development up to 1806. For this ideal is not something Hegel simply sloughs off with *The German Constitution;* it continues to play a prominent role in the concept of *Sittlichkeit* that he proceeds to develop in the course of his Jena writings.

JENA WRITINGS (1)

In 1801 Hegel moved from Frankfurt to Jena. Roughly coinciding with this move, Hegel's thought takes a new direction, assuming a more systematic and philosophical form and explicitly engaging the epistemological and metaphysical debate stemming from Kant's "Copernican Revolution" in philosophy and Fichte's and Schelling's respective "extensions" of it. This shift in orientation is captured well in a letter Hegel wrote to Schelling shortly before moving to Jena: "In my scientific development, which started from the more subordinate needs of man, I was inevitably driven toward science, and the ideal of [my] youth had to take the form of reflection and thus at once of a system. I now ask myself, while I am still occupied with it, what return to intervention in the life of men can be found" (*L*, 64/1:59–60). The turn to systematic philosophy at Jena, culminating in the *Phenomenology of Spirit* in 1807, marks the decisive turning point in Hegel's philosophical development. It is at Jena that Hegel truly becomes Hegel. It is there that the issues and terms—if not the conclusions—of Hegel's later philosophy, both theoretical and practical, definitively emerge.

Hegel's first important writing at Jena was the essay *The Difference between Fichte's and Schelling's System of Philosophy* (1801). Published in *The Critical Journal of Philosophy*, which Hegel coedited with Schelling, the essay shows the obvious influence of Schelling's "identity philosophy." Yet it also displays continuities with the social-cultural concerns of Hegel's earlier writings, especially the concern for social and cultural wholeness, for overcoming the dualisms of modern life, that was so prominent in "The Spirit Christianity." In *Difference*, philosophy emerges as one of the ways—along with religion—that reason (*Vernunft*) can overcome the antitheses and dichotomies set up by the intellect (*Verstand*). "Dichotomy (*Entzweiung*)," Hegel tells us, "is the source of *the need of philosophy*" (*DFS*, 89/20). "When the might of union vanishes from the life of men and the antitheses lose their living connection and reciprocity and gain independence, the need of philosophy arises" (*DFS*, 91/22). The task of philosophy is to suspend these dichotomies and antitheses and restore the sense of the whole, or absolute, out of which they have been constructed by the intellect.

It is in the light of this project of overcoming dualism and dichotomy that Fichte's and Schelling's philosophies are compared in *Difference* and Fichte's ultimately found wanting. Hegel does not begin by criticizing Fichte. Indeed, he finds in Fichte's principle of transcendental or intellectual intuition—the famous I=I that refers to the self's prereflective awareness of itself in all of its acts, the ineluctable element of self-consciousness attending every act of consciousness—"the authentic principle of speculation [i.e., the identity of subject and object] boldly expressed" (*DFS*, 81/11). Fichte radically articulates the "determinate and express principle of idealism," namely, that "the world is a product of the freedom of intelligence" (*DFS*, 130/65–66). But, though Fichte's philosophy thus begins with the original identity of subject and object in self-consciousness—begins, as Hegel puts it, with the absolute—it ultimately falls into dualism. For Fichte goes on to argue that the I or self, in order to become *reflectively* aware of itself, must oppose to itself a not-I; it is only through opposition to something outside of it that the self becomes something determinate. Out of such opposition, however, the self never finds its way back to identity, or the absolute. Though the self, in practical activity, directs itself against the not-I, it can never completely eliminate it without, at the same time, eliminating the very condition upon which it exists. The Fichtean self is thus condemned to endless "striving" and "infinite progress." And the complete resolution of the dualism of subject and object remains, as in Kant, an "ought" never to be realized (*DFS*, 124–35/58–72).[34]

Hegel epitomizes his criticism of Fichte's philosophy by saying that it turns the "subject-object"—the original identity of subject and object in transcendental intuition—into a "subjective subject-object"—a one-sided identity achieved only through the subject's acting on and subduing the object (*DFS*, 81/11, 117/50, 135/72, 155/94). He introduces his discussion of Schelling's philosophy by arguing that Fichte's "subjective subject-object needs an objective subject-object to complete it, so that the absolute presents itself in each of the two subject-objects, and finds itself perfected only in both together as the highest synthesis that nullifies both insofar as they are opposed. As their absolute point of indifference, the absolute encloses both, gives birth to both and is born of both" (*DFS*, 155/94). Schelling advances beyond the one-sided subjectivism of Fichte's philosophy, according to Hegel, by providing an account of the "objective subject-object" in his philosophy of nature. For Fichte, in keeping with his subjectivist outlook, nature is something dead and unmeaning in itself, having significance only in relation to human ends and activity (*DFS*, 135–41/72–79). For Schelling, on the other hand, nature is something living, freely self-organizing, and (as Hegel later puts it) "spiritual." Schelling's philosophy of nature, of objective subject-object, is thus the necessary complement to Fichte's subjective transcendental philosophy. Together the two sciences constitute the essential phases of the absolute, described not a little obscurely in the passage above in terms of the Schellingian notion of an "indifference point" (*DFS*, 155–74/94–115).[35]

This is the gist of the difference Hegel sees between Fichte's and Schelling's philosophies in *Difference*. Hegel is very much under the influence of Schelling's "identity philosophy" in this essay, though some have argued there are already signs of Hegel's eventual break with his friend.[36] Be that as it may, Hegel's criticisms of Fichte in this essay remain vital for understanding the development of his own idealism, and, indeed, they are roughly the same criticisms he will make of Fichte throughout his career (see *HP,* III, 479–505/387–413). Of special interest to us are the criticisms Hegel makes of Fichte's practical—moral and political—philosophy in *Difference*. These criticisms, partly canvased in chapter 1, relate back to the critique of Kantian morality in "The Spirit of Christianity" as well as to that of the "machine state" in *The*

German Constitution; they also look forward to the important critique of Kantian and Fichtean formalism in *Natural Law.*

Hegel's critique of Fichte's practical philosophy appears in the context of his treatment of Fichte's understanding of the relation of the I to nature alluded to above. For Fichte, the freedom of the I is utterly opposed to the necessity associated with nature. In the human being, this opposition takes the form of the opposition between intelligence and natural drive, between reflection and impulse, or between reason and passion. And Fichte, no less than Kant, demands the subordination of the latter to the former, the subordination of the necessity of nature to the freedom of intelligence. The human being's final purpose, an infinite task never to be completely achieved, is "absolute freedom, absolute independence from nature" (*DFS,* 135–44/72–81).

From this general characterization of the opposition of nature and freedom in Fichte's practical philosophy, Hegel goes on to consider its application in Fichte's political and moral philosophy. In Fichte's political philosophy as presented in the *Foundations of Natural Right,* Hegel maintains, "the absolute opposition of nature and reason and the domination of reflection reveal themselves in all their harshness." Freedom is, of course, the supreme value in Fichte's political philosophy, but, Hegel argues, "freedom is here something merely negative, namely, absolute indeterminateness," opposition to the determinacy of nature. Such a notion of freedom leads to a community characterized throughout by the "lordship of the intellect" or "concept" and the "bondage of nature." In the Fichtean community of rational beings, every action, every "stirring of life," is subjected to the dominion of the concept in the form of law and to the supervision of the police. Here Hegel refers to Fichte's comment about the police knowing where every citizen is at every hour of the day as well as to his demand that citizens carry identity cards at all times as evidence of the tyrannical potential of Fichte's state (*DFS,* 142/79, 144–47/81–85). Hegel's discussion of the Fichtean "police-state" here, which he also refers to as a "machine-state," recalls his discussion of the "machine-state" in *The German Constitution.*

To the Fichtean police- or machine-state, the state under the dominion of intellect, Hegel opposes "the true infinity of a beautiful community where laws are made superfluous by customs" (*DFS,* 146/84). Once again he seems to have in mind something like the organic political life of the Greek polis. The contrast he wishes to draw is most clear in a passage already quoted in chapter 1:

> [Fichtean] natural right offers us a picture of the complete lordship of the intellect and the complete bondage of the living being. It is an edifice in which reason has no

part and which it therefore repudiates. For reason is bound to find itself most explicitly in its self-shaping as a people (*Volk*), which is the most perfect organization that it can give itself. But that state as conceived by the intellect is not an organization at all, but a machine; and the people is not the organic body of a communal and rich life, but an atomistic, life-impoverished multitude. The elements of this multitude are absolutely opposed substances . . . The unity of these elements is a concept; what binds them together is an endless domination. This absolute substantiality of points makes the basis for an atomistic system of practical philosophy in which, as in the atomistic system of nature, an intellect alien to the atom becomes law in the practical sphere under the name of *Right*. . . . *Fiat justitia, pereat mundus* is the law, and not even in the sense Kant gave it: "let right be done though all the scoundrels in the world perish." But rather in this sense: right must be done, even though for its sake, all trust, all joy and love, all the potencies of a genuinely ethical (*sittlichen*) identity, must be eradicated root and branch. (*DFS*, 148–49/87)

Fichte's moral philosophy, as presented in the *Sittenlehre* or *Doctrine of Ethics,* exhibits the same opposition of freedom and nature, the same lordship of intellect and bondage of nature, that is found in his political philosophy, only now the lordship and bondage have been internalized. Hegel's discussion here parallels his critique of Kantian ethics in "The Spirit of Christianity." In Fichte's *Ethics,* he writes, "the commander is transferred within man himself, and the absolute opposition of the command and the subservience is internalized, the inner harmony is destroyed; not to be at one, but to be an absolute dichotomy (*Entzweiung*) constitutes the essence of man." And as with Kant, the opposition in Fichte's ethics between the "formal unity of the concept" and the "manifold of nature" leads to "collisions of duty." Such collisions can be avoided only if virtue is understood, not as the reflective application of the formal and empty unity of the concept to the manifold of nature, but, as Hegel put it in "The Spirit of Christianity," as a modification of "one living spirit" (*DFS*, 149–51/87–90).

Hegel develops these criticisms of Fichte's practical philosophy—and by implication Kant's—in *Faith and Knowledge* (1802–3), deploying for the first time the distinction between *Sittlichkeit* and *Moralität,* ethical life and morality, which will play an enormous role in his mature moral and political philosophy. Fichte's practical philosophy, Hegel argues, is thoroughly formalistic; his practical ideal is a pure and empty concept utterly opposed to empirical content. "Content and ideal are incapable of union in an ethical (*sittlichen*) totality." In Fichte's political philosophy, this leads to a notion of legal right as something that has an independent being and is absolutely opposed to the sphere of life and individuality. It is not the living being itself which posits itself at the same time in the law as universal and becomes truly objective in a people (*Volk*). Rather, the universal, fixed apart, confronts life as rigorous law. Individuality finds itself under an absolute tyranny. Right shall prevail; not, however, as the inner freedom of the individuals, but as their external freedom, which is their subsumption under a concept that is alien to them. (*FK,* 182–83/425)

In Fichte's moral philosophy, the opposition of the pure will, duty for duty's sake, to empirical content leads not only to the collisions of duty mentioned above but ultimately to indecision, hypocrisy, arbitrariness, and ethical subjectivism. In an analysis that again recalls his critique of Kantian ethics in "The Spirit of Christianity," Hegel argues that in any concrete and complex situation a number of different formal duties will necessarily apply, thus giving rise to a conflict of duties. Because these formal duties are equally absolute, the choice between them becomes subjective, contingent. Such contingency allows the bad man to justify his unethical conduct by picking out an aspect of it that fulfills some duty, while it reduces the decent man to a state of weakness and indecision. Hegel's overall conclusion is that the pure, formal will is incapable of generating a necessary, determinate content; such content must be supplied by a genuine ethic (*Sittlichkeit*) in the form of the life of a people. "In a true *Sittlichkeit,* subjectivity is suspended," whereas in *Moralität,* "subjectivity is held on to and saved." It is only in *Sittlichkeit,* as opposed to *Moralität,* that "a true identity of the universal and the particular, matter and form" is achieved (*FK,* 183–86/425–28).

The idea of *Sittlichkeit* alluded to in *Faith and Knowledge* and the emerging critique of Fichtean-Kantian practical philosophy in terms of its formalism and emptiness receive their fullest treatment, at least in the early Jena period, in the essay *On the Scientific Ways of Treating Natural Law, Its Place in Moral Philosophy, and Its Relation to the Positive Sciences of Law* (1802–3), otherwise known as the *Natural Law* essay. It may be, as Manfred Riedel has argued, that this essay is still too indebted to the classical outlook and not yet sufficiently informed by the individualistic principles of modern natural law to be seen as completely anticipating the *Philosophy of Right*.[37] Nevertheless, the essay does suggest something fundamental about the direction of Hegel's political philosophy— just where he has problems with the political philosophies of his predecessors and how he uses the notion of *Sittlichkeit* to address those problems.

Hegel begins *Natural Law* by considering the two principal modern approaches to the science of natural law, both of which he regards as defective and inadequately philosophical. The first is the empirical approach, exemplified by such thinkers (though Hegel mentions no names) as Hobbes, Locke, and Hume. This approach, when it aspires to a scientific form as opposed to pure empiricism, is characterized by picking out a single aspect of a complex phenomenon and making it into the essence or purpose of the whole. Such an approach Hegel finds exemplified in the notion of the "state of nature," in which everything that is thought accidental in the civil state is stripped away, leaving behind what is essential—for example, the desire to dominate, self-preservation, or gregarious instinct. But empiricism, Hegel argues, lacks all criteria for drawing this boundary between the accidental and the essential. And when it proceeds to deduce civil society from the fictional state of nature, it becomes clear that the desired outcome was presupposed all the time. Better than such an abstractive scientific empiricism, Hegel maintains, would be a pure empiricism that did not allow itself to be confused by the understanding or by simplifying reflection. Such pure empiricism proves more often than not to be illusory, having already been contaminated by abstract reflection and concepts drawn from the culture of the day. There really is no escape from theory into immediate intuition (*NL*, 59–70/434–53).

Hegel's attitude toward the empirical approach to natural law, however, is not altogether negative. He does concede that the empirical natural law theories of Hobbes and Locke do attempt to derive political authority from the will or freedom of the subject: "infinity, regarded as the absoluteness of the subject . . . is stressed in the particular field of natural law by the systems which are called anti-socialistic and posit the being of the individual as the primary and supreme thing." Unfortunately, though, these modern theories of natural law do not think through the infinity or absoluteness of the subject in a radical enough fashion, identifying it for the most part with the empirical drives and desires of the individual. As Hegel somewhat abstractly puts it: "infinity is not raised there to the pure abstraction which it has received in the idealism of Kant and Fichte" (*NL*, 70/453–54).[38] It is to the idealism of Kant and Fichte, whose formal approach to the science of natural law lies at the opposite pole from the empirical approach, that Hegel therefore turns next.

In treating the formal approach of Kant and Fichte, Hegel returns to the line of argument that he has been developing in *Difference* and *Faith and Knowledge*. As he did in those works, he begins by characterizing Kant's and Fichte's formalism fairly abstractly in terms of the opposition of the unity of the concept and the manifold of nature, of pure reason and empirical reality, of the ideal and the real, form and content, the infinite and the finite. The principle of this formalistic philosophy is said to be, not the absolute, but the "negative absolute" (*NL*, 71–74/454–58). Hegel then goes on to consider the practical philosophy following from this formalistic point of view, this conception of the negative absolute, first in the form of Kant's ethics, and second in the form of Fichte's science of natural law.

Hegel's famous critique of Kant's ethics in *Natural Law* revolves around the charge of the "emptiness" of the categorical imperative, specifically in its first formulation, "Act only according to that maxim by which you can at the same time will that it should become a universal law."[39] Hegel's argument has two basic prongs. According to the first, Kant's so-called formula of universal law is said to be productive only of tautologies; there is no specific content that cannot be universalized in conformity with the formula. Hegel adduces Kant's example of appropriating a deposit with which one has been entrusted, in the event the owner of the deposit dies without leaving a record of it. Kant argues that such a maxim, if universalized, would contradict itself, because no deposits would then exist. "But," Hegel asks, "where is the contradiction if there were no deposits?" The non-existence of deposits is no more contradictory than their existence. Kant's formula of universal law is ultimately incapable of saying anything about the substantive issue of whether there should or shouldn't be deposits, whether there should or shouldn't be property. It issues only in the tautology that, if there is property, then there should be property. But any specific thing may be justified by such tautologous legislation—both property and non-property. For this reason, Hegel maintains that Kant's formula of universal law turns into a principle of immorality (*NL*, 76–79/461–64).

The second prong of Hegel's critique of Kant's first formulation of the categorical imperative argues that, when applied, it is self-contradictory. Moral action is generally directed against something specific, for example, the sensuous self, cruelty, or poverty. Kant's formula of universal law enjoins that such action be universalized, but in doing so it negates the specific thing that called the action forth in the first place. By universalizing moral duty, the formula of universal law negates precisely what it presupposes. Hegel puts it this way: if duty involves "the supersession of something specific, then, by the elevation of the supersession to universality or to the state of having been superseded, not only the specific thing which is to be superseded, but the superseding itself, is cancelled." Hegel then applies this to the specific injunction, "Help the poor."

This injunction, when universalized, annihilates itself. If everyone helped the poor, there would be no poor left to help. As Blake, quoted by F. H. Bradley,[40] comically writes:

> Pity would be no more
> If we did not make somebody poor.

Hegel goes on to say that this self-canceling character also belongs to the universalization of such maxims as "honorably defending one's country against its enemies," though he does not really explain how, remarking only that "when so universalized . . . the specification of country, enemies, and defense is cancelled." His basic point seems to be that patriotism, at its core, involves allegiance to a *particular* country; to see such allegiance in terms of subscription to some general principle about patriotism is to miss the particularity that is the essence of the phenomenon (*NL*, 79–80).

It must be said that Kantians (and even many non-Kantians) have not been overly impressed by these criticisms, which Hegel continues to deploy in his later writings (see *PS*, 252–59/311–19, 374–83/453–64; *PR*, §135, R, A). It is usually pointed out, for example, that Hegel's charge of the emptiness of Kant's ethics relies exclusively on the first and most formalistic formulation of the categorical imperative. In his second formulation, which enjoins us to "treat humanity, whether in your own person or in that of another, always as an end and never as a means only," Kant provides the "matter" or end that is missing from the first.[41] This second formulation, as well as the third "formula of autonomy," is much more helpful for resolving casuistic questions than the first, providing more determinate guidance as to what our positive duties are. Nor have Hegel's arguments against the first formulation of the categorical imperative gone unchallenged. In his discussion of the case of the deposit, for example, Hegel seems to distort Kant's point, which is not that deposits must exist simply, but only that they must exist if someone is to profit by appropriating them. The maxim of gaining money by appropriating deposits is self-contradictory because, when universalized, it undermines the condition, i.e., the entrusting with deposits, upon which it depends. Hegel's argument against the injunction, "Help the poor," seems similarly flawed. If the injunction is understood to be directed at abolishing the condition of poverty rather than perpetuating charitable activity (perhaps for selfish reasons, as Blake's lines suggest), there is no self-contradiction if everyone follows the injunction and poverty is indeed abolished.[42]

Though some of Hegel's specific arguments in *Natural Law* about the emptiness of Kant's categorical imperative no doubt misfire, this should not blind us to the important issue that his overall critique of Kantian ethics raises. This issue concerns the nature of practical rationality. From "The Spirit of Christianity" on, Hegel has objected to the way in which universal and particular, form and content, concept and empirical nature, are opposed to one another in Kant's moral philosophy, and the way in which the former member of each of these antitheses supervenes externally upon the latter. Kantian practical reason, according to Hegel, consists in a kind of "external reflection" whereby general principles are applied to specific contents. But because there is no essential or organic relationship between the general and the specific here, a certain amount of arbitrariness arises. Almost any particular content, duly purged of its particularity and concreteness, can be brought under general principles by such reflective reason. This, for Hegel, constitutes the formalism, indeterminateness, and essential abstractness of Kant's moral philosophy and of the reflective model of practical rationality that it embodies. In his own account of practical rationality—epitomized by his doctrine of *Sittlichkeit*—Hegel tries to bring universal and particular, form and content, into closer conjunction with one another and thus avoid the arbitrariness and subjectivism he associates with the standpoint of reflection.

The larger point Hegel is making about Kant's reflective model of practical rationality has been captured well by F. H. Bradley in his Hegelian and wonderfully provocative essay "My Station and Its Duties." Bradley argues there that in ordinary situations of moral action our judgments as to what is right or wrong are generally not the product of explicit reflection but of a nonexplicit, nondiscursive, "intuitive" type of reasoning. It is only in the comparatively rare cases where there is a difficulty of application that we reflect on our principles and engage in the self-consciously deliberative enterprise of subsuming the particular under the universal. Ordinary moral judgment is more akin to perception or intuition than it is to reflection or discursive reasoning, and the basis of such moral perception or intuition is the "morality of the community." Thus, Bradley concludes, "To the question, How am I to know what is right? the answer must be, By the *aisthēsis* of the *phronimos;* and the *phronimos* is the man who has identified his will with the moral spirit of the community, and judges accordingly."[43] Hans-Georg Gadamer makes a similar point in defending the cogency of Hegel's critique of Kant's moral philosophy. The categorical imperative demands that we self-consciously bring our particular actions under universal principles, "but it is obvious that situations of moral action are not generally ones in which we have the inner freedom for reflection of this kind."

The situation in which moral reflection can appear is always an exceptional one, a situation of conflict between duty and inclination, a situation of moral seriousness and distanced self-examination. It is impossible for us to treat the totality of moral phenomena in this way. The moral must be something different. Hegel expressed this point in a provokingly simple formula: morality is living in accordance with the customs of one's land.[44]

Bradley's and Gadamer's Hegelian appeals to the "morality of the community" and the "customs of one's land" are not, of course, without their own difficulties. And the specter of relativism that they raise might also be thought to hover over Hegel's notion of *Sittlichkeit* as well. This question cannot be answered within the confines of this chapter or the early writings it examines. A considered response to it must await our detailed analysis of the *Philosophy of Right* in later chapters. There we will find that Hegel's doctrine of *Sittlichkeit* does not reduce to a simple communitarian pluralism or relativism; that, rather, it provides a rational standard by which to judge various social orders, communities, or national customs. For the moment, though, we must be satisfied with having established that Hegel has indeed located an important problem in Kant's conception of practical rationality.

From Kant's ethics, Hegel turns to consider the application of the formal point of view to the science of natural law, which he finds most clearly and consistently worked out in Fichte's *Foundations of Natural Right*. As in *Difference* and *Faith and Knowledge,* Hegel here focuses on the external and coercive relation of law, or right, to the individual will in Fichte's political philosophy. Although the unity of right and duty, on the one hand, and the thinking and willing subject, on the other, constitutes "the great element in the philosophy of Kant and Fichte," this unity is confined to morality. The linchpin of Fichte's (and Kant's) political philosophy is the distinction between morality and legality. In deducing the latter, we cannot presuppose the former; we must proceed on the assumption of mutual distrust among human beings, or, as Fichte puts it, the assumption that "faith and constancy are lost." Legality is neither based on nor essentially concerned with the pure intentions and good will that constitute the essence of morality; rather, it is concerned with external actions—injuries to human bodies and property—which it regulates by means of "compulsion." Externality and compulsion are the hallmarks of the relation of law to the individual will in the legal sphere as Fichte conceives it, whereas morality is characterized by internality and freedom (*NL,* 83–85/469–71). It is against this notion of legality derived independently of morality, of right divorced from (as Hegel put it in *Difference*) "all trust, all joy and love, all the potencies of a genuinely ethical identity," that Hegel's notion of *Sittlichkeit* in *Natural Law* will chiefly take shape.

Hegel goes on to sketch how Fichte's system of natural law based on externality and compulsion operates and ultimately falls into self-contradiction. The key task for Fichte is to create a supreme power that can compel the individual will to accord with the general will, these two wills being presupposed as different. This immediately raises the problem of how the "supreme will, by compulsion and supervision, is also to become correspondent with the concept of the general will." Fichte's solution to this problem, according to Hegel, leading to an absurd and self-canceling circularity, is to distribute the power of the whole in such a way "between the two sides that stand over against one another that the governed are compelled by the government and *vice versa*." Fichte's ultimate solution to the problem is to create a check on the supreme power in the form of the ephorate. The ephorate would have the power to determine whether the will of the government is in tune with the general will and, if not, to suspend the government and call a constitutional convention of the people. But Hegel sees in this only more circularity. Who will judge whether the ephorate's will truly corresponds to the general will? And why would the government submit its judgment in this regard to that of the ephorate? Finally, if the people are called upon to decide the issue between the government and the ephorate, what could be expected from "such a mob . . . whose life is even less public, and who is simply not educated to be conscious of the general will, or to act in the spirit of the whole, but exactly the opposite?" All of this points, for Hegel, to the nullity of a system of law deduced independently of morality and based exclusively upon external compulsion (*NL*, 85–89/471–76).

Hegel concludes his treatment of Fichte with a discussion of the incompatibility of freedom and coercion. The discussion is rather obscure, but it is crucial insofar as it constitutes the transition to Hegel's consideration of ethical life. He begins by making a distinction between "empirical" freedom, the freedom to choose between opposed entities (+A or −A, as Hegel not very luminously refers to them throughout this discussion), and "absolute" freedom, which is not bound to either side of such an opposition and therefore stands beyond it. Hegel's basic point is that, if freedom is conceived, not as something empirical (as it is by Fichte), but as something absolute, it cannot be coerced (*gezwungen*); it can only be subdued, or subjugated (*bezwungen*). Such absolute freedom is at issue when the individual refuses to curb his lawless will under the threat of punishment but rather willingly risks the penalty, even, or rather especially, if the penalty is death. "[B]y his ability to die," Hegel writes, "the subject proves himself free and entirely above all coercion. Death is the absolute subjugator." This has implications for our notion of punishment. For if the criminal as a free man willingly risks the penalty in committing a crime, then punishment must be understood as a necessary complement to the crime, not as some external and coercive deterrent. In language anticipating his later view that the criminal wills his own punishment, Hegel writes: "Thus the punishment is the restoration of freedom, and the criminal has remained, or rather been made, free" (*NL*, 89–92/476–80).[45]

The link between freedom and death, freedom and risk of life, in the above passage—a link that will again appear in Hegel's accounts of the struggle for recognition—forms the starting-point for Hegel's crucial discussion of what he now refers to as "absolute ethical life" (*absolute Sittlichkeit*). "[T]he absolute ethical totality," Hegel tells us, "is nothing other than a *people.*" And by calling it absolute, he means to deny the view, belonging to Fichte and the entire individualistic tradition, that the ethical totality is merely instrumental to something else, the guarantor of individual freedom and security. The ethical totality as a people is an end in itself. And its character as an end reveals itself most clearly in war:

> In war there is the free possibility that not only certain individual things but the whole of them, as life, will be annihilated and destroyed for the absolute itself or for the people; and therefore war preserves the ethical health of peoples in their indifference to specific institutions, preserves it from habituation to such institutions and their hardening. Just as the blowing of the winds preserves the sea from the foulness which would result from a continual calm, so also corruption would result for peoples under continual or indeed "perpetual" peace. (*NL*, 92–93/480–82)

Apart from the dig at Kant, this notorious passage—which Hegel will later repeat in the *Philosophy of Right* (§324R)—reflects the primacy of the political whole over the particular interests comprising it that was a feature of Hegel's civic republicanism in his early theological writings and of his definition of the state in *The German Constitution.* This emphasis on the primacy of the political, or ethical, whole dominates Hegel's ensuing discussion of economic life, the "system of universal mutual dependence in relation to physical needs and work and the amassing [of wealth] for these needs." He stresses that this system of economic needs must be subordinated to the ethical whole, must be prevented from "becoming a self-constituting and independent power." "[T]he ethical whole must . . . preserve in this system the awareness of its inner nullity, and impede both its burgeoning in point of quantity, and the development of ever greater difference and inequality for which its nature strives" (*NL*, 94/482–83).

From his discussion of the subordination of economic life to absolute ethical life, Hegel goes on to discuss the two classes or estates (*Stände*) corresponding to these two dimensions of social reality. Corresponding to absolute ethical life and serving as custodians of the political whole is the estate of the free, a military estate distinguished by the virtue of courage and a willingness to risk violent death for the sake of the whole. Corresponding to economic life is the estate of the unfree, the *bourgeoisie*, which "exists in the difference of need and work, and in the law of justice of possession and property; its work concerns the individual and thus does not include the danger of death." To these Hegel actually adds a third, agricultural estate, but his interest is primarily in the first two, and especially in preventing the first from mixing with and being over-whelmed by the second. In a passage recalling his description of the decline of ancient republicanism in "The Positivity of the Christian Religion," Hegel speaks eloquently, quoting Gibbon, of the corruption and degradation arising from the universalization of private life in the Roman Empire whereby the first, ethical estate was canceled and the nation consisted solely of the economic estate. This situation, above all, must be avoided. The economic estate must be kept separate from the free, political estate; and economic life, while it must be conceded a certain autonomy, must not be allowed to overwhelm absolute ethical life (*NL*, 99–104/489–95).

One cannot help but be struck by the "oddly archaic"[46] quality of these passages from *Natural Law*. There is a recognition of the social and economic realities of modern life, but these remain tightly bound within the still domi-nant model of the organic ethical life of the Greek polis. Indeed, the roughly contemporary essay on *The German Constitution*, as we have seen, shows a greater appreciation for modern social and political reality and its differences from the ancient than what we find here in *Natural Law*. The generally classi-cal, nonmodern, and nonindividualistic perspective of *Natural Law* receives its supreme expression in the climactic section of the essay on the relationship of the individual's ethical life to absolute ethical life and the correlative relation-ship of morality to natural law.

With respect to the first relationship, Hegel argues that absolute ethical life simply is the ethical life of the individual; there is no individual ethical life apart from the ethical life of the political or social totality; "the ethical life of the individual is one pulse beat of the whole system and is itself the whole system." *Sittlichkeit*, like the Greek *ethos*, expresses this social character of individual morality perfectly, which is why the "newer systems of ethics" based on individuality and independence have adopted the word *Moralität* instead. Against the whole individualistic tradition from Hobbes through Kant and Fichte, Hegel quotes Aristotle on the priority of absolute ethical life to individual ethical life: "The people (*Volk*) is by nature prior to the individual; if the individual in isolation is not anything self-sufficient, he must be related to the whole in one unity, just as other parts are to their whole" (*NL*, 112–13/504–5). In keeping with this view, Hegel characterizes moral education—much as he will characterize it throughout his career—as the "cancellation of the subjective," the disciplining of the child to universality: "the essence of the child is that it is suckled at the breast of universal ethical life; it lives first in an absolute vision of that life as alien to it, but comprehends it more and more and so passes over into the universal spirit." And he caps his assault on moral subjectivity with a saying he will repeat in both the *Phenomenology* and the *Philosophy of Right:*

> [I]t is vain and inherently impossible to strive after a private positive ethical life. As regards ethical life, the saying of the wisest men of antiquity is alone true, that "to be ethical is to live in accordance with the customs of one's country." And as regards education, the reply of a Pythagorean to the question: "What is the best education for my son?" is "Make him a citizen of a well-ordered people." (*NL*, 115/507–8; compare *PS*, 214/266 and *PR*, §153A)

It follows from this, as regards the second relationship mentioned above, that natural law is prior to morality; the latter is nothing apart from the former. Hegel emphatically rejects the distinction between legality and morality that undergirds the political philosophies of Kant and Fichte (*NL*, 113/505–6, 116/509). Natural law is not simply a system of external security, protecting individual rights through the imposition of coercive duties. Nor is morality something purely internal and individual, divorced from the social or political totality. It is against this opposition of a purely external and coercive system of natural law and a purely internal and formal system of morality that Hegel's own understanding of natural law based on the idea of absolute ethical life is primarily directed.

The last two interrelated claims about the relationship of absolute ethical life to the ethical life of the individual and the relationship of natural law to morality seem to support Riedel's contention, alluded to above, that *Natural Law* is very much indebted to the classical outlook and not yet sufficiently informed by the individualistic principles of modern natural law (as represented by Hobbes, Rousseau, Kant, and Fichte) to be seen as completely anticipating the *Philosophy of Right*.[47] There are two things, however, that might be said to qualify Riedel's contention. First, though *Natural Law* does not show the appreciation of individuality and subjectivity that will characterize Hegel's mature political philosophy, it does contain a number of important anticipations of the latter. The critique of Kant's formalistic ethics and of Fichte's individualistic doctrine of natural law and the postulation of the notion of *Sittlichkeit* to remedy the defects discerned in these doctrines form an important and permanent part of Hegel's mature outlook. Second, it is not clear that Hegel in *Natural Law* fully subscribes to the naturalism, classical or Schellingian, that Riedel attributes to him. It is true that Hegel is not as explicit in *Natural Law* as he will later be about his affinity with the nonnaturalistic, voluntaristic tradition of natural law inaugurated by Hobbes and radicalized by Rousseau, Kant, and Fichte. Nor does he draw the line between nature and spirit as sharply as he soon will. Nevertheless, there are intimations of his later point of view in what he says about absolute freedom, the role of the negative absolute, and the fact that "spirit is higher than nature" (*NL*, 111/503).

For all that, it remains the case that *Natural Law* tries to incorporate a number of features of the classical polis, giving the essay, as noted before, a certain archaic quality. The essay also pays insufficient attention to the modern principles of individuality and subjectivity. These defects begin to be addressed in some of Hegel's later Jena writings.

JENA WRITINGS (2)

In this concluding section, I consider three related writings, the *System of Ethical Life* (1802–3), the *Philosophy of Spirit of 1803–4,* and the *Philosophy of Spirit of 1805–6.* These three writings all belong to the systematic presentations of Hegel's philosophy at Jena, and they are all united by a common structure, moving from prepolitical life—what Hegel calls "natural ethical life" (*natürliche Sittlichkeit*) in *System of Ethical Life*—through a negative moment characterized by "the struggle for recognition" to ethical life proper in the state. We will be concerned with the middle moment marked by the struggle for recognition, as it plays an important role in Hegel's later philosophy, most famously in the *Phenomenology*.[48]

Despite the structural similarities between these writings, there are a number of important differences. Indeed, the *System of Ethical Life,* written shortly after *Natural Law,* seems to have more in common with that work in terms of its overall perspective than it does with the *Philosophy of Spirit of 1805–6.* Riedel (again) has argued that the latter manuscript reflects an important change in Hegel's political philosophical outlook: the abandonment of the model of the classical polis and a growing appreciation for modern individuality.[49] There is some truth in this claim, though the change may not be quite as stark as Riedel draws it. At any rate, what and how much changes in Hegel's outlook as he moves from *Natural Law* and the *System of Ethical Life* to the *Philosophy of Spirit of 1805–6* is a question that will hover over the following analysis.

As he did in *Natural Law,* Hegel makes a distinction in the *System of Ethical Life* between absolute ethical life and economic life, or, as he puts it now, between absolute ethical life and "relative ethical life." This is a distinction within ethical or political life. In the *System of Ethical Life,* unlike *Natural Law,* Hegel also makes an analogous distinction between prepolitical life, or "natural ethical life," and ethical life proper, and he shows how the latter arises out of the former via the struggle for recognition. It is in its account of these two prepolitical moments, and of how political life proper develops out of them, that the *System of Ethical Life* is chiefly distinguished from *Natural Law.*[50]

Hegel divides his account of natural ethical life in the *System of Ethical Life* into two levels, or *Potenzen*—the latter term, like so many others in this obscure manuscript, is a Schellingian term of art. The first level is that of "Feeling," in which the concept, or universal, is subsumed under intuition, or the particular. Here Hegel is concerned primarily with human needs and their satisfaction. He begins with the most elementary form of need-satisfaction in which the subject simply annihilates the object, as in eating and drinking, and he goes on to trace the progressive mediation or spiritualization of need-satisfaction through labor, possession, the production of tools, and the use of that most spiritual of tools, speech. Despite such mediation, the concept, or thought, remains subordinate at this stage to intuition, the particular, desire (*SEL,* 103–16/9–24).

The second level of natural ethical life consists in the subsumption of intuition under the concept. In his account of this level, Hegel is largely concerned with the conceptualization of the laboring process and of possession. His account moves from the division of labor to the production of surplus, the transformation of possession into property, the emergence of legal right, and the institution of exchange, contract, and money. This conceptualization or universalization of the laboring process and of possession is paralleled by the conceptualization or universalization of the subject of labor and possession, moving from the relation of abstract "persons" through the relation of lordship and bondage and culminating in the relation of the family. It is only in the latter relation that human beings arrive at a genuine union, beyond the relation, dependence, and inequality characteristic of the previous stages of natural ethical life. In the family, according to Hegel, "the entire foregoing particularity is transformed . . . into the universal." And insofar as the family is a genuine union to which the individual gives him- or herself entirely, Hegel insists, against Kant, that it cannot be understood in terms of contract (*SEL,* 116–29/24–38).

Nevertheless, the universality achieved in the family remains, for Hegel, imperfect; it is merely natural, inner, implicit; it has not yet become an object of consciousness. Also, the "really objective intuition of one individual in another" remains "afflicted with a difference; the intuition [of the father] in the wife, the child, and the servant is not an absolutely perfect equality; equality remains inward, unspoken, still unborn; there is an invincible aspect of involvement in nature in it" (*SEL,* 128/37, 142/52, 143/53). These defects of natural ethical life are remedied in ethical life proper, the ethical life of a people. But how do we get from natural ethical life to the genuinely universal ethical life of a people? It is the task of the section entitled "The Negative or Freedom or Transgression," which contains Hegel's first account of the struggle for recognition, to explain this transformation of natural ethical life into ethical life proper (*SEL,* 129–42/38–52). As this first account of the struggle for recognition, in keeping with the rest of the *System of Ethical Life,* is quite obscure—indeed, the connections drawn in this paragraph concerning its structural role in the work as a whole are not made explicit there—I rely on the comparable, but much clearer account in the *Philosophy of Spirit of 1803–4.*

As in the *System of Ethical Life,* Hegel's account of the struggle for recognition in the *Philosophy of Spirit* is preceded by an account of natural ethical life as it is evinced in the satisfaction of human desires and in the family. Again as in the *System of Ethical Life,* Hegel is concerned to show how human desire comes to be mediated, how it transcends the immediacy and opposition between subject and object characteristic of animal desire. In the first instance, such mediation is accomplished through labor and the tool. In labor the object of desire is not simply canceled or consumed; enjoyment is deferred, and the object of desire is brought into connection with the subject by being worked on. The tool mediates the antithesis between the subject and object of desire in a similar fashion. In the tool we have an object of practical activity that is not simply an other-to-be-canceled for the subject; the tool is something that abides through the alternation of desire and its satisfaction. Analogously to the tool, the family mediates the opposition and annihilation characteristic of sexual desire. In love, marriage, and the family we come upon something that, like the tool, does not die away in the enjoyment but rather abides through it. Hegel defines love here as the "intuiting of oneself in the being of the other consciousness," a phrase that points forward to his later definition of freedom as "being with oneself in the other" (see *PR*, §7A). Such "being with oneself in the other" contrasts sharply with the animal, for whom other-being always remains opposite and outside it. Because marriage involves this idea of "being with oneself in the other," this overcoming of the opposition of subject and object, Hegel again insists that it cannot be understood as a contract. And he sees the child as the embodiment of the unity, the subject-objectivity, of the marriage partners (*FPS*, 207/266, 229–33/299–305).

Here again, though, the identity or universality attained in the family is seen by Hegel to be imperfect, merely natural, afflicted with difference and singularity; it is tested and purified only through the struggle for recognition. "[I]t is absolutely necessary," Hegel writes, "that the totality which consciousness has reached in the family recognizes itself as the totality it is in another consciousness." Here, of course, Hegel appropriates the theme of recognition that we saw Fichte first develop. Hegel's and Fichte's respective accounts of recognition share the same basic idea, namely, that free individuality cannot be achieved alone but ultimately rests on intersubjective recognition, the formation of a "community of consciousness"; but they develop this idea in different ways. The most obvious difference is that Hegel's account of recognition involves a life-and-death struggle. This points to an even more fundamental difference. Fichte's account of recognition is developed in the context of a transcendental argument designed to explain the possibility of self-consciousness; this is what gives it a certain abstractness and obscurity. In Hegel's account, on the other hand, the struggle for recognition sheds this abstract transcendental character and becomes almost completely a genetic account (albeit idealized) of the process by which the individual consciousness achieves genuine being-for-self or freedom. In this way, Hegel provides (as Fichte did not) a philosophic image as dramatic and compelling as the war of all against all in Hobbes's state of nature.

It is important to point out that the story Hegel tells, like earlier accounts of the state of nature, is not intended to be an historical account of the origins of political society but, rather, a fiction designed to bring out the necessary presuppositions of rational consciousness and rational social institutions. At the heart of this story is the motive of honor. Each family head identifies himself with every aspect of his possessions. Injury to any single aspect constitutes an offense to his integrity and honor. Such injury, Hegel maintains, is inevitable, and from it ensues the struggle for recognition. This struggle must be to the death, for it is only by going for the death of the other and thus exposing oneself to death that one proves that it is the totality of the self that is at issue in the maintenance of the single detail. This is the paradox that interests Hegel in the struggle for recognition:

> I perpetrate the contradiction of wanting to affirm the singularity of my being and my property; and this affirmation passes over into its contrary, that I offer up everything I possess, and the very possibility of all possession and enjoyment, my life itself; in that I posit myself as totality of singularity, I suspend myself as totality of singularity; I want to be recognized in this [outward] extension of my existence, in my being and possessions, but I transform this will in affirming it, because I cancel this existence and get recognition only as rational, as totality in truth, since when I go for the death of the other, I myself wager my own life, too, and cancel this extension of my existence, the very totality of my singularity. (*FPS*, 242/315)

The paradoxical result of the struggle for recognition is that the singular consciousness that originally sought recognition for itself is canceled, superseded. This canceling or superseding of singularity paves the way for the true universality and mutuality—what Hegel refers to in the *System of Ethical Life* as the "supreme subject-objectivity" (*SEL*, 144/54)—that is characteristic of absolute, as opposed to merely natural, ethical life. Not self-preservation or the protection of property lies at the basis of free political life, for Hegel, but rather the noble consciousness's contempt for these, its willingness to sacrifice life and property for the recognition of its independence. Again our attention is drawn to the civic republican ideal that underpins Hegel's account of the transition from natural ethical life to the genuinely universal ethical life of a people via the struggle for recognition. As one commentator has rightly put it, what Hegel is principally interested in in this account is the great transition "from the natural bondage of self-preservation to the freedom of self-sacrifice for the *polis*."[51] Hegel's opposition to the individualistic social contract tradition in this regard is made clear in a marginal comment he makes toward the end of the section on the struggle for recognition: "No composition, no [social] contract, no tacit or stated original contract; [to the effect that] the single [person] gives up part of his freedom, [he surrenders] the whole of it rather, his singular freedom is only his stubbornness, his death" (*FPS*, 242).

Hegel's civic republican emphasis on the freedom and universality of the ethical life of a people versus the bondage and singularity of natural ethical life pervades his entire discussion of the former. Here we must return to the *System of Ethical Life,* which contains a fuller description of the articulations of the ethical life of a people than does the more fragmentary *Philosophy of Spirit of 1803–4.* Hegel's discussion here closely parallels his discussion of absolute ethical life in *Natural Law.* As he did in *Natural Law,* Hegel sharply distinguishes between absolute ethical life, for which courage is the defining virtue and war, which "makes the emptiness of specific things emerge," the defining moment, and relative ethical life, which is largely concerned with economic satisfaction and for which honesty is the defining virtue. To these two forms of ethical life Hegel adds a third, that of trust, based on agricultural life. Corresponding to these three forms of ethical life are the three classes or estates: first, the absolute estate, or military nobility; second, the estate of honesty, or the bourgeoisie; and third, the peasantry (*SEL,* 147–56/57–68).

From this discussion of the estates comprising ethical life, the "constitution" of the state, Hegel goes on to discuss ethical life in its more active mode as "government." Here there appears Hegel's odd notion of "absolute government," presided over by elders and priests, and charged with maintaining the distinction between the three estates (*SEL,* 157–63/69–76). Somewhat more familiar is what Hegel discusses under the rubric of "universal government," consisting of the legislature, the judiciary, and the executive (*SEL,* 163–76/76–89). Especially important in this regard is what Hegel says about the role of government with respect to the economy, or system of need.

Hegel's deep interest in political economy can be traced to his careful reading of and (unfortunately lost) commentary on James Steuart's *Inquiry Into the Principles of Political Economy* in 1799 while he was in Berne.[52] This interest does not manifest itself fully, however, until we reach Hegel's analysis of the system of need in the *System of Ethical Life* (167–73/80–86)—and in a parallel passage from the *Philosophy of Spirit of 1803–4* (247–49/321–24)—an analysis far more developed than anything found in *Natural Law.* Here Hegel shows an acute awareness of the dislocation arising from the mechanism of the market and the dehumanization arising from the division of labor. In this connection, commentators feel obliged to see anticipations of Marx,[53] though Hegel himself relies mainly on Adam Smith. Nevertheless, Hegel makes essentially the same point in these writings that he made in *Natural Law:* namely, that government must bring under the control of the universal the blind and unconscious necessity characterizing the system of needs. As he vividly puts it in the *Philosophy of Spirit of 1803–4:* the "monstrous system of community" created by the system of needs "requires continual strict dominance and taming like a wild beast" (*FPS,* 249/324). Hegel is particularly concerned about the gross inequality of wealth created by the system of need, leading to the dissolution of the ethical bond of the people. "The government," he writes, "has to work as hard as possible"—primarily through taxation—"against this inequality and the destruction of private and public life wrought by it" (*SEL*, 171/84).

In the end, Hegel's conception of ethical life proper in the *System of Ethical Life* does not differ all that much from his conception of absolute ethical life in *Natural Law*. In both conceptions, Hegel's emphasis is on the primacy of the political, or ethical, whole over the particular—especially economic—interests comprising it. What is new in the *System of Ethical Life*—the account of the prepolitical moments of natural ethical life and the struggle for recognition—serves only to reinforce the distinction between the freedom of universal ethical life and the bondage of natural needs and private interests. As in *Natural Law*, too, a number of features of absolute ethical life in the *System of Ethical Life* seem "oddly archaic"—for example, what Hegel says about the estate of elders and priests. As Hyppolite comments: "The polis and the Platonic ideal mingle with eighteenth-century states in a completely unhistorical exposition."[54] This defect is redressed in the final work considered in this chapter, the *Philosophy of Spirit of 1805–6*.

Though the *Philosophy of Spirit of 1805–6* bears a certain structural affinity with the *System of Ethical Life* and the *Philosophy of Spirit of 1803–4*, it nevertheless *looks* very different from them. Gone for the most part is the Schellingian conceptual vocabulary that framed and frequently occluded the arguments of the earlier works. This is symptomatic of the larger change in Hegel's general philosophical outlook in the second half of the Jena period, marked by the waning influence of Schelling and the renewed influence of Fichte, with his radical Kantian antithesis between nature and freedom.[55] Gone also are the archaisms, the attempts to fit modern social reality into an ancient institutional framework. Indeed, the characterization of modernity vis-à-vis antiquity in terms of the "higher principle" of subjectivity and individuality emerges here for the first time. In general, we can discern in the *Philosophy of Spirit of 1805–6* the outlines of the later *Philosophy of Right* much more clearly than in any previous work. Because this is so, I sketch here only the general drift of the argument of the 1805–6 *Philosophy of Spirit*, postponing until later a full analysis of the details that it shares with the *Philosophy of Right*.

In the first part of the *Philosophy of Spirit of 1805–6*, entitled "Spirit According to Its Concept," Hegel covers roughly the same ground—albeit in a more sophisticated and perspicuous manner—that he covered in his earlier analyses of natural ethical life. He first considers "intellect," the process by which the immediacy of intuition comes to be mediated and universalized by spirit, a process in which language plays a crucial role. He then considers "will," which follows a similar process of mediation and universalization. The key mediating factors here, again recalling the earlier analyses of natural ethical life, are the tool and family possession. In the first instance, human will moves from the bare satisfaction of desire, in which the object is extinguished, through labor, to the more stable content of the tool. This process of mediation is further developed in the cognition (*Erkennen*) of love between the sexes, in which each party comes to know itself immediately in the other. The unity of male and female in love becomes objective to itself in family possession and, more spiritually, in the child. Such unity, however, remains merely natural, incompletely universal; a unity of natural, "uncultivated" selves instead of free and independent selves. Hence the necessity, as we have seen before, of one "family, as a totality [confronting] another self-enclosed totality, comprising individuals who are complete, free individualities for one another"; that is, of the struggle for recognition (*HHS*, 85–110/185–213).

Hegel's account of the struggle for recognition in the *Philosophy of Spirit of 1805–6* is by far the clearest and most developed of the accounts we have considered so far. It also makes explicit the connection of the struggle for recognition to the familiar political philosophical notions of the state of nature and natural right. The situation Hegel describes in terms of two families as self-enclosed totalities confronting one another is what, traditionally, has been referred to as the state of nature, "the free indifferent being of individuals toward one another." In the state of nature, individuals have "no rights, no obligations towards one another, but acquire them only in leaving that situation." How individuals come to have such rights and obligations, how individuals come to be related in terms of "right," is what Hegel's account of the struggle for recognition seeks to demonstrate. His central point is that right, as "the relation of persons in their behavior to others . . . the universal element of their free being, the determination, the limitation of their empty freedom," is essentially the relation of recognition. As he succinctly puts it in a marginal note, again echoing Fichte: "[R]ecognition is the [basis of] right" (*HHS*, 110–112/213–15).

The story Hegel tells—which, again, is concerned less with historical origins than with philosophical presuppositions—goes as follows. A member of one family takes possession of an unpossessed piece of land. This act is not unproblematic, however, nor is the possession necessarily recognized, insofar as it has the effect of excluding someone else from the land and of depriving them of something that otherwise could have been theirs. The two parties are thus not for one another what they are for themselves, and the struggle for recognition ensues to rectify this mutual misunderstanding. The excluded party takes the first action, since he is explicitly aware, in a way the excluding party is not, of the discrepancy between his being-for-himself and his being-for-the-other: he introduces his excluded being-for-himself into the other's possession by ruining something in it. The excluding party now realizes that his own being-for-himself does not accord with his being-for-the-other, and he "resolves not to expose his existence any further, but to arrive at a knowledge of himself, i.e., to become recognized." He no longer seeks such recognition, however, in the unstable form of a thing but rather as something "absolute, as will, i.e., as someone for whom his existence (which he had as property) no longer counts." Again we encounter the paradox that, in order to gain absolute recognition as will, the individual must risk his life. Through the "life and death struggle" that ensues, the two parties come to "know themselves as being-for-themselves . . . each sees the other as pure self, and it is a *knowledge of the will.*" The experience of separation and exclusivity gives way to the recognition of the spiritual element the two parties have in common: the "universal will" (*allgemeine Willen*) (*HHS*, 110/214, 111–18/215–21).

Once again we see how Hegel's story about the struggle for recognition differs from the stories earlier contract theorists told about the struggle of all against all in the state of nature. The key difference is, of course, that what is at issue is *recognition,* not some finite or empirical object such as self-preservation or property. It is only through the risk of these finite things, of life and property, that recognition of something absolute—free personality—can be gained. For Hegel, the transition from the state of nature to ethical, or political, life involves something far more grandiose—namely, absolutely free personality, the universal will—than anything found in Hobbes or Locke. And it is on the basis of this grandiose idea of absolute freedom that political life goes on to be constructed.

Unlike in Hegel's previous accounts of the struggle for recognition, however, the struggle for recognition in the *Philosophy of Spirit of 1805–6* does not lead directly to absolute ethical life; rather, it issues only in the "immediate" form of ethical life as "right" (*HHS*, 118/222). This is significant because it endows the sphere of right—the sphere of property, contracts, legal justice, and punishment—with an ethical importance not seen in any of Hegel's previous writings. In the *Philosophy of Spirit of 1805–6,* Hegel no longer seems to be operating with a simple contrast between an organic, holistic *Sittlichkeit* and the legalistic, individualistic bourgeois state. Ethical life here is clearly connected to legal right and incorporates considerable individuality. In its treatment of right as an essential moment following on the struggle for recognition and preceding the constitution of the state, the *Philosophy of Spirit of 1805–6* begins to intimate the structure of the later *Philosophy of Right*.

Hegel now goes on to show how the sphere of recognition itself undergoes development. In the section entitled "Actual Spirit," he takes up certain social practices and institutions that he previously, in the *System of Ethical Life*, relegated to the sphere of natural ethical life: division of labor, money, exchange, property right, contract, and legal right. The development he traces in this section is toward ever more explicit identification of the individual with the universal will. He begins by taking up some of the same topics he discussed earlier—tools, work, and possession—considering them now, however, in a social or intersubjective context. In this context, needs multiply, labor becomes mechanical, money and exchange are instituted, and mere possession is transformed into property right. Recognition takes on an even more spiritual form in contract, in which declarations, not objects, are exchanged and "the will of the other counts as such." But here a contradiction emerges between the ideal universal will expressed in the contract and the existent particular will of the individual. This contradiction is made explicit in crime, the assertion of the existent particular will against the universal one. Finally, punishment in the form of individual revenge comes on the scene as the restoration of right, "the inversion of the injured universal recognition." In all this can be discerned, not just the outlines, but even some of the specifics, of the argument of the *Philosophy of Right* (*HHS*, 119–32/222–36).[56]

A higher degree of universality is attained in "coercive law." In this sphere, "the individual person is transcended, negated [*aufgehhoben*]. That is, the totality alone is provided for, not the individual as such, who is rather sacrificed to the universal" (*HHS*, 133/237). But Hegel does not see the universal law here as simply imposing itself on the individual from the outside as something external or alien. In the first place, the law is understood to be the individual's "essence as pure universal will, i.e., as the disappearance of his will as a particular being" (*HHS*, 145/249). In the second, the individual must come to know himself in the law. Indeed, Hegel envisions the sphere of law as, in an important way, an educational process in which the individual is cultivated to universality, in which he comes to see himself in the universal (*HHS*, 132n.1/236–37n.3, 133/237, 143n.15/247n.2).

One of the most important functions of the law is to regulate property-relations among individuals. Here Hegel returns to the analysis of political economy that he began to develop in the *System of Ethical Life* and the *Philosophy of Spirit of 1803–4;* and once again he shows an acute awareness of the problems arising from modern commercial and industrial society. In the economic sphere, the universal is not yet something with which the individual consciously identifies but, rather, a blind necessity upon which he depends. Here needs are multiplied and refined, and labor becomes increasingly divided and abstract. As a result of the latter development, the individual worker becomes "more mechanical, duller, spiritless." And with the invention of machinery to further simplify and increase the productivity of labor, "a vast number of people are condemned to a labor that is totally stupefying, unhealthy, and unsafe." Modern industrial conditions also expose the worker to ever increasing contingency: "entire branches of industry, which supported a large class of people, go dry all at once because of [changes in] fashion or a fall in price due to inventions in other countries, etc.—and this large population is thrown into helpless poverty." Modern economic life comes to be characterized by the "contrast between great wealth and poverty," and this radical inequality leads "to the utmost dismemberment of the will, to inner indignation [*Empörung*] and hatred," on the part of the worker (*HHS*, 138–40/242–44).[57]

Hegel, unlike his epigone Marx, has no complete or magical solution to the problems he sees arising from modern commercial and industrial society. Nevertheless, he does envisage an important role for the state. In order to abate some of the contingency of the market, the state must serve as "universal overseer," regulating various aspects of commerce. Hegel adds, though, that such interference in the market "must be as inconspicuous as possible, since commerce is the field of arbitrariness." The state must also provide relief for the poor through "poor-taxes and institutions" (*HHS*, 140/244–45). Not a terribly profound solution to the problem of modern poverty, it might be thought, given the acuteness of Hegel's diagnosis. But then again, it is not clear we have found any better solutions to this problem that (as Hegel later commented) "agitates and torments modern societies especially" (*PR*, §244A).

The third and final part of the *Philosophy of Spirit of 1805–6*, titled "Constitution," corresponds to the absolute ethical life of a people, being concerned with the political organization of ethical life in the state. Here Hegel takes up the classical question of how a people, state, or, recalling Rousseau, "universal will" (*allgemeine Willen*) comes to be constituted. And like Rousseau, only somewhat more consistently, he denies that the universal will can be understood simply as the product of individual wills, the will of all. Rather, the universal will must be understood as "primary and the essence—and individuals have to make themselves into the universal will through the negation of their own will [in] externalization and cultivation. The universal will is prior to them, it is absolutely *there* for them." In the margin, Hegel here refers—as he did in *Natural Law*—to Aristotle's dictum that the whole is prior to the parts (*HHS*, 153–54/256–57).

With respect to the actual process by which the state is constituted, Hegel rejects the idea of a social contract as fanciful. It is more realistic, he maintains, to see states as having been established through "the noble force of great men." The passage elaborating this point is striking in its candor and underlines just how far Hegel has departed from the individualism of the social contract tradition:

> It is not [a matter of] physical strength, since many are physically stronger than one. Rather, the great man has something in him by [virtue of] which others may call him their lord. They obey him against their will. Against their will, his will is their will. Their immediate pure will is his, but their conscious will is different. The great man has the former on his side, and they must obey, even if they do not want to. This is what is preeminent in the great man—to know the absolute will [and] to express it— so that all flock to his banner [and] he is their god. In this way Theseus established the Athenian state. And thus, in the French Revolution, it was a fearful force that sustained the state [and] the totality in general. This force is not despotism but tyranny, pure frightening domination. Yet it is necessary and just, insofar as it constitutes and sustains the state as this actual individual. (*HHS*, 154–55/257–58)

Recalling *The German Constitution*, Hegel cites Machiavelli as having understood the necessity of tyranny spoken of in this passage, and he refers to contemporary Germany as suffering from the disease of particularism for which Machiavelli prescribed so acutely. Tyranny, Hegel concludes, educates the people toward the universal and toward obedience. It is only through such education that tyranny eventually becomes superfluous and the rule of law possible (*HHS*, 155–57/258–60).

If Hegel seems singularly non-, if not anti-, individualistic in his treatment of the founding of the state, the act by which a people becomes a people, our view of him changes as he goes on to consider the form the state takes after such founding. Initially, Hegel argues, the state had a democratic character. All citizens participated in public affairs, and there was an immediate identity between the individual and the universal. "This [was] the beautiful [and] happy freedom of the Greeks, which is and has been so envied." But it could not last, according to Hegel; "a higher level of abstraction [was] needed, a greater [degree of] contrast and cultivation, a deeper spirit." According to this "higher abstraction," which Hegel associates with modern times, "each individual *goes back into himself* completely, knows his own *self as such,* as the essence, comes to this sense of self-will (*Eigensinn*), of being absolute although separated from the existing universal, possessing his absolute immediately in his knowing. As an individual, he leaves the universal free, he has complete independence in himself" (*HHS,* 158–59/261–62). This emergence of individuality in the modern sense is partnered by a change in the form of government. In place of the direct democracy and the citizen consumed by public affairs of the ancient polis, there now appears a monarch and a representative legislative assembly. The relationship between individual and government becomes more mediate, less direct. "This is the higher principle of the modern era," Hegel writes in a passage that sums up the distinction he is drawing between antiquity and modernity,

> a principle unknown to Plato and the ancients. In ancient times, the common morality consisted of the beautiful public life—beauty [as the] immediate unity of the universal and the individual, [the polis as] a work of art wherein no part separates itself from the whole, but is rather this genial unity of the self-knowing Self and its [outer] presentation. Yet individuality's knowledge of itself as absolute—this absolute being-within-itself—was not there. The Platonic Republic is, like Sparta, [characterized by] this disappearance of the self-knowing individuality. (*HHS,* 159–60/262–63)

Commentators such as Riedel fix on this passage as providing the clearest evidence of Hegel's break with his earlier Hellenic ideal and of his turn toward the appreciation of modern individuality that characterizes his mature political philosophy.[58] They are largely right to do so. Nevertheless, a few provisos are necessary. First, the distinction Hegel draws here between antiquity and modernity is not entirely unprecedented in his work. He makes a similar distinction in *The German Constitution* between ancient republicanism and modern representative institutions. It is true that there we do not find modern individuality evoked in exactly the same way as it is here—a way that will become definitive in Hegel's reflections on history and politics from the *Phenomenology* to the *Philosophy of Right.* Nevertheless, there is enough similarity to suggest—as I have suggested before—that there is a certain fluidity in Hegel's "Hellenism" and "modernity" throughout these early writings; it is not always clear where the one ends and the other begins.

This leads to a second proviso, namely, that there is still a great deal in the *Philosophy of Spirit of 1805–6* that is nonindividualistic and reflects an important strand of the "Hellenism" running through Hegel's earlier writings. One need only recall the reflections immediately preceding the discussion of the "higher principle of modernity" on the priority of the universal will to the individual will to realize that Hegel has not utterly changed his stripes.[59] As noted before, Hegel here invokes the authority of Aristotle in much the same way he did in *Natural Law*—the essay Riedel sees as embodying Hegel's earlier, classical outlook. There is something here—"Hellenic ideal" is undoubtedly an inadequate expression—that runs through all of Hegel's political writings, early and late. It points to a permanent feature of his political philosophy, not something transitory, which he simply sloughs off.

This is an appropriate place to conclude our analysis of the *Philosophy of Spirit of 1805–6*. Hegel goes on to discuss the classes or estates comprising the state, adding a fourth estate—the public or bureaucratic estate—to the peasant, business, and military estates he has delineated in earlier discussions (*HHS*, 162–71/266–75). Hegel's theory of the estates here achieves the form it will for the most part retain all the way through the *Philosophy of Right*. Hegel also makes the familiar point about the ethical moment of war, in which personal security and property "vanishes in the power of the universal" (*HHS*, 171/276). But what for us is the key innovation of this work has already emerged, namely, Hegel's candid recognition of the importance of modern subjectivity and individuality. The development of this new insight, its meaning and implications for moral and political life, belongs among the many tasks of Hegel's first and most fascinating book, published one year after the *Philosophy of Spirit of 1805–6*, the *Phenomenology of Spirit*.

Chapter 3 The Moral
and Political Ideas of the
Phenomenology of Spirit

The *Phenomenology of Spirit* is one of the greatest, as well as one of the most difficult, books in the literature of philosophy. It is not primarily a book of moral or political philosophy, although much of its argument is fraught with moral and political implications. It is with these that I am concerned in this chapter, drawing out the continuities between them and the moral and political themes pursued in the previous chapter. Two themes, somewhat paradoxically related, dominate my analysis: first, Hegel's critique of individualism and his concomitant emphasis on ethical life or, as he refers to it here, "spirit" as the necessary context for ethical reason and action; second, Hegel's understanding of the role of subjectivity and individuality in the historic development of spirit. The latter theme we saw emerge in the last of the Jena manuscripts considered in the previous chapter, the *Philosophy of Spirit of 1805–6.* In the *Phenomenology,* this theme, which plays an important role in Hegel's mature political philosophy, is fully explored and developed. In many ways it constitutes the central interest of the work, filling out the final piece in Hegel's moral-political development. Again, my focus on the moral and political themes of the *Phenomenology* represents only a part of the total intention of the book. Therefore, I begin by considering the basic "epistemological" problem of the *Phenomenology*.[1]

BASIC PROBLEM OF THE PHENOMENOLOGY

The first sentence of the Introduction to the *Phenomenology* gives a good idea of the central problem of the book: "It is a natural assumption that in philosophy, before we start to deal with its proper subject matter, viz. the actual cognition of what truly is, one must first of all come to an understanding about cognition, which is regarded either as the instrument to get hold of the absolute, or as the medium through which one discovers it" (*PS*, 46/68). The *Phenomenology* is first and foremost devoted to the traditional problem of coming "to an understanding about cognition." But it rejects the traditional ways of conceiving of cognition as either an active instrument by which to get hold of the absolute—that is, ultimate reality—or a passive medium through which to apprehend it. For these ways of conceiving of cognition ultimately presuppose "a boundary between cognition and the absolute that completely separates them" (*PS*, 46/68); and they lead to a skepticism over our ability to grasp ultimate reality in knowledge. It is to refute such skepticism over cognition's or science's ability to grasp the absolute—a skepticism Hegel identifies with the philosophies of Kant and Fichte—that Hegel undertakes his exposition of how true knowledge or science makes its appearance.

The first few pages of the Preface to the *Phenomenology*, written after the rest of the book was complete, disclose the same central preoccupation with defending science's ability to reach ultimate truth against the skepticism of Kant and his followers. "The true shape in which truth exists," Hegel declares, "can only be the scientific system of such truth" (*PS*, 3/14). And he immediately counterposes this understanding of the relationship between science and ultimate truth to the increasingly influential, what might be called romantic view of thinkers like Jacobi and Schlegel that it is only in immediate intuition and feeling, not discursive thought, that one can grasp the absolute (*PS*, 4–6/14–18). This subjectivist identification of ultimate truth with immediate intuition Hegel sees as the direct result of the critical philosophy's denial of our knowledge of the absolute, the thing in itself.[2] And it is because the Kantian critique of pure reason inevitably leads to the abandonment of reason and the turn toward subjective feeling that Hegel seeks to establish knowledge on a different, surer foundation.

Hegel is not concerned at this point to refute the errors of this romantic doctrine of intuition or feeling. Instead, he simply holds up against what he regards as its complacency the fact that "ours is a birth-time and a period of transition to a new era." What is dawning is the possibility of a scientific grasp of the whole in which the absolute is no longer transposed to some remote and mysterious "beyond." Of course, this idea of science is still in its infancy; it is not yet a complete actuality but, rather, appears in an immediate and simple form, without articulation. As a result, "Science lacks universal intelligibility, and gives the appearance of being the esoteric possession of a few individuals." Ordinary consciousness, which justly demands intelligibility of science, revolts against this esotericism. This, according to Hegel, is the "Gordian knot with which scientific culture is at present struggling . . . One side boasts of its wealth of material and intelligibility, the other side at least scorns this intelligibility, and flaunts its immediate rationality and divinity" (*PS*, 6–8/18–20).[3]

Schelling and his doctrine of "intellectual intuition" are, of course, the immediate targets of Hegel's charge of esotericism here. This charge mainly concerns the form of Schelling's conception of the absolute. Hegel goes on, however, to criticize the way in which Schelling's absolute is related to content. In Schelling's system, it "appears that everything has been subjected to the absolute Idea, which therefore seems to be cognized in everything and to have matured into an expanded science." But on closer inspection, it becomes evident that Schelling's absolute is only externally applied to the diversity of the finite world "through the shapeless repetition of one and the same formula." With this pantheistic conception of the relation of the absolute to the finite world Hegel wants nothing to do, referring to it as a "monochromatic formalism" and, most famously, as "the night in which all cows are black" (*PS*, 8–9/21–22).

In the next few pages of the Preface, Hegel concisely sums up his own conception of the absolute and how it differs from Schelling's more metaphysical conception. It is crucial to grasp Hegel's departure from Schelling here, for it indicates just how little his conception of the absolute has in common with the romantic and untenable metaphysics of "cosmic spirit" with which it has been frequently identified.[4] He begins, of course, with the famous statement that "everything turns on grasping and expressing the true, not only as *substance*, but equally as *subject*" (*PS*, 9–10/23). By this Hegel does not mean to conjure up the image of a cosmic subject "ejecting the world in its becoming self-conscious,"[5] which would be simply to conceive of the absolute as a special sort of substance. Rather, he means to suggest that the absolute refers to the essentially self-conscious and self-constituting character of human experience, insight into which comes only at the end of an arduous process of such self-constitution and self-understanding. Thus, in one of his most telling statements, Hegel writes: "Of the absolute it must be said that it is essentially a *result*, that only in the *end* is it what it truly is; and that precisely in this consists its nature, viz. to be actual, subject, the spontaneous becoming of itself" (*PS*, 11/24). Precisely because the absolute is not something other than human subjectivity, it does not, as Schelling's absolute does, exclude reflection. "It is reflection that makes the true a result, but it is equally reflection that overcomes the antithesis between the process of its becoming and the result" (*PS*, 11–12/25). For Hegel, unlike Schelling, it is through reflection, not intuition or the revelatory power of art, that the absolute becomes manifest.

The most profound expression of the view that substance is essentially subject, according to Hegel, is to be found in the "representation of the absolute as *spirit*—the most sublime concept [*Begriff*] and the one which belongs to the modern age and its religion" (*PS*, 14/28). I will have much more to say about Hegel's concept of spirit, or *Geist*, below. Here I only want to point out that it is not necessary to import into this concept any dubious metaphysical or cosmic connotations. In referring to the absolute as spirit, Hegel once again seems to have in mind the essentially self-conscious and self-constituting character of human experience, the fact that what we have, and all we have, is self-determining human subjectivity. Again, insight into this ultimate fact comes only at the end of an arduous process, at which point spirit becomes *for itself* what it is *in itself*, that is, knows itself as spirit. This moment corresponds to what Hegel calls "science" and what he describes in the final chapter of the *Phenomenology* as "absolute knowing."

Such is the nature of the Hegelian absolute, different from both Spinoza's inert nature-substance and Schelling's more dynamic subject-substance. But the problem of the *Phenomenology* remains: to refute skepticism over our ability to grasp the absolute in knowledge or science, and to do so in such a way that is persuasive to ordinary consciousness, thus undoing the "Gordian knot" of scientific culture to which Schelling's intuitive and esoteric conception of the absolute gives rise. Hegel's solution to this twofold problem is, as has already been indicated, to show how true knowledge or science makes its appearance; or, put somewhat differently, to trace the formative education (*Bildung*) by which natural consciousness arrives at the standpoint of science. "[T]he individual," Hegel writes, "has the right to demand that science should at least provide him with the ladder to this standpoint [of science], should show him this standpoint within himself" (*PS*, 14–15/29). It is just such a ladder that Hegel, again in contradistinction to Schelling, intends to provide in his phenomenology of science and of spirit.

As to the exact nature of the formative process by which natural consciousness ascends to the standpoint of science, I will be brief, it being beyond the scope of this chapter to add anything of significance to the vast literature on this subject. Hegel begins by characterizing the process as a "pathway of doubt" (*Weg des Zweifels*) and of "despair" (*Verzweiflung*), since in the course of it natural consciousness comes to realize that what it takes as knowledge is not, in fact, real knowledge (*PS*, 49/72). But the procedure by which the untruth of natural consciousness is revealed is not an entirely negative one. To negate something that is untrue is not to leave behind pure nothingness but, rather, a nothingness that is specifically related to that which is negated, a "*determinate* nothingness, one which has a *content.*" What Hegel calls "determinate negation" always gives rise to a new content, and it is this that allows for the progressive character of the essentially negative process natural consciousness undergoes (*PS*, 50–51/73–74). Nor is this progress endless; it has a goal, which Hegel characterizes as "the point where knowledge no longer needs to go beyond itself, where knowledge finds itself, where concept corresponds to object and object to concept" (*PS*, 51/74), or, more simply, as "spirit's insight into what knowing is" (*PS*, 17/33).

Hegel also maintains that "progress toward this goal is . . . unhalting, and short of it no satisfaction is to be found at any of the stations on the way" (*PS*, 51/74). Why is this so? Why is consciousness impelled to pursue this "dialectical" path of negation and self-criticism, refusing to rest until it achieves nonself-undermining or absolute knowledge? It is at this point that something of an assumption creeps into Hegel's thought in the form of a distinction between the inertia of animal life and the dynamism of human consciousness:

> Whatever is confined within the limits of natural life cannot by its own efforts go beyond its immediate existence; but it is driven beyond it by something else, and this uprooting entails its death. Consciousness, however, is explicitly the *concept* of itself. Hence it is something that goes beyond limits, and since these limits are its own, it is something which goes beyond itself. . . . Thus consciousness suffers this violence at its own hands: it spoils its own limited satisfaction. When consciousness feels this violence, its anxiety may well make it retreat from the truth, and strive to hold on to what it is in danger of losing. But it can find no peace. If it wishes to remain in a state of unthinking inertia, then thought troubles its thoughtlessness, and its own unrest disturbs its inertia. (*PS*, 51/74–75)[6]

Hegel goes on to specify more precisely the dialectical character of the process by which natural consciousness is raised to absolute knowledge.[7] His principal point is that the criterion which impels this progressive development is not something that comes from the outside but, rather, is something internal to consciousness itself. "Consciousness provides its own criterion from within itself, so that the investigation becomes a comparison of consciousness with itself." The specific comparison involved is between consciousness's actual knowledge and what it claims that knowledge presupposes or is about. And what consciousness generally finds out is that there is a contradiction between these two things, that what it actually knows does not correspond to the criterion it sets up for itself. Thus, in the dialectic of "Consciousness" with which the *Phenomenology* opens, consciousness comes to realize that its knowledge is not about a reality out there and independent of it but, rather, about something to which it is self-related. What changes here is not simply consciousness's knowledge but, perhaps even more importantly, its conception of what that knowledge involves or is about, the object of its knowledge, its original criterion. Thus there arises a new form of consciousness, with a new criterion and a new ostensible object. To the consciousness being studied this new object seems to be something it comes upon externally and by chance. It is only *we* phenomenologists looking on at this development who grasp the necessary relationship between this second object and the first, this new form of consciousness and the preceding one (*PS*, 52–56/75–80).

This gets us to a major controversy in the interpretation of Hegel's dialectic. Hegel claims that the progression traced by consciousness in the *Phenomenology* is a "necessary" progression (*PS*, 20/38, 50/73, 56/80), and scholars have tried to figure out just what this "necessity" consists in and whether the dialectic of the *Phenomenology* lives up to it.[8] Views on this subject range from Findlay's suggestion that Hegel's conception of necessary development in the *Phenomenology* does not preclude the possibility of alternative paths to absolute knowledge—Hegel does not confuse the necessary with the unique—to Plant's contention that Hegel's entire philosophical project demands a much stricter, more deductive and ontological notion of necessity.[9] Again, given the scope of this chapter, I can only indicate, without fully defending, my position on this vexed and much-written-about issue. Distinguishing between the stronger claim that Hegel's dialectical progressions constitute the *only possible* resolutions to the internal contradictions of previous forms of consciousness and the weaker claim that they represent the *best possible* resolutions *so far,* I think all that is important about Hegel's general approach can be defended on the latter, weaker, and philosophically more satisfying view. Hegel's dialectical accounts in the *Phenomenology* lose none of their power or persuasiveness by being viewed in terms of general plausibility rather than in terms of strict or deductive necessity.[10]

There is one further issue about the basic structure of the *Phenomenology*—this one, too, having had much scholarly ink spilled over it—which needs to be addressed before descending to Hegel's concrete analyses. It concerns the over-all unity or coherence of the *Phenomenology*, specifically, the relation between the earlier, transcendental part of the book (up through the chapter on "Reason") and the later, historical part (comprising the chapters on "Spirit" and "Religion"). A number of commentators have argued that these two parts do not cohere and, further, that the book should have ended with the discussion of "Reason," the later historical sections being merely digressive and ultimately dispensable. Rudolf Haym's early articulation of the incoherence or "palimp-sest" view remains the *locus classicus:* "Put all at once, the *Phenomenology* is a psychology brought into confusion and disorder through a history, and a history brought to ruin through a psychology."[11] Hegel himself contributes to this view in some of his later comments on the *Phenomenology*, especially in the *Encyclopedia*.[12]

The position one takes on this question of the unity or coherence of the *Phenomenology* ultimately depends on what one sees as the central philosophi-cal claim of the book. If one takes, as I do, the central claim to be about the essentially social and historical character of human subjectivity, then the histor-ical portions of the *Phenomenology* become absolutely crucial to providing a complete account of that subjectivity.[13] The following concrete analyses will bear out this thesis about the general meaning of the *Phenomenology*, although my focus will necessarily be restricted to the more practical—ethical and political—portions of the book. Of crucial importance to confirming and clarifying the thesis will be unpacking what Hegel means by "spirit," or *Geist*. To this end we must first turn to Hegel's treatment of recognition in the chapter on "Self-Consciousness."

SELF-CONSCIOUSNESS AND RECOGNITION

The chapter on self-consciousness, with its master-slave dialectic, is, of course, one of the most famous of the whole *Phenomenology*. It has been particularly highlighted in predominantly "socio-historical" interpretations of the *Phenom-enology*, of which Alexandre Kojève's *Introduction to the Reading of Hegel* remains the *locus classicus*.[14] More recently, there has been an attempt to deemphasize the social and historical themes of the chapter on self-consciousness and to interpret it in terms of the more general "epistemological" problematic of the *Phenomenology* as a whole.[15] My approach to this chapter lies somewhere in between these two. Given my focus on Hegel's practical philosophy, I am primarily interested in the ethical and political implications of Hegel's account of the struggle for recognition and the master-slave dialectic. Nevertheless, I try to avoid the distortion that afflicts interpretations such as Kojève's in which these episodes are taken as the key to the *Phenomenology* or to Hegel's political philosophy as a whole.[16]

The chapter on self-consciousness of course follows on the first three chapters of the *Phenomenology* devoted to "Consciousness." In these chapters, Hegel explores various realist accounts of experience or knowledge and in each case demonstrates their inadequacy to account for the determinacy of experience, our ability to discriminate among the objects of experience. The root presupposition of "consciousness" is that the determinations and discriminations we make in experience are somehow the result of the world out there and independent of us, that "what is true for consciousness is something other than itself" (*PS*, 104/137). What is learned in the course of the dialectic of "consciousness" is that consciousness of anything presupposes some sort of active self-relation to it, that "consciousness" is always a form of "self-consciousness." Hegel puts this point strongly in the chapter on "Force and the Understanding": "The reason why 'explaining' affords so much self-satisfaction is just because in it consciousness is, so to speak, communing directly with itself, enjoying only itself; although it seems to be busy with something else, it is in fact occupied only with itself" (*PS*, 101/134).

Hegel now turns his attention to self-consciousness, which (he simply asserts) takes the form of "desire [*Begierde*] in general" (*PS*, 105/139). In desire, in contradistinction to "consciousness," the self does not seek truth in something other than itself but, rather, seeks certainty of itself by treating all otherness as something to be negated, destroyed, consumed. Even animals, Hegel tells us, are privy to the higher truth that belongs to desire over against mere "consciousness": "for they do not just stand idly in front of sensuous things as if they possessed intrinsic being, but, despairing of their reality, and completely assured of their nothingness, they fall to without ceremony and eat them up" (*PS*, 65/91).

This immediate form of satisfaction of desire, however, turns out to be somewhat problematic. Self-consciousness discovers that, having superseded one object of desire, it requires another to sustain its self-certainty. Every achievement of satisfaction calls forth a new desire, and it is in this endless succession of satisfaction and desire that self-consciousness becomes aware of the independence of the object. This leads to one of the most crucial transitions in Hegel's argument: "On account of the independence of the object, . . . [self-consciousness] can achieve satisfaction only when the object itself effects the negation within itself." Only another self-consciousness can effect such nega-tion within itself, and from this follows Hegel's fundamental conclusion: "self-consciousness achieves its satisfaction only in another self-consciousness." It is only in being recognized by another self-consciousness that self-consciousness can achieve unity in its otherness. With such unity-in-otherness, Hegel tells us, we have before us, albeit in rudimentary form, the "concept of spirit": the " 'I' that is 'We' and 'We' that is 'I' " (*PS*, 109–10/143–45).

Hegel next expounds in greater detail the process of recognition that issues in the relationship of mastery and servitude. Because this account is so well-known, I do not dwell on its details. But I do want to bring out just where this account departs from and where it coincides with Hegel's earlier accounts of the struggle for recognition.

The first difference with the earlier accounts is that here there is no mention of families or of property. The struggle takes place between two isolated indi-viduals or self-consciousnesses, and it is motivated, in keeping with the epis-temological problematic of the *Phenomenology*, by the pure desire for recogni-tion and self-certainty. In the first instance, the two individuals appear to one another, not as self-consciousnesses, but as ordinary objects submerged in the immediacy of "life." In order to appear to one another as self-consciousnesses, beings-for-self—which is what genuine recognition and absolute self-certainty require—each must show that he is not attached to "any specific existence" or to mere life. Each must risk his own life and, at the same time, seek the death of the other. There must be a life-and-death struggle. Here Hegel picks up the thread that runs through all his earlier accounts of recognition: genuine recog-nition and freedom require risking one's life. As he puts it here: "[I]t is only through staking one's life that freedom is won; only thus is it proved that for self-consciousness, its essential being is not [just] being, not the *immediate* form in which it appears, not its submergence in the expanse of life, but rather that there is nothing present in it which could not be regarded as a vanishing moment, that it is only pure *being-for-self*" (*PS*, 113–14/147–49).

One outcome of the life-and-death struggle is that one or both of the parties is killed. But such an outcome "does away with the truth which was supposed to issue from [the struggle]." The recognition and self-certainty for which the battle was initiated cannot take place unless both parties survive. But Hegel does not infer from this, as he had in his earlier accounts of the struggle for recognition, the necessity of a kind of mutual recognition among equals. Rather, perhaps assuming less, he postulates the emergence of an unequal relationship between an independent consciousness willing to risk its life for recognition and a dependent consciousness that prefers life to such risk (*PS*, 114–15/149–50). This outcome marks the greatest difference between the *Phenomenology*'s account of the struggle for recognition and Hegel's earlier accounts. Instead of leading directly to absolute ethical life, as in the *System of Ethical Life* and the *Philosophy of Spirit of 1803–4*, or even to ethical life in the immediate form of right, as in the *Philosophy of Spirit of 1805–6*, the struggle for recognition in the *Phenomenology* leads only to the unequal relationship of master and servant. We still have a way to go before arriving at the mutuality and universality of ethical life.

Hegel goes on to anatomize the respective consciousnesses of the master and servant. The master is, of course, the one who achieves the recognition for which the life-and-death struggle was initiated. His being-for-self is now reflected in and mediated through the consciousness of the servant, who does to himself what the master would do to him. But this recognition is ultimately flawed, for the servant has turned out to be something quite different from the independent consciousness required for genuine recognition. This is the famous impasse of the master: the recognition he receives from the servant is ultimately worthless. The being-for-self of the master is not adequately reflected in objective existence, and thus the master fails to achieve genuine self-certainty (*PS*, 115–17/150–52).

The other side of this paradox is that the truth of independent consciousness turns out to be the consciousness of the servant. At first it appeared that the servant was characterized, in contradistinction to the master, by an inadequate amount of negativity, by too great an attachment to life. But now Hegel argues that the servile consciousness

> does contain within itself this truth of pure negativity and being-for self . . . For this consciousness has been fearful, not of this or that particular thing or just at odd moments, but its whole being has been seized with dread; for it has experienced the fear of death, the absolute Lord. In that experience it has been quite unmanned, has trembled in every fibre of its being, and everything solid and stable has been shaken to its foundations. (*PS*, 117/153)

The importance Hegel here ascribes to the fear of death in the dialectical development of the servile consciousness cannot but remind one of Hobbes's emphasis on the decisive role of this fundamental passion in the state of nature.[17] But the fear of death in Hegel's analysis ultimately has a very different significance than it has in Hobbes's. To Hobbes, the fear of death remains tied to empirical and naturalistic self-preservation. To Hegel, on the other hand, the servant's fear of death signifies the melting away of everything solid, stable, empirical, and merely natural; it constitutes the beginning of the servant's overcoming of his attachment to natural existence. This is what Hegel means when he quotes the biblical saying that "the fear of the lord is the beginning of wisdom" (*PS*, 117–118/153).[18]

The overcoming of the servant's attachment to natural existence that is begun in fear is carried out in work. "Through his service [the servant] rids himself of his attachment to natural existence in every single detail; and gets rid of it by working on it." In work the fleetingness of desire and the independence of the thing that results from such fleetingness are overcome. "Work . . . is desire held in check, fleetingness staved off; in other words, work forms and shapes the thing." In the formative activity of the servant, his being-for-self acquires permanence and objectivity. In this way, the servant achieves the independence and self-certainty that eluded the master (*PS*, 117–18/153–54). Both fear and work play an important role in disciplining and educating the will of the servant, purging it of its immediacy, singularity, and egoism. This aspect of servitude is brought out particularly well in the 1825 lecture notes on the abbreviated version of "The Phenomenology of Spirit" in the *Encyclopedia*. There Hegel argues that it is through service that self-consciousness

> acquires the habit of renouncing its own will, of not allowing a free rein to desire. For the servant, fear of the lord is the beginning of wisdom. Everyone has to learn to obey, and he who is to command must have obeyed and learnt to obey i.e. must not follow his immediate and single will, his egoistic desire.—Whoever wants to command must do so reasonably, for only he who commands reasonably will be obeyed. . . . Command involves understanding how to avoid what is preposterous and absurd, and knowing what is universal involves the renunciation of the singularity of self-consciousness. This is a moment which occurs in the life of everyone, and persons who have been spoiled, who have had no curb put upon their will, are subsequently the weakest, being incapable of true purposes and interests, of acting in a genuinely purposeful manner. (*BP*, 89)

The universalizing aspect of servitude underlined in this passage leads directly, in the *Encyclopedia* "Phenomenology," to the notion of "reason." In the *Phenomenology* of 1807, on the other hand, Hegel moves from the master-slave dialectic to a consideration of the various dualistic strategies adopted by the slave to affirm his independence in the face of his external or worldly dependence: Stoicism, Skepticism, and the Unhappy Consciousness. I do not go into these important moments of self-consciousness, which (the last in particular) recall some of the religious themes from Hegel's early writings. Instead, I conclude this section with a few remarks about the relationship of Hegel's account of the struggle for recognition in the *Phenomenology* to his earlier accounts and the role of the struggle for recognition in general in Hegel's later political philosophy.

What most distinguishes Hegel's account of the struggle for recognition in the *Phenomenology* from his earlier accounts is the diminished political role that it plays. No longer does this struggle lead directly, as it did in Hegel's earlier writings, to the absolute ethical life of a people or to the legal relationships characteristic of civil society. No doubt part of this is due to the more epistemological orientation of the *Phenomenology*. But this cannot be the whole explanation, since Hegel takes up the idea of ethical life later in the chapters devoted to "Reason" and "Spirit." The diminished ethical and political significance of the struggle for recognition and master-slave dialectic is also reflected in Hegel's later writings. In the lecture notes on the *Encyclopedia* "Phenomenology," for example, Hegel stresses the priority of the struggle for recognition to the familiar relationships of family, civil society, and state (*BP,* 77–79). And in the *Philosophy of Right,* he insists that

> the point of view of the free will, with which right and the science of right begin, is already beyond that false point of view whereby the human being exists as a natural being . . . and is therefore capable of enslavement. This earlier and false appearance is associated with the spirit that has not yet gone beyond the point of view of its consciousness; the dialectic of the concept and of the as yet only immediate consciousness of freedom gives rise at this stage to the *struggle for recognition* and the relationship of *lordship and servitude.* (*PR,* §57)

The struggle for recognition and the master-slave dialectic play almost no role in Hegel's later political philosophy, and for this reason Kojève's use of these episodes as synoptic keys to Hegel's whole philosophy is misleading.[19]

Nevertheless, although its direct political significance has been diminished, the struggle for recognition in the *Phenomenology* still retains a paradigmatic meaning in Hegel's overall political philosophy. It still reflects the fundamental anti-atomistic point contained in Hegel's (and Fichte's) earlier accounts of recognition, namely, that genuine freedom cannot be achieved alone but ultimately rests on intersubjective recognition, the formation of (as he puts it in the *Encyclopedia Philosophy of Spirit*) a "universal self-consciousness" (*EPS*, §436). And it still points, even if it does not directly lead, to ethical life and the ideal of objective spirit. In recognition, Hegel has already told us, we have the concept of spirit, an intimation of the " 'I' that is 'We' and the 'We' that is 'I.' " And again in the *Encyclopedia Philosophy of Spirit*, he tells us that the universal self-consciousness that issues from the struggle for recognition "constitutes the *substance* of all the essential spirituality of the family, fatherland, and state, as well as of all the virtues of love, friendship, valor, honor, and fame" (*EPS*, §436R). Despite all this, it is in the chapter of the *Phenomenology* entitled "Reason" that we get Hegel's most explicit critique of individualist models of agency, as well as the actual transition to spirit and ethical life.

OVERCOMING INDIVIDUALISM
AND THE IDEA OF SPIRIT

The shapes of consciousness treated in the latter part of the chapter on self-consciousness—Stoicism, Skepticism, and Unhappy Consciousness—are all characterized by negation of and flight from the world. In the chapter on reason, consciousness now moves beyond its alienation from the world and comes to see itself as the whole of reality. This is the standpoint of idealism.

> Up till now [self-consciousness] has been concerned only with its independence and freedom, concerned to save and maintain itself for itself at the expense of the *world*, or of its own actuality, both of which appeared to it as the negative of its essence. But as reason, assured of itself, it is at peace with them, and can endure them; for it is certain that it is itself reality, or that everything actual is none other than itself; its thinking is itself directly actuality, and thus its relationship to the latter is that of idealism. Apprehending itself in this way, it is as if the world had for it only now come into being; previously it did not understand the world; it desired it and worked on it, withdrew from it into itself and abolished it as an existence on its own account . . . [Now] it discovers the world as *its* new real world, which in its permanence holds an interest which previously lay only in its transiency; for the *existence* of the world becomes for self-consciousness its own *truth* and *presence;* it is certain of experiencing only itself therein. (*PS*, 139–40/178–79)

In the first instance, reason appears as "Observing Reason," or the kind of reason which Hegel associates with natural science. Though bearing a certain resemblance to the apprehension characteristic of "consciousness," observing reason does not stand passively before things but, rather, actively engages them, classifying them, making experiments, and transforming sensuous particulars into universals. Observing reason is not itself aware, however, of the active role it plays in constituting the world it observes; this insight is available only to us looking on (*PS*, 145–47/185–87). At this stage, observing reason directs itself both to physical nature and to self-consciousness, and it is in relation to the latter that its limitations reveal themselves. Reducing self-consciousness to a mere thing, observing reason is ultimately incapable of accounting for free, spiritual activity and thus of accounting for itself. The absurdity of this enterprise of constructing a natural science of self-consciousness is epitomized for Hegel in the judgment of phrenology that "the being of spirit is a bone" (*PS*, 208/260).

The failure of observing reason to account for free, spiritual activity and hence for itself leads Hegel to consider a more adequate expression of reason, namely, practical or "active" reason. Here, as in the earlier transition from consciousness to self-consciousness, Hegel concedes a certain primacy to practical reason over theoretical reason. In active reason, the objectivism of observing reason is superseded by the assertion of the self through practical activity. Whereas observing reason sought to find itself as a thing, active reason seeks to produce only itself. And whereas observing reason remained unaware of its own activity in constituting the world it observed, in active reason this awareness, previously available only to us, becomes explicit for consciousness (*PS*, 211/263).

To begin with, Hegel tells us, active reason is merely individual and seeks to produce itself in a clearly counterposed "other." The burden of the ensuing sections on active reason is to expose the contradictions involved in various models of agency that start from this individualistic premise—to expose, as Judith Shklar puts it in her somewhat exaggerated account, "the moral failures of asocial men."[20] But before going through these defective individualistic models of agency, Hegel draws a picture of the goal toward which they are leading, the true, social model of agency before which they are to go under: namely, the ethical life (*Sittlichkeit*) of a people. As in his earlier writings, Hegel describes the ethical life of a people as the consummate expression of universality and reciprocity, of the identity of self and others, subject and substance:

> The *labour* of the individual for his own needs is just as much the satisfaction of the needs of others as of his own, and the satisfaction of his own needs he obtains only

through the labour of others. As the individual in his *individual* work already *unconsciously* performs a *universal* work, so again he also performs the universal work as his *conscious* object; the whole becomes, as *a* whole, his own work, for which he sacrifices himself and precisely in so doing receives back from it his own self. There is nothing here which would not be reciprocal, nothing in relation to which the independence of the individual would not, in the dissolution of its being-for-self in the *negation* of itself, give itself its *positive* significance of being *for itself.* This unity of being-for-another or making oneself a thing, and of being-for-self, this universal substance, speaks its *universal language* in the customs and laws of its nation. But this existent unchangeable essence is the expression of the very individuality which seems opposed to it; the laws proclaim what each individual is and does; the individual knows them not only as his universal objective thinghood, but equally knows himself in them, or knows them as *particularized* in his own individuality, and in each of his fellow citizens. In the universal spirit, therefore, each has only the certainty of himself, of finding in the actual world nothing but himself; he is as certain of the others as he is of himself. I perceive in all of them the fact that they know themselves to be only these independent beings, just as I am. I perceive in them the free unity with others in such wise that, just as this unity exists through me, so it exists through the others too—I regard them as myself and myself as them. (*PS*, 213–14/265–66)

Hegel concludes this evocation of the reciprocity of ethical life by repeating the saying he first uttered in the *Natural Law* essay: "The wisest men of antiquity have therefore declared that wisdom and virtue consist in living in accordance with the custom's of one's nation" (*PS*, 214/266).

The ethical life of a people is the goal toward which active reason is leading. But Hegel now complicates his story by telling us that this goal can be regarded in one of two ways. It can be regarded either as having not yet been attained, in which case the development traced would be one in which the individual will is gradually purged of its immediacy and the rawness of its impulses and is educated up to genuine universality. Or the happy state of ethical life can be regarded as already having been realized, but only "immediately and in principle," in which case "reason *must* withdraw from this happy state," for it exists as "something given," mere "being," inert substance without subjectivity or individuality. Hegel opts for the latter alternative, "since in our times that form of these [individualistic] moments is more familiar in which they appear after consciousness has lost its ethical life." He presents us with three different forms of modern, largely romantic individualism: hedonism, "the law of the heart," and virtue that opposes itself to "the way of the world" (*PS*, 214–17/266–70).

In making the transition from observing reason to the first form of active reason, hedonism, Hegel refers to Goethe's Faust, who despised intellect and science and plunged into the life of pure pleasure. There is a certain parallel between pleasure here and what Hegel earlier treated under the rubric of desire. But unlike desire, pleasure—and here Hegel principally has in mind sexual pleasure—does not seek to consume the other but to unify with it, to become one with the other without destroying it. The tragedy of sexual pleasure is that, while self-consciousness does to some extent become objective to itself through it, it does so in an utterly generic and therefore impoverished way. The unity that is attained in sexual pleasure is one that obliterates the particular individual, a unity in which the particular individual can find no reflection. Thus, for Hegel, the other side of pleasure is necessity, a kind of empty universality in which "the individual has simply perished and the absolute unyieldingness of individual existence is pulverized on the equally unrelenting but continuous world of actuality" (*PS,* 217–21/270–75).

The next form of active reason, "the law of the heart," represents an advance on hedonism in that it incorporates necessity or universality within it. This necessity or law is understood to spring from the individual heart, the natural goodness of human beings, and it is directed against the perverting and oppressive conventions of society. Hegel clearly has Rousseau in mind here and his lesser Romantic epigones, and it comes as no great surprise that he is quite contemptuous of their subjectivistic sentimentalism. He sees the law of the heart as subject to two fundamental self-contradictions. First, in being carried out, the law of the heart "ceases to be a law of the *heart,*" becoming instead a part of the alien conventional social order against which the authentic self necessarily defines itself. Second, if the injunction to follow the law of one's own heart is universalized, the law of the individual's heart must necessarily encounter resistance from others insofar as it is not the law of their hearts. In the face of this second contradiction, the law of the heart turns into the "frenzy of self-conceit." The individual explains the resistance of others and of the universal order in general in terms of the machinations of "fanatical priests" and "gluttonous despots." But the real source of perversion, Hegel tells us, lies not in these external enemies but in the immediately legislative heart itself (*PS,* 221–26/275–81).

In the course of the dialectic of the law of the heart, the conception of the universal order against which the untainted individual heart originally posed itself changes somewhat. Originally conceived as a dead, unconscious, and unspiritual necessity, the universal order that resists the law of the individual's heart comes to be seen as the law of all hearts. On the one hand, this constitutes a vivification and spiritualization of the universal order, endowing it with consciousness. On the other, it reveals the universal order to be not genuinely universal but only a kind of Hobbesian state of war:

> The universal that we have here is, then, only a universal resistance and struggle of all against one another, in which each claims validity for his own individuality, but at the same time does not succeed in his efforts, because each meets with the same resistance from others, and is nullified by their reciprocal resistance. What seems to be public *order*, then, is this universal state of war, in which each wrests what he can for himself, executes justice on the individuality of others and establishes his own, which is nullified through the action of others. (*PS*, 227/282)

Hegel calls this universal state of war masquerading as public order the "way of the world." And it is against the unfettered individualism of the way of the world that the next figure of active reason, the man of virtue, takes arms.

The man of virtue, however, does not set himself entirely against the way of the world. He seeks only to destroy the implicit form the universal takes there: the unconscious, unintended way in which the universal emerges from the play of individuality. It is precisely because the man of virtue recognizes that the universal already exists in the way of the world that Hegel calls his struggle with it a "sham-fight." Like Don Quixote, the "knight of virtue" cannot take this fight seriously or allow it to become serious, knowing "that his true strength lies in the fact that the good exists in its own right, i.e. brings itself to fulfilment." Instead, he contents himself with rhetoric and fine phrases; he "glories in this pompous talk about doing what is best for humanity, about the oppression of humanity, about making sacrifices for the sake of the good." Here Hegel expresses a disdain for a certain sort of self-conscious moralism or idealism—so different from ancient virtue, which "had in the *spiritual substance* of the nation a foundation full of meaning, and for its purpose an actual good already in existence"—that will become a staple of his ethical outlook. "Ideal entities and purposes of this kind," he acidly comments, "are empty, ineffectual words which lift up the heart but leave reason unsatisfied, which edify, but raise no edifice." Because of its purely rhetorical character, and because it seeks to suppress that individuality without which there is no actuality, virtue is finally defeated by the way of the world:

> [Virtue] wanted to consist in bringing the good into actual existence by the sacrifice of individuality, but the side of reality is nothing else but the side of individuality. . . . The "way of the world" was supposed to be the perversion of the good because it had individuality for its principle; only, individuality is the principle of the

real world; for it is precisely individuality that is consciousness, whereby what exists *in itself* exists equally *for an other;* it does pervert the unchangeable, but it perverts it in fact from the *nothing of abstraction into the being of reality.* (*PS,* 230–35/285–91)

With the breakdown of the sham and rhetorical stance of virtue, we leave behind those forms of abstract individualism in which the individual pits himself against the world and against actuality. The opposition between self and world gives way to transparency, and the individual now seeks simply to manifest himself in the world through action:

[C]onsciousness has cast away all opposition and every condition affecting its action; it starts afresh from *itself,* and is occupied not with an *other,* but with *itself.* . . . Action has, therefore, the appearance of the movement of a circle which moves freely within itself in a void, which, unimpeded, now expands, now contracts, and is perfectly content to operate in and with its own self. . . . Action alters nothing and opposes nothing. It is the pure form of transition from a state of not being seen to one of being seen, and the content which is brought out into the daylight and displayed, is nothing else but what this action is in itself. (*PS,* 237/293)

It is this purely individualistic, almost solipsistic conception of action that Hegel now proceeds to develop dialectically. His aim is to show how this conception refutes itself and leads to a more intersubjective understanding of action—leads, in fact, to spirit.

Hegel begins by specifying more precisely the presuppositions of this form of individuality that "takes itself to be real in and for itself." Such individuality postulates first an original determinate nature. Action is understood to consist simply in making this original or implicit nature explicit and actual, in translating it "from the night of possibility into the daylight of the present." It is only through action, Hegel tells us, anticipating Sartre's assertion of the priority of existence to essence, that an individual learns who or what he really is. Nor can the deed or work that results from such action be said to be good or bad; it simply expresses the original nature of the individual, and beyond that no other standard is relevant. All this suggests why Hegel entitles this section "The Spiritual Animal Kingdom." The complete absence of mediation or difference between an originally given nature and action is characteristic of animal consciousness. That this immediate harmony breaks down suggests that we are dealing with something more than animal consciousness, too (*PS,* 237–42/294–300).

The seeds of the breakdown of this self-enclosed model of action lie in the deed or work produced. Once the work is let go into the world, it encounters other determinate natures, all of which are concerned to make of it something that reflects *their* interests, *their* original natures. In this way, the work ceases to reflect simply the original nature of the individual and reveals itself to be "something perishable, which is obliterated by the counter-action of other forces and interests, and really exhibits the reality of individuality as vanishing rather than as achieved." In order to escape this contingency of action, the individual now goes from a one-sidedly subjective model of agency to a one-sidedly objective one. No longer seeking the purpose or value of an action in its ability to express his original nature, he finds it instead in its ability to express some larger, more impersonal cause or task—what Hegel refers to as *die Sache selbst,* or "the thing itself" (also translated, depending on the context, as "the matter in hand" or "the heart of the matter") (*PS,* 243–46/300–4).

Here we have the "honest consciousness": the artist creating, not to express himself, but only for art's sake; the scholar toiling selflessly to advance science. And the main point Hegel makes with respect to this consciousness is that it is not as honest or selfless as it appears to be. The individual's devotion to the abstract "thing itself" is never devoid of some personal interest or concern. Thus, when an individual carries out an action, and others, assuming that his interest is in the "thing itself" as such, come along and offer their assistance or point out that the thing has already been accomplished by them, the individual is forced to confess that "it is its *own* action and its *own* effort that constitute its interest in the 'matter in hand.'" When the others find out that this is the real motivation behind the action, they feel deceived. But Hegel points out that they themselves are guilty of the same deception, since their original offer of help was itself motivated by a desire to exhibit their own action, their own effort, and not by the pure "thing itself." He concludes:

> It is, then, equally a deception of oneself and of others if it is pretended that what one is concerned with is the *"matter in hand" alone.* A consciousness that opens up a subject-matter soon learns that others hurry along like flies to freshly poured-out milk, and want to busy themselves with it; and they learn about the individual that he, too, is concerned with the subject-matter, not as an *object,* but as his *own* affair. (*PS,* 247–51/305–10)

Hegel makes this point not because he is interested in unmasking the self-interested or self-expressive basis of all action. As we have already seen, he rejects this one-sidedly subjective account of agency. Action is never simply for oneself but always also for others. "Actualization is . . . a display of what is one's own in the element of universality whereby it becomes, and should become, the affair of everyone." It is this intersubjective dimension of agency that Hegel draws our attention to here, a dimension missing in the foregoing individualistic accounts of action as either an expression of one's original nature or an expression of some abstract and impersonal "thing itself." The real "thing itself" is the "*action* of the *single* individual and of all individuals," or, in the more memorable phrase, the "doing of all and each" (*das Tun Aller und Jeder*). This "thing itself" socially understood Hegel refers to as "spiritual essence" (*geistige Wesen*) (*PS*, 251–52/310).

We are now on the threshold of the idea of spirit and of ethical substance prefigured at the beginning of the section on individualistic reason. But before making the transition to the authentic expression of this idea in the life of a people, Hegel considers two individualistic refractions of it: law-giving reason and law-testing reason. In the first, individual self-consciousness believes that it knows immediately what is right and good and expresses this immediate knowledge in unconditional laws such as "Everyone ought to speak the truth" and "Love thy neighbor as thyself." But these laws, Hegel points out, are not as unconditional or universal as they appear, for they are contingent on one's knowing the truth or on one's loving intelligently. "To legislate immediately in [this] way is thus the tyrannical insolence which makes caprice into law and ethical behaviour into obedience to such caprice." The failure to find a universal content for its laws leads individual self-consciousness to the more modest task of establishing their formal universality, testing them for the absence of self-contradiction. Hegel clearly has Kant's categorical imperative in mind here, and the criticism he makes of it is the same one he made in *Natural Law:* the universalization test issues only in empty tautologies according to which any specific content (Hegel again uses the example of property) can be justified. Once again, we end up with arbitrariness and caprice (*PS*, 252–60/311–20).

In both law-giving reason and law-testing reason the individual remains primary: "[ethical] substance is at first only a *willing* and *knowing* by this particular individual." In becoming genuinely ethical, self-consciousness now leaves behind this individualism and relates itself to laws that are understood to have "intrinsic being." These laws are eternal; they are not grounded "in the will of a particular individual," nor are they "validated by *my* insight"; they are valid in and for themselves. As Hegel puts it at his most anti-subjectivistic, these laws simply "*are,* and nothing more; this is what constitutes [self-consciousness's] relationship to them." He goes on to quote Sophocles' *Antigone:*

They are not of yesterday or today, but everlasting,
Though where they came from, none of us can tell.

The ethical disposition (*die sittliche Gesinnung*) consists not in making laws or in testing them for self-consistency; it "consists just in sticking steadfastly to what is right, and abstaining from all attempts to move or shake it, or derive it" (*PS,* 260–62/320–23).

In this way, reason becomes spirit (*Geist*). This transition, as well as the critique of the various forms of individualism leading up to it, essentially mirrors the move from individuality to ethical life found in Hegel's earlier Jena writings, from the *Natural Law* essay on. Though the depiction and critique of the various strategies adopted by individualistic practical reason are undoubtedly richer, more detailed, and more dramatic in the *Phenomenology,* Hegel's fundamental point remains the same: individual reason alone is inadequate to determine our ethical duties; these duties must ultimately be grounded in some sort of intersubjective context, must be related to the social whole. In this regard at least, the *Phenomenology* does not depart from Hegel's earlier writings; it simply provides the most elaborate defense so far for the social character of practical reason or morality.

Along these same lines, one cannot help but be struck—in the same way we were struck in some of his earlier Jena writings—by the harshness of Hegel's criticism of individualism and subjectivism as he makes the transition from reason to spirit, or from individuality to ethical life, in the *Phenomenology*. And, of course, Hegel means us to be. He seems to delight in driving home the objectivity and substantiality of the social whole against the arbitrariness and incompleteness of merely individual reason. At the same time, though, he is concerned to show that spiritual or ethical substance is not uninformed by or simply opposed to human subjectivity or being-for-self. Spirit is both substance *and* subject. As substance, spirit "is the unmoved solid *ground* and *starting-point* for the action of all, and it is their purpose and goal, the in-itself of every self-consciousness expressed in thought." But as subject or being-for self, spirit

> is a fragmented being, self-sacrificing and benevolent, in which each accomplishes his own work, rends asunder the universal being, and takes from it his own share. This resolving of the essence into individuals is precisely the *moment* of the action and the self of all; it is the movement and soul of substance and the resultant universal being. Just because it is a being that is resolved in the self, it is not a dead essence, but is *actual* and *alive*. (*PS,* 264/325)

The idea of spirit or *Geist* is, of course, one of the most important in Hegel's philosophy. We have encountered it already in Hegel's earlier writings, but it is only here, in the transition from reason to spirit in the *Phenomenology*, that we gain a more precise understanding of this crucial Hegelian concept. In the first instance, of course, spirit simply refers to the realm of human awareness, doing, and understanding that Hegel counterposes to the unself-conscious realm of nature. This is the meaning of spirit in the title of the *Phenomenology of Spirit* as well as in the rubrics of Hegel's various philosophies of spirit, early and late. But spirit also has a more specific meaning for Hegel, which is disclosed in the passages from the *Phenomenology* discussed above. Here spirit refers to that union of substantiality and subjectivity, of universality and individuality, which is embodied in the ethical life of a people. Substantiality devoid of subjectivity is unspiritual, as Hegel illustrates in his early attacks on the positivity of dogmatic religion, both Jewish and Christian,[21] as well as in his later construction of the almost purely substantialistic ethics of the Oriental world (see *IPH*, 93–95/135–37). On the other hand, subjectivity that is not tethered to substance is equally unspiritual. This is the point Hegel makes in his critique of the various individualistic models of agency in the *Phenomenology*. It is also a point he makes later, in the *Philosophy of Right*, in his critique of the individualistic or atomistic understanding of ethical life. There he sums up the point about spirit I am making here: "[T]here are always only two possible viewpoints in the ethical realm: either one starts from substantiality, or one proceeds atomistically and moves upward from the basis of individuality. This latter viewpoint excludes spirit, because it leads only to an aggregation, whereas spirit is not something individual but the unity of the individual and the universal" (*PR*, §156A).

At the present stage of the *Phenomenology*, however, Hegel insists that the ethical life of a people constitutes only the immediate form of spirit. As we have just seen, the ethical disposition is one that is governed by unmediated custom and habit; for it the laws simply *are*, eternal and unquestionable. In this immediate form, spirit appears as something natural and does not yet recognize itself as free, self-determining subjectivity. For this reason, Hegel tells us, spirit "must advance to the consciousness of what it is immediately, must leave behind it the beauty of ethical life, and by passing through a series of shapes attain to a knowledge of itself" (265/326). This superseding of customary ethical life by spirit and its coming to grasp itself as free, self-determining subjectivity is the theme of the longest chapter of the *Phenomenology*, entitled "Spirit."

THE HISTORY OF SPIRIT: FROM THE GREEK
POLIS TO THE FRENCH REVOLUTION

With the chapter on spirit, Hegel moves from a consideration of "shapes merely of consciousness" to the consideration of real, historical "shapes of a world" (*PS*, 265/326). The historical movement he traces—in keeping with the overall aspiration of the *Phenomenology* to grasp the true not only as substance but also as subject—is from the immediate substantiality of the Greek polis to the complete mediation of this substantiality by subjectivity in the modern world. Here Hegel picks up the thread of the *Philosophy of Spirit of 1805–6*, where we saw the first signs of his abandonment of his early Hellenic ideal and his increasing appreciation of modern subjectivity and individuality. It is of the utmost importance for understanding the *Phenomenology* and, indeed, Hegel's political philosophy as a whole to give due weight to his reincorporation of subjectivity and individuality into his argument, after his critique of these ideas in the previous chapters on self-consciousness and reason. Contrary to what Judith Shklar argues, the *Phenomenology* cannot be seen simply as a "massive assault upon the 'subjectivity' of individualism" or as an "elegy for Hellas."[22] Indeed, James Schmidt exaggerates only slightly when he writes that the *Phenomenology* "is not so much an elegy for Hellas as an exorcism of Hegel's own obsession with Athens."[23]

There is, of course, considerable overlap between this historical portion of the *Phenomenology* and Hegel's later *Lectures on the Philosophy of History*. Indeed, I occasionally refer to the latter to illuminate what is sometimes less clearly stated in the former. Nevertheless, it is important to recognize the difference in point of view between these two works. In the *Phenomenology*, Hegel is less concerned with history per se than with "the self-movement of phenomenological thought from standpoint to standpoint."[24] For this reason, his use of history there is less inclusive and in some ways more arbitrary from a strictly historical point of view than it is in the *Philosophy of History*. Thus, he begins his account in the *Phenomenology* with Greek ethical life, instead of returning to earlier forms of historical spirit. And instead of concluding his account by passing from the French Revolution to the post-Revolutionary rational state, as he does in the *Philosophy of History*, he moves from the French Revolution to a consideration of Kantian-Fichtean morality and thence to religion. Whether this latter transition says something significant about the political outlook of the *Phenomenology* vis-à-vis that of his later (and, indeed, earlier) political philosophy is a question I will take up in the next section.

Hegel's dialectical analysis of Greek ethical life through an interpretation of Greek tragedy is one of the most famous and beautiful sections in the *Phenomenology*. It begins by dividing the ethical substance of the Greeks into two powers: the human law, which corresponds to the public or political realm; and the divine law, which is bound with the family and the cult of dead over which the family presides. Whereas the former is associated with light, self-consciousness, and universality, the latter is associated with darkness, the unconscious, particularity, and privacy. The difference between the two powers also expresses itself in the difference between the sexes, man being identified with the political community and woman with the family. And as with the relationship between man and woman, the two powers are understood to be utterly complementary and interdependent: "Just as the family . . . possesses in the community its substance and enduring being, so, conversely, the community possesses in the family the formal element of its actual existence, and in the divine law its power and authentication" (*PS,* 267–78/328–42).

The breakdown of Greek ethical life comes about as a result of the immediate way in which the individual ethical consciousness relates to one or the other of these two powers. For such an ethical consciousness, in contrast to the slipperiness of modern moral consciousness, its duty is clear: "there is no caprice and equally no struggle, no indecision, since the making and testing of laws has been given up; on the contrary, the essence of ethical life is for this consciousness immediate, unwavering, without contradiction." Ethical consciousness in this immediate form is essentially the pathos of "character." And it is precisely because of its immediacy that this ethical consciousness, embodied in either man or woman and adhering either to human or divine law, fails to recognize the opposing law and thus transgresses it. Hegel illustrates this with reference to Sophocles' *Antigone.* Creon as the embodiment of the human law of the state decrees that Polyneices shall not have a proper burial. And Antigone as the embodiment of the family and divine law defies this decree and attempts to bury her brother. Each acts out his or her necessary role or "character" without really grasping the consequences. The tragic outcome points up the limits and leads to the supersession of the individual's immediate identification with ethical substance (*PS,* 279–89/342–54).

In the *Philosophy of History,* this breakdown of Greek ethical life in the immediate form of custom is presented more straightforwardly, if somewhat less ingeniously. There Hegel argues—again as he did in the *Philosophy of Spirit of 1805–6*—that Greek ethical life was utterly lacking in the principle of subjectivity that forms the basis of modern political life, and it was for that reason that direct democracy was an appropriate and stable form of government for it:

> Of the Greeks in the first and genuine form of their freedom, we may assert, that they had no conscience; the habit of living for their country without further reflection was the principle dominant among them. The consideration of the state in the abstract—which to our understanding is the essential point—was alien to them. Their grand object was their country in its living and real aspect: this Athens, this Sparta, these altars, this form of social life, this union of fellow citizens, these manners and customs. To the Greek his country was a necessity, without which he could not live. (*PH*, 250–53/306–9)

The corruption of Greek ethical life came about as a result of the introduction of subjective reflection by the Sophists and especially Socrates. Socrates—whom Hegel here calls the "inventor of morality"—questioned the customary and unreflective way in which the Greeks held their moral beliefs and sought to make them conscious of what they were doing. For this he was justly condemned to death, since such subjective reflection spelled the ruin of Greek ethical life. On the other hand, this subjective reflection constituted the "higher principle" upon which the future progress of spirit would be built (*PH*, 268–70/327–30).

In both the *Phenomenology* and the *Philosophy of History*, the breakdown of Greek ethical life is followed by the abstractly universal and atomistic state Hegel associates with the Roman Empire. Here the immediate unity of the individual with ethical substance gives way to alienation: "The universal unity into which the living immediate unity of individuality and substance withdraws is the soulless community which has ceased to be the substance . . . of individuals, and in which they now have the value of selves and substances, possessing a separate being-for-self" (*PS*, 290/355). On the one side stands the emperor, who embodies the abstractly universal character of the state. On the other stand private individuals who exist outside of and to some extent in opposition to the universality of the state—abstract legal "persons" whose freedom consists mainly in the right of private property instead of in active participation in public life (*PS*, 290–93/355–59).[25] Hegel's description here of the transition from the integrated ethical life of the Greek polis to the atomistic individualism of the Roman Empire recalls the famous passage from "The Positivity of the Christian Religion" that begins, "The picture of the state as a product of his own energies disappeared from the citizen's soul" ("PC," 156/206). In the *Philosophy of History*, Hegel describes the alienation of the individual under the Roman Empire in this way:

[T]he equitable and moral medium between sovereign and subjects was wanting—the bond of a constitution and organization of the state, in which a gradation of circles of social life, enjoying independent recognition, exists in communities and provinces, which, devoting their energies to the general interest, exert an influence on the general government. . . . That, therefore, which was abidingly present to the minds of men was not their country, or such moral unity as that supplies: the whole state of things urged them to yield themselves to fate, and to strive for a perfect indifference to life—an indifference which they sought either in freedom of thought [i.e, Stoicism and Skepticism] or in directly sensuous enjoyment [i.e., Epicureanism]. (*PH,* 317/384–85)

In the *Phenomenology,* of course, in contrast to the earlier "Positivity" essay, Hegel no longer regards this individualism and alienation of the Roman world as an entirely bad thing. It marks the beginning of that long process by which the individual, instead of simply finding himself immediately in ethical substance, molds himself into a being that is capable of a self-conscious relation to such substance. This development, however, presupposes a concept of individuality more profound than that found in the Roman world. In legal "personality," the self is still immediate, natural, undeveloped. This self must be deepened or, as Hegel puts it, "cultivated" (*gebildet*). The legal "person" must be transformed into the more profound and inward notion of the human "subject." This transformation is the theme of the next section of the *Phenomenology,* "Self-Alienated Spirit: Culture" (*Der sich entfremdete Geist: die Bildung*).

This section elaborates the development touched on previously in *The Philosophy of Spirit of 1805–6* whereby "each individual *goes back into himself* completely, comes to this sense of self-will, of being absolute although separated from the existing universal, possessing his absolute immediately in his knowing" (*HHS,* 159/262). As the title of the section indicates, Hegel sees this process of subjectivization and self-cultivation as essentially a process of self-alienation. The self's sense of its subjectivity and independence develops not naturally or in a linear fashion but out of the experience of self-opposition, the experience of finding the world and its substance inadequate to it, alien. Hegel here shows as acute a sense of the "bad faith" involved in the self's coinciding with itself or any of its objects as any modern existentialist. The experience of self-alienation is, of course, a painful experience, and Hegel sometimes speaks of it as the "terrible discipline of culture" (*die fürchterliche Zucht der Bildung*) (*PH,* 344/416). In the course of this discipline, the self sets aside the immediacy and naturalness belonging to the individual in the Greek and Roman worlds and transforms itself into a universal. But it is not just the self that changes in this process. Through the self's alienation in culture, the universal substance also loses its abstractness and becomes actual, becomes filled with self-consciousness and individuality (*PS*, 294–95/359–60, 297–99/363–65).[26]

It is possible here to give only the briefest outline of the rich dialectic leading up to the Enlightenment and French Revolution. In the world corresponding roughly to medieval and early modern Europe, substance appears in one of two forms, either as state power or as wealth. Hegel describes two possible attitudes toward these subtantialities: that of the "noble" consciousness, which sees in state power and wealth something positive with which it can identify; and that of the "ignoble" consciousness, which sees in these substantialities something negative and disparate from itself. The latter, for example, "sees in the sovereign power a fetter and a suppression of its own *being-for-self,* and therefore hates the ruler, obeys only with a secret malice, and is always on the point of revolt" (*PS,* 305; 372). The upshot of the dialectic Hegel proceeds to go through is that the noble consciousness inevitably turns into the ignoble consciousness. Initially alienating its immediate self and identifying with state power in the "heroism of [military] service," the noble consciousness is impelled to ever more radical self-alienations in which not only it but also state power and wealth are progressively debased. Thus the "heroism of service" gives way to the more alienating and spiritual "heroism of flattery," and the "heroism of flattery" itself prepares the ground for the replacement of state power by wealth and the dissolution of political loyalty into economic dependence. At this point, the noble consciousness is well on its way to becoming ignoble: "in the genuine renunciation of its personality, it actually rends in pieces the universal substance," bringing it "under the control of being-for-self" (*PS,* 312/380).

The culmination of this process of self-alienation and self-cultivation comes in Hegel's magnificent treatment of the "disrupted consciousness," loosely based on Diderot's *Rameau's Nephew* (which had been translated into German by Goethe). The world now exists under the supremely alienating sway of wealth. Nor is it only the poor man, the economically dependent man, who experiences the world of wealth in this way. For the rich man, too, the benefactor who "knows that what it dispenses is the self of another," the world of wealth is devoid of identity and profoundly out of joint: "[He] stands on the very edge of this innermost abyss, of this bottomless depth, in which all stability and substance have vanished; and in this depth [he] sees nothing but a common thing, a plaything of [his] whims, an accident of [his] caprice." In this context, self-consciousness develops a language to correspond to its utterly disrupted state: a witty, cosmopolitan and ultimately nihilistic language which jumbles and inverts all values and "strips of their significance all those moments which are supposed to count as the true being and as actual members of the whole." Rameau's mad nephew is taken as the exemplar of this language of disruption, this language of "pure culture," and Hegel contrasts him to the slow-footed "honest" consciousness that still believes in the old verities but which also appears at a distinct disadvantage in comparison with his witty and shameless counterpart. There is no going back, Hegel tells us, after spirit has attained this degree of subjectivity, no Rousseauan retreat to the simplicity and innocence of nature. If consciousness is to overcome its disrupted condition, it must do so by following the experience of subjectivity to its end (*PS*, 313–19/381–89).[27]

The realm of culture culminates in consciousness's explicit awareness of its alienated and disrupted condition and of the vanity of all reality (i.e., state power and wealth). Two ways of transcending this alienation of self and hollowness of the world now suggest themselves to Hegel. The first consists in flight from the real world and the location of true being and unalienated consciousness in a realm "beyond." This is "faith," which is distinguished from what Hegel later describes under the rubric of "religion" insofar as it is characterized by flight from the world and opposition to actuality and self-consciousness. The content of such faith is immediate, objective, outside of self-consciousness—what Hegel used to refer to as "positive"—and takes the imaginative form of the Christian Trinity. The second way of transcending the self-alienation of spirit in culture consists simply in the consummation of the corrosive movement of culture in what Hegel calls "pure insight" (*reine Einsicht*). In contradistinction to the positivity of faith, pure insight or intellection "apprehends nothing but self and everything as self, i.e. it *comprehends* everything, wipes out the objectivity of things and converts all *intrinsic* being into a being for *itself*." To this moment of pure insight corresponds the Enlightenment, and it is to the struggle of the Enlightenment against faith that Hegel turns his attention next (*PS*, 295–97/360–63, 319–28/389–98).

Here Hegel returns, of course, to one of the dominant themes of his early theological writings. There he largely took the position of the Enlightenment—the position of Lessing, Mendelssohn, Kant, and Fichte—against what he considered to be the positivity of a good deal of Christian theology. In the *Phenomenology*, though, he is concerned with the Enlightenment's critique of the positivity of religion more in its Voltairian than its Lessingian or Kantian guise, and he directs a number of criticisms at this critique. His most fundamental criticism is that the Enlightenment's critique of faith is self-contradictory. The Enlightenment points out to faith that the object of its worship is really the creation of its own consciousness. Not only is this insight not fatal to religious consciousness, it also reveals that faith is not something fundamentally opposed to or other than the Enlightenment. In criticizing faith on this basis, the Enlightenment is only criticizing—that is, failing to recognize—itself. Shifting its ground somewhat, the Enlightenment also claims that the object of faith is something alien to its consciousness, the product of priestly deception and delusion of the people. But here, Hegel argues, the "Enlightenment is foolish." In such matters involving consciousness's certainty of itself and of its essential being, deception and delusion are impossible. Finally, Hegel takes issue with the way in which the Enlightenment distorts faith by focusing on the inessential, "positive" moment in it: for example, when the Enlightenment declares that the absolute Being of faith is a piece of stone, a block of wood, or a piece of dough; or when the Enlightenment claims that faith is based on questionable historical evidence of questionable historical events. The essence of faith, Hegel argues, has nothing to do with such sensuous things or historical proofs; it is a matter of spirit (*PS*, 332–38/404–11).

Despite these criticisms, Hegel maintains that the Enlightenment holds a superior right over faith: the right of self-consciousness. For all its misunderstanding of faith, the Enlightenment does manage to point up the inconsistency that lies at the heart of faith, the inconsistent way in which faith brings together the sensuous or merely positive and the spiritual. In the end, faith cannot resist the Enlightenment's critique, which merely confronts it with the self-contradiction that is implicit in it. As a result, faith loses its content and turns into the "sheer yearning" Hegel associates with Romantic thinkers such as Jacobi and Schleiermacher. At this point, faith has in effect become the same thing as Enlightenment. The only difference lies in its being "unsatisfied Enlightenment" (*PS*, 343–44/417–18, 346–49/420–24).

It remains for Hegel to consider the positive teaching—as opposed to the merely negative polemic—of the Enlightenment. Having criticized faith for yoking the idea of God to determinate contents such as wood, stone, or dough, the Enlightenment now conceives of the absolute Being as a contentless and predicateless vacuum the empty *Être suprême* of French deism. Correlative to this idea of a predicateless absolute Being is the idea of finite reality as purely sensible or material, devoid of any significance beyond itself. Mediating between these two ideas is the concept of the useful, the quintessential object of the Enlightenment, according to Hegel. The way in which Hegel makes the transition to utility here is somewhat artificial. His argument seems to be that, while finite reality does not point to anything beyond itself and therefore has positive existence in itself, it must also display its negative relation to absolute Being, its nothingness, by existing only for another. A more straightforward explanation of the nexus between the Enlightenment and utility can, however, be constructed. In a world bereft of any "higher" purpose, meaning can come only from human purposes and interests. The idea of utility completes the reduction of reality to being-for-self that has been the thrust of the entire movement of culture. As Hegel puts it, the useful represents the object par excellence of pure insight and the Enlightenment insofar as "self-consciousness penetrates it and has in it the *certainty* of its *individual self,* its enjoyment (its *being-for-self*); self-consciousness sees right into the object, and this insight contains the *true* essence of the object (which is to be something that is penetrated, or to be *for an 'other'*)." In the idea of utility, heaven is finally brought down to earth, and the stage is set for the "absolute freedom" of the French Revolution (*PS,* 340–43/413–16, 353–55/428–31).

The French Revolution was, of course, the decisive political event of Hegel's lifetime, the event, as Charles Taylor has noted, "against which all of his generation had to think out their political philosophy, and had to rethink their stance to the Enlightenment."[28] It is well known that Hegel's youthful reaction to the initial stages of the Revolution was enthusiastic, as evidenced by the famous (though probably apocryphal) story of the planting of the "Tree of Liberty" by him and his fellow seminarians, Schelling and Hölderlin. But Hegel soon became disenchanted with the direction taken by the French Revolution under the Jacobins.[29] By the time he writes *The German Constitution* (1799–1802), his references to the French Revolution are predominantly negative. In that essay, as we have seen, he identifies the French Revolution in its Jacobin guise with the centralized "machine state" and criticizes it, in a manner reminiscent of Burke, for having destroyed the differentiated system of representation inherited from the feudal constitution (see *GC,* 159–64/479–85, 205–6/535–37, 207/538, 234–35/572). In the section of the *Phenomenology* we are about to consider, which contains Hegel's first sustained discussion of the French Revolution, this critical note is again sounded and extended. Nevertheless, despite his predominantly critical remarks, it is important to bear in mind that Hegel's attitude toward the French Revolution was never entirely negative. This is what ultimately differentiates it from Burke's more conservative reaction. Throughout his life Hegel continued to regard the French Revolution as signaling the dawn, if not the actualization, of a new era of freedom. This more favorable assessment of the French Revolution is captured in the following passage from the *Philosophy of History:*

The thought, the concept of right asserted its authority *all at once,* and the old framework of injustice could offer no resistance to its onslaught. A constitution, therefore, was established in harmony with the thought of right, and on this foundation all future legislation was to be based. Never since the sun had stood in the firmament and the planets revolved around it had it been perceived that man's existence centres in his head, i.e. in thought, inspired by which he builds up the world of reality. This was accordingly a glorious mental dawn. All thinking beings shared in the jubilation of this epoch. Emotions of a lofty character stirred men's minds at that time; an enthusiasm of spirit thrilled through the world, as if the reconciliation between the Divine and the world was now accomplished. (*PH,* 447/529)[30]

Hegel's specific account of the French Revolution in the *Phenomenology* begins by making the transition from the Enlightenment idea of utility to the idea of absolute freedom embodied by the Revolution. The main problem with utility, according to Hegel, is that it leaves open the question: useful for whom or for what? The being-for-another of the useful object does not necessarily coincide with my being-for-self, and therefore a certain objectivity attaches to it which my self cannot penetrate. "Utility is still a predicate of the object, not itself a subject or the immediate and sole *actuality* of the object." Self-consciousness overcomes this last vestige of objectivity and achieves certainty of itself only when it sees everything as an emanation of its own will. This is what Hegel means by "absolute freedom": "the world is for [self-consciousness] simply its own will" (*PS,* 355–57/431–32).

Hegel specifies what he means by such absolute freedom by referring to the notion of the "general will," which he interprets in the following way:

[The general] will is not the empty thought of will which consists in silent assent, or assent by a representative, but a real general will, the will of all *individuals* as such. For will is in itself the consciousness of personality, or of each, and it is as this genuine actual will that it ought to be . . . so that each, undivided from the whole, always does everything, and what appears as done by the whole is the direct and conscious deed of each. (*PS,* 357/432–33)

It is, of course, Rousseau that Hegel has in mind here. And while one might object that his interpretation of the general will is one-sidedly individualistic, it does capture certain elements of Rousseau's complex (not to say inconsistent) teaching: his contention that in joining civil society and submitting to the general will each "nevertheless obeys only himself and remains as free as before"; his insistence that the general will cannot be represented and demands some sort of directly democratic arrangement; and so forth.[31] As we saw in chapter 1, this individualistic and purely democratic interpretation of Rousseau's doctrine of the general will appears at several points in Hegel's later writings, frequently in conjunction with references to the French Revolution.[32] Although it may not capture the whole of Rousseau's complex teaching, it certainly expresses what Hegel believes was made of that teaching by the French Revolution. Thus, in the *Philosophy of History*, he writes that the legacy of the French Revolution in the post-Napoleonic state has spawned the "liberal" demand

> that the ideal general will should also be the *empirically* general—i.e. that the units of the state, in their individual capacity, should rule, or at any rate take part in the government. Not satisfied with the establishment of rational rights, with freedom of person and property, with the existence of a political organization in which are to be found various circles of civil life each having its own functions to perform, and with that influence over the people which is exercised by the intelligent members of the community, and the confidence that is felt in them, *Liberalism* sets up in opposition to all this the atomistic principle, that which insists upon the sway of individual wills; maintaining that all government should emanate from their express power, and have their express sanction. (*PH*, 452/534)

What happens when this doctrine of absolute freedom, this doctrine that every act of government should emanate from the self-conscious decision of each individual, "ascends the throne of the world" and tries to realize itself? In the first place, there is a liquidation of all meaningful social differentiation. This, as I have already indicated, is the Burkean point. The articulation of ethical life into different classes and estates that was such a prominent part of Hegel's analysis in his earlier writings (and will be in his mature political philosophy) is something that the individualism of absolute freedom cannot tolerate. Here

> each individual consciousness raises itself out of its allotted sphere, no longer finds its essence and its work in this particular sphere, but grasps itself as the *concept* of will, grasps all spheres as the essence of this will, and therefore can only realize itself in a work which is the work of the whole. In this absolute freedom, therefore, all social groups or classes which are the spiritual spheres into which the whole is articulated are abolished; the individual consciousness that belonged to any such sphere, and willed and fulfilled itself in it, has put aside its limitation; its purpose is the general purpose, its language universal law, its work the universal work. (*PS*, 357/433)[33]

But even in trying to accomplish directly the universal work of the state, the absolutely free individual consciousness encounters problems. In the political realm, too, there is differentiation—into legislative, judicial, and executive powers—and governmental action must ultimately concentrate itself in a single individuality. As a result, individual consciousness comes to be merely represented and does not experience government as the "direct and conscious deed of each." The basic flaw of the absolutely free individual consciousness when it comes to the state is that "it lets nothing break loose to become a *free object* standing over against it. It follows from this that it cannot achieve anything positive, either universal works of language or of reality, either of laws and general institutions of *conscious* freedom, or of deeds and works of a freedom that *wills* them." Unable to produce a positive work or deed, the only thing left for the individual consciousness characterized by absolute freedom is "negative action" and the "fury of destruction" (*PS*, 358–59/434–36).

Hegel proceeds to deduce various features of the Reign of Terror from this purely negative and destructive will of absolute freedom. Having destroyed the actual organization of the state, this will now turns on itself, specifically that part of itself which falls outside of its pure freedom: namely, its "abstract existence as such." "The sole work and deed of universal freedom is therefore *death,* a death too which has no inner significance or filling . . . It is thus the coldest and meanest of all deaths, with no more significance than cutting off the head of a cabbage or swallowing a mouthful of water." Moreover, mere suspicion takes the place of guilt as the basis for such executions. No revolutionary government, insofar as it is constituted by specific individuals who take specific actions, can be regarded as anything but a faction from the point of view of the pure universal will. Knowing that such a judgment exists against it, even in the absence of explicit rebellious acts, a revolutionary government must proceed to prosecute individuals on the basis of mere suspicion instead of actual guilt. Hence the Committee of Public Safety's "law of suspects" (*PS*, 359–60/436–37).

This brings us to the end of Hegel's discussion of the French Revolution. For all intents and purposes, the point of view it articulates remains definitive for Hegel's later discussions of the French Revolution in the *Philosophy of Right* and the *Philosophy of History*. The recurrent point is that the abstract and atomistic notion of freedom embodied in the French Revolution and deriving from Rousseau is ultimately incapable of allowing anything positive, whether it be social classes, laws, or political institutions, "to become a free object standing over against" the individual; the logic of this abstract freedom leads only to "negative action" and the "fury of destruction." This point has obvious affinities, as noted in several places, with Burke's famous critique of the French

Revolution. Unlike Burke, however, Hegel will not have recourse to some sort of nonhuman natural law or providential order to correct the abuses of human will and reason evinced in the French Revolution. Instead, he will think through human will or freedom in such a way that it does not alienate itself when linked with the otherness and positivity of historical laws and institutions. This will be the task of the *Philosophy of Right*.

MORALITY, RELIGION, AND POLITICS

By the end of Hegel's discussion of the French Revolution, we seem to be on the verge of a more satisfactory understanding of political freedom and the state. In the *Philosophy of History,* as noted, Hegel follows up his discussion of the French Revolution with a consideration of the rational state in the post-Revolutionary period. This is not, however, the course he takes in the *Phenomenology*. Indeed, he never returns to the subject of politics again in the book, going on instead to discuss morality, religion, and finally absolute knowledge. Whether this suggests something important about Hegel's attitude toward politics and the state in the *Phenomenology* is a question I will take up at the end of this section. But before doing so, we must first consider the important section of the *Phenomenology* titled "Spirit That Is Certain of Itself: Morality," in which Hegel takes up the moral outlook of post-Revolutionary German philosophy: Kant and Fichte and their Romantic successors.

With the section on self-certain spirit or "morality," we have arrived at the most extreme expression of the subjectivity that has been developing and deepening since the collapse of the objective ethical order of the Greeks. The object of consciousness is now nothing other than its own subjective self-certainty. As Hegel puts it: "Here, then, knowledge appears to have become completely identical with its truth . . . [T]he object is for itself the certainty of itself, viz. knowledge." We have arrived at the most extreme idealism: "What consciousness did not know would have no significance for consciousness and can have no power over it. Into its conscious will all objectivity, the whole world, has withdrawn. It is absolutely free in that it knows its freedom, and just this knowledge is its substance and purpose and its sole content" (*PS,* 364–65/441–42). Although Hegel will end up criticizing the form of subjectivity embodied in self-certain spirit, it is important to remember that it represents a necessary stage in the development of spirit, one that is higher than any previous stage and one that is the immediate prelude to Hegel's own absolute idealism.[34]

The first form of self-certain spirit Hegel takes up is "The Moral View of the World," corresponding (though Hegel nowhere mentions their names) to the philosophies of Kant and Fichte. As in his earlier critiques of Kant and Fichte, Hegel focuses on the opposition between freedom and nature, duty and inclination, in the moral view of the world. Moral self-consciousness takes duty to be "its sole aim and object" and "behaves with perfect freedom and indifference" toward the otherness that is nature. Both sides of the equation, morality and nature, are thus self-enclosed and assume an absolute independence with respect to one another. As Hegel succinctly puts it, "The freer self-consciousness becomes, the freer also is the negative object of its consciousness," i.e., nature. This situation of mutual indifference between morality and nature, however, is deeply unsatisfying to moral self-consciousness, and Kant puts forward his postulates of practical reason in order to remedy it (*PS*, 365–66/442–443).

The first of these postulates addresses the problem posed by the absence of a preestablished harmony between morality and happiness. The moral will, as Kant continually reminds us, cannot strive for happiness but only to be *worthy* of happiness. But this lack of connection between morality and happiness is, again, not very satisfying to moral self-consciousness: "The moral consciousness cannot forego happiness and leave this element out of its absolute purpose." Therefore, the harmony between morality and happiness is postulated: it is an idea demanded by reason to complete morality and to encourage moral self-consciousness, though it is not actual in the world of sensuous appearances. The second postulate, that of the existence of God, is closely connected with the first. God serves as the intelligible cause that brings about and guarantees, through a system of divine rewards and punishments, the harmony between morality and happiness. Finally, the third postulate, that of the infinite progress in morality, relates to the opposition between morality and the nature within us in the form of sensuousness and inclination. This opposition is presupposed by morality, and yet reason also demands that it be overcome. The antithesis between morality and sensuousness, duty and inclination, is simultaneously preserved and overcome by postulating the idea of an infinite progress in morality. "[T]he consummation of this progress has to be projected into a future infinitely remote; for if it actually came about, this would do away with the moral consciousness" (*PS*, 366–74/443–52).[35]

The three postulates of practical reason that Hegel adapts from Kant are designed to resolve the dualism between freedom and nature, duty and inclination, upon which Kant's entire philosophy rests. Hegel argues, however, that they only end up disguising and distracting attention away from the real contradictions of the moral view of the world. The reconciliation of morality and nature never really takes place but is simply displaced to some nebulous "beyond." This is perhaps most clearly seen in the postulate of infinite moral progress. The contradiction to which this postulate is addressed—a contradiction that Hegel first articulated in the *Natural Law* essay under the rubric of the self-canceling character of morality—consists in the fact that Kantian morality both requires and seeks to destroy the sensuous inclinations. Kant tries to evade this contradiction by postulating an infinite moral progress in which the inclinations are progressively conquered without being completely eliminated. But this does not represent a genuine solution for Hegel. Even to progress toward perfection without completely achieving it is to diminish the possibility of morality; "for to advance toward morality would really be to move toward its disappearance." Here, as also with the other postulates, the moral consciousness shows itself to be not completely in earnest about morality (*PS*, 374–81/453–62).

Hegel's criticisms of Kant here, as in the earlier *Natural Law* essay, may be more ingenious than they are fair. Nevertheless, they point to what remains for him the fundamental flaw of Kant's philosophy, namely, its dualism of morality and nature, duty and inclination. This dualism is overcome in the next figure of consciousness Hegel takes up, namely, "conscience," corresponding to the generation of post-Kantian Romantic thinkers—Jacobi, Schleiermacher, Novalis, and so forth—who abandoned Kant's rigid dualism between duty and inclination and grounded morality in subjective, authentic conviction. In conscience, self-consciousness renounces the opposition between duty and reality that characterized the moral view of the world and fills the emptiness of pure duty with a content consisting of the agent's own contingent self or immediate individuality. "Duty is no longer the universal that stands over against the self; on the contrary, it is known to have no validity when thus separated. It is now the law that exists for the sake of the self, not the self that exists for the sake of law." With conscience (*Gewissen*), self-consciousness has reached the furthest extreme of subjectivity and the most complete self-certainty (*Selbstgewissheit*) (*PS*, 383–87/464–69).[36]

Conscience, then, marks an advance over the emptiness of the Kantian moral will. Nevertheless, Hegel argues, it too is afflicted with a certain emptiness or indeterminacy. True, conscience provides the will with a certain content and thereby creates the possibility for concrete moral action. But this content is ultimately determined by the "caprice of the individual and the contingency of his unconscious natural being." On this basis, any action can be justified with reference to the subjective conviction of the individual. What some might regard as violence and wrongdoing in the acquisition of property, others might justify in terms of the duty to provide for the support of oneself and one's family. Duty here is "capable of any content." Thus, Hegel can write that "conscience is free from any content whatever; it absolves itself from any specific duty which is supposed to have the validity of law. In the strength of its own self-assurance it possesses the majesty of absolute autarky, to bind and loose" (*PS*, 390–93/472–76).

Despite this subjectivism or relativism, conscience is not completely locked up in itself but retains an element of universality in the form of the desire to have its subjective conviction recognized by others. Such recognition, however, is not easy to come by. There always exists a certain disparity between an action, once it has been carried out and exists in the medium of being, and the conscientious intention that lies behind it. Here, as in several other places in the *Phenomenology*, language serves as the crucial mediating factor between particularity and universality, self and others. "Language is self-consciousness existing *for others*, self-consciousness which *as such* is immediately *present*, and as *this* self-consciousness is universal." It is only by supplementing an action with language, commenting on it, explaining it, that the disparity between the objective deed and the conscientious intention that lies behind it can be overcome. In this way, conscience leads to a community of consciences, the "spirit and substance" of which is the "mutual assurance of their conscientiousness, good intentions, the rejoicing over this mutual purity, and the refreshing of themselves in the glory of knowing and uttering, of cherishing and fostering, such an excellent state of affairs" (*PS*, 388/469–70, 393–98/476–81).

In this way, also, talk replaces action. The conscientious soul prefers the purity and universality of speech to the finitude and impurity of action. This is the predicament of the "beautiful soul," who "lives in dread of besmirching the splendour of its inner being by action and an existence; and, in order to preserve the purity of its heart, it flees from contact with the actual world."[37] The rest of the section on conscience consists of a dialectic between the beautiful soul and acting conscience—the dialectic of "evil and its forgiveness." In the course of this dialectic, acting conscience comes to recognize its guilt, and the beautiful soul comes to accept the necessity of finite action. In connection with the latter, Hegel criticizes the way in which the beautiful soul condemns concrete action by focusing only on what is particular and self-interested in it, deploying the *mot* he will repeat on several other occasions: "No man is a hero to his valet;

not, however, because the man is not a hero, but because the valet—is a valet."[38] In the beautiful soul's forgiveness of acting conscience, universal is finally reconciled with particular. This reconciliation brings the long chapter on spirit to a close and marks the transition to absolute spirit in the form of religion (*PS,* 399–409/483–94).

I do not intend to go into the penultimate chapter of the *Phenomenology* devoted to religion, in which Hegel recapitulates the whole history of spirit, but now from the standpoint spirit's absolute self-consciousness in religious experience. Nor do I intend to discuss the final chapter on philosophy or "absolute knowing." These chapters are obviously crucial to understanding the whole purpose of the *Phenomenology*—the raising of natural consciousness to the standpoint of philosophy or absolute knowledge—but they are less important for our narrower focus on the moral and political themes of the book. With respect to these themes, the section on morality and conscience, in which self-consciousness reaches the furthest extreme of subjectivity, constitutes an appropriate stopping-point. Later on, in the *Philosophy of Right* (§§136–40), Hegel will again take up the issue of conscience—indeed, he refers the reader there back to his discussion in the *Phenomenology*—though there as the immediate prelude to the transition to ethical life instead of to religion.

This last point raises an important question about the overall structure of the *Phenomenology* and its possible political implications. As noted, after the discussion of the French Revolution, politics disappears from the pages of the *Phenomenology,* giving way first to morality, and then to religion and philosophy. This structural feature of the book has led some commentators to argue that Hegel abandons in the *Phenomenology* the glorification of the state and of ethical life that characterized his earlier writings. In the *Phenomenology,* so this argument goes, we find not only a rejection of the objective ethical order of the Greek polis but also a critique of the modern attempt to bring heaven down to earth and divinize the state in the French Revolution. The failure of the French Revolution, its necessary culmination in the Terror, leads spirit to seek satisfaction in the nonpolitical realms of morality, religion, and philosophy. Franz Rosenzweig sums up this line of argument by saying that "Hegel was never further from his state absolutism" than in the *Phenomenology.* He is forced to concede, however, that Hegel does eventually return to his earlier, statist view in the *Philosophy of Right* and the *Philosophy of History.*[39]

There is not much to recommend this argument. The vacillating pattern it imputes to Hegel whereby he abandons his original view of the state only later to return to it is not attractive. And there is no reason to suppose that just because Hegel does not mention the state in the final chapters of the *Phenomenology* he somehow thinks it does not have a further history or development after the French Revolution. The transitions from the French Revolution to morality and from morality to religion and absolute knowledge are ultimately dictated by the knowledge problematic of the *Phenomenology*. They do not suggest that the state or politics have completely dropped out of the picture. It is perfectly possible to imagine a new and more satisfying understanding of the state emerging out of the radical subjectivism expressed in the French Revolution and Kantian morality, as indeed is the case in the *Philosophy of Right* and the *Philosophy of History*.[40] And the various moments of religion traced in the *Phenomenology* actually seem to presuppose some relationship to actual, objective spirit or the state. Religion is seen, not as an alternative to political community, but as its supreme self-intuition.[41]

For all that, it must be admitted that the *Phenomenology* is not primarily a political work. Its principal concern is epistemological, the grounding of absolute knowledge by showing how natural consciousness is inexorably led to it. For this reason, politics and the state play a comparatively small role in the final chapters of the book. Nevertheless, the *Phenomenology* does contain a number of important political themes, and they are the ones we have focused on in this chapter: the idea of recognition, the critique of individualism, the crucial role of objective spirit and ethical life, the limitations of Greek ethical life and the corresponding importance of modern subjectivity, and the critique of the extreme forms of subjectivism found in the French Revolution, Kantian morality, and Romantic conscience. With the exception of his understanding of the limitations of Greek ethical life and his positive appreciation of modern subjectivity, all these themes had appeared in Hegel's earlier writings, albeit not always in as powerful or well-developed form. Even Hegel's privileging of modern subjectivity over Greek customary morality we glimpsed in the *Philosophy of Spirit of 1805–6,* though it was necessary to go through the *Phenomenology* to appreciate its full significance. These themes also appear again in the *Philosophy of Right*. Though the overall purposes of the *Phenomenology* and the *Philosophy of Right* are no doubt different, their overall ethico-political perspectives completely coincide.[42] Thus it can be said that Hegel's development with respect to his moral and political philosophy, as with respect to almost everything else, comes to its conclusion in the *Phenomenology*.

Chapter 4 Hegel's Idea
of Political Philosophy

Having considered the development of Hegel's moral and political thought up through the *Phenomenology,* we are now ready to examine the *Philosophy of Right.* In this chapter, I take up the methodological issues that first confront the reader immediately upon opening the book, in the Preface and the first few paragraphs of the Introduction. The first issue concerns Hegel's understanding of the relationship between philosophy and historical-political actuality. This, of course, is the great theme of the Preface to the *Philosophy of Right,* encapsulated in the famous (or infamous) dictum, "What is rational is actual; and what is actual is rational" (*PR,* 20/24). In the first section of this chapter, I carefully analyze the Preface to the *Philosophy of Right,* explicating this dictum, showing that it does not imply a complete abdication to the historical process nor deprive Hegel's political philosophy of all normative or critical force with respect to historical-political reality. The second methodological issue concerns Hegel's understanding of philosophy as "conceptual" analysis. Here we will have recourse to Hegel's logic, and I will show that this logic—and the idea of "conceptual" analysis it involves—is not as "incredible" as some of its critics have portrayed it.

Before turning to these issues, however, I would first like to sketch briefly Hegel's attitude toward political events in Germany as they unfolded from the battle of Jena in 1806 to the publication of the *Philosophy of Right* in 1821, especially since some of these events form the immediate background of Hegel's argument in the Preface to the *Philosophy of Right*.[1] Of course, the period of history from 1806 to 1821 in Germany was an extremely tumultuous one. It began, after the Napoleonic conquests, as an era of great and liberalizing reform. In Prussia, the ministers Karl vom Stein and Karl von Hardenberg led this reform movement. They sought to transform the absolute monarchy into a constitutional monarchy, "to replace the arbitrary and irresponsible rule of royal cronies with orderly and responsible ministerial government." They also introduced reforms designed to bring about civil equality—for example, the civil emancipation of the Jews—social mobility, and economic freedom. They were less successful in opening up the political process to greater popular participation.[2]

With this movement of progressive reform in Germany Hegel was in complete accord. This is reflected in his correspondence and elsewhere by his tremendous admiration for Napoleon, who represents the forward movement of history for Hegel against the backwardness of German political life. Never a nationalist, Hegel rejoiced at the Prussian defeat at Jena in 1806. On the eve of the battle, he writes to his friend and patron Friedrich Niethammer that he "saw the Emperor—this world-soul—riding out of the city on reconnaissance. It is indeed a wonderful sensation to see such an individual, who, concentrated here at a single point, astride a horse, reaches out over the world and masters it." And he goes on, "As I [myself] did earlier, all now wish the French army luck" (*L*, 114–15/1:120–21).[3] In August of 1807, Hegel, again writing to Niethammer, refers to Napoleon as the "great professor of constitutional law" who now "sits in Paris" and contrasts him favorably with German princes who "have neither grasped the concept of a free monarchy yet nor sought to make it real" (*L*, 141/1:185). In November of 1807, he comments that "so far we have seen that in all imitations of the French only half the example is ever taken up. The other half, the noblest part, is left aside: liberty of the people; popular participation in elections; government decisions taken in full view of the people" (*L*, 151/1:197). And finally, in February of 1808, he prays for the introduction of the Napoleonic Code in Germany so that "the characteristic *modes of centralization* and organization prevalent up to now will disappear—forms in which there is no justice, no popular participation, but only the arbitrariness and sophistry of a single individual" (*L*, 159–60/1:218–19).

In 1813, during the wars of national liberation, there was a tremendous upsurge of anti-French, nationalist sentiment in Germany, but Hegel remained coolly unaffected by it.[4] Even after Napoleon's final defeat at Waterloo in 1815, he still maintains that the reaction against Napoleon "is chiefly restricted to matters of vanity" and cannot undo the historic changes the latter has introduced into the political world (*L*, 325/2:86–87). But Hegel's moderate, anti-nationalist constitutionalism—shared by government ministers such as Hardenberg and Karl von Altenstein, who recruited Hegel to come to the University of Berlin in 1818—was not to prevail in the polarizing political atmosphere in Germany after Waterloo. In 1815, in reaction to the conservative proposal for German confederation that emerged from the Congress of Vienna, the *Burschenschaft* (student fraternity) movement was formed, advocating not only liberal constitutional reform but also nationalism and sometimes anti-semitism. In 1817, the *Burschenschaft* movement held a gigantic festival at Wartburg celebrating the German nation, at which the Jacobian philosopher and personal rival to Hegel, Jacob Fries, delivered an impassioned speech. In 1819, a fringe and no doubt disturbed member of the student movement, Karl Sand, murdered the reactionary playwright August von Kotzebue. This led to the promulgation of the reactionary Carlsbad Decrees, which clamped down on the universities and imposed strict censorship on the press.[5]

These, of course, are the events that form the immediate background of the Preface to the *Philosophy of Right,* in which Hegel explicitly disparages Fries and the Wartburg Festival and even offers a partial defense of the Carlsbad Decrees. This should not lead us to conclude, however, that Hegel has suddenly turned conservative and joined with the forces of reaction. Though he certainly did not share the nationalism, much less the anti-semitism, of the *Burschenschaft* movement, he was not entirely unsympathetic with some of its liberal constitutional goals. He also defended a number of his students and assistants who belonged to the *Burschenschaft* movement from government persecution.[6] As we shall soon see, it was mainly the subjectivist or emotivist turn that Fries gave the *Burschenschaft* movement that Hegel objected to, a turn for which Sand's desperate act of conviction seemed the logical conclusion. That Hegel's political outlook has little in common with the reactionary Prussian state of 1819 is also confirmed by the entire argument of the *Philosophy of Right,* but the demonstration of this point must await our analysis in this and later chapters.

Before turning to that analysis, there is one final preliminary point that needs to be made concerning the various versions of the *Philosophy of Right.* Though the *Philosophy of Right* was published in 1821, Hegel had lectured on it several times before that: once in Heidelberg, in 1817–18, and twice in Berlin, in 1818–19 and 1819–20. The notes taken by students from these lectures are all now available, and I draw on them extensively. Scholars such as K.-H. Ilting and Shlomo Avineri, believing the published version of the *Philosophy of Right* to be compromised by the reactionary atmosphere that set in after the Carlsbad Decrees, have argued that the earlier lectures reveal a more liberal and open-ended political philosophy.[7] I find such claims for the differences between the lecture notes and the published version of the *Philosophy of Right*, however, to be highly exaggerated. For the most part, Hegel's political outlook remains unchanged throughout these versions. Nevertheless, the lectures do reveal a great deal about the development of Hegel's thinking on the philosophy of right, and they are extremely helpful in illuminating some of the darker passages of the *Philosophy of Right*.

THE RATIONAL AND THE ACTUAL

Toward the end of the Preface to the *Philosophy of Right*, Hegel, displaying his usual disdain toward prefaces in general, downplays its importance, saying it contains only "some external and subjective comments on the point of view of the work" (*PR*, 23/28). Despite this disclaimer, the Preface has always been the focus of considerable scholarly and polemical attention, as it should be. For it contains Hegel's most succinct, not to say provocative, statement of his views on the crucial issue of the relationship between philosophy and historical-political actuality, or between theory and practice.[8] Hegel's position has, of course, been famously misunderstood. Beginning with Rudolf Haym in the mid-nineteenth century, Hegel's assertion of the rationality of the actual has been taken as a formula for the most conservative glorification of the status quo and specifically of the Prussian state in 1821.[9] More recent scholarship, however, in keeping with what I have argued above, has uncovered historical and biographical evidence that Hegel's political views were not particularly conservative but, rather, moderately liberal or progressive, in line with the reforms of Stein, Hardenberg, and Humboldt.[10] Though such historical research has been important in correcting some of the grosser distortions of Hegel's political views, my focus here is on the text of the Preface. My concern is not apologetic but with understanding Hegel's conception of political philosophy, what exactly he means by the "science of right."

The Preface begins by drawing our attention to this "scientific" character of the *Philosophy of Right*. Hegel tells us that what distinguishes the *Philosophy of*

Right from other works of political philosophy is the speculative or "scientific" method on which it is based, a method Hegel has fully developed in his logic. "[I]t will readily be noticed that the work as a whole, like the construction of its parts, is based on the logical spirit. It is also chiefly from this point of view that I would wish this treatise to be understood and judged. For what it deals with is *science,* and in science, the content is essentially inseparable from the *form*" (*PR,* 10/12–13).[11] In the second section of this chapter, I examine the connection between Hegel's logic and the method of the *Philosophy of Right* alluded to in this passage. For now I am interested only in the contrast Hegel draws between his own emphasis on the importance of scientific form and those writers who depreciate the importance of such form, focusing instead exclusively on content. For the latter writers—whom Hegel associates with the post-Kantian, Romantic doctrine of immediate intuition, feeling, or conviction—the task of philosophy consists "in the discovery of *truths,* the statement of *truths,* and the dissemination of *truths.*" This exclusive emphasis on content or "truths," however, has led nowhere except to a chaos of conflicting truths, according to Hegel. And the only way to resolve this chaos is through "scientific means" (*PR,* 10–11/13).

It is at this point that Hegel puts forward his first statement about the relationship between philosophy or science and historical-political actuality. Contrary to those writers who insist that the task of philosophy consists in the discovery and dissemination of new ethical or political truths, Hegel argues that the "*truth* concerning *right, ethics, and the state* is at any rate *as old* as its *exposition and promulgation* in *public laws and in public morality and religion.*" That the truth about ethics and politics is already embodied in existing laws and institutions does not mean, however, that there remains nothing left for philosophy to do with respect to it. "What more does this truth require, inasmuch as the thinking mind [*Geist*] is not content to possess it in this proximate manner?" Hegel asks. "What it needs is to be *comprehended* [*begreifen*] as well, so that the content which is already rational in itself may also gain a rational form and therefore appear justified to free thinking. For such thinking does not stop at what is *given* . . . but starts out from itself and thereby demands to know itself as united in its innermost being with the truth" (*PR,* 11/13–14).

The idea of philosophy as "comprehension" of the rationality implicit in a given content that Hegel articulates here runs through the entire Preface. It receives perhaps its clearest expression in the first paragraphs of Hegel's Introduction to the *Encyclopedia.* There Hegel defines philosophy as the "meditation" or "thinking-over" (*nachdenken*) of the content that is originally given in prephilosophical experience—for example, in feeling, intuition, desire, and willing, all of which Hegel refers to collectively as "representation." In such prephilosophical modes of experience thinking is active, but it remains implicit, submerged in an immediate form. It is only in philosophy that this thinking becomes explicit. Philosophy is the translation of representations into explicit thoughts and concepts. But such translation does not involve a change in the essential content of our prephilosophical experience, only in the form of our awareness of it. "Philosophy should be quite clear," Hegel tells us, "about the fact that its content is nothing other than the basic import that is originally produced and produces itself in the domain of the living spirit, the content that is made into the *world,* the outer and inner world of consciousness." Using the term "actuality" (*Wirklichkeit*) to designate this content, Hegel argues that philosophy must be in accord with it. "Indeed," he writes, "this accord [with actuality] can be viewed as an outward touchstone . . . for the truth of a philosophy" (*EL,* §§1–6).[12]

From this initial understanding of philosophy as "thinking-over" or "comprehension" of a content that is already rational in itself, Hegel goes on to expand his critique of the subjectivism he discerns in current—again, post-Kantian, Romantic—conceptions of political philosophy. This critique is highly polemical; and it sometimes seems that Hegel wishes to oppose to modern subjectivism the most unreflective and customary form of morality—more in the manner of the *Natural Law* essay than the *Phenomenology.* Thus, he compares unfavorably the modern attitude that prides itself on the difficulty of discovering, "among the *infinite variety of opinions,* what is universally acknowledged and valid in them" with the "simple attitude of ingenuous emotion" that adheres "with trusting conviction to the publicly recognized truth" and bases its "conduct and fixed position in life on this firm foundation." But Hegel's point is not as simple as that; nor does he completely ignore the subjective dimension. A few sentences further, for example, he suggests that the simple attitude alluded to above itself encounters a difficulty, one that arises "from the fact that human beings *think* and look for their freedom and the basis of ethics in [the realm of] thought." That the political order must be justified to free thinking is a "divine right," according to Hegel, but, he quickly adds, "it is nevertheless turned into wrong if the only criterion of thought and the only way in which thought can know itself to be free is the extent to which it *diverges from what is universally acknowledged and valid* and manages to invent something *particular* for itself" (*PR,* 11–12/14–15).

Hegel develops his complex position on the relation between reflection and ethical substance, or between subjectivity and objective spirit, in the next paragraph of the Preface, and in particular in the Addition attached to it. He begins by noting that those writers who identify freedom of thought with "divergence from, and even hostility towards, what is publicly acknowledged," in particular, the state, seem to regard the ethical world very differently from the world of nature:

> As far as *nature* is concerned, it is readily admitted that philosophy must recognize it *as it is,* that the philosopher's stone lies hidden *somewhere,* but *within nature itself,* that nature is *rational within itself,* and that it is this *actual* reason present within it which knowledge must investigate and grasp conceptually—not the shapes and contingencies which are visible on the surface, but nature's eternal harmony, conceived, however, as the law and essence *immanent* within it.

In contrast to this, the ethical world, the world of spirit, is supposed not to be rational in itself; it is "supposed rather to be at the mercy of contingency and arbitrariness, to be *god-forsaken,* so that, according to this atheism of the ethical world, *truth* lies *outside* it" (*PR,* 12–14/15–16).

This obviously makes no sense to Hegel, but he does not really explain why we should regard the ethical world as inherently rational in the same way we do the natural world. Is it simply a matter of faith? To raise this question is, in a way, to raise the question hovering over the entire Preface, the question of the rationality of the actual. In the present context, it is perhaps possible to grasp what Hegel has in mind without imputing to him some large, metaphysical doctrine about the providential character of human history. The thrust of his argument seems to be directed against a certain sort of subjectivism that refuses to accord rationality to anything that has not been constructed by or brought before the tribunal of individual reason. On such a subjectivist outlook, everything that has been built up in the ethical world—the world of historical, objective spirit—appears arbitrary and contingent, to be razed and reconstructed from the ground up. Hegel has, of course, criticized a version of this type of subjectivism in the section of the *Phenomenology* devoted to the French Revolution. There he makes the Burkean point that the attempt to justify and construct everything in the ethical world on the basis of subjective reason—the attempt, as Burke put it, to build everything anew "as if you had never been moulded into civil society"[13]—leads inevitably to the "fury of destruction" and the Reign of Terror. There is an echo of this point in the paragraph under consideration from the Preface, when Hegel says of those who deny the rationality of the ethical world that they seem to suppose "that no state or constitution had ever previously existed or were in existence today, but that we had *now* (and this 'now' is of indefinite duration) to start right from the beginning, and that the ethical world had been waiting only for such intellectual constructions, discoveries, and proofs as are *now* available" (*PR,* 12/15).

The analogy Hegel draws between the ethical world and nature, however, should not be overstressed. In a crucial Addition to the paragraph under consideration, he points out the equally important differences between these two realms. Like Kant,[14] he distinguishes between laws of nature and laws of right. The former, he writes, "are simply there and are valid as they stand . . . our cognition adds nothing to them and does not advance them." The laws of right, on the other hand, "are something *laid down* (*Gesetztes*), something *derived from* human beings," and therefore they are not simply accepted or acquiesced in but must somehow be justified to human reason. This is what makes the inquiry into the nature of right of crucial practical importance. "In right, the human being must encounter his own reason; he must therefore consider the rationality of right, and this is the business of our science." Hegel also believes that such an investigation into the rationality of right is of particular importance in today's world because of the distinctively modern demand, stemming from the Reformation, that everything be justified at the bar of human reason (*PR,* 13–14A/15–17A). As he puts it toward the end of the Preface: "It is a great obstinacy, the kind of obstinacy which does honour to human beings, that they are unwilling to acknowledge in their attitudes anything which has not been justified by thought—and this obstinacy is the characteristic property of the modern age, as well as being the distinctive principle of Protestantism" (*PR,* 22/27).

In this Addition, Hegel makes clear once again that, despite his polemic against the excesses of contemporary subjectivism, he has not altogether neglected the claims of modern subjectivity. This recognition of the claims of modern subjectivity is, as we have seen, a major theme in both the *Phenomenology* and the *Philosophy of History,* and it is ultimately what distinguishes Hegel from the anti-rationalist, Burkean outlook to which we compared him above. For Hegel, unlike Burke, the political order must ultimately be justified to human reason, although not in the individualistic manner that typifies Enlightenment rationalism. It is the latter proviso that Hegel emphasizes in the concluding sentences of the Addition we are considering. By admitting that the laws of right must ultimately be justified to human thought or reason, it might seem that the door is being thrown open to "contingent opinions." But Hegel quickly dismisses this fear by distinguishing between "genuine thought" based on the "concept of the thing" (*der Begriff der Sache*) and mere opinion. It is only the former that is relevant to justifying the laws of right to human reason. And such "genuine" or "conceptual" thought is not available to everyone but only to the Hegelian "scientist":

> The concept of the thing does not come to us by nature. Everyone has fingers and can take a brush and paint, but that does not make him a painter. It is precisely the same with thinking. The thought of right is not, for example, what everybody knows at first hand; on the contrary, correct thinking is knowing and recognizing the thing [*Sache*], and our cognition should therefore be scientific. (*PR*, 14A/17A)

What Hegel means by "conceptual" or "scientific" cognition is something that will occupy us in the second section of this chapter. For now we must follow to the end the critique of subjectivism that takes up the better part of the Preface. There is not a great deal of development to this critique. For the most part Hegel simply repeats, with various rhetorical twists, the charge that the ethics and politics of conviction—an outlook he has already criticized in the section devoted to "conscience" in the *Phenomenology*—leads to a dangerous relativism and ultimately to the destruction of all law and public order. With Sand's murder of Kotzebue no doubt on his mind, he writes: "the concepts of truth and the laws of ethics are reduced to mere opinions and subjective convictions, and the most criminal principles—since they, too, are *convictions*—are accorded the same status as those laws" (*PR*, 19/23). It is in this context that Hegel attacks the philosopher Jacob Fries, an exponent of the ethics of conviction he is criticizing and a radical democrat, and refers disparagingly to the Wartburg Festival of 1817 held by the student fraternities or *Burschenschaften*. It is here, too, that Hegel offers a mild—and not entirely unambiguous—defense of the Carlsbad Decrees of 1819 (*PR*, 15–19/17–23). These remarks on the events of the day have, of course, added fuel to the image of Hegel as a conservative defender of the reactionary Prussian state, but my comments above as well as recent historical scholarship have shown that Hegel's relationships to Fries, the *Burschenschaften*, and the Prussian government were more complex than these remarks suggest, and that his actual political views were much more in line with those of liberal reformers such as Stein and Hardenberg than with the reactionary elements in the Prussian state.[15]

Hegel's comments on the split that has occurred between the state and philosophy due to the latter's superficiality and subjectivism conclude the critical portion of the Preface and form the transition to a more positive consideration of the relationship between philosophy and actuality. Here we enter a thicket of some of Hegel's most famous pronouncements on the relationship between philosophy and actuality, including "What is rational is actual; and what is actual is rational." Because these pronouncements are so familiar and seductively epigrammatic, and because the reasons or arguments that lie behind them are not always apparent, we must subject them to careful analysis, reconstructing what lies concealed beneath their magisterial surface.

Let us begin by considering what seem to be the earliest formulations of the so-called *Doppelsatz* in the lectures on the philosophy of right of 1817–18 and 1819; for these early formulations provide an important clue as to the meaning of the dictum that the rational is actual and the actual rational in the *Philosophy of Right*. In the Heidelberg lectures of 1817–18, the antecedent to the assertion that the rational is actual appears in the context of Hegel's discussion of the question, Who is to make the constitution of a people or nation? Hegel's answer is that the constitution of a people is not something "made," nor is it the product of a social contract; rather, the constitution is a determination or development of the already existent spirit of a people (*Volksgeist*): "The *Volksgeist* is the substance; what is rational must be [*was vernünftig ist, muss geschehen*]. . . . [G]enuine rationality is the inner authority, being in harmony with the *Volksgeist*" (*LNR*, §134R).[16] The context here clearly suggests that when Hegel says that the rational must be or happen he is referring to the fact that the rational is not to be equated with some sort of abstract ideal divorced from actual or historical circumstances; rather, the rational is always grounded in history and actuality. The rational constitution is not an abstract blueprint or metaphysical construction (as Burke would say) conceived of independently of historical circumstances; rather, it is an outgrowth of the developing—not static—self-consciousness of a people.[17]

Hegel makes this point even more clearly in the Berlin lectures of 1819–20, where the formulation of the *Doppelsatz* also begins to approach the canonical form it assumes in the *Philosophy of Right*. The assertion of the actuality of the rational and the rationality of the actual now appears in the Introduction to the lectures, instead of in the later discussion of the constitution of the state. This Introduction resembles in many respects the Preface to the *Philosophy of Right*, but without the polemical tone or references to recent events. Here Hegel writes that philosophy "does not conduct its business beyond [*jenseits*] the business of the world." And he goes on to argue, as he did in the Heidelberg lectures, that the rational constitution is one that is grounded in the historic spirit of a people:

[P]hilosophy knows that only what is present in the concept of a people can be valid in the actual world [*der wirklichen Welt*]. It would be folly to force on a people arrangements to which it has not yet progressed by itself. What the age possesses in its inner spirit, this certainly happens [*geschiet*] and is necessary. A constitution is the arrangement of this inner spirit. It is the foundation [*Boden*]; there is no power in heaven or on earth against the right of the spirit. This is obviously something other than reflection and imagination [*Reflexion und Vorstellung*] which one can draw at will out of abstract thinking or out of the goodness of one's heart. What is rational becomes actual, and the actual becomes rational [*Was vernünftig ist, wird wirklich, und das Wirkliche wird vernünftig*]. (*VPR₁₉*, 50–51)

Many scholars have claimed that the version of the *Doppelsatz* in this passage differs significantly from the one found in the *Philosophy of Right* in that it pictures the relationship between rationality and actuality as a dynamic, unfinished process instead of as a conservative, static equation.[18] These claims for the difference between the version of the *Doppelsatz* in the lectures of 1819–20 and the canonical version in the *Philosophy of Right* are, I think, exaggerated.[19] The assertion of the rationality of the actual in the *Philosophy of Right* does not involve a static equation between the two or deny the possibility of development; and it certainly is not meant to sanctify the status quo. The importance of the formulation of the *Doppelsatz* in the lectures of 1819–20 is not so much that it uses the word "becomes"—in many ways this word obscures Hegel's fundamental point—but that it once again points to the fact that the rational is not to be found in some abstract and imaginary "beyond" but, rather, in what is effective and actual in the world.

As we turn back to the Preface to the *Philosophy of Right* now, this is the point that stands in the forefront of Hegel's mind as he discusses the relationship between philosophy and actuality. He begins by stating that, in the face of the various misunderstandings of the relationship between philosophy and actuality,

I accordingly come back to my earlier observation that, since philosophy is *exploration of the rational*, it is for that very reason the *comprehension of the present and the actual*, not the setting up of a *world beyond* [*Jenseitigen*] which exists God knows where—or rather, of which we can very well say that we know where it exists, namely in the errors of a one-sided and empty ratiocination [*einseitigen, leeren Räsonierens*]. (*PR*, 20/24)

This passage immediately confronts us with some difficulties. In the first place, it is not clear what "earlier observation" Hegel is referring to here. Or, rather, it is clear—it can only be the passage treated above in which Hegel characterizes philosophy as the "comprehension" of the rationality already implicit in the state (*PR,* 11/13–14)—but it is not clear that this earlier observation exactly coincides with the one in the passage just quoted. In this latter passage, Hegel does not seem to be saying that, because the actual is rational, philosophy must consist in the "thinking-over" and comprehension of this actuality. The inference seems to go in the other direction. Because philosophy is the exploration of the rational, it must be the comprehension of the present and the actual. As in the earlier lectures, this statement seems be more about the nature of rationality than about the nature of actuality. It says that the rational is actual rather than that the actual is rational.

That Hegel is more concerned in this passage with asserting the actuality of the rational rather than the rationality of the actual is confirmed by the way in which he rounds off the passage. Because philosophy is the exploration of the rational, it is "not the setting up of a *world beyond* which exists God knows where—or rather, of which we can very well say that we know where it exists, namely in the errors of a one-sided and empty ratiocination." The rational is not to be sought outside the actual in a "world beyond"; such idealism leads only to the most extreme and self-contradictory subjectivism. This is a recurrent—and by now quite familiar—theme in Hegel's philosophy. It is, in a way, the central lesson of the *Phenomenology.* From the "unhappy consciousness" to the "beautiful soul," Hegel exposes the self-defeat involved in the attempt to flee the actual world and set up an ideal world "beyond." He summarizes his basic point on this score in the *Philosophy of History:*

> [N]othing is more common today than the complaint that the *ideals* raised by fantasy are not being realized, that these glorious dreams are being destroyed by cold actuality. On their life-voyage, these ideals smash up on the rock of hard reality. They can only be subjective, after all; they belong to that individuality of the solitary subject which takes itself to be the highest and wisest. Ideals of that sort do not belong here [i.e., in reflections on the state]—for what the individual spins out for himself in his isolation cannot serve as law for the universal reality. (*IPH,* 38/52)

He reiterates this point in the important paragraph on "actuality" in the *Encyclopedia Logic.* The thesis that the rational is actual, he writes, sets itself against "the notion that ideas or ideals are something far too excellent to have actuality, or equally something too impotent to achieve actuality" (*EL,* §6R).

When Hegel utters his dictum about the actuality of the rational and the rationality of the actual, it is, of course, the assertion of the actuality of the rational that comes first. And this, from what we have just seen, is no accident.

The rational is not something that is simply in our heads or merely inward; it is what is effective and actual. In Aristotelian terms, the rational is not mere *dynamis* but also *energeia.*[20] It is, thus, a doctrine about the nature of rationality that stands first in Hegel's understanding of the identification of the rational and the actual. And it is only after he has made this fundamental point about actuality's being an essential component of rationality that he makes the further claim, in the second half of the *Doppelsatz,* that the actual is rational.[21]

It is, of course, this second part of the *Doppelsatz* which has (wrongly in my view) received the most attention and also caused the most difficulties. Hegel's assertion of the rationality of the actual has been construed as a kind of blanket sanctification of the status quo and of everything that exists. Hegel, however, explicitly rejects this understanding of his dictum in an important Addition to the 1830 edition of the *Encyclopedia Logic.* There he quite clearly distinguishes between "actuality" (*Wirklichkeit*), on the one hand, and "being-there" (*Dasein*) and "existence" (*Existenz*), on the other. Not everything that exists is actual. Much of what exists is mere "appearance," transient and insignificant. "Actuality" refers only to the substantial or essential part of what is there:

> [W]hat is there [*Dasein*] is partly *appearance* and only partly actuality. In common life people may happen to call every brain wave, error, evil, and suchlike "actual," as well as every existence, however wilted and transient it may be. But even for our ordinary feeling, a contingent existence does not deserve to be called something-actual in the emphatic sense of the word; what contingently exists has no greater value than that which something-*possible* has; it is an existence which (although it is) can just as well *not be.* (*EL,* §6)

Later in the *Encyclopedia Logic,* Hegel goes so far as to identify actuality with the rational part of what exists: actuality is "what is rational through and through; and what is not rational must, for that very reason, be considered not to be actual" (*EL,* §142A).

Though Hegel clearly distinguishes here between the actual and the merely existent and thus keeps his assertion of the rationality of the actual from being reduced to the absurd claim that everything that exists is rational, his clarification is not without its difficulties. In the first place, it seems to reduce the statement that the actual is rational to something of a tautology: the actual is rational because the actual refers only to that part of existence which is rational.[22] But the connection Hegel is trying to make between actuality and rationality is more than merely analytic or definitional. Again, the central and philosophically controversial point seems to be that actualization is an essential aspect of rationality. The rational is not something that is simply in our heads or merely inward; it is the unity of inner and outer, of ideal and efficacy; and this is what Hegel means by actuality. In other words, though the second half of the *Doppelsatz,* which asserts the rationality of the actual, may be something of tautology, the first half, which asserts the actuality of the rational, certainly is not.

A second difficulty arises from Hegel's distinction between the actual and the merely existent: it is not clear what standard he is using to distinguish the former from the latter. Before taking up this complicated issue, however, I will close out Hegel's discussion of the relationship of philosophy to actuality by briefly considering some of the famous pronouncements with which he concludes this discussion. Given what he has said about the actuality of the rational and the rationality of the actual, Hegel concludes that the philosophy of right "must distance itself as far as possible from the obligation to construct a *state as it ought to be;* such instruction as it may contain cannot be aimed at instructing the state on how it ought to be, but rather at showing how the state, as the ethical universe, should be recognized." Not the construction of what ought to be but the comprehension of "*what is* is the task of philosophy." Hegel then proceeds to make the point he makes repeatedly from the early lectures on with respect to the relationship between philosophy and actuality: if philosophy does not concern itself with comprehending the actual-historical world before it but instead seeks to construct a "world beyond" which merely "ought to be," then it risks falling into the most extreme and relativistic subjectivism:

> [T]hus philosophy, too, is *its own time comprehended in thoughts.* It is just as foolish to imagine that any philosophy can transcend its own contemporary world as that an individual can overleap his own time or leap over Rhodes. If his theory does indeed transcend his own time, if it builds itself a world *as it ought to be,* then it certainly has an existence, but only within his opinions—a pliant medium in which the imagination can construct anything it pleases. (*PR,* 21–22/26)

It is in connection with the statement that every philosophy "is its own time comprehended in thoughts" that we must consider Hegel's treatment of Plato's *Republic* in the Preface to the *Philosophy of Right.*[23] If any philosophy would seem to contradict Hegel's contention about the relationship of philosophy to actuality, it is Plato's idealistic philosophy. Nevertheless, Hegel maintains that "even Plato's *Republic,* a proverbial example of an *empty ideal,* is essentially the embodiment of nothing other than the nature of Greek ethics." Plato saw that the substantialistic ethics of his time were being penetrated by the "deeper principle" of subjective freedom in the guise of the Sophists and the reflective morality of Socrates. But he also realized that this deeper principle could appear only as a destructive force in the context of Greek culture. Therefore, he sought to counteract it by constructing his republic on a purely substantial basis devoid of subjective freedom (*PR*, 20/24).

By seeing Plato's philosophy as a reflection of the spirit of his time, Hegel does not mean to debunk it in crude historicistic fashion. This becomes clear in his discussion of Plato's *Republic* in the *Lectures on the History of Philosophy*. There Hegel defends Plato against the criticism (most famously expressed by Machiavelli)[24] that his ideal republic is a mere chimera, "capable of being carried out, but only on the condition that men should be of an excellence such as may possibly be present among the dwellers in the moon, but that it is not realizable for men like those on the earth." Plato's republic is not ideal in this sense; rather, it represents a "true ideal" that "is not what *ought* to be actual but what *is* actual and alone the actual." Plato is not a subjective idealist of the sort Hegel despises: "Plato is not the man to dabble in abstract theories and principles; his truth-loving mind has recognized and represented the truth, and this could not be anything else than the truth of the world he lived in, the truth of the *one* spirit which lived in him as well as in Greece." In words reminiscent of the Preface to the *Philosophy of Right*, Hegel concludes: "No man can overleap his time; the spirit of his time is his spirit also" (*HP*, II, 93–96/109–11).

That every philosophy is a product of its time does not mean, for Hegel, that all philosophies are equal. On this basis, he criticizes Plato's philosophy, not because it is too idealistic, but because it is not idealistic enough in the authentic sense of that term: the Platonic republic is "a chimera, not because excellence such as it depicts is lacking to mankind, but because it, this excellence, falls short of man's requirements" (*HP*, II, 95/110). As he constantly reminds us throughout the *Philosophy of Right*, the Platonic republic falls short of man's requirements in that it rests on a purely substantial basis and fails to take into account the modern principle of subjective freedom. For this reason, it is destined to be superseded (*HP*, II, 98–99/113–14). By the same token, Hegel argues that not all constitutions are equal. Though every constitution must be related to the spirit of the people that is current, there is a "true constitution" toward which every nation must advance. Such a true constitution cannot be externally or prematurely imposed on a people, but it stands as the telos of all rational constitutional development. "It is of essential importance," Hegel writes, "to know what the true constitution is; for what is in opposition to it has no stability, no truth, and passes away [*aufhebt*]. It has a temporary existence but cannot maintain itself; it has been accepted but cannot secure permanent acceptance; that it must be cast aside lies in the Idea of the constitution" (*HP,* II, 96–98/111–13).

We now move from Hegel's interpretation of Plato to the difficulty mentioned above concerning the criterion or standard by which Hegel distinguishes the actual from the merely existent—a difficulty which also suggests itself in the distinctions Hegel draws above between true and temporary philosophies and true and temporary constitutions. To this difficulty, however, Hegel seems to have a ready response. As he has at various other points in the Preface to the *Philosophy of Right,* he refers to the "concept" (*Begriff*) as the means by which the actual (and the rational) can be distinguished from what merely exists.

> For what matters is to recognize in the semblance of the temporal and the transient the substance which is immanent and the eternal which is present. For since the rational, which is synonymous with the Idea, becomes actual by entering into external existence, it emerges in an infinite wealth of forms, appearances, and shapes and surrounds its core with a brightly coloured covering in which consciousness at first resides, but which only the concept can penetrate in order to find the inner pulse, and detect its continued beat even within the external shapes. (*PR,* 20–21/25)

Hegel repeats this claim that it is the concept that provides the standard by which the actual is distinguished from the merely existent in the first paragraph of the Introduction to the *Philosophy of Right:* "[I]t is the *concept* alone . . . which has *actuality,* and in such a way that it gives actuality to itself. Everything other than this actuality which is posited by the concept itself is transitory *existence* [*Dasein*], external contingency, opinion, appearance without essence, untruth, deception, etc." (*PR,* §1R).

The rationality of the actual, then, can only be determined in relation to the Hegelian "concept." Although at first it might seem that Hegel's assertion of the rationality of the actual rests on a controversial doctrine about the necessary rationality of the historical process, the real meaning of the assertion turns out to be much less historicistic. In the first place, as we have seen, not everything in history can be deemed actual or, therefore, rational. In the second, what is actual or rational in history cannot be determined by the historical process alone but only with the aid of the philosophical concept. This is not to deny that history tells us something important about the rationality or actuality of a particular social practice or institution. Whatever cannot maintain itself in history as a stable entity cannot be considered fully rational. This is why Hegel ultimately judges the substantial and "beautiful" ethical life of the Greeks to be defective, as the discussion of Plato above suggested. Such an ethical life depended on the exclusion of the principle of subjective freedom, and this made it "inherently unstable" and destined to fall apart "under the influence of reflection" (*LPHI*, 202–3/249–50). But historical success or survival alone does not tell us whether a particular social form is rational or actual; this can only be definitively determined with reference to the philosophical concept.[25] The concept comes first and the philosophy of history second. The reason in history can only be discerned if we already possess, in the concept, the criterion by which to assess it (see *EL*, §16R).

The priority of the philosophical concept to history to which I point here does not, of course, resolve all the difficulties involved in Hegel's assertion of the rationality of the actual. Indeed, it may only seem to displace them from a controversial philosophy of history to an even more controversial logic of the concept. Be that as it may—and I will have more to say about this in the next section—it certainly proves that Hegel's dictum does not involve a crude historicism, a complete abdication to the historical process, the "deification of success," or the "idolatry of the factual."[26]

What I am calling the priority of the philosophical concept to historical reality—the fact that there exists a standard of rationality, discoverable by philosophy, which is not reducible to what simply exists—receives perhaps its clearest expression in the third paragraph of the Introduction to the *Philosophy of Right*. Here Hegel is concerned to distinguish "natural law" (*Naturrecht*) or "philosophical right" from "positive right."[27] More specifically, he distinguishes the philosophical deduction or justification of right in terms of the concept from the historical approach to right—embodied by the historical school of law in Germany led by Savigny—which seeks to justify laws and institutions in terms of their coherence with historical circumstances and existing legal tradition. The latter, historical view, Hegel argues, is valuable in its own place. Montesquieu hit upon a genuine insight when he argued that "legislation in general and its particular determinations should not be considered in the abstract, but rather as a dependent moment within *one* totality, in the context of all the other determinations which constitute the character of a nation and age." But this historical outlook turns into most profound error when it oversteps its bounds and seeks to usurp the role of philosophical or conceptual justification—when it confuses historical justification, which possesses only relative validity, with a justification which is "valid in and for itself."

This distinction, which is very important and should be firmly borne in mind, is at the same time a very obvious one; a determination of right may be shown to be entirely *grounded in* and *consistent with* the prevailing *circumstances* and *existing* legal institutions, yet it may be contrary to right and irrational in and for itself, like numerous determinations of Roman civil law which followed quite consistently from such institutions as Roman paternal authority and Roman matrimony. (*PR*, §3R)

The distinction Hegel draws in this paragraph between philosophical or conceptual justification and historical justification is determinative of the argument of the *Philosophy of Right* as a whole. This argument proceeds philosophically; the development it traces is conceptual; at no point does it appeal to history or "what is" as a justification of what it sets out to prove. It is true that Hegel tries at various points to connect his philosophical argument to existing institutions and arrangements; this much is demanded by his belief in the actuality of the rational and the rationality of the actual. But this in no way implies that agreement with existing institutions and arrangements constitutes the measure or criterion of truth of his argument. Indeed, as we shall see more fully later on, the idea of the state Hegel elaborates in the *Philosophy of Right* diverges in important respects from the Prussian state as it exists at the time he is writing. This gives his argument a certain normative and even critical power and contradicts, once again, the image of Hegel as simply a conservative apologist for the status quo.

One would not want to exaggerate this normative or critical aspect of Hegel's argument in the *Philosophy of Right*, however.[28] Although the philosophical concept of the state he elaborates in the *Philosophy of Right* is not reducible to what simply exists and, indeed, serves as a criterion for the rationality of the actual, Hegel still does not see the task of philosophy as being primarily critical or practical. There is certainly much that can be criticized in existing arrangements and existing states. But such "negative fault-finding," Hegel maintains, is "all too easy" (*IPH*, 38/53). Philosophy needs to concern itself with the more difficult task of detecting and understanding the affirmative aspect that lies beneath the motley surface of existing arrangements. As Hegel expresses this nonpractical conception of the task of philosophy in the *Encyclopedia Logic*:

When the understanding turns against trivial, external, and perishable objects, institutions, situations, etc., with its "ought"—objects that may have a great relative importance for a certain time, and for particular circles—it may very well be in the right; and in such cases it may find much that does not correspond to correct universal determinations. Who is not smart enough to be able to see around him quite a lot that is not, in fact, as it ought to be? But this smartness is wrong when it has the illusion that, in its dealings with objects of this kind and with their "ought," it is operating within the [true] concerns of philosophical science. This science deals only with the Idea—which is not so impotent that it merely ought to be, and is not actual—and further with an actuality of which those objects, institutions, and situations are only the superficial rind. (*EL,* §6R)

The same conception of the affirmative task of philosophy can be found in the *Philosophy of Right:*

Any state, even if we pronounce it bad in the light of our own principles, and even if we discover this or that defect in it, invariably has the essential moments of its existence within itself (provided it is one of the more advanced states of our time). But since it is easier to discover deficiencies than to comprehend the affirmative, one may easily fall into the mistake of overlooking the inner organism of the state in favour of individual aspects. The state is not a work of art; it exists in the world, and hence in the sphere of arbitrariness, contingency, and error, and bad behavior may disfigure it in many respects. But the ugliest man, the criminal, the invalid, or the cripple is still a living human being; the affirmative aspect—life—survives in spite of such deficiencies, and it is with this affirmative aspect that we are here concerned. (*PR,* §258A)

Besides the fact that it falls outside of what he considers to be the proper business of philosophy, Hegel gives one other reason for philosophy's refraining from criticizing the state or "issuing instructions on how the world ought to be." Put simply, philosophy "always comes too late to perform this function." It is only after "actuality has gone through its formative process and attained its completed state," Hegel argues, that it can finally be grasped and comprehended in thought. This somewhat melancholy observation on the practical limitations of philosophy is beautifully captured in the oft-quoted passage on the owl of Minerva: "When philosophy paints its grey in grey, a shape of life has grown old, and it cannot be rejuvenated, but only recognized, by the grey in grey of philosophy; the owl of Minerva begins its flight only with the onset of dusk" (*PR,* 23/27–28).[29] Some read into this passage the announcement of the "end of history,"[30] others Hegel's recognition of the flawed character and imminent demise of his own age.[31] I doubt whether either of these interpretations can be completely sustained. The former misses the fact that the passage seems to point to a condition of all philosophies, not just the "final" one. The latter suggests a pessimism and critical attitude that find little resonance in the rest of the Hegelian corpus. Without reading too much into the passage, the least that can be said is that it reflects Hegel's belief that (*pace* Marx) philosophy cannot change the world but only interpret it, that philosophy always remains a matter of *nachdenken* in the most literal sense.

We have been following Hegel's understanding of the relationship between philosophy or "science" and actuality in the Preface to the *Philosophy of Right*, and it turns out that this understanding is rather complex. On the one hand, Hegel holds that philosophy must take its start from the actual world. Philosophy consists in the "thinking-over" and "comprehension" of the rationality that is implicit in the actual world. To sever this link between philosophy and actuality, to see philosophy as independent of or, worse, in opposition to historical-political actuality, is to condemn it to a subjectivism in which, as we have seen Hegel say, "the imagination can construct anything it pleases" (*PR*, 22/26). On the other hand, philosophy does not simply acquiesce to the actual world or uncritically attribute rationality to whatever exists. The actual is rational, but a good deal of what exists is contingent, arbitrary, and neither rational nor actual in Hegel's sense of the term. The rationality of the actual can only, finally, be determined through philosophical or conceptual analysis. This is the point stressed throughout my discussion. What such conceptual analysis actually involves, however—what exactly Hegel means by the concept—is a question I have not yet addressed. To answer it properly, we must consider more carefully Hegel's ideas on philosophical method, which are most fully expounded in his logic.

LOGIC AND METHOD

We have seen that the argument of the *Philosophy of Right* consists in a kind of conceptual analysis. In order to grasp what such conceptual analysis involves, we must examine Hegel's speculative logic. This at least is Hegel's view of the matter. In the Introduction to the *Philosophy of Right*, he writes that the "method whereby the concept, in science, develops out of itself and is merely an *immanent* progression and production of its own determinations is . . . assumed to be familiar from logic" (*PR*, §31). This connection between the method of the *Philosophy of Right* and Hegel's logic is most clearly stated in a passage from the Preface from which I now quote in full:

> [T]he primary difference between the present outline and an ordinary compendium is the method which constitutes its guiding principle. But I am here presupposing that the philosophical manner of progressing from one topic to another and of conducting a scientific proof—this entire speculative mode of cognition—is essentially different from other modes of cognition. . . . Since I have fully developed the

nature of speculative knowledge in my *Science of Logic,* I have only occasionally added an explanatory comment on procedure and method in the present outline. . . . [I]t will readily be noticed that the work as a whole, like the construction of its parts, is based on the logical spirit. It is also chiefly from this point of view that I would wish this treatise to be understood and judged. For what it deals with is *science,* and in science, the content is essentially inseparable from the *form.* (*PR,* 10/12–13)

There is, of course, considerable debate over the relation of Hegel's logic or speculative philosophy to his political philosophy. There are those who, like Charles Taylor, argue that Hegel's political philosophy can and should be detached from the "incredible" claims of his speculative logic.[32] Allen Wood provides a recent version of this social reading of Hegel's philosophy. Pronouncing Hegel's speculative logic dead and a failure, Wood denies that this implies that there remains nothing of interest in Hegel's philosophy: "The fact is rather that Hegel's great positive achievements as a philosopher do not lie where he thought they did, in his system of speculative logic, but in a quite different realm, in his reflections on the social and spiritual predicament of modern Western European culture."[33] On the other hand, there are those who, offering a more "nonmetaphysical" and philosophically plausible reading of Hegel's speculative logic, see a more intimate connection between it and his political philosophy.[34]

My position is more in accord with that of the latter set of interpreters. Ultimately, I do not think Hegel's political philosophy can be separated from his speculative logic insofar as the latter articulates and justifies his views on philosophical method—his views on how philosophical explanation differs from and is indeed superior to other, empirical forms of explanation. Nevertheless, I do avoid the implication that Hegel's political philosophy is somehow "founded" on or "deducible" from his speculative philosophy. Hegel's political philosophy as it is found in the *Philosophy of Right* is itself philosophical and does not acquire its sole justification through appeal to the logic. Much of the argument of the *Philosophy of Right* is intelligible on its own and can be evaluated without reference to the logic. Nevertheless, there is a certain mystery about the book, especially about the way it proceeds, the order in which Hegel takes up various topics and resolves certain issues, that can only be clarified through an analysis of his ideas on philosophical method as they present themselves most fully in the logic. Besides, it is not very satisfying as an interpretive principle to detach and take seriously only one part of a philosopher's thought while dismissing as worthless what he considered to be the very soul and basis of that part.

In this section, then, taking off from the remarks quoted above from the

Preface and Introduction to the *Philosophy of Right,* I explore Hegel's specula-tive logic and its bearing on his philosophical method, trying to show that it is not as dead or implausible as it has sometimes been depicted. I begin by indicating how the project of this logic takes up where the argument of the *Phenomenology* left off.

In the years following the publication of the *Phenomenology,* Hegel wrote what he considered to be his magnum opus, the *Science of Logic,* the first volume of which was published in 1812 and the second in 1816. The *Science of Logic,* of course, does not merely follow the *Phenomenology* in a chronological sense; it also occupies the absolute standpoint, the standpoint of "science," to which the *Phenomenology* served as introduction and ladder. This absolute or "scientific" standpoint is characterized by the complete identity of subject and object, knowledge and being, certainty and truth. Whereas the movement of the *Phenomenology* was driven by the difference between knowledge and truth and its progressive cancellation, the standpoint of Hegelian science in the form of the *Logic*

> does not contain this difference. On the contrary, since the moment has the form of the concept, it unites the objective form of truth and of the knowing self in an immediate unity. The moment does not appear as this movement of passing back and forth, from consciousness or picture-thinking into self-consciousness, and con-versely; on the contrary, its pure shape, freed from its appearance in consciousness, the pure concept and its onward movement, depends solely on its pure *determinate-ness. (PS,* 491/589)

This idea of the "pure determinateness" of the concept, of the self-determina-tion of thought by itself, lies at the heart of the project of the *Logic.*

There is, of course, tremendous controversy over the exact relation of the *Phenomenology* to the *Logic,* most of it fueled by Hegel's shifting views on the final organization of his system. Whereas in the *Phenomenology* and the first edition of the *Science of Logic* he clearly sees the former as a necessary introduction to the latter and as the first part of his system, in later remarks he seems to modify his position somewhat.[35] None of these later remarks, however, seriously under-mines the justificatory role Hegel originally assigned the *Phenomenology.* Hegel's succinct statement of the relation of the *Phenomenology* to the *Science of Logic* in the Introduction to the latter remains for the most part definitive:

> The concept of pure science and its deduction is therefore presupposed in the present work in so far as the *Phenomenology of Spirit* is nothing other than the deduction of it. Absolute knowing is the *truth* of every mode of consciousness because, as the course

of the *Phenomenology* showed, it is only in absolute knowing that the separation of the *object* from the *certainty of itself* is completely eliminated: truth is now equated with certainty and this certainty with truth. (*SL,* I, 49/43)

The *Logic* starts, then, from the absolute and thoroughly idealist standpoint it was the task of the *Phenomenology* to justify. And it is this starting-point that ultimately distinguishes Hegel's speculative logic from traditional formal logic. Hegel devotes a good deal of his introductory discussions in both the *Science of Logic* and the *Encyclopedia Logic* to bringing out the difference between his speculative logic and traditional formal logic. The defect of the latter, he argues, is that it treats thinking as something subjective and separate from objects, that it treats thought-determinations (*Denkbestimmungen*) as external forms distinct from the content or matter of thought. This defect belongs also to Kant's critical philosophy, which, on the one hand, characterizes concepts as empty unless applied to or filled with sensible intuitions, and on the other, distinguishes between our subjective thought-determinations and what things are in themselves (see *SL,* I, 36–40/26–30, 44–45/36–38, 50–51/44–45; *EL,* §§19–24).

In contrast to this formal logic, Hegel's speculative logic embraces both subject and object, form and content: "What we are dealing with in logic is not a thinking *about* something which exists independently as a base for our thinking and apart from it, nor forms which are supposed to provide mere signs or distinguishing marks of truth; on the contrary, the necessary forms and self-determinations of thought are the content and the ultimate truth itself" (*SL,* I, 50/44). And in contrast to the Kantian view that our thinking is ultimately subjective and shut off from things in themselves, Hegel's logic treats thinking as what is finally objective and substantial in things. In this regard, Hegel rates ancient metaphysics more highly than modern critical philosophy:

> Ancient metaphysics had . . . a higher conception of thinking than is current today. For it based itself on the fact that the knowledge of things obtained through thinking is alone what is really true in them, that is, things not in their immediacy but as first raised into the form of thought, as things *thought*. Thus this metaphysics believed that thinking (and its determinations) is not anything alien to the object, but rather its essential nature, or that things and the thinking of them . . . are explicitly in full agreement, thinking in its immanent determinations and the true nature of things forming one and the same content. (*SL,* I, 45/38)[36]

It is because Hegel regards our thought-determinations as expressing what is finally objective and substantial in things that he identifies logic with metaphysics: "Thus *logic* coincides with *metaphysics,* with the science of *things* grasped in *thoughts* that used to be taken to express the *essentialities* of the things" (*EL*, §24).

Of course, such passages have been cited in support of the most implausibly metaphysical interpretations of Hegel's logic, interpretations which see this logic as lapsing into some sort of precritical metaphysics and as involving "incredible" ontological claims.[37] Although I cannot offer an adequate treatment of this vast and complex issue here, I do want to indicate my basic position. By arguing that thinking expresses what is objective and substantial in things, Hegel is not primarily making an ontological claim about the nature of reality, how it is somehow homologous with our thinking and therefore posited by cosmic mind. Rather, he makes an "epistemological" claim about the possibility of experience, namely, that there are no objects of experience, no determinate "things," that are not somehow constituted by or infected with thought. Deprive a thing of its universal determinations, Hegel tells us—an individual human being of its humanness or a dog of its animality—and "we could not say what it is" (*EL*, §24A1). Or as he puts it in the *Science of Logic:* "[E]ach human being though infinitely unique is so primarily because he is a *man,* and each individual animal is such an individual primarily because it is an animal . . . it would be impossible to say what such an individual could still be if this foundation were removed, no matter how richly endowed the individual might be with other predicates" (*SL*, I, 36–37/26).

All this is to say that Hegel's project in the *Logic* is far more continuous with Kant's critical philosophy than may at first appear. Where Hegel departs from Kant—and, of course, follows Fichte—is in rejecting the distinction between the conceptual and intuitional elements of knowledge, between the spontaneity of thinking and the receptivity of sense-experience.[38] For Hegel, as we have seen, all experience is conceptual or involves thinking. This is a point he makes over and over again in connection with his assertion of the objectivity of thought. He rejects the view of thinking as just one faculty existing alongside others such as sensation, intuition, and volition. Thinking pervades all our activities:

> In all human intuiting there is thinking; similarly, thinking is what is universal in all representations, recollections, and in every spiritual activity whatsoever, in all willing, wishing, etc. These are all of them just further specifications of thinking. When thinking is interpreted in this way, it appears in quite a different light than when we simply say that, along with and beside other faculties such as intuiting, representing, willing, and the like, we have a faculty of thinking. If we regard thinking as what is genuinely universal in everything natural and everything spiritual, too, then it overgrasps all of them and is the foundation of them all. (*EL*, §24A1)

This doctrine of the ubiquity of thought entails a complete transformation of Kant's transcendental logic, albeit in a postcritical, not a precritical, direction. For Kant, the objective validity of concepts ultimately depends on their being tethered to sensible intuition. Once this Kantian anchor in intuition is abandoned, however, the objective validity of concepts, their "really" possible as opposed to merely logically possible status, can only be determined in relation to other concepts. With this appears the distinctive project of Hegel's logic, namely, the self-determination of thought, or, as he puts it at the outset of the *Encyclopedia Logic,* thinking's development from within itself "of its own peculiar determinations and laws, which thinking does not already *have* and find given within itself, but which it gives to itself" (*EL,* §19R).[39] Hegel credits Fichte with being the first to attempt such a genuine deduction of the categories of thought, in contrast with Kant, who merely accepted the categories as empirically given through observation (*EL,* §§42R, 60A2). The strangeness and radically groundless character of the project of the self-determination of thought is captured beautifully later when Hegel says that, in the *Logic,* "thought is free and withdrawn into itself, free of all [given] material, purely at home with itself. When we think freely, voyaging on the open sea, with nothing under us and nothing over us, in solitude, alone by ourselves—then we are purely at home with ourselves" (*EL,* §31A; see also §24A2).

Hegel's rejection of Kant's account of the objectivity of concepts in terms of intuition and his replacement of it with a doctrine of thought's self-determination also entail an abandonment of Kant's distinction between appearances and things in themselves. It is not that Hegel wishes to return to the precritical metaphysical tradition that simply assumed that thought grasps directly what things are in themselves. Indeed, Hegel criticizes this older metaphysics for its uncritical use of the categories of ordinary representation and of the understanding, its tendency to regard them as somehow ultimate and unquestionable (see especially *EL,* §28); and he praises Kant for having subjected these categories to critical scrutiny and having established the finitude and merely apparent character of empirical cognition. Hegel agrees with Kant that "the objects of which we have immediate knowledge are mere appearances, i.e., they do not have the ground of their being within themselves, but within something else." But instead of seeing the ground of these appearances in things in themselves, he sees it in the absolute Idea:

> According to the Kantian philosophy, the things that we know about are only appearances for *us,* and what they are *in-themselves* remains for us an inaccessible

beyond. . . . In fact, the true situation is that things of which we have immediate knowledge are mere appearances, not only *for us,* but also *in themselves,* and that the proper determination of these things, which are in this sense "finite," consists in having the ground of their being not within themselves but in the universal divine Idea. (*EL,* §45A; see also §60A1)

For Hegel, the status of the categories and their relation to reality can only be determined in relation to the sequence of thought's self-determination and ultimately in relation to the final term of that sequence, namely, the absolute, not in relation to the ghostly thing in itself.

It is to the details of the process by which thought or, as Hegel generally refers to it, the "concept," determines itself in the *Logic* that I now turn. My account of the movement from "being" to "essence" to "concept" is, given my overall focus on Hegel's political philosophy, necessarily brief and therefore somewhat superficial. Nevertheless, it is important to have a general idea of this movement and its underlying rationale, because it serves as a model for Hegel's procedure in the *Philosophy of Right.* As Hegel tells us, the philosophies of nature and spirit are both merely "applied logic," concerned "to [re]cognise the logical forms in the shapes of nature and spirit, shapes that are only a particular mode of expression of the forms of pure thinking" (*EL,* §24A2). For my account of the movement of the *Logic* I generally rely on the shorter and more accessible *Encyclopedia Logic* instead of on the mammoth *Science of Logic.* There are, of course, many important differences between these two works, especially in the second large subdivision devoted to the "Logic of Essence," but for my general purposes the *Encyclopedia Logic* will suffice.

Hegel's logic is divided into three main parts, the logic of being, the logic of essence, and the logic of the concept. The movement from the first of these to the second and third is, in the main, a movement from less determinate categories to more determinate categories, from simpler categories that do not include the context which makes possible their application to more complex categories which precisely make explicit this presupposed context. Another and more Hegelian way of expressing this movement is that it goes from what is partial and abstract to what is concrete and self-complete. The motor of this movement is, of course, the dialectic, about which (again) I say little here, because the argument of the *Logic* as a whole is an illustration and demonstration of it. Generally this method consists in showing how the fixed and one-sided thought-determinations of the abstract understanding pass over into their opposites and thus reveal themselves to be self-contradictory. As in the *Phenomenology,* though, such self-contradiction does not result in pure negation or abstract nothingness but in a "determinate negation" which has a positive content embracing both sides of the opposition (*EL*, §§79–82; also §89R).[40]

Let us turn first to the logic of being. In keeping with his project of tracing the course of thought's self-determination, the path by which thought moves from indeterminacy to complete determinacy, Hegel begins with the most indeterminate thought, the emptiest and most immediate thought, that of being. There follows the famous dialectic of being and nothing, by which Hegel shows that being in its complete lack of determination is the same as nothing. The speculative "synthesis" of these two ideas is becoming, the positive result of which is the first (albeit minimally) determinate thought of the logic, namely, determinate being or being-there (*Dasein*). There is, no doubt, a certain artificiality to this opening dialectic of the logic, and it has generated a fair amount of controversy. Nevertheless, the justification for starting the logic in this way is tolerably clear within Hegel's overall scheme, and it does succeed in getting us to the philosophically important topic of being-there in the form of "quality."[41]

Quality is the simplest and most immediate determination of reality, its point of view being most succinctly expressed in Bishop Butler's famous line that "everything is what it is, and not another thing." We say, "there is a meadow," or, "that is a tree," and we are making what Hegel understands to be qualitative determinations. Such determinations are purely positive, immediate in the sense that they are not explicitly related to or mediated by anything other than themselves. Therein lies their deficiency for Hegel. For the determinacy of all such qualitative determinations, he argues, ultimately depends on their being differentiated from or related to that which they are not. By failing to include explicitly the otherness or negation which they presuppose, qualitative determinations ultimately remain inadequately determinate (*EL*, §§90–92). The self-contradiction that Hegel exposes in quality here—between what qualitative determination explicitly claims to be and what it implicitly presupposes—has nothing to do with finding some sort of ontological contradiction in finite things or reality itself.[42] Rather, it has to do with elucidating the possibility-conditions of a certain abstract category of thought. The key claim is that, within its own terms, quality is unable to successfully pick out, discriminate, or determine anything.

Hegel goes on to show how the breakdown of quality leads to its dialectical opposite, "quantity," which in turn yields to the synthetic category of "measure" or qualitative quantity. Both of these further determinations, however, remain tied to the immediacy and pure positivity that are characteristic of quality and are the hallmark of the entire logic of being. Like quality, quantity and measure both fail to include explicitly relation, mediation, or negation, in their point of view, and they are thus subject to the same "passing over" into their opposite, the same instability and indeterminateness, that afflicted quality. This instability and indeterminateness lead to the idea of "essence." In the logic of essence, the relationality or mediation missing from the logic of being is explicitly included or "posited" (to use the Hegelian term of art). Hegel clearly describes the transition in the following way:

> Ordinary consciousness interprets things as [simply] being, and considers them in terms of quality, quantity, and measure. But these immediate determinations then prove not to be fixed, but to pass into something else, and essence is the result of their dialectic. In essence no passing-over takes place any more; instead, there is only relation. In being, the relational form is only [due to] our reflection; in essence, by contrast, the relation belongs to it as its own determination. When something becomes other (in the sphere of being) the something has thereby vanished. Not so in essence: here we do not have a genuine other, but only a diversity, relation between the one and *its* other. (*EL*, §111A)

The sphere of essence is the sphere of relation. Here things are no longer understood to be what they immediately show themselves to be, as in the logic of being; this immediate being of things is now regarded as a mere semblance (*Schein*). Instead, things are understood to be mediated or posited by something else, their essence. "The immediate being of things is here represented as a sort of rind or curtain behind which the essence is concealed." Hegel explains further:

> [W]hen we say . . . that all things have an essence, what we mean is they are not truly what they immediately show themselves to be. A mere rushing about from one quality to another, and a mere advance from the qualitative to the quantitative and back again, is not the last word; on the contrary, there is something that abides in things, and this is, in the first instance, their essence. (*EL*, §112A)

In the course of the logic of essence, Hegel goes through the various forms this essence-existence or essence-appearance relationship has traditionally assumed: in the relationships between ground and grounded, thing and properties, content and form, whole and parts, force and utterance, inner and outer, and so forth. In all these relationships he exposes a common defect: the tendency to treat the two terms of the relationship as independent of one another, with one being primary or foundational. In fact, Hegel maintains, both sides of the relationship should be seen as inseparable and coequal. Thus, in the case of the content-form distinction, he tells us that the "essential" content of a book or work of art cannot be separated from or regarded as independent of the form.

"The only genuine works of art are precisely the ones whose content and form show themselves to be completely identical." The abstract content of *Romeo and Juliet* may be said to be "the ruin of two lovers brought about by the strife between their families; but by itself this is not yet Shakespeare's immortal tragedy" (*EL,* §133A). Likewise with the whole-parts distinction. The whole is not something different from the parts, nor are the parts somehow separable from and indifferent to the whole. Here Hegel adverts to his favorite and Aristotelian analogy of organic life: "[T]he members and organs of a living body should not be considered merely as parts of it, for they are what they are only in their unity and are not indifferent to that unity at all" (*EL,* §135A).

The fallacy Hegel is pointing out with respect to these essence-appearance relationships is perhaps most intelligibly expressed in what he says about the inner-outer distinction as it relates to ethical conduct. In a manner reminiscent of his critique of romantic and subjective inwardness in the *Phenomenology,* Hegel here criticizes the appeal to one's essential inner self, one's "allegedly excellent intentions and sentiments, in the face of [one's] inadequate performances and even of [one's] discreditable acts." He is willing to concede that there may "be single instances where, through the adversity of external circumstances, well-meant intentions come to nothing and the execution of well-thought out plans is frustrated." But these discrepancies between inner intention and outer performance must remain the exception and not the rule in our interpretation of human action; otherwise the door is opened to a mendacious subjectivism. In general, Hegel tells us, "the essential unity between inward and outward" in human conduct "holds good; and hence it must be said that a person *is* what he *does*." And he criticizes, as an instance of the false understanding of the relationship between inner motive and outer performance, those valet historians who trace the great deeds of historical heroes to base motives or passions (*EL,* §140A; also §112A).

The unity of the inner and outer that has just been disclosed leads to the third and final major category of the logic of essence, "actuality" (*Wirklichkeit*). In actuality, essence no longer lies behind external existence or appearance but, rather, is unified with it and manifests itself therein. As we saw in relation to Hegel's dictum concerning the actuality of the rational and the rationality of the actual, however, actuality is not simply to be identified with whatever exists or with what is immediately present. Hegel sharply distinguishes between actuality and mere contingency. Actuality refers only to what is essential in external existence, and this essentiality is construed in terms of the necessary or lawful relationship between appearances (*EL,* §§142–49).

In the first instance, such necessary or lawful relationship is exemplified in the relationship of cause and effect. For Hegel, though, the relationship of cause and effect suffers from the same defect all the other two-tiered explanations in the logic of essence suffer from: the two terms of the relationship are treated as distinct from or independent of one another and the cause is regarded as somehow primary or foundational. Properly or conceptually understood, Hegel argues, cause and effect "are not only distinct, but are just as much identical too." Both of them have "one and the same content, and the distinction between them is primarily just between *positing* and *being posited*" (*EL,* §153A). Hegel's point here is that the relationship between cause and effect is one of interdependence and mutual implication rather than of mechanical interaction between discrete substances. In the end, cause and effect must be seen as moments in an overall system of necessity in which no single element has complete independence or primacy. It is only from their place in such a system that cause and effect derive their true determinacy.

There is a recognition of this interdependence and mutual mediation between cause and effect in the final relationship Hegel considers in the logic of essence, that of "reciprocal action." In this relationship, neither cause nor effect is seen to be independent or primary; each affects or mediates the other reciprocally. Hegel illustrates what he has in mind by considering the historical question of whether the character and customs of a people are to be regarded as the cause or the effect of its constitution and laws. According to the standpoint of reciprocal action, the answer is both. The customs are the effect of the constitution and the constitution is the effect of the customs. Neither side is foundational or exclusively causal. The same reciprocal relationship can also be seen in the organs and members of a living organism. With the relationship of reciprocal action, Hegel tells us, we stand "on the threshold of the concept." Nevertheless, it, too, falls somewhat short of truly conceptual comprehension. For the two sides of the relationship remain immediately given and are not grasped in terms of a more comprehensive category which explains them both:

> [T]he use of the relationship of reciprocal action is unsatisfactory because, instead of being able to count as an equivalent of the concept, this relationship itself still requires to be comprehended. And comprehension comes when its two sides are not left as something immediately given, but . . . when they are recognised as the moments of a third, higher [whole], which is, in fact, precisely the concept. (*EL,* §156A)

This is the transition to the logic of the concept. In the logic of the concept, the externality characteristic of the logic of essence is overcome. Here we no longer have to do with relationships in which the terms are independent or lie outside of one another. The logic of the concept deals only with wholes that are inwardly or self-differentiated. Here "the terms that appear initially to be bound together are not in fact alien to one another; instead, they are only moments of *one* whole, each of which, being related to the other, is at home with itself, and goes together with itself" (*EL*, §158A). Similarly, the dialectical movement belonging to the concept is no longer the "passing-over into another" characteristic of the logic of being nor the "shining into another" characteristic of the logic of essence but, rather, purely immanent "development" in which "only that is posited which is already implicitly present." Hegel once again uses the analogy of organic life to illustrate his meaning. The development of the concept is like that of the plant in which the germ already contains implicitly within itself the root, stem, and leaves. And once again he refers to the distinguishing fact that the concept "remains at home with itself in the course of its process" (*EL*, §161A).

The moments of the concept are the universal, the particular (*das Besondere*), and the singular (*das Einzelne*). These are the terms in which conceptuality has traditionally been understood, but Hegel has a very untraditional understanding of them. Traditionally, the universal—and hence the concept—has been understood in terms of what a set of particulars or individuals has in common. Hegel, however, rejects this abstract understanding of universality—and of conceptuality—in terms of mere communality. "It is of the greatest importance, both for cognition and for our practical behaviour, too, that we should not confuse what is merely communal with what is truly universal." Instead, he sees a much more intimate connection between the universal and the particular and the singular. The universal is not merely "something common against which the particular stands on its own" but "what particularises (specifies) itself, remaining at home with itself in its other" (*EL*, §163A1). Hegel elaborates on this doctrine of "concrete," as opposed to merely abstract, universality by arguing that when we characterize a group of individuals as human beings we are not pointing to something they simply have in common; on the contrary, their being human "is what is *universal* in them, it is their *kind*, and none of them would be what he is at all without this kind." The universal here is not simply "an external bond that embraces all the singular instances which subsist on their own account"; rather, it "is the ground and soil, the root and substance of the single instance" (*EL*, §175A). In an interesting aside, Hegel adds that the distinction he is drawing between what is merely held in common and what is genuinely universal is also expressed in Rousseau's distinction between the general will and the will of all, though Rousseau himself did not consistently adhere to this distinction. "The general will is the *concept* of willing, and the laws are the particular determinations of willing as grounded in this concept" (*EL*, §163A1).

With this understanding of the essential unity of universality, particularity, and singularity in the concept, Hegel analyzes the various forms of judgment and syllogism found in traditional or formal logic. His basic point is to reveal the unity of universal, particular, and singular that is obscured in traditional logic. Thus, with respect to judgment, he rejects the notion that the subject and predicate are to be understood as independent of one another, arguing instead that they are originally unified in the concept. The German *Urteil* profoundly expresses this idea of judgment as an "original division" of what is first unified in the concept (*EL*, §166R). This identity of subject and predicate also serves as a criterion by which to judge the value of judgments. In simple, qualitative judgments such as "This rose is red," the relationship between subject and predicate is loose and external. The rose is many other things besides red, and red is a quality that belongs to many other things besides this rose. In the more determinate and "genuine" judgments of the concept, on the other hand, for example, "This art work is beautiful," or "This action is good," the relationship between subject and predicate is no longer loose and external. The predicate expresses something essential about the subject, something without which that subject would not be what it is, as in the example above concerning the humanity of a set of individuals. "[I]n the judgment of the Concept," Hegel writes, "the predicate is, as it were, the soul of the subject, by which the latter, as the body of this soul, is determined through and through" (*EL*, §§171–72). The interdependence between universal, particular, and singular becomes even more transparent in the syllogism.

In judgment and the syllogism we are dealing with what Hegel calls the "subjective concept." From his account of the subjective concept Hegel turns to a consideration of the "object" to which the subjective concept applies. For Hegel, of course, as against Kant, there can ultimately be no distinction between subject and object, concept and reality. And in this context, that means that the purposiveness that has already been attributed to the concept must also be attributed to objective reality. Accordingly, Hegel tries to demonstrate the necessity of a teleological understanding of the natural world. This demonstration is not entirely convincing, and it is likely to promote the misunderstanding that Hegel is trying to establish a strongly metaphysical interpretation of the teleological and spiritual character of nature in the manner of his friend Schelling. Nevertheless, Hegel's point here is less metaphysical than epistemologi-cal—though, again, these two perspectives are ultimately inseparable for him. He is trying to show what a concrete understanding of the objective world must look like, given the purposiveness of the concept and of thinking in general. It is this purposiveness of the concept and of thinking in general that becomes thematic in the culminating section of the *Logic* on the "Idea."

Hegel defines the Idea as the "absolute unity of concept and objectivity" (*EL*, §213). What exactly this resolution and telos of the entire *Logic* involves, however, is not immediately clear. Is the Idea some sort of final insight into the nature of the universe or absolute substance? Or is it ultimately, like absolute knowing in the *Phenomenology,* a kind of self-consciousness, an insight into "what it is to be a thinking subject"?[43] Though there is not space here to resolve definitively this complex and controversial issue, Hegel's characterization of the Idea as "essentially process" (*EL*, §215), his tracing of its development from "life" through cognition and willing, and finally his account of the "absolute Idea" in terms of an account of speculative method all suggest the latter, what might be called "metalogical" reading of the conclusion of the *Logic*. The case for this metalogical reading of the resolution and telos of the *Logic* has been put most powerfully by Robert Pippin. The resolution of the *Logic,* he writes,

> appears to consist in a self-consciousness about the spontaneity of Notional determi-nation, a generally antiempiricist, antinaturalist account of any possible conceptual scheme, and a self-consciousness about the wholly internal ground of thought in itself—that Notional distinctions can be understood and assessed only in terms of each other—and such self-consciousness appears to be the *extent* of the "resolution." The entire "Subjective Logic" [i.e., logic of the concept] section would thus appear to be a reflective account of the subjectivity of the Objective Logic [i.e., the logics of being and essence], and beyond such a metalevel claim, not to resolve or conclude in some permanent, traditionally "absolute" way, thought's "process."[44]

That self-consciousness about the nature of conceptuality and not some more substantial or metaphysical cognition constitutes the telos of the *Logic* is most clearly revealed by the fact that Hegel's account of the absolute Idea resolves itself into an account of the speculative method. The absolute Idea is nothing more than the recollective apprehension of the "absolute form" or method by which the overall movement of the *Logic* has been determined. Here Hegel recapitulates in abstract form the basic moments of the *Logic*. The speculative method begins, first, with the immediate or being, passes through a moment of mediation in which the immediate is related to an other, and concludes with the sublation (*Aufhebung*) of this otherness in the inwardly differentiated or self-mediating concept (see *EL*, §§237–42; also *SL*, II, 825–43/550–73). The overall force of this method, however, gains little from its abstract formulation. Its validity ultimately depends on the validity of the specific argument which constitutes the movement of the *Logic* as a whole.

This concludes our brief analysis of Hegel's logic and returns us to the issue which impelled us to undertake this analysis in the first place, namely, the issue of philosophical method in the *Philosophy of Right* and of the nature of Hegelian conceptual analysis. We began by quoting the Preface and Introduction to the *Philosophy of Right* to the effect that the arrangement of the entire work is based on the speculative method developed in the *Logic*. This understanding of the relationship between Hegel's logic and his political philosophy we also saw reiterated in the *Logic* itself, where Hegel tells us the philosophy of spirit is to be understood as "applied logic," a science concerned to recognize the logical forms of pure thinking in the shape of spirit (*EL*, §24A2). As we turn to the *Philosophy of Right*, we find this connection to the *Logic* confirmed in the basic structure of the work, which moves from the immediacy of "Abstract Right" to the pure mediacy and reflectedness of "Morality" and finally to the synthesis and sublation of these two moments in "Ethical Life." This dialectical pattern is again repeated in the movement within "Ethical Life" from the family to civil society and finally to the state. And within each of these moments there are further involutions of this three-stage dialectic.

To note the correspondence between the overall movement of the *Logic* and the overall movement of the *Philosophy of Right* provides, of course, only the most formal understanding of Hegel's procedure in the latter work. What was said above about the abstract formulation of Hegel's speculative method toward the end of the *Logic* goes as well for the application of this method to the realm of spirit and politics. The validity of this method can only finally be assessed in terms of the specific argument in which it is deployed. The purpose of this chapter was not to prove that the argument of the *Philosophy of Right* rests on indisputable logical foundations. Its aim was more modest than that: to gain a clearer understanding of the nature of and rationale for the speculative logic which constitutes the basis of Hegel's procedure in the *Philosophy of Right*. I also showed that this logic is not as "incredible" as it has often been portrayed, though this should not be taken to imply that it is completely without difficulties. Beyond that, we must turn to the specific argument of the *Philosophy of Right* to amplify the meaning of Hegel's speculative logic and method and to determine their final validity.

Chapter 5 Hegel's Concept
of Freedom

In this chapter, I explicate Hegel's concept of freedom through a careful analysis of the Introduction to the *Philosophy of Right*. In the writings examined so far, freedom has, of course, played a central role. Hegel's earliest writings, directed against the "positivity" of Judaism and Christianity, are suffused with the idea of freedom, which he largely interprets in terms of the Kantian notion of autonomy. "Reason and Freedom," he writes to Schelling in 1795, "remain our password" (*L,* 32/1:18). And he enthusiastically agrees when Schelling writes back, "The alpha and omega of all philosophy is freedom" (*L,* 32/22 and 35–36/1:23–25). Toward the end of the 1790s, however, Hegel begins to revise the notion of freedom or autonomy he finds in Kant's and Fichte's practical philosophies, rejecting the dualism of pure reason and sensuous impulse implied in it. While he continues to accept Kant's and Fichte's equation of freedom with radical self-determination and self-dependence, he nevertheless seeks to ground freedom in a more positive, less oppositional relationship to nature, the world, and otherness in general.

This critique of Kantian-Fichtean autonomy, in which freedom is opposed to nature and sensuous inclination, runs through all of Hegel's ethical writings at Jena, culminating in the *Phenomenology*. From one point of view, the *Phenomenology* may be said to consist in an inventory and critique of all the various and inevitably unsuccessful strategies adopted by consciousness—from Stoicism and the "unhappy consciousness" to Kantian-Fichtean "morality" and the "beautiful soul"—to secure freedom apart from, above, or beyond the empirical self and the actual world. Even in Hegel's *Logic* the theme of freedom is not absent. He writes there: "In the Logic, thoughts are grasped in such a way that they have no content other than one that belongs to thinking itself, and is brought forth by thinking. . . . Spirit is here purely at home with itself, and thereby free." And he goes on to state a formula for freedom that recurs throughout his discussion of freedom in the *Philosophy of Right* and that encapsulates his revision of the Kantian-Fichtean idea of autonomy: "for that is just what freedom is: being at home with oneself in one's other, depending upon oneself, and being one's own determinant" (*EL,* §24A2).

It is only in the *Philosophy of Right,* though, that the idea of freedom receives full and thematic treatment. This book is nothing other than a complete elaboration of the meaning and implications of human freedom properly understood. That freedom is the starting-point and, indeed, sole object of the *Philosophy of Right* is made clear in §4 of the Introduction: "The basis of right is the *realm of spirit* in general and its precise location and point of departure is the *will;* the will is *free,* so that freedom constitutes its substance and destiny and the system of right is the realm of actualized freedom, the world of spirit produced from within itself as a second nature" (*PR,* §4). We will analyze fully this important paragraph that not only forms the starting-point for Hegel's argument concerning freedom in the *Philosophy of Right* but in many respects encapsulates the whole of it. Here I only observe that it places Hegel squarely in the voluntarist tradition of modern political philosophy—the tradition inaugurated by Hobbes and deepened by Rousseau, Kant, and Fichte—which we considered in the first chapter of this book. In contradistinction to ancient political philosophy, whose master concepts are reason and nature, modern political philosophy makes will or freedom the basis of the state.[1] It is true that Hegel, following Kant, identifies freedom with reason in a certain sense. And it is also true that he does not make will the basis of the state in the traditional contractarian sense of individual consent. Nevertheless, despite these modifications of the voluntarist tradition of modern political philosophy, there remains an important sense in which Hegel can still be said to belong to it. One purpose of this chapter—and, indeed, of the ensuing chapters—will be to bring out what this sense consists in.[2]

Whether Hegel ultimately belongs to the voluntarist tradition of modern political philosophy has, of course, been seriously questioned by many critics. Some have questioned whether Hegel ultimately maintains the primacy of the will that is suggested in the paragraph quoted above; whether he doesn't, in the final analysis, lapse back into the standpoint of reason and nature—as opposed to will and artifice—belonging to ancient political philosophy.[3] Others have questioned whether what Hegel calls freedom really corresponds to what we ordinarily and properly understand by freedom. As E. F. Carritt, a liberal English critic of Hegel, once put it: "No doubt Hegel professed (as who does not?) and even persuaded himself (as who cannot?) that he was an admirer of freedom. And he managed this by giving the word a peculiar meaning of his own."[4] Connected with this latter criticism is the one made famous by Isaiah Berlin, which raises the question whether Hegel's "positive" conception of freedom doesn't lead to the very opposite of freedom ordinarily and properly understood.[5]

In general, I defend Hegel against the charges that his teaching on freedom turns into something else, showing that it does not abandon the modern standpoint of will or freedom for ancient reason, and that, while it certainly does not simply correspond with our ordinary understanding of freedom, it is not directly opposed to that understanding either but, rather, incorporates it in a more comprehensive notion. Hegel's positive conception of freedom ultimately captures more of what we mean by freedom and why we find it valuable than the competing negative conception of doing what we please without hindrance. The latter may be an aspect of the more comprehensive, positive notion of freedom, but it cannot be the ultimate meaning or justification of freedom. These issues, however, can only be definitely resolved after a complete analysis of the Introduction to the *Philosophy of Right*, which is devoted to the concept of freedom apart from its embodiment in specific practices or institutions—the latter aspect being taken up in the rest of the book.

THE CONCEPT OF WILL

Let us return to the paragraph quoted above, in which Hegel states that free will is the basis of right. We must inquire further into what Hegel means by "free will" here. And to simplify our task, let us take the words separately, beginning with the word "will."

The concept of will is, of course, one of the most problematic in the history of philosophical psychology. From Augustine down to Descartes and his progeny, the will has been conceived as a separate faculty mediating between thought and action. This notion of the will as a separate entity serving to translate thoughts into actions has come under intense criticism.[6] Fortunately, it has nothing to do with Hegel's concept of will. Indeed, Hegel begins his discussion of the will by rejecting the idea that it is a separate faculty distinct from thinking. "Those who regard thinking as a distinct *faculty*," he writes, "divorced from the will as an equally distinct *faculty*, and who in addition even consider that thinking is prejudicial to the will—especially the good will—show from the outset that they are totally ignorant of the nature of the will" (*PR*, §5R). He puts the same point in a slightly different way in the Addition to §4: "[I]t must not be imagined that a human being thinks on the one hand and wills on the other, and that he has thought in one pocket and volition in the other, for this would be an empty representation" (*PR*, §4A).[7] For Hegel, the will is not a faculty separate from thinking but, rather, "a particular way of thinking—thinking translating itself into existence, thinking as the drive to give itself existence" (*PR*, §4A). It is thinking in its practical, as opposed to theoretical, guise—what Kant referred to as "practical reason."

What exactly does this mean, though? What exactly is Hegel getting at when he asserts that willing is inseparable from thinking? To answer this question, we must probe further into what Hegel means by thinking. In the Addition to §4, he gives a brief account of thinking, characteristically emphasizing its "ideality," its tendency to overcome the externality and independence of objects:

> When I think of an object, I make it into a thought and deprive it of its sensuous quality; I make it into something which is essentially and immediately mine. For it is only when I think that I am with myself [*bei mir*], and it is only by comprehending it that I can penetrate an object; it then no longer stands opposed to me, and I have deprived it of that quality of its own which it had for itself in opposition to me. (*PR*, §4A)[8]

This idealization, this overcoming of the externality and independence of objects, is accomplished through generalization. Thinking is nothing but generalization, thinking the universal. And it is exemplified at the simplest and most fundamental level—here Hegel returns to the opening arguments of the *Phenomenology*, as well as to Kant's "transcendental unity of apperception" and Fichte's "intellectual intuition"—in the utterance of the "I." When I say "I," I abstract from all particularity and reduce the manifold to the simplicity of the universal (*PR*, §4A).[9] This, for Hegel, is the essence of thinking.

The thinking Hegel describes here belongs in the first instance to the theoretical attitude. Theoretical reason differs from practical reason in that it internalizes and assimilates alien objects, whereas practical reason seeks to externalize and objectify its subjective aims and interests (*PR,* §4A).[10] Despite this difference, though, the thinking that belongs to theoretical reason also belongs to practical reason. Indeed, Hegel sees such thinking as the essential precondition for willing: "The theoretical is essentially contained within the practical; the idea that the two are separate must be rejected, for one cannot have a will without intelligence" (*PR,* §4A). Hegel gives a full account of the way in which theoretical intelligence is presupposed by and resolves itself into practical will in the *Encyclopedia Philosophy of Spirit* (see §§445–68). In the *Philosophy of Right,* he simply points out that the will begins with thought or abstraction in the form of the "I," and that willing is always accompanied by a generalized representation of the object willed. This thinking, generalizing, representing aspect of human willing is what distinguishes it from the instinctive behavior of an animal: "The will determines itself, and this determination is primarily of an inward nature, for what I will I represent to myself as my object. The animal acts by instinct . . . it has no will, because it does not represent to itself what it desires" (*PR,* §4A; see also §11A).[11]

We now turn to the word that forms the other half of the starting-point of the *Philosophy of Right,* namely, "free." Of course, Hegel does not see freedom as something separable from the will. He makes this clear in the first few sentences of the Addition to §4:

> The freedom of the will can best be explained by reference to physical nature. For freedom is just as much a basic determination of the will as weight is a basic determination of bodies. If matter is described as heavy, one might think this predicate is merely contingent; but this is not so, for nothing in matter is weightless: on the contrary, matter is weight itself. Heaviness constitutes the body and is the body. It is just the same with freedom and the will, for that which is free is the will. Will without freedom is an empty word. (*PR,* §4A)

From this passage, too, it is clear that Hegel is not at this point in his argument concerned with freedom in the "positive" sense of being substantively self-directed or autonomous—a condition which may or may not be achieved by a human being—but, rather, with freedom as a formal condition inherent in all willing.[12] As weight is a basic determination of all bodies, so freedom in this formal sense is a basic determination of all wills. Nevertheless, as we will see more clearly below, Hegel does not conceive of this formal freedom intrinsic to agency simply as a negative capacity but, rather, as itself marked by a certain sort of—even if deficient—self-dependence and autonomy.

In what, then, does this formal freedom inherent in willing consist for Hegel? As it turns out, it is closely connected with the intelligent or thinking aspect of willing brought out above. Thinking, as we have seen, is characterized by ideality, the overcoming of externality, being with oneself. But this is precisely how Hegel tends to characterize the freedom inherent in willing as well. In the *Philosophy of History*, for example, he returns to the matter-weight analogy deployed in the passage above to show that the freedom belonging to spirit consists essentially in self-dependence, being with oneself. He writes, whereas "matter has weight insofar as it strives toward a central point outside itself," spirit

> is that which has its center in itself. Its unity is not outside itself; rather, it has found it within its own self. It is in its own self and alone unto itself. While matter has its "substance" outside itself, spirit is autonomous and self-sufficient, a being-with-itself [*Bei-sich-selbst-sein*]. But this, precisely, is freedom—for when I am dependent, I relate myself to something else, something which I am not; as dependent, I cannot be without something which is external. I am free when I exist independently, all by myself. (*IPH*, 20/30)

Hegel makes the same point in the *Encyclopedia Philosophy of Spirit*, when he characterizes freedom as a formal feature of spirit that allows it to "withdraw itself from everything external and from its own externality, its very existence"; also as "the absence of dependence on an other, the relating of self to self" (*EPS*, §382). In other words, even the formal freedom inherent in willing Hegel conceives of in terms of autonomy; and the dialectic of freedom he will pursue will consist in transforming this abstract self-identity into one which incorporates otherness.

Freedom in this sense—of ideality, the overcoming of externality, self-dependence—is brought specifically to bear on the concept of the will in §5 of the Introduction to the *Philosophy of Right*. In §§5–7, Hegel develops the concept of will in accordance with the three moments of the logical concept, that is, abstract universality, particularity, and singularity. Paragraph 5 corresponds to the moment of abstract universality. Here the will—and freedom— is understood as the "*absolute possibility of abstracting* from every determination in which I find myself or which I have posited in myself, the flight from every content as a limitation" (*PR*, §5R). Though this represents only a very limited or abstract understanding of human will and freedom, according to Hegel, it nevertheless corresponds to something essential. For it is precisely this capacity to abstract from all determinacy and particularity, to withdraw from all externality and be with oneself, which—as we have already seen—distinguishes human beings from animals. As he did in the passage from the *Encyclopedia Philosophy of Spirit* quoted above, Hegel sees this distinctive human capacity as revealing itself in an extreme form in the possibility of suicide: "The human being alone is able to abandon all things, even his own life: he can commit suicide" (*PR*, §5A). It also reveals itself in the master's willingness to risk his life in the struggle for recognition.[13]

Hegel calls freedom understood as the flight from all content and the abstraction from all determinacy and particularity "negative freedom." By this he does not mean what Isaiah Berlin means when he uses the same expression. For Berlin, negative freedom refers, not to the ultimate source of human action, but merely to the area in which a human being may act in an unobstructed fashion. This is the Hobbesian (or Benthamite) and wholly empirical notion of freedom as the "absence of external impediments" in pursuing whatever we have a desire to pursue.[14] For Hegel, negative freedom *is* ultimately concerned with the source of human actions, whether they emanate from and ultimately express one's self or not. And it has nothing to do with the unfettered pursuit of our empirical desires and inclinations but precisely abstracts from all such determinacy and particularity. It is not the empiricist tradition of Hobbes and Bentham that Hegel has in mind when he talks about negative freedom but, rather, the rationalist tradition of Kant and especially Fichte. Indeed, Hegel's earliest references to negative freedom come in connection with Fichte and the dominion of reason or intellect over empirical desire and natural inclination that is found in his ethical and political philosophy (see *DFS*, 133/69, 144–45/82).[15] Again, all this has little to do with negative freedom in Berlin's sense and, indeed, it shares a number of features with what Berlin describes under the rubric of "positive freedom."

For Hegel, the most dramatic and frightening example of the attempt to actualize the notion of negative freedom is the French Revolution. Here Hegel returns to his analysis of the French Revolution in the *Phenomenology*, where he argued that the "absolute freedom" embodied in the French Revolution was ultimately incapable of allowing anything positive—whether it be social classes, laws, or political institutions—"to become a free object standing over against" the individual. The logic of this absolute freedom led only "negative action" and the "fury of destruction" (*PS*, 357–59/433–36). It is just this emphasis on destruction and the intolerance of anything positive or determinate that runs through Hegel's discussion of negative freedom and the French Revolution in the *Philosophy of Right*. Such negative freedom, he writes,

> may well believe that it wills some positive condition, for instance the condition of universal equality . . . but it does not in fact will the positive actuality of this condition, for this at once gives rise to some kind of order, a particularization both of institutions and of individuals; but it is precisely through the annihilation of particularity and of objective determination that the self-consciousness of this negative freedom arises. Thus . . . its actualization can only be the fury of destruction. (*PR*, §5R)

Hegel applies this insight into the destructive logic of negative freedom to the Reign of Terror in the French Revolution:

> This was a time of trembling and quaking and of intolerance towards everything particular. For fanaticism wills only what is abstract, not what is articulated, so that whenever differences emerge, it finds them incompatible with its own indeterminacy and cancels them. This is why the people, during the French Revolution, destroyed once more the institutions they had themselves created, because all institutions are incompatible with the abstract self consciousness of equality. (*PR*, §5A)

From the utter indeterminacy of the first moment of the concept of the will, Hegel moves on to the second moment, the moment of determination and of particularization. Though this transition from the indeterminacy and abstract universality of the first moment of the will to the particularity of the second moment obviously follows from Hegel's understanding of the logical concept, it can also be explained in more ordinary and "phenomenological" terms. Just as willing always involves the ability to abstract from whatever is simply given—this is the formal freedom that distinguishes human beings from animals—so it also involves that *something* be willed. This is not a particularly obscure or controversial point—it is easily grasped by the understanding. Nor does it constitute an insight that is any less one-sided than the insight into the formal freedom of the will. All that is asserted in this second moment of the concept of the will is that the will must will *something*. What that something consists in is not further specified at this point. The content of the will at this stage, Hegel tells us, may be either "given by nature" or "generated by the concept of spirit" (*PR*, §6).

It is only with the third moment of the concept of the will, treated in §7 of the Introduction, that we arrive at a concrete understanding of the freedom of the will. This moment—the moment of singularity or individuality—is the unity of the two preceding moments of abstract universality and particularity.

Here the universal "I" determines itself, wills a determinate something, but in such a way that it does not cease to be universal or with itself (*bei sich*). This is Hegel's definitive formula for freedom: "Freedom is to will something determinate, yet to be with oneself [*bei sich*] in this determinacy and to return once more to the universal." Nor is this understanding of freedom simply a speculative idea remote from our experience. Hegel tells us that we have access to it, in "the form of feeling," in love and friendship. "Here," he writes, "we are not one-sidedly within ourselves, but willingly limit ourselves with reference to an other, even while knowing ourselves in this limitation as ourselves. In this determinacy the human being should not feel determined; on the contrary, he attains his self-awareness only by regarding the other as other" (*PR*, §5A).

Hegel's idea of freedom as "being with oneself in an other" encapsulates his revision of the Kantian and (again) especially Fichtean idea of freedom as rational autonomy.[16] While this latter notion expresses an essential aspect of freedom, the aspect of self-dependence or being with oneself which Hegel treats under the rubric of negative freedom, it never successfully incorporates otherness or particularity. Hegel's concept of freedom aims to redress this defect of the Kantian-Fichtean outlook, breaking down the abstract opposition between self-dependence and otherness or determinacy. As he puts it in the *Encyclopedia Philosophy of Spirit:* "The freedom of spirit is not merely an absence of dependence on the other won outside of the other but won in the other; it attains actuality not by fleeing from the other but by overcoming it" (*EPS*, §382A). How exactly this notion of being with oneself in the other and in determinacy is to be accomplished Hegel does not say at this point in his argument. In §§4–7 he has been mainly concerned with achieving a satisfactory definition or concept of freedom and the will. This definition or concept now serves as a criterion by which to judge the various forms the will takes as it determines itself—the subject to which Hegel turns his attention in the rest of the Introduction.

THE NATURAL WILL, ARBITRARINESS, AND HAPPINESS

Having grasped the concept of the freedom of the will essentially as being with oneself in the other and in determinacy, Hegel must now show in what sort of actual will this concept comes to be realized. To this end he considers the various ways in which the will determines itself. He begins by distinguishing two points of view from which the determination of the will may be considered.

The first, treated in §8, considers the determination of the will from the point of view of form. Here determination refers essentially to the translation of a subjective end or purpose into objectivity. The second, outlined in §9, considers the determination of the will from the point of view of its content, of what specifically is willed. Whereas the former, formal point of view is concerned with the determination of the will insofar as it is *mine,* the latter is concerned with it insofar as it is *true,* that is, insofar as it corresponds not merely to my subjective intention but also to the concept of the will.

It is with the latter consideration, the determination of the will with respect to content, that Hegel concerns himself in the ensuing paragraphs of the Introduction. In the first instance, he argues, this content is merely immediate, consisting of our natural drives (*Triebe*), desires, and inclinations. Here "the will is *free* only *in itself* or *for us*"; it does not yet have itself or freedom for its content. Such a will exists in a sort of self-contradiction, according to Hegel: its content does not match its form; what it is explicitly or for itself does not correspond to what it is implicitly or in itself. It is only when the will has freedom as its object instead of what is merely immediate or natural, when it is for itself what it is in itself, that this self-contradiction is surmounted and the will is genuinely free (*PR,* §§10–11).

This is the general process of the determination of the will that Hegel describes in the rest of the Introduction. But before taking up the will that is completely free, free in and for itself, we must first examine what Hegel calls the "immediate" or "natural" will. Again, the content of this will consists in our "immediately present" and naturally given "drives, desires, and inclinations." And the first point Hegel wishes to make with respect to this natural will is that it is not natural in the same sense as an animal will. Whereas the animal is strictly determined by and must simply obey its drives, the human being (as we have already learned in §§4 and 5) is "wholly indeterminate"; he "stands above his drives and can determine and posit them as his own" (*PR,* §11A). The natural will is not exempt from the formal freedom that is inherent in all human agency.

While Hegel is ultimately critical of the natural will, insofar as it does not yet have freedom as its object, he does not simply dismiss it as nugatory. The natural will plays an important role in the process by which the will gradually determines itself. Initially, the natural will is completely indeterminate. It "exists only as a multitude of varied drives, each of which is mine *in general* along with others, and at the same time something universal and indeterminate which has all kinds of objects and can be satisfied in all kinds of ways." The first task of the natural will is to cancel this "double indeterminacy" by "resolving" (*Beschliessen*) on something (*PR,* §12). Here the will picks out from the multitude of drives of which it originally consists one drive with which to identify itself. Further, it transforms this indeterminate drive—say, hunger—into a desire for a determinate object—say, a banana. For Hegel, such resolving constitutes an essential stage in the self-determination of the will. And, as he did in the *Phenomenology,* he criticizes the "beautiful soul" that refuses to resolve on or commit itself to anything determinate, preferring the false infinity of possibility to the finitude of actuality:

> A will which resolves on nothing is not an actual will; the characterless man can never resolve on anything. The reason for such indecision may also lie in an over-refined sensibility which knows that, in determining something, it enters the realm of finitude, imposing a limit on itself and relinquishing infinity. . . . Such a disposition is dead, even if its aspiration is to be beautiful. "Whoever aspires to great things," says Goethe, "must be able to limit himself." Only by making resolutions can the human being enter actuality, however painful the process may be; for inertia would rather not emerge from that inward brooding in which it reserves a universal possibility for itself. But possibility is not yet actuality. The will which is sure of itself does not therefore lose itself in what it determines. (*PR,* §13A)[17]

As determinate as the content of the resolving will is, its form remains wholly indeterminate, marked by the infinite "I" capable of abstracting from any determinate content which Hegel has already described in §5 of the Introduction. This "I" "*stands above* its content, i.e. its various drives, and also above the further individual ways in which these drives are actualized and satisfied" (*PR,* §14). Hegel has already mentioned this formally infinite and indeterminate aspect of the will in differentiating the natural will from a purely animal will. But at the level of the natural will this indeterminacy remained implicit, whereas here, at the level of what Hegel now calls the "reflective will," it becomes explicit. The content of the reflective will of course remains our natural drives, desires, and inclinations. But what is new is that the "I" stands above these natural drives and desires, "choosing" (*Wählen*) among them, but in no way identifying itself completely with any of them, in fact regarding what it chooses as external to its essential capacity to choose (*PR,* §14).[18] What Hegel describes here under the rubric of the reflective will looks very much like the deontological self prior to its ends which Michael Sandel has ascribed to John Rawls.[19] And it is interesting to note that Hegel himself cites Kant as embodying this notion of the will as "formal self-activity" (*PR,* §15R). Of course, Kant goes beyond this negative concept of freedom as the capacity to choose (*Willkür*) with his notion of the autonomous will (*Wille*).[20]

Hegel goes on to point out that the freedom which belongs to the reflective will is "arbitrariness" (*Willkür*). This is "the commonest idea we have of freedom," he says, namely, freedom of choice, freedom as "being able to do as one pleases." But it is also clearly a defective idea of freedom. It is defective because the form of the will here—namely, "free reflection which abstracts from everything"—is in contradiction with the content of the will—namely, our drives and inclinations that are simply given by nature. It is the given character of the content of the arbitrary will, the fact that this content "is not determined as mine by the nature of my will, but by *contingency*," that makes arbitrariness a radically defective notion of freedom (*PR*, §15). Hegel here refers to the "contingent" (*zufällig*) character of the arbitrary will. This word has a special meaning in his philosophy and captures exactly what he finds wrong with the notion of freedom as arbitrariness. In the *Encyclopedia Logic,* contingency is treated under the rubric of "actuality" as a primitive form of that logical category. "The contingent," Hegel writes there, "is generally what has the ground of its being not within itself but elsewhere." And he goes on to relate this notion of contingency to the notion of freedom as arbitrariness: "The content of arbitrariness is something given and known to be grounded, not within the will itself, but in external circumstances" (*EL*, §145A). Once again Hegel's fundamental criticism of freedom as arbitrariness comes down to this: that the content of such freedom remains something given by nature and not determined by me or by the concept of the free will. The arbitrary will remains free in itself but not yet for itself.

Hegel caps his critique of the notion of freedom as arbitrariness with an analogy to art. It is an illuminating analogy in that it confronts us with an application of Hegel's rationalistic conception of freedom that the modern reader might find difficult to subscribe to, thus providing a useful test for our acceptance of this conception. Hegel begins by stating that an individual is not free when he acts arbitrarily but only when he wills what is rational: "When I will what is rational, I act not as a particular individual, but in accordance with the concepts of ethics [*Sittlichkeit*] in general: in an ethical act, I vindicate not myself but the thing [*die Sache*]." Then comes the analogy to art:

> The rational is the high road which everyone follows and where no one stands out from the rest. When great artists complete a work, we can say that it *had* to be so; that is, the artist's particularity has completely disappeared and no *mannerism* is apparent

in it. Phidias has no mannerisms; the shape itself lives and stands out. But the poorer the artist is, the more we see of himself, of his particularity and arbitrariness. (*PR,* §15A)[21]

Hegel here takes aim at the Romantic doctrine of art which holds that what is most important about a work of art is that it should express the particularity and personal idiosyncrasies of the artist. This Romantic attitude toward art is perhaps nowhere better expressed than in Novalis's remark that "the more personal, local, peculiar, of its own time, a poem is, the nearer it stands to the centre of poetry."[22] Modern aesthetic sensibility no doubt stands closer to Novalis's Romanticism than to Hegel's classicism. And yet, in the light of the wearisome excesses to which the doctrine of art as subjective expression has led, Hegel's rational, objective conception of art becomes more compelling. At any rate, the analogy forces us to realize how deeply embedded (if not questionable) the idea of freedom as arbitrariness is in our culture, beyond the sphere of action and morality.

Hegel further amplifies on the idea of the arbitrary will by indicating that its contradictory character reveals itself at the phenomenal level "as a *dialectic* of drives and inclinations which conflict with each other in such a way that the satisfaction of one demands that the satisfaction of the other be subordinated or sacrificed, and so on." The main point Hegel makes here is that there is no criterion or yardstick by which to determine which of these drives should be satisfied and which should be sacrificed. It all comes down to the "contingent decision of arbitrariness." When the understanding applies itself to the task of arranging these drives into some sort of order or hierarchy, it usually ends up uttering "tedious platitudes" along the lines of Kant's "counsels of prudence." There are ultimately no universal principles by which to organize our drives and inclinations into a rational system (*PR,* §17).[23]

What Hegel says here about the attempt to achieve some sort of comprehensive satisfaction of our drives and inclinations necessarily leads him to consider more carefully the issue of happiness. For it is precisely such comprehensive satisfaction, as opposed to the individual satisfaction of particular drives, that is at issue in happiness. We would do well to follow what Hegel has to say here about happiness, since happiness constitutes, in the history of ethics, the great alternative to his own designation of the final human good, namely, freedom. As Allen Wood has written, "Hegel shares with classical ethics the idea that practical philosophy is focused on a single encompassing human good, consisting in the self-actualization of human beings as agents." But Hegel differs from the classics in that his "name for the final human good is not 'happiness' but 'freedom.'"[24]

On first glance, Hegel's reasons for rejecting happiness as the final human good resemble Kant's. Like Kant, as we have already seen from §17 of the Introduction, Hegel emphasizes the indeterminacy of happiness, the fact that there is no yardstick or universal principle by which our drives and inclinations might be arranged into a hierarchical order or more comprehensive satisfaction.[25] But there is another aspect to Hegel's argument about happiness which, unlike Kant's, suggests a certain continuity between the end of happiness and the end of freedom—which suggests that the satisfaction really aimed at in happiness points to and is ultimately more adequately realized in freedom. The key to this aspect of Hegel's argument lies in what he says about the "universality" aimed at in happiness. In the transition to the theme of happiness in the *Encyclopedia Philosophy of Spirit,* he writes that "the truth of the particular satisfactions [of the drives and inclinations] is the universal, which under the name of *happiness* the thinking will makes its aim" (*EPS,* §478). And he elaborates on this universal aspect of happiness: "In this representation [*Vorstellung*] brought forth by reflective thinking of a universal satisfaction, the drives, in so far as their particularity is concerned, are posited as negative; and they are to be partly sacrificed to each other for the benefit of that aim, and partly sacrificed to that aim directly, either altogether or in part" (*EPS,* §479).

What comes through in this passage is the way in which happiness subordinates our particular drives and desires to a universal aim, the way it reduces them to merely negative moments in its quest for a more comprehensive satisfaction. In happiness, in other words, the will takes its first steps toward overcoming the merely natural character of its content that has afflicted it since we first began considering the natural will. Hegel makes the same point in the Introduction to the *Philosophy of Right,* where he speaks of the educative role of happiness in purifying and systematizing our drives: "In happiness, thought already has some power over the natural force of the drives, for it is not content with the instantaneous, but requires a whole of happiness. This is connected with education to the extent that education likewise implements a universal" (*PR,* §20A). And the anti-Kantian implication of this point is brought out clearly in Hegel's discussion of practical education in the Nuremberg *Philosophical Propaedeutic:*

> The freedom of man, as regards natural impulses, consists not in his *being rid* of such impulses altogether and thus striving to escape from his nature but in his recognition of them as a necessity and as something rational; and in realizing them accordingly through his will, he finds himself constrained only so far as he creates for himself

accidental and arbitrary impressions and purposes in opposition to the universal. (*PP,* 43/261)

Of course, happiness ultimately fails in its aspiration to universality. It never completely escapes the naturalness and particularity of its content. In the end, "it is subjective feeling and pleasure which must have the casting vote as to where happiness is to be placed" (*EPS,* §479). And if we think of the ideal of happiness in terms of the universal happiness of everyone, we are still no better off, "since the content of this universal is in turn merely universal pleasure . . . and we are compelled to return to the drive. Since the content of happiness lies in the subjectivity and feeling of everyone, this universal end is itself particular, so that no true unity of content and form is present within it" (*PR,* §20A). In happiness we are still dealing only with formal universality, that is, a universality in which the content remains external to the form and is not yet produced out of the universal itself.

Despite this, we ought not to lose sight of the positive element Hegel ascribes to happiness, namely, its aspiration to universality and its attempt, albeit unsuccessful, to overcome the naturalness and particularity of the drives. It is this that links happiness to freedom for Hegel. And it is this that ultimately differentiates his analysis of happiness from that of Kant. For Kant, happiness is merely indeterminate and shares little with the moral or autonomous will; and this reflects the larger dualism running through his practical philosophy between freedom and nature, reason and sense. As we know, Hegel rejects this dualism in Kant's thought, and his analysis of happiness and how it ultimately points to freedom is emblematic of this. Of course, Hegel does not mean to blur the distinction between freedom and happiness. Indeed, he is quite clear that the former is not only different from but prior to the latter, and that it ultimately serves as a more complete expression of the final human good. But he does want to argue that happiness and freedom are not simply opposed to one another, and that the latter in many respects expresses the deepest, albeit incompletely realized, aspirations of the former. How this is so will become clearer as we consider the final step in Hegel's argument concerning the free will.

THE RATIONAL WILL AND RIGHT

Hegel takes the final step in his argument concerning the free will in §21 of the Introduction to the *Philosophy of Right.* Here the contradiction between the universal form of the will and the particularity of its content that marked the natural will, arbitrariness, and happiness is finally overcome. The will no longer makes natural drive or inclination its content but, rather, freedom, the universal, itself. In this way the will becomes free not only in itself but for itself. "When the will has universality, or itself as infinite form, as its content, object, and end, it is free not only *in itself* but also *for itself*— it is the Idea in its truth" (*PR*, §21). Hegel puts this idea even more succinctly in the Addition to this paragraph: "The will in its truth is such that what it wills, i.e. its content, is identical with the will itself, so that freedom is willed by freedom" (*PR*, §21A).[26]

Yet another way in which Hegel characterizes the freedom of the will at this final stage is in terms of "self-determining universality" (*PR*, §21). From the outset of our analysis in this chapter, we have seen how important the idea of self-determination or self-dependence—what Hegel frequently refers to as "being with oneself"—is to his concept of freedom. This idea is already prominent in the treatment of "negative freedom" in §5 of the Introduction to the *Philosophy of Right;* and it receives perhaps its clearest expression in Hegel's comment that the essential characteristic of spirit is that it is "autonomous and self-sufficient, a being-with-itself (*Bei-sich-selbst-sein*). But this, precisely, is freedom—for when I am dependent, I relate myself to something else, something which I am not . . . I am free when I exist independently, all by myself" (*IPH*, 20/30). Of course, this aspiration to self-determination remains unfulfilled in the earlier stages of the will—in the natural will and the arbitrary will. The content of the will here is at odds with its universal and infinite form. The will does not remain with itself in the other. It is only now, when the will makes freedom or the universal its content, that it achieves complete self-determination, absolute self-dependence. Only now "is the will completely *with itself* [*bei sich*], because it has reference to nothing but itself, so that every relationship of *dependence* on something *other* than itself is thereby eliminated" (*PR*, §23).[27]

How exactly does the will begin to make freedom, the universal, its content? In the Remark to §21, Hegel makes a great deal of the role of thought in this development. He writes that the "process whereby the particular is superseded and raised to the universal is what is called the activity of *thought.* The self-consciousness which purifies and raises its object, content, and end to this universality, does so as *thought asserting itself* in the will. Here is the *point at which it becomes clear* that it is only as *thinking* intelligence that the will is truly itself and free (*PR*, §21R)."[28] It is not immediately clear what Hegel has in mind here. Of course, thinking has played a crucial role in Hegel's conception of the will from the start. In the first part of the Introduction, Hegel underlines the thinking aspect of willing largely to distinguish human willing from the instinctive behavior of an animal. In human willing, unlike animal behavior, the object willed is posited in the "I" and appears as something "I represent to myself as my object" (*PR*, §4A). But Hegel has more in mind in §21 than this formal role of thinking in willing. Here he draws attention to the way in which thinking purifies and raises the *content* of the will to universality.

What Hegel has in mind becomes clearer in the remainder of the Remark to §21, where he refers to slavery. "The slave," he writes, "does not know his essence, his infinity and freedom; he does not know himself as an essence—he does know himself as such, for he does not *think* himself. This self-consciousness which comprehends itself as essence through thought and thereby divests itself of the contingent and the untrue constitutes the principle of right, of morality, and of all ethics" (*PR*, §21R). From this passage it becomes clear that what Hegel is referring to when he speaks of "thought asserting itself in the will" or the will "thinking itself" (*EPS*, §469) is the self-consciousness of the will as free in its essence. This self-consciousness is missing in the slave; and it is missing (Hegel tells us elsewhere) in all those civilizations that have tolerated slavery, for example, the Orient, Greece, and Rome. It is only with Christianity that there first emerged "the awareness that "*every* human is free by virtue of being human, and the freedom of spirit comprises our most human nature" (*IPH*, 21/31).[29] It is just this awareness that Hegel sees as the crucial first step in the will's becoming free not only in itself but for itself.

Apart from Christianity, there is one figure above all with whom Hegel identifies the development whereby thought is made the content of the will: this is Rousseau. In a later passage of the *Philosophy of Right*—and one already considered in chapter 1—Hegel writes: "[I]t was the achievement of Rousseau to put forward the *will* as the principle of the state, a principle which has *thought* not only as its form (as with the social instinct, for example, or divine authority) but also as its content, and which is in fact *thinking* itself" (*PR*, §258R). Hegel repeats this assessment of Rousseau's contribution to political philosophy in his *Lectures on the History of Philosophy*, quoting the *Social Contract* to the effect that "to renounce one's freedom is to renounce that one is a man. To not be free is a renunciation of all duties and rights" (*HP*, III, 401/306–7). In both of these passages, Hegel criticizes Rousseau's misunderstanding of the general will. But he does not allow this misunderstanding to detract from what he sees as Rousseau's great achievement, namely, the setting up of thought as the content of the will, the recognition of freedom as the essence of human beings. Rousseau's misunderstanding of the general will, Hegel writes,

> does not concern us. What does concern us is this, that thereby there should come into consciousness the sense that man has freedom in his spirit as the altogether absolute, that free will is the concept of man. Freedom is just thought itself; he who casts thought aside and speaks of freedom knows not what he is talking of. The unity of thought with itself is freedom, the free will. . . . It is only as having the power of thinking that the will is free. (*HP,* III, 402/407–8)

We have been pursuing Hegel's initial discussion of the will that is free in and for itself in §21 of the Introduction to the *Philosophy of Right.* In particular, we unpacked what Hegel means when he says that the will begins to make freedom or the universal its content through thought, or as thinking will. In §§22–24, Hegel connects the notion of the will that is free in and for itself with some of the key concepts from his logic and metaphysics. Thus, in §22, he tells us that the "will which has being in and for itself is *truly infinite,* because its object is itself, and therefore not something which it sees as *other* or as a *limitation.*" By the same token, this will is also said to be "true" (*PR,* §23)—"truth" for Hegel referring to the fact that the content or reality of something corresponds to its concept (*PR,* §21A).[30] Finally, the will that has being in and for itself is said to be "universal" (*PR,* §24)—not in the "abstract" sense of something common which stands outside of and opposed to the particular, but in the "concrete" sense of particularizing itself and "remaining at home with itself in its other" (*EL,* §163A1).

With respect to the last point, Hegel also remarks that the "universal which has being in and for itself is in general what is called *rational*" (*PR,* §24R). We can extrapolate from this that the will that has being in and for itself can also be called "rational." Hegel nowhere in the *Philosophy of Right* explicitly defines the crucial notion of the "rational will." The expression first appears in the Remark to §29 of the Introduction, where it is simply identified with the will which has being in and for itself (see also *PR,* §258R). In the *Encyclopedia Philosophy of Spirit,* he provides a more formal definition: "The spirit which knows itself as free and wills itself as this its object, i.e. which has its essence for its determination and aim, is in the first instance the rational will [*der verünftige Wille*] in general" (*EPS,* §482). All this is simply to say that what Hegel has been describing as the will that is free in and for itself is also what he calls elsewhere the rational will. This is worth noting, not simply because it is convenient to have a brief expression to stand for the concept of free will Hegel is defining here, but also because this particular expression, the rational will, has been the subject of so much controversy in the interpretation of Hegel's political philosophy.

With the rational will, the will that knows itself as free and makes freedom its content, Hegel has arrived at a complete definition of the *concept* of free will. Nevertheless, there remains one final step in his argument in the Introduction. The "concept" of free will must be developed into what he calls the "Idea" of freedom. For Hegel, the Idea of something is the concept of it plus its actualization. Thus he writes in the first paragraph of the *Philosophy of Right* that the Idea of right consists in the "concept of right and its actualization." In the *Encyclopedia Logic,* he provides a more general definition: "The Idea is what is true *in and for itself, the absolute unity of concept and objectivity.* Its ideal content is nothing but the concept in its determinations; its real content is only the presentation that the concept gives itself in the form of external thereness [*Dasein*]" (*EL,* §213). The rational will is only the "implicit" or "abstract" Idea, Hegel tells us in the *Encyclopedia Philosophy of Spirit* (§482). In order to become the explicit Idea, the Idea which exists in and for itself, the rational will must develop itself into objectivity and give itself the form of external thereness or existence.

In §§25–28 of the Introduction to the *Philosophy of Right,* Hegel is mainly concerned to clarify what he means by the objectivity into which the concept of free will must develop itself in order to exist as Idea. He begins by listing the various senses in which objectivity and subjectivity can be used, with a view to showing that the meanings of these terms are by no means stable or absolutely opposed, and that, "like other distinctions and antithetical determinations of reflection, they pass over into their opposites on account of their finitude and hence of their dialectical nature" (*PR,* §26R). Nevertheless, he goes on to argue that, in considering the development of the concept of free will into the Idea, he is concerned with objectivity in two specific senses: "in the sense that [freedom] becomes the rational system of the spirit itself, and in the sense that this system becomes immediate actuality." It is only by becoming objective in this way, in developing itself into immediate and external existence, that the "abstract concept of the Idea of the will," namely, the rational will or "the free will which wills the free will," can become the fully developed or explicit Idea (*PR,* §27).

The stage is now set for Hegel's momentous definition of "right" (*Recht*) in §29: "*Right* is any existence [*Dasein*] in general which is the existence of the *free will.* Right is therefore in general freedom, as Idea" (*PR,* §29).[31] In a certain way this definition embodies the paradox—or at least what has been seen as the paradox—that lies at the heart of Hegel's teaching concerning freedom:

namely, its identification of freedom with right, or *Recht*. But in order to see what is paradoxical in this, we must first say something more about the crucial word *Recht*.

As is generally observed, the word *Recht* in German has a wider meaning than "right" does in English, at least so far as the latter is conventionally used. Whereas "right" in English generally refers to a subjective claim in some sense distinguishable from our legal obligations or duties, *Recht*, like equivalent words in other European languages—*ius* in Latin, *droit* in French, *diritto* in Italian—can also refer to law or the objective conditions to which our subjective will must conform. *Recht* refers to law, of course, not in the narrow sense of specific legal statutes or positive law—for this Hegel uses the word *Gesetz*— but in the comprehensive sense of the whole basis and system of law—again like *ius, droit,* and *diritto*. As Hegel puts it in the *Encyclopedia Philosophy of Spirit: Recht* is here "to be taken, not merely in the sense of limited juristic law, but in the comprehensive sense of the actual body [*Dasein*] of all the conditions of freedom" (*EPS,* §486). And in the *Philosophy of Right,* he remarks that "when we speak here of right, we mean not merely civil right [*bürgerliche Recht*], which is what is usually understood by this term, but also morality, ethics, and world history" (*PR,* §33A). The important point, though, at least as we compare *Recht* to the English "right," is not simply that *Recht* refers to law in a comprehensive sense, but that it refers to law at all and not merely to a subjective claim in some way distinguishable from legal obligation or duty.

Of course, what gives Hegel's definition of *Recht* its peculiarly paradoxical character is that, while it certainly retains the primary German reference to law in the comprehensive sense, Hegel also wants to preserve its reference—primary in the English "right"—to freedom. And this is what leads to the striking identification of rights and duties—so strange to the English and empiricist ear—which runs through Hegel's discussion of freedom. As he writes in the *Encyclopedia Philosophy of Spirit,* having just defined *Recht* exactly as he did in the *Philosophy of Right* as a reality that is the "existence of the free will":

> What is a right is also a duty, and what is a duty is also a right. For an existence is a right only insofar as it is grounded in the free substantial will; and the same content in relation to the will distinguished as subjective and individual is a duty. It is the same content which the subjective consciousness recognizes as a duty and brings into existence in others. The finitude of the objective will thus creates the semblance of a distinction between rights and duties. (*EPS,* §486)

It is important not to turn Hegel's point here into something more common-place than it is. By identifying rights and duties he does not simply mean to assert that rights and duties are correlative, that for every right on my part there corresponds a duty in someone else. Rather, he wants to argue that my rights, insofar as they are existences of freedom, *are* duties in relation to my subjective will, and vice versa. Thus he writes with respect to the right of property: "[M]y right to a thing is not merely possession, but as possession by a *person* it is *property*, or legal possession, and it is a *duty* to possess things as property, i.e. to be as a person" (*EPS*, §486).[32] He sums up his point about the utter coinci-dence of right and duty in the following remark from the *Philosophy of Right*:

> *Duty* is primarily an attitude *towards* something which, for me, is *substantial* and universal in and for itself. Right, on the other hand, is in general the *existence* of this substantial element, and is consequently the latter's *particular* aspect and that of my own *particular* freedom. . . . In the state, as an ethical entity and the interpenetra-tion of the substantial and the particular, my obligation towards the substantial is at the same time the existence of my particular freedom; that is, duty and right are *united* within the state *in one and the same relation*. (*PR*, §261R; see also §155)[33]

Hegel's reflections on the identity of rights and duties brings us back to what I earlier referred to as the paradox that is contained in his definition of *Recht* and the paradox which in some ways lies at the heart of his teaching on freedom in general: namely, the paradox that freedom is compatible with constraint. This is the paradox to which Rousseau gave expression in his notorious line that "whoever refuses to obey the general will will be forced to do so," that is, "he will be forced to be free."[34] I am not, of course, the first to notice this paradox in Hegel; in one way or another, it is the focus of almost every noteworthy criticism of his "positive" doctrine of freedom. Before dealing with some of these criticisms, there is one passage from the *Philosophy of Right* that I will quote, because it perfectly captures the identification of right and duty, freedom and law, toward which the entire discussion of freedom in the Introduction has been leading. The point of the passage is encapsulated in the striking sentence, "The individual, however, finds his *liberation* in duty," but the surrounding context amplifies Hegel's meaning and underscores the importance of his critique of the natural will in the Introduction:

> A binding duty can appear as a *limitation* only in relation to indeterminate subjec-tivity or abstract freedom, and to the drives of the natural will or the moral will which arbitrarily determines its own indeterminate good. The individual, however, finds his *liberation* in duty. On the one hand, he is liberated from his dependence on mere

natural drives, . . . and on the other hand, he is liberated from that indeterminate subjectivity which does not attain existence or the objective determinacy of action, but remains *within itself* and has no actuality. In duty, the individual liberates himself so as to attain substantial freedom. (*PR,* §149)

Hegel's discussion of freedom in the Introduction to the *Philosophy of Right* culminates with the identification of right or law with freedom (in §29), and this identification leads directly to the paradoxical conclusion drawn in the passage just quoted: that the individual finds his liberation, his substantial or "affirmative" freedom, only in duty. Hegel, of course, is aware of how strange this must sound and how much of a departure it marks from the tradition of modern political philosophy. And he goes on, in the Remark to §29, to make this departure explicit by commenting on and criticizing his great predecessors in the modern tradition, Kant, Rousseau, and (by implication) Fichte.

Of all thinkers, Kant might seem to be the least likely for Hegel to contrast his position with here. No thinker has been more eloquent about the liberating effects of duty than Kant. But, as we saw in chapter 1, there is a tension between Kant's moral philosophy, in which the liberating effects of duty are spoken of, and his political philosophy, in which liberty is conceived of in a more conventional, "negative" fashion. And it is with the latter that Hegel is now concerned. He quotes, not entirely accurately, Kant's definition of right in the *Rechtslehre* as "the *limitation* of my freedom or *arbitrary will* in such a way that it may coexist with the arbitrary will of everyone else in accordance with a universal law." The inaccuracy does not fundamentally alter Kant's meaning, which does imply a very different understanding of right from the one we have found in Hegel. As Hegel himself points out, Kant's definition of right "contains only a *negative* determination—that of limitation"; and it leaves the arbitrary wills of individuals intact, uniting them through a "universal law" in an utterly formal way (*PR,* §29R). In Hegel's definition of right, by contrast, right is not a negative limitation of the arbitrary will of the individual but, rather, the positive realization of freedom understood in terms of the rational will.

There certainly is a difference in the way Kant and Hegel formulate their definitions of right here. But it is not immediately clear what the significance of this difference is, or why Hegel finds the Kantian formulation so problematic. This becomes somewhat clearer when he traces Kant's definition back to its source in Rousseau. He writes:

The definition of right in question embodies the view, especially prevalent since Rousseau, according to which the substantial and primary factor is supposed to be not the will as rational will which has being in and for itself or the spirit as *true* spirit, but will and spirit as the *particular* individual, as the will of the single person in his distinctive arbitrariness. Once this principle is accepted, the rational can appear only as a limitation on the freedom in question, and not as immanent rationality, but only as an external and formal universal. (*PR,* §29R)

I will say more about the idea of rationality and of the rational will that this passage intimates in a moment. Here I only want to draw attention to the difficulties Hegel sees as flowing from this Rousseauan outlook. In the first place, he points out that this outlook "is devoid of any speculative thought and is refuted by the philosophical concept." In place of the immanent rationality of the Hegelian concept we have a merely external and formal rationality that supervenes upon a nonrational material, the arbitrary will of the individual. But more important than this, at least from a practical point of view, the Rousseauan outlook has "produced phenomena in people's minds and in the actual world whose terrifying nature is matched only by the shallowness of the thoughts on which they are based" (*PR,* §29R). The reference here is, of course, to the French Revolution. And Hegel makes clear, as he has earlier in the Introduction to the *Philosophy of Right* (in §5), as well as in the *Phenomenology,* that this is a real danger that flows from the individualistic conception of freedom found in Rousseau and preserved in Kant's definition of right.

The latter point is amplified in Hegel's most extensive discussion of Rousseau in the *Philosophy of Right,* in the Remark to §258. We already referred to this Remark in connection with Hegel's statement that "it was the great achievement of Rousseau to put forward the *will* as the principle of the state, a principle which has *thought* not only as its form . . . but also as its content." But Hegel goes on from this to criticize Rousseau's particular conception of the will, in basically the same way he did in §29:

> But Rousseau considered the will only in the determinate form of the *individual* will (as Fichte subsequently also did) and regarded the universal will not as the will's rationality in and for itself, but only as the *common element* arising out of this individual will *as a conscious will.* The union of individuals within the state thus becomes a *contract,* which is accordingly based on their arbitrary will and opinions, and on their express consent given at their own discretion; and the further consequences which follow from this . . . destroy the divine [element] which has being in and for itself and its absolute authority and majesty. (*PR,* §258R)

This is Hegel's principal worry. When right is reduced to the harmony of my arbitrary will with the arbitrary will of everyone else, when the state is reduced to a contract based on the arbitrary wills of individuals, the majesty of the law and the divine quality of the state are destroyed. This is the danger Hegel wishes to avert with his definition of right as the realization of rational freedom. For him right "is something *utterly sacred*" (*PR,* §30), and the Rousseauan-Kantian definition of right somehow undermines this sanctity. Hegel proceeds to draw the expected connection between Rousseau's abstract and individualistic conception of freedom and the French Revolution:

> Consequently, when these abstractions were invested with power, they afforded the tremendous spectacle, for the first time we know of in human history, of the overthrow of all existing and given conditions within an actual major state and the revision of its constitution from first principles and purely in terms of *thought;* the *intention* behind this was to give it what was *supposed* to be a purely *rational* basis. On the other hand, since these were only abstractions divorced from the Idea, they turned the attempt into the most terrible and drastic event. (*PR,* §258R)

Throughout his discussion of Rousseau, in both §§29 and 258, Hegel contrasts Rousseau's emphasis on the arbitrary will of the individual with his own notion of the rational will. Even Rousseau's conception of the general will, Hegel argues, fails to grasp the universal will "as the will's rationality in and for itself," understanding it instead "only as the *common element* arising out of [the] individual will *as a conscious will.*" As was pointed out in chapter 1, it can be doubted that Hegel's individualistic interpretation of the general will here entirely captures all that is contained in Rousseau's complex and not always coherent doctrine, although it certainly corresponds to some of the things that Rousseau says about the general will.[35] But whether Hegel is ultimately right about Rousseau is less important here than what is disclosed in these passages about Hegel's own notion of the rational will, the notion that marks the pinnacle of his reflections on freedom in the Introduction to the *Philosophy of Right.* The main point is, of course, that the rational will is not to be confused with the arbitrary will of the individual. The content of the rational will, unlike that of the arbitrary will, is not simply at the discretion of the individual but, rather, corresponds directly to the free nature of the will. This is what Hegel means when he says that the rational will is for itself what it is in itself. And what he wants to emphasize more than anything else about the rational will at this point, as he contrasts it with the arbitrary will, is that it is rational "in itself," that it has an objective character which cannot be reduced to the subjective consent of the individual. He puts the point this way:

In opposition to the principle of the individual will, we should remember the fundamental concept according to which the objective will is rational in itself, i.e. in its *concept*, whether or not it is recognized by individuals and willed by them at their discretion—and that its opposite, knowledge and volition, the subjectivity of freedom (which is the *sole* content of the principle of the individual will) embodies only *one* (consequently one-sided) moment of the *Idea of the rational* will, which is rational solely because it has being both *in itself* and *for itself.* (*PR,* §258R)

The sharp contrast Hegel draws here between the rational will, on the one hand, and the individual will, on the other, underlines once again the way in which the former concept—which simply encapsulates the main thrust of Hegel's teaching about freedom—cuts against our ordinary notions of will and freedom. It is true that Hegel does not overlook the importance of the subjective element, of the "for itself," in this passage, but he clearly subordinates it to the objective, "in itself" rationality of the genuinely free will. As he succinctly puts it in the Addition to §258: "Any discussion of freedom must begin not with individuality or the individual self-consciousness, but only with the essence of self-consciousness; for whether human beings know it or not, this essence realizes itself as a self-sufficient power of which single individuals are only moments" (*PR,* §258A). This is what usually provokes the objections to Hegel's doctrine of freedom that the rational will really abandons the will for something else—reason or intellect—and that Hegelian freedom no longer corresponds to what we ordinarily or plausibly mean by that term. Having fully explicated Hegel's conception of freedom and of will as it is definitively presented in the Introduction to the *Philosophy of Right,* it is time to consider these objections more carefully.

FREEDOM AND REASON

Before taking up some of the more common objections to Hegel's concept of freedom, let us try to reduce that concept to its essence. The core idea, as we have seen, is that freedom consists in thoroughgoing self-determination, self-dependence, or, in Hegel's language, "being with oneself." The will is free only when it is determined by or has as its object its own freedom. For this reason, freedom does not consist in arbitrariness or simply doing as we please; for here the will is determined by something other than its own freedom and universality, namely, by its natural inclinations and particular desires. Only the rational will is genuinely free because only the rational will has itself, its freedom and its universality, for its content; only the rational will is for itself what it is in itself. To recur to the sentence that best summarizes the idea of freedom as self-determination which is embodied by the rational will: only in the rational will "is the will completely *with itself,* because it has reference to nothing but itself, so that every relationship of *dependence* on something *other* than itself is thereby eliminated" (*PR*, §23).

This is, no doubt, a rather grandiose notion of freedom, but it is not without its distinguished antecedents in the tradition of modern philosophy. One thinks of Spinoza's definition of freedom in terms of self-determination: "A thing is said to be free when it exists solely from the necessity of its nature, and is determined to act by itself alone."[36] But most of all one thinks of Kant's notion of autonomy, the notion of the will as determined, not by natural inclination or sensible impulse, but by the rational nature of the individual. This Kantian notion of autonomy, prepared by Rousseau, radicalized by Fichte, and in some ways representing the deepest current of modern moral sensibility, remains the animating idea behind Hegel's conception of freedom as radical self-determination or being with oneself.[37]

Of course, Hegel criticizes the Kantian-Fichtean idea of freedom as autonomy. He maintains that, in the end, this idea fails to come to terms with nature, particularity, and otherness in general. It represents a merely "negative" (again in the Hegelian, not in the Berlinian, sense) conception of liberty, abstracting from all determinacy and fleeing from all content. Its logical outcome, when put into practice, is the fury and destruction of the French Revolution. Freedom is not just being with oneself but "being with oneself in the other." This formula encapsulates Hegel's distinctive appropriation and modification of the Kantian-Fichtean notion of autonomy. Hegel not only deepens and extends the quintessentially modern notion of freedom as self-determination and autonomy, he also represents one of the first and most profound critics of its excesses. This is what makes his conception of freedom so important.

Though not without distinguished antecedents in the modern philosophical tradition, Hegel's conception of freedom as radical self-determination nevertheless departs from the typical definition of freedom found in the better part of modern, and to a large extent liberal, political philosophy. According to this definition, freedom consists in the ability to pursue one's wants and desires without obstruction or interference. This is, of course, the notion of freedom that Hegel dismisses as mere arbitrariness. It is a notion to be found in its purest form, on the one hand, in Hobbes's definition of liberty as the "absence of external impediments," and on the other, in Bentham's definition of law as always being a fetter or constraint on liberty.[38] It can also be found, albeit not so starkly, in such classically liberal writers as Locke and Mill. While Locke does not necessarily oppose freedom to law, he still largely sees it in terms of doing whatever one pleases within the space carved out by the law: "a liberty to follow my own will where the rule prescribes not"; "a liberty to dispose, and order, as [a man] lists, his person, actions, possessions, and his whole property, within the allowance of those laws under which he is."[39] And for Mill, the "only liberty which deserves the name is that of pursuing our own good in our own way, so long as we do not attempt to deprive others of theirs or impede their efforts to obtain it."[40]

This is, of course, what Isaiah Berlin termed the "negative" concept of freedom. And in his famous essay, "Two Concepts of Liberty," he defends it against what he considers to be the insidious confusions of the concept of "positive freedom," which he associates with Rousseau, Kant, Fichte, and Hegel, among others. Because Berlin's criticisms of the latter, positive (and, by implication, Hegelian) concept of freedom have been so influential, it is necessary to give them some consideration. We find that Berlin imports much into this positive concept of freedom which has little to do with Hegel's own thinking about freedom. Nevertheless, his argument is valuable insofar as it crystallizes the prejudices of a certain empiricist and (one might say) English way of thinking about freedom which refuses to consider freedom in any but a negative way.

Let us start with the distinction between negative and positive freedom itself. Berlin defines negative freedom pretty much in the way we defined it above, as the ability to pursue our wants and desires without obstruction or intrusion. The only thing that is noteworthy in his account of negative freedom is that he chooses to defend it in its most implausible Hobbesian-Benthamite form.[41] To this notion that law always represents a restriction on freedom Locke's reply to Filmer remains decisive: "that ill deserves the name of confinement which hedges us in only from bogs and precipices."[42] In contradistinction to the unfettered character of negative freedom, positive freedom involves the idea of self-mastery, the mastery of one's empirical, passional self by one's "real" or "rational" self; it involves the idea of self-direction in the sense of direction by one's "true" self. Berlin's characterization of positive freedom here does bear some resemblance to Hegel's notion of freedom as radical self-determination, though it should be noted that his language of self-mastery or mastery by one's "real" self suggests a dualism between reason and passion that is more congenial to Kant and Fichte and possibly some of the later British idealists than it is to Hegel.

Berlin argues that the idea of positive freedom, the idea of being self-directed or directed by one's "true" self, has historically taken two forms. In the first, self-mastery is achieved and independence won through the denial or overcoming of our passions and desires. Berlin characterizes this strategy of self-emancipation as the "retreat to the inner citadel," and he associates it with such thinkers as Kant and the Stoics. The second form the idea of positive freedom has taken, and the one that Berlin associates specifically with Hegel, is that of "self-realization, or total self-identification with a specific principle or ideal in order to attain the selfsame end."[43] Here freedom is understood as comprehending the necessity of the world. Berlin gives the examples of the mathematician and the musician. For the mathematician, the truths of mathematics do not appear as an alien necessity but as a product of his own rational capacity with which he freely identifies. Likewise, the musician does not see a piece of music as something externally imposed upon him by the composer but, rather, as something that he has so completely absorbed and understood that it loses its alien or unfree character. Understanding equals freedom. "That," Berlin writes, "is the programme of enlightened rationalism from Spinoza to the latest (at times unconscious) disciples of Hegel. *Sapere aude*. What you know, that of which you understand the necessity—the rational necessity—you cannot, while remaining rational, want to be otherwise."[44] And it is a programme which Berlin sees as leading from Hegel to the naturalisms of Marx and Freud: "We are enslaved by despots—institutions or beliefs or neuroses—which can be removed only by being analyzed and understood. We are imprisoned by evil spirits which we have ourselves—albeit not consciously—created, and can exorcise them only by becoming conscious and acting accordingly."[45]

It is not clear how all this actually relates to Hegel. While it is true that Hegel does, at some level, identify freedom with rational necessity, he does not see this necessity as a kind of fact that first exists outside of human freedom and only later comes to lose its alien character by being understood. For Hegel, the rational necessity of right or of the state, for example, is itself derived from freedom, is produced by the logic of freedom, consists in the immanent development of freedom. This is what makes Berlin's examples of the mathematician and the musician somewhat misleading. The truths of mathematics exist independently of the mathematician, and the musical score is composed by somebody other than the musician. In neither case is the rational necessity that is to be appropriated itself understood to be the product of the agent's own freedom.[46] In the end, Berlin makes Hegel's understanding of the relationship between freedom and necessity here too

Spinozistic, mistakenly assimilating it to the outlook of what he calls "enlightened rationalism."

Berlin's most famous claim regarding the positive notion of freedom as rational self-direction is that, when applied to the realm of society and politics, it leads to authoritarianism or totalitarianism. In order to sustain this claim, Berlin finds it necessary to attribute to adherents of positive freedom the assumption that in morals and politics "there must exist one and only one true solution to any problem."[47] Once this assumption is admitted, it is not difficult to derive the features of a full-blown totalitarian rationalism, replete with the "rule of experts" and an "elite of Platonic guardians."[48] The problem is, of course, that the assumption has nothing to do with Hegel. Nowhere in his thought do we find such a rigid and simple-minded rationalism. Indeed, as we shall see later on, the Hegelian state accommodates a considerable amount of diversity in the form of what he calls the "right to the satisfaction of the subject's particularity" (*PR,* §124R; see also §185R, etc.). Of course, Hegel does not ultimately subscribe to Berlin's radical and irreducible value-pluralism. In the end, he does try to forge some sort of unity out of diversity and articulate a framework "whereby all the diverse ends of men can be harmoniously realized."[49] But it is a serious flaw in Berlin's argument that he takes this reasonable aspiration of any political philosophy and necessarily links it with an extravagant and tyrannical rationalism. In the end, one is forced to agree with Allen Wood's judgment that "perhaps Berlin's only point is that *any* idea (however true and noble) may be perverted into its virtual opposite if it falls into the hands of people who are sufficiently deranged, self-deceiving, or opportunistic."[50]

We have seen that Hegel's identification of freedom with rationality need not lead to the totalitarian nightmare Berlin depicts. Nevertheless, there exist other, less crude versions of the Berlinian criticism that would repay consideration. According to one version, Hegel's identification of freedom with rationality or the rational will, while it may not lead to totalitarianism, does lead to a displacement of the distinctively modern emphasis on freedom and the primacy of the will and returns us to the rationalistic outlook characteristic of ancient political philosophy. This criticism of Hegel's doctrine of freedom and of the rational will has been made most powerfully by M. B. Foster in his early and extremely suggestive *The Political Philosophies of Plato and Hegel* and by Patrick Riley in his *Will and Political Legitimacy.*

Foster's critique of Hegel's doctrine of freedom starts from the distinction between ancient political philosophy and modern political philosophy cited at the beginning of this book. Whereas the ruling ideas of the ancient outlook are reason and nature, the ruling idea of the modern outlook is will, freedom, self-actualization:

> Modern political theories differ from ancient principally in making freedom the ground, end, and limit of the state; however much modern theories may differ from one another, according to the variety of meanings freedom may bear, these differences sink into relative insignificance when they are seen to be differences only in the interpretation of the principle which all have in common and in virtue of which they may be all contrasted with the ancient theories that the state is natural.[51]

With respect to this grand distinction between ancient and modern political philosophy, Foster argues that Hegel's position is equivocal. On the one hand, Hegel criticizes Plato and the ancients for not giving enough recognition to the "subjective element," or individual will and freedom—here Foster shows a sensitivity to this aspect of Hegel's thought that is missing from cruder critiques. On the other hand, Hegel's conception of the rational will is ultimately only "imperfectly differentiated from reason"[52] and does not escape the rationalism characteristic of Plato's political philosophy. Foster's argument here is too intricate to go into. The gist is that Hegel's rational will ultimately lacks the spontaneity and creativity that Foster sees as essential to the concept of will and that he traces back, for its metaphysical expression, to the Judeo-Christian doctrine of Creation. While Hegel tentatively admits the individual will into his political philosophy in a variety of ways, he fails to recognize completely "a worth in will other than its conformity to reason."[53]

Riley elaborates on Foster's criticism of Hegel's rationalism. Like Foster, he distinguishes the tradition of modern political philosophy from that of ancient political philosophy in terms of its voluntarism. Whereas ancient political philosophy conceived of political obligation largely in terms of the notions of reason and nature, having only an indistinct notion of will or voluntary action, modern political philosophy grounds political obligation squarely in will and consent.[54] Like Foster, Riley too criticizes Hegel for compromising the modern voluntarist standpoint and incorporating only a very "attenuated" notion of will into his political philosophy, ultimately subordinating will to reason. With respect to this latter point, Riley does not simplistically overlook Hegel's attempt to "preserve the will as a moral concept." He distinguishes Hegel's outlook, for example, from the nonvoluntaristic outlook of Burke. Nevertheless, he ultimately sees Hegel as preserving the will in only a passive and attenuated form—as "recognition" of the rational—and canceling it "in every form thought politically important since the time of Hobbes."[55]

What can be said against these criticisms of Hegel's conception of will and freedom by Foster and Riley? On the one hand, not a great deal. Foster and Riley legitimately point out that Hegel's voluntarism departs in significant ways from the voluntarism of early modern social-contract theory as well as from the voluntarism implied in early Christian doctrine. On the other hand, this point still begs the most important question. In the end, Foster's and Riley's criticism of Hegel reduces to the claim that Hegel's notion of will is "attenuated" or insufficiently spontaneous or "creative" because it is not indeterminate or arbitrary.[56] But this is only to point out what Hegel already acknowledges: the rational will is not the arbitrary will, and freedom is not to be identified with indeterminate choice. The question remains whether this teaching of Hegel's does not constitute a deeper insight into human freedom than the conception of will Foster and Riley hold up against it. Below I will argue that it does.

Another way to approach Foster's and Riley's critique of Hegel is by reconsidering their understanding of Hegel's relationship to the great tradition of political philosophy. Their critique rests largely on a sharp division of the tradition of political philosophy into two parts, the ancient labeled "reason," and the modern labeled "will," and on the further contention that insofar as Hegel departs from the conventional interpretation of the latter he must lapse back into the standpoint of the former. But is this necessarily so? Does not Hegel's conception of freedom as rational self-determination differ in important ways from the classical ideal of rational self-realization?

Despite important similarities, the classical ideal of rational self-realization is ultimately partnered by an idea of nature that is alien to Hegel and to the modern tradition in general. To bring reason to bear on practical life, according to the classical view, is to bring the individual into line with the rational order that inheres in nature. Rational self-direction is ultimately a matter of discovering one's place in the rational order of a purposive cosmos. This link to nature is what enables the classics to describe the final human good in terms of "happiness." A very different spirit informs Hegel's conception of freedom as rational self-determination, and one which is more consonant with modern presuppositions. This conception is in no way linked to a teleological understanding of nature. Rational self-determination does not involve conformity to some sort of end or purpose given by nature. Rather, it involves the overcoming of all merely contingent determination by nature and the spinning out of freedom itself a content that is congruent with it.[57] This is what lies behind Hegel's rejection of the natural will for the rational will in the Introduction to the *Philosophy of Right*. And it is what lies behind his adoption of "freedom" instead of "happiness" as the name for the final human good.

By contrasting Hegel's conception of freedom as rational self-determination with the classical ideal of rational self-realization in this way, we are again reminded of Kant. For it is to the Kantian ideal of autonomy that Hegel's conception of rational self-determination ultimately harks back, not to the classical ideal of rational self-realization. For all of his criticism of Kant's dualism, Hegel never really abandons the Kantian principle of autonomy. His philosophy represents an attempt to extend and deepen this principle, allowing it to penetrate reality even more profoundly than it does in Kant's philosophy, but it never abandons or compromises this principle. Nor is the Kantian ideal of autonomy to be confused with the classical ideal of rational self-realization. Despite a common emphasis on reason and rational self-control, the Kantian ideal of autonomy, unlike the classical ideal, is not tied to a teleological conception of nature that provides reason with its end. For Kant, as for Hegel, reason liberates us from nature; it does not seek conformity with it. As Robert Pippin has put it: "Reason itself, in all its manifestations, does not, in Kant, discover the human place within Nature or serve some natural end or passion; it 'legislates to Nature'; it does not discover the good life, it prescribes the rules for human activity, be Nature as it may."[58]

Kantian autonomy is the name for the deepest current of modernity: the determination to rely on human reason alone, without metaphysical support from God or nature. And insofar as Hegel's conception of rational self-determination represents an extension and deepening of the Kantian ideal of autonomy, it, too, very much belongs to this modern current. This is the point to be urged against Foster's and Riley's contention that Hegel's conception of freedom in terms of the rational will somehow represents a betrayal of the voluntarism of modern political philosophy and a lapsing back into the rationalistic standpoint of ancient political philosophy. The rationality Hegel invokes is not, like the reason of the ancients, something independent of or opposed to human will or freedom; rather, it is its consummate expression. The rational will is the will that has itself for its content and is utterly self-dependent. Such self-dependence is what Hegel, not implausibly, understands by freedom. To repeat once more the sentence which I quoted at the beginning of this chapter: "[F]or that is just what freedom is: being at home with oneself in one's other, depending upon oneself, and being one's own determinant" (*EL*, §24A2). Freedom thus understood does not constitute an abandonment of the voluntarist tradition of modern political philosophy. Quite the contrary, in many ways it represents the most radical and self-consistent expression of the modern emphasis on the primacy of the will.

To distinguish Hegel's conception of freedom as rational self-determination from the more naturalistic classical ideal of rational self-determination in this way is not, however, to deny that it has any metaphysical status whatsoever. A number of recent commentators, trying to push Hegel ever further in a non-metaphysical direction and thus make him more palatable to contemporary philosophical taste, have denied that there is anything metaphysical about Hegel's conception of freedom or agency; but the evidence for this position is quite slim.[59] As we have seen repeatedly throughout this chapter, Hegel is quite comfortable with arguing that freedom understood as self-determination or being at home with oneself is the essence of human beings. To have the capacity for self-determination is not simply a contingent or historic acquisition; it is what it is to be a human being, what distinguishes human beings from animals. And the desire to cultivate or realize this essential human capacity for self-determination, to transform this implicit, in-itself character of human beings into an explicit, for-itself actuality, is not merely a contingent or historic disposition; it is the rational destiny of human beings. It is true that Hegel does not, like Kant and Fichte, ground his positive conception of freedom in a questionable metaphysic of a higher and lower—or true and false—self. But he does ultimately justify the rational or universal will in terms of its correspondence to the free or universal nature of human beings, and he rejects the natural will for its failure to correspond to the same. The metaphysical status of this argument would seem hard to deny.

To admit this metaphysical dimension of Hegel's conception of freedom is, of course, from the standpoint of much contemporary political theory, to weaken it. Even if it is not seen as dangerous, the attempt to ground human freedom and the disposition to cultivate it in some sort of conception of human nature is at the very least regarded as unnecessary or redundant. Without defending this metaphysical aspect of Hegel's teaching, I maintain that it does not necessarily undermine the value of his overall conception of freedom as rational self-determination. Regardless of whether we follow Hegel in thinking that freedom as he understands it is the essence of human beings, what differentiates us from animals, we can still concede that his positive conception of freedom brings out more clearly than other—especially negative—conceptions just what we understand by freedom and why we find it valuable. Our deepest intuitions about freedom suggest that it does not involve simply doing what we please but, rather, self-control, self-coherence, cultivation of capacities, and fulfillment of significant purposes. As Charles Taylor has written, "Freedom is important to us because we are purposive beings."[60] It is this purposive, self-realizing dimension of freedom that Hegel captures with his positive conception of freedom as rational self-determination. It may be that the disposition to cultivate and not suppress the capacity for self-determination is a contingent and historic disposition—albeit one that runs rather deep in the modern European tradition—but Hegel provides us with an account of it that, for its penetration and subtlety, surpasses the accounts of his predecessors as well as many metaphysically more parsimonious contemporary theories.

In defending Hegel's concept of freedom in this section, I do not imply that there is nothing to be said against it. My main point has been that this concept, as a concept, is not necessarily vulnerable to turning into something other than or opposed to freedom, whether it be totalitarianism (*a là* Berlin) or a version of classical rationalism (*a là* Foster and Riley). But there are other and potentially more serious questions that might be raised about Hegel's doctrine of freedom. These questions do not have to do so much with the internal coherence of Hegel's concept of freedom as they do with his identification of freedom with certain historic practices and institutions and ultimately with the modern state. They are questions that we will consider as we go through the rest of the argument of the *Philosophy of Right*, concerned with the embodiment of freedom in the various forms of right, in the following chapters.

Chapter 6 The Basic Structure of the *Philosophy of Right:* From Abstract Right to Ethical Life

In this chapter, I follow the movement of the *Philosophy of Right* through the three major moments that constitute its basic structure: the movement from abstract right through morality to ethical life. The chapter focuses on the first two of these moments—abstract right and morality—showing what exactly they involve, wherein their significance lies, and why, in Hegel's view, they are ultimately abstract and must give way to the more concrete standpoint of ethical life. The chapter will conclude with an examination of the general concept of ethical life, leaving to the ensuing chapters the consideration of the specific articulations of ethical life in the family, civil society, and the state.

This, of course, is a lot of ground to cover in a single chapter. Each of these moments could warrant a separate chapter of its own, if not several. This has been the usual way of dealing with the immense and complicated architecture of the *Philosophy of Right:* picking out a single room—whether it be property, or punishment, or the concept of morality—and exploring it in detail on its own. Although there are good reasons for proceeding in this way with the *Philosophy of Right—*

the architecture of the book *is* immense and complicated—such a procedure tends to distract attention from the overall movement of the book and from the central philosophical point this movement expresses. This is what I hope to convey in the present chapter: a sense of the overall dialectical movement of the *Philosophy of Right* by which the individualistic standpoints of abstract right and morality are shown to be incomplete and to necessitate the more concrete standpoint of ethical life.[1]

It is to the elucidation of the latter notion that the present chapter is ultimately directed. *Sittlichkeit,* or ethical life, is, of course, a crucial notion in Hegel's political philosophy, encapsulating in many ways the crux of his critique of the theoretical—largely individualistic—foundations of liberalism and of modern political philosophy in general. It is also an incredibly ambiguous notion. In Hegel's earlier writings, as we have seen, the idea of ethical life is still very much bound up with his early Hellenic ideal. Indeed, in the *Phenomenology,* the term is used almost exclusively to refer to the ancient Greek polis, now no longer perceived to be an ideal. And yet, Hegel never simply identified the concept of ethical life with the Greek polis; and this is nowhere more true than in the *Philosophy of Right,* in which the modern state is portrayed as a form of ethical life quite different from the ancient polis. It is to the account of ethical life in the *Philosophy of Right* that we must turn, then, to clarify this crucial concept and determine its relevance to modern moral and political conditions.

Finally, stemming from its ambiguity, ethical life is a philosophically controversial notion. The most common criticism of ethical life is that it is a conservative or traditionalist notion that sanctifies customary morality and is hostile to individuality or any sort of moral reflection or criticism. The analysis of ethical life found toward the end of this chapter begins to address this issue, showing that the concept of ethical life is far more rationalistic and universalistic—in keeping with Hegel's doctrine of freedom treated in the previous chapter—than conservative, traditionalist, romantic, relativistic, and communitarian interpretations of it have suggested.[2] A final determination on this important issue, however, must await our discussion of the various articulations of ethical life in the next two chapters, especially that most complex and comprehensive articulation embodied by the modern state.

NATURE OF THE ARGUMENT

Before descending to the details of the three major parts of the *Philosophy of Right,* we need to consider more generally the nature of the argument they compose. Hegel provides some guidance on this issue in §§30–33 of the Introduction. In §29, as we saw in the previous chapter, he defines right as any existence of the free will. By defining right in this way, he considerably expands its conventional denotation. Right no longer refers simply to "civil right, which is what is usually understood by this term, but also to morality, ethics, and world history" (*PR,* §33A) In §§30–33, Hegel goes on to explain in general terms how we are to view the relationship between these various forms of right.

He begins, in §30, by indicating that the various forms of right are not coequal but form a hierarchy corresponding to the "different stages in the development of the concept of freedom." There are lower forms of right, which are said to be "more formal," "more abstract," "more limited"; and there are higher forms of right, which are said to be "more concrete," "richer," and "more truly universal." Nor is it simply that the latter are higher than the former; they also, Hegel tells us, possess a "higher right" in relation to the former, overriding or trumping their claims. This is an idea that appears with some frequency throughout the *Philosophy of Right,* in particular when Hegel wants to talk about the higher right of the state vis-à-vis the more abstract rights of private property and of particular welfare (*PR,* §§33A, 46R, 126, 130, 261, 323).[3] Because he sees rights—and duties, which are merely the counterparts of rights—as being arranged hierarchically from more abstract to more concrete, there are, for Hegel, no ultimate or unresolvable conflicts or collisions between rights or duties, as there were for Kant. Every collision, he writes, "also contains this further moment: it imposes a limitation whereby one right is subordinated to another; only the right of the world spirit is absolute in an unlimited sense" (*PR,* §30R).

In §31, Hegel describes the process by which the stages in the development of the concept of freedom and of right are going to be determined in the *Philosophy of Right.* It is, of course, going to be a "dialectical" process whereby the concept of freedom develops out of itself its own determinations in the form of rights. Here again we encounter what in some ways is the cardinal principle of Hegel's philosophical method, namely, the self-determining or self-productive character of the concept. In §1 of the Introduction, as we have seen, Hegel maintains that "it is the *concept* alone . . . which has *actuality,* and in such a way that it gives actuality to itself" (*PR,* §1R). Now, in §31, he draws our attention again to the self-actualizing, self-determining, character of the concept of freedom and how this forms the basis of the movement of the entire philosophy of right: "it is the spirit in its freedom . . . which here gives itself actuality and engenders itself as an existing world; and the sole business of science is to make conscious this work which is accomplished by the reason of the thing" (*PR*, §31R).

In §32, Hegel further specifies the dialectical process of conceptual self-determination that forms the basis of the structure of the *Philosophy of Right*. In the course of its actualization, he tells us, the concept of freedom assumes different "shapes": the right of property, morality, the family, and so forth. The sequence in which these shapes or existences of freedom are taken up in the *Philosophy of Right* will be strictly dictated by the dialectical development of the concept of freedom itself. Nor, Hegel points out, does this conceptual sequence of the shapes or forms of right necessarily coincide with the sequence of their temporal appearance. The right of property and the idea of the infinite subjectivity of morality, for example, did not come into existence before the family, and yet they are treated first in the argument of the *Philosophy of Right* (*PR*, §32).

Why does Hegel begin with the abstract and historically posterior instead of with the "concretely true" and historically prior? The answer has to do with Hegel's conception of the task of philosophy, which, as he puts it here, is "to see the truth precisely in the form of a result," or, as he puts it in another place, to see the truth as "validating" itself (*EL*, §83A). Philosophy begins with the abstract only to show that it is not self-complete and requires what is concretely true as its essential ground and support. "The course we follow," Hegel writes, summing up a good deal about his philosophical procedure in the *Philosophy of Right*, "is that whereby the abstract forms reveal themselves not as existing for themselves, but as untrue" (*PR*, §32A).

The philosophical procedure Hegel describes here, which moves from the abstract to the concrete, is perfectly exemplified in the two major transitions of the *Philosophy of Right*, that from morality to ethical life, and that from civil society to the state. In the first transition—the one with which we will be primarily concerned in this chapter—Hegel tells us that abstract right and morality have shown themselves to be abstractions that cannot exist on their own. Ethical life is the "truth" of these two moments insofar as they "can be seen to return to this Idea as their own *result* (*PR*, §141R). Put less abstractly: "The sphere of right and that of morality cannot exist independently; they must have the ethical as their support and foundation" (*PR*, §141A). A similar movement from the abstract and nonself-sufficient to the concrete and self-complete can be seen in the transition from civil society to the state. Here Hegel describes the state as emerging from the family and civil society as their "true ground" and "result." Though in terms of the conceptual development pursued by the *Philosophy of Right* the state is subsequent to the moments of family life and civil society, "in actuality" and as the concrete truth of these two abstract moments, it "is in fact the *primary* factor; only within the state does the family first develop into civil society, and it is the idea of the state which itself divides into these two moments" (*PR,* §256R).[4]

The arguments by which Hegel "deduces" or "proves" the ideas of ethical life and the state in the *Philosophy of Right* will be examined in detail later on. Here I bring out only the general nature of the conceptual development he pursues in the book. In §33, he finally lays out the major subdivisions of the *Philosophy of Right* and provides a minimal rationale for them. The major subdivisions are abstract right, morality, and ethical life. And the rationale for them ultimately derives from Hegel's speculative logic: the principle by which the stages in the development of right have been determined "is presupposed from speculative logic" (*PR,* §33R). Here Hegel refers to the speculative method that he elaborates toward the end of his *Logic* and that is itself nothing more than the recollective apprehension of the "absolute form" or method by which the overall movement of the *Logic* has been determined. The three moments of this speculative method are: (1) the moment of being or the immediate, which is characterized by abstract self-identity, without explicit relation to an other; (2) the moment of reflection or mediation, in which the immediate is understood to be posited or mediated by an other, an essence or some other such foundational term; (3) the synthetic moment, which is the truth and unity of the previous two (*EL,* §§237–42; *SL,* II, 825–38/550–66). In terms of the structure of the *Philosophy of Right,* abstract right corresponds to the moment of being or the immediate, morality corresponds to the moment of reflection or mediation, and ethical life corresponds to the synthetic moment which is the truth and unity of the previous two.

There is more that could be said to flesh out the relationship between Hegel's logic and the structure of the *Philosophy of Right.,* But it is not clear that saying more at this point would render the structure of the *Philosophy of Right* more intelligible or compelling. Although the formal correspondences between the speculative logic and the structure of the *Philosophy of Right* are no doubt important for Hegel's systematic purposes, it is not from them that the power or even the justification of the structure of the *Philosophy of Right* ultimately derives. Rather, the power of this structure ultimately derives from its embodying a genuine development toward a richer, more concrete and self-complete conception of right understood as the actualization of freedom. Before subjecting the individual moments that make up the basic structure of the *Philosophy of Right* to more detailed examination, then, let us encapsulate how this structure reflects the movement from abstract to concrete of which I have been speaking.

The argument begins with abstract right. This is the sphere of legal personality and of property. It represents a crucial determination of freedom insofar as, in it, human beings are recognized as bearers of rights that cannot be violated. It is abstract, however, insofar as it does not reach to the particularity of human beings, which particularity thus remains only contingently related to the universal claims of this legal sphere. In other words, abstract right does not contain within itself the minimal moral disposition necessary to motivate and enforce its juridical claims. This defect leads Hegel to consider morality, the sphere of the moral subject as opposed to the merely legal personality. This sphere is more concrete than that of abstract right in that, in it, the will seeks to realize itself in ends that are more consonant with its spiritual nature—motives, intentions, and so forth, instead of external things. Nevertheless, it, too, is abstract in that it fails to arrive at a determinate criterion for action and thus dissolves into a radical subjectivism. Here, of course, we encounter Hegel's critique of the moral point of view which goes all the way back to his *Natural Law* essay.

The thrust of Hegel's analysis in the first two parts of the *Philosophy of Right* is that formal right and morality are abstract spheres that cannot stand alone. Each lacks what the other possesses. Formal right "lacks the moment of subjectivity, which in turn belongs solely to morality" (*PR*, §141A); and morality lacks a determinate universal content, which alone belongs to abstract right. It is only by unifying these two abstract points of view that a concrete standpoint can be achieved. This is what happens in ethical life. Ethical life is the concrete truth or unity of the abstract moments of right and morality, combining the objectivity and universality of the former with the subjectivity of the latter. Thus Hegel writes: "The *ethical* [*das Sittliche*] is a subjective disposition [*subjektive Gesinnung*], but of that right which has being in itself" (*PR*, §141R). Put another way: ethical life is the "subjective form and self-determination of the will" that "has its own concept, namely freedom, as its content" (*PR*, §141A). But these are only formulas. In order to give them meaning, we must carefully go through the three moments that are brought together in them.

ABSTRACT RIGHT

Abstract right represents the first essential determination or existence of the free will, of the will that is free in and for itself. It is the sphere of the right to life, liberty (understood as arbitrariness), and property. By characterizing it thus, I obviously mean to draw attention to the connection between abstract right and the central tenets of liberalism as they are found in the tradition of modern natural right from Locke to Kant. Given this connection, the significance of Hegel's treatment of abstract right is twofold. It is significant, first, in that it clearly recognizes the fundamental importance of the rights and freedoms which form the core of liberalism. But it is significant, second, in that it reveals the incompleteness of these liberal rights and freedoms and the insufficiency of liberal theory to ground them.[5]

I have spoken of the relationship between abstract right and liberalism or the tradition of modern natural right, but this needs to be refined. For it is not the liberal tradition or the tradition of modern natural right in general from which Hegel derives the specific features of abstract right; rather, it is the version of this tradition found in Kant and Fichte, with its sharp distinction between legality and morality. Abstract right, according to Hegel, is preeminently the sphere of legality as Kant and Fichte understood it: it is the sphere of legal personality, concerned only with the external actions of individuals insofar as they impinge on the external freedom of others, and indifferent to the motives in which those actions are performed. As Hegel puts it early on in the section devoted to abstract right: "In formal right . . . it is not a question of particular interests, of my advantage or welfare, and just as little of the particular ground by which my will is determined, i.e. of my insight and intention" (*PR,* §37). And later on, he writes that, in relation to abstract right as a coercive right, "special attention must be paid to the distinction between right and morality." Legal coercion "cannot claim to extend to a person's disposition [*Gesinnung*], for in the moral sphere, I exist [only] for myself, and force is meaningless in this context" (*PR,* §94A).

The connection between Hegel's understanding of abstract right and Kant's and Fichte's understanding of the legal state in which right is divorced from ethical considerations—the state constructed by Kant's nation of rational devils or in the event, as Fichte put it, that constancy and faith between persons has been lost—is clear in Hegel's Nuremberg Gymnasium lectures. These lectures, written between 1808 and 1811, are important in that they mark the first unambiguous appearance of the tripartite abstract right-morality-state structure that was to become definitive for Hegel's mature political philosophy (see *PP,* 162–66/59–63). They are also important in that they clearly show how this structure grows out of the distinction between legality and morality drawn by Kant and Fichte. In several places, Hegel sharply distinguishes between right—by which he means abstract right—and morality—which he generally identifies with subjective "disposition" (*Gesinnung*) or intention. "*Right* must be distinguished from *morality*," he writes in one place. "Right, in general, leaves the disposition out of consideration. Morality, on the other hand, is concerned essentially with the intention and demands the deed should be done out of simple *respect* for duty" (*PP,* 19/228, 36/251; see also 20–21/230, 22/232, 164/61).

Of course, Hegel, unlike Kant and Fichte, does not accord absolute status to this distinction between legality and morality. Indeed, one of the principal points of the section of the *Philosophy of Right* devoted to abstract right is to show that the sphere of legality ultimately cannot stand alone; that it is an abstraction that requires moral disposition in order to be a concrete or actual existence. It is ethical life, and specifically the state, which ultimately accomplishes this synthesis between legality and morality, right and subjective disposition. Hegel's rejection of the Kantian-Fichtean distinction between morality and legality here is not, of course, something new to his political philosophical outlook. It can be found as early as the *Natural Law* essay. In this essay, and, indeed, throughout his writings at Jena, Hegel severely criticizes the notion of natural right that he particularly associates with Fichte's political philosophy as a system of external security designed to protect individual rights but divorced from ethical intentions or motives. On this fundamental issue Hegel's position does not change, from his early writings to the *Philosophy of Right*.

With this understanding of the general idea of abstract right, we now turn to Hegel's specific analysis of this form of right and of the central ideas and institutions he associates with it: personality, property, contract, and punishment. He begins with the idea of personality. This is the crucial image of the human being that underlies everything that belongs to abstract right. According to Hegel, the idea of personality has two aspects to it. In the first place, personality is characterized by freedom and universality. But this freedom or universality is wholly abstract; it consists in pure self-identity, total abstraction from everything determinate. Analogous to the "negative freedom" of the will treated in §5 of the Introduction, the freedom of personality is that of the "completely abstract 'I' in which all concrete limitation and validity are negated and invalidated" (*PR,* §35R). Because the freedom or universality of personality is thus abstract, it exists alongside the finite and natural being of the individual without determining or transforming it. This is the second aspect of personality and constitutes its "immediacy." The abstract universality of personality coexists with the immediate or natural being of the individual. Hegel expresses the duplicity of personality in this way: on the one hand, "I am completely determined in all respects (in my inner arbitrary will, drive, and desire, as well as in relation to my immediate external existence)" and am thus "finite"; on the other, I am "totally pure self-reference, and thus know myself in my finitude as *infinite, universal,* and *free*" (*PR,* §35).[6] Because of this duplicity, Hegel says of personality that it is "at the same time the sublime and the wholly ordinary; it contains this unity of the infinite and the utterly finite . . . The supreme achievement of the person is to support this contradiction, which nothing in the natural realm contains or could endure" (*PR,* §35A).

The reference to "achievement" in the last sentence draws attention to something that should not be overlooked in Hegel's treatment of personality: namely, that he sees it *as an achievement,* as a crucial, albeit abstract, determination of freedom. He remarks, for example, that the "highest achievement of a human being is to be a person," though he quickly qualifies this by saying that "the simple abstraction 'person' has something contemptuous about it, even as an expression" (*PR,* §35A). He also indicates that there have been individuals and peoples who did not have a personality, "insofar as they [had] not yet arrived at this pure thought and knowledge of themselves" (*PR,* §35R). Historically Hegel associates the achievement of personality with Rome and with Christianity, and he always connects this achievement with the disappearance of slavery. In Rome we begin to see the emergence of legal personality and the concomitant disappearance, in contrast with Greece, of slavery (see *PS,* 290–92/355–57; *PH,* 254–55/310–11, 278–79/339–40, 316–17/383–84; *PR,* §185R). But it is only with Christianity that "*freedom of personality* [begins] to flourish . . . and [becomes] a universal principle for part—if only a small part—of the human race" (*PR,* §62R). Likewise, it is only with Christianity that slavery becomes utterly impossible (see *IPH,* 21/31; *PH,* 334/403–4). The connection Hegel sees between Christianity, the idea of personality, and the disappearance of slavery comes out nicely in the following passage:

> [T]he genuine reason why there are no longer any slaves in Christian Europe is to be sought in nothing but the principle of Christianity itself. The Christian religion is the religion of absolute freedom, and only for Christians does man count as such, man in his infinity and universality. What the slave lacks is the recognition of his personality; but the principle of personality is universality. The master considers the slave not as a person, but as a thing devoid of self; and the slave himself does not count as an "I," for his master is his "I" instead. (*EL,* §163A1)

What Hegel says here about the incompatibility of personality and slavery discloses something else about the former notion that Hegel only alludes to at various points in his discussion of abstract right: namely, that personality presupposes mutual recognition.[7] This dependence of personality on the prior moment of recognition was evident in the *Philosophy of Spirit of 1805–6*, where Hegel saw the arrangements of abstract right as emerging directly from the struggle for recognition and, indeed, referred to recognition as the "basis of right" (*HHS*, 118–20/222–23, 112n.28/215n.). In the *Philosophy of Right*, this dependence is not so apparent, largely because Hegel has relegated the struggle for recognition to an earlier part of his system. Nevertheless, he alludes to it at a couple of crucial points. The first time comes in his discussion of slavery in the Remark to §57. There he tells us that the point of view with which the *Philosophy of Right* begins is already beyond the stage of the struggle for recognition and the relationship of lordship and bondage in which it issues: "The point of view of the free will with which right and the science of right begin is already beyond that false point of view whereby the human being exists as a natural being and as a concept which has being only in itself and is therefore capable of enslavement" (*PR*, §57R). Hegel is even more explicit about the dependence of personality and of abstract right on recognition a little later on when he takes up the subject of contract: "Contract presupposes that the contracting parties *recognize* each other as persons and owners of property; and since it is a relationship of objective spirit, the moment of recognition is already contained and presupposed within it" (*PR*, §71R).

As already pointed out, personality constitutes the basis of abstract right for Hegel, and it therefore provides the formula for the general imperative of this purely legal sphere: "be a person and respect others as persons" (*PR*, §36). Two implications follow from this general imperative of abstract right. First, given the abstractness of personality, respecting it does not involve any positive relationship to the particularity of the individual will—its needs, desires, and so forth. "[E]verything which depends on particularity is here a *matter of indifference*" (*PR*, §37A), Hegel says. Though particularity is certainly present in personality, in the form of natural drives, needs, and desires, this particularity falls completely outside the freedom, universality, and infinity of personality. This, again, is what constitutes the immediacy of personality and of the entire sphere of abstract right: the particularity of the individual subsists alongside the freedom and universality of personality and thus retains its merely immediate or natural character; it "is not yet present as freedom." Abstract right is the sphere of legality; it is concerned only with protecting and respecting the abstract universality of personality and therefore leaves out of consideration particular interests and particular welfare as well as moral insight and intention (*PR*, §37).

The second implication Hegel draws from the general imperative to "be a person and respect others as persons" is that it imposes only negative duties or prohibitions. The general thrust of all legal duties is "*not to violate* personality and what ensues from personality." Beyond that, the law leaves our conduct undetermined. The law protects the freedom of personality, but because that freedom is abstract and contains no particular content, the law does not tell us whether or how to use it. By the same token, the law protects our rights, but "it is not absolutely necessary that I should pursue my rights." For this reason, Hegel says the determinations of abstract right are mere "permissions" or "warrants." They specify what we *can* do, but, unlike moral imperatives, they do not specify what we *must* do (*PR*, §37A, 38).[8] The point Hegel makes here about the permissive character of abstract right again recalls the distinction between legality and morality drawn by Kant and Fichte. Fichte in particular emphasizes the permissive character of legal right in contradistinction to the categorical character of morality.[9]

From the idea of personality, Hegel goes on to discuss the right of property, in some ways the quintessential right of the legal sphere, according to Kant and Fichte, and, ever since Locke, the cornerstone of liberal political philosophy. The move from personality to property is, for Hegel, quite simple. "The person must give himself an external *sphere of freedom* in order to have being as Idea" (*PR*, §41). Personality must supersede its subjectivity and give itself objective existence. This it does in property. Property is nothing more (or less) than the embodiment of the freedom of personality. The distinctiveness and appeal of Hegel's doctrine of property lie precisely in its singleminded attempt to trace property back and connect it to the freedom of the will. Hegel eschews any sort of utilitarian justification of property in the *Philosophy of Right*. He insists throughout his discussion that the "rational aspect of property is to be found not in the satisfaction of needs" but, rather, in its being the "first *existence* of freedom" (*PR*, §§41A, 45R).

Why is property particularly connected with personality? For Hegel, the reason lies, once again, with the immediacy of personality. Because the freedom or universality of personality is abstract, the moment of particularity falls outside of it; personality is at one and the same time sublimely infinite and utterly finite. This means, in the first place, as we have seen, that personality remains tied to the immediate or natural being of the individual. It also means that personality seeks to embody itself in a world of immediate external things, a world that is "*immediately different* and *separable* from" the free will (*PR*, §41). The immediacy of property thus corresponds to the immediacy of personality.

As Hegel writes: "Even if this first reality of my freedom is in an external thing and is thus a poor kind of reality, the abstract personality in its very immediacy can have no other existence than in the determination of immediacy" (*PR*, §41A).

The first thing Hegel establishes with respect to the will's giving itself existence in immediate external things as property is its right to do so. In this regard, he speaks of the "*absolute right of appropriation* which human beings have over all things" (*PR*, §44). Here Hegel links property to one of the largest themes of his whole philosophy, namely, idealism. Contrary to what realism holds, he tells us, things—which include the immediate, natural attributes of the person as well as external things more conventionally understood (*PR*, §§43, 47)—are not self-sufficient or ends in themselves. "Only the will is infinite, *absolute* in relation to everything else"; and "to appropriate something means basically only to manifest the supremacy of my will in relation to the thing and to demonstrate that the latter does not have being in and for itself and is not an end in itself." This is the "idealism" contained in the moment of property, "whereas realism declares [things] to be absolute." To cap his point, Hegel recalls the animal's simple "refutation" of realism that he first adduced in the *Phenomenology:* "Even the animal has gone beyond this realist philosophy, for it consumes things and thereby proves they are not absolutely self-sufficient" (*PR*, §44A; compare *PS*, 65/91).

The property that serves as an existence and embodiment of the free will is necessarily private property, according to Hegel. Hegel's argument for private property here is not fully developed, and to some it has not appeared very convincing.[10] Nevertheless, the logic of the argument seems tolerably clear. The privacy of property follows from the fact that property is an objectification or embodiment of the will, and specifically of the will at the stage of personality. But the will at the stage of personality, the personal will, is an exclusively individual will (*PR*, §§46, 34). Private property is simply the objective correlate of the individualism of personality. Not that the standpoint of personality or of the right of private property is any sense ultimate. Hegel is quite clear that the "determinations which concern private property may have to be subordinated to the higher spheres of right, such as a community or the state." Nevertheless, such subordination is understood to be of an exceptional nature. The state cannot simply ride roughshod over the person and the right of private property; otherwise there would be no point in going through abstract right in the way that Hegel does. Apropos of this, Hegel criticizes Plato for forbidding the guardians to own private property in the

Republic and thus failing to comprehend the freedom of spirit "in its determinate moments" (*PR*, §46R).

Hegel provides a fairly elaborate discussion of the ways in which the will appropriates things and thus comes to embody itself in property—far too elaborate to give anything but the barest outline here. Consistent with the idealism theme mentioned above, the general movement he describes—from "taking possession" to "use" to "alienation"—is one whereby the will gains ever greater mastery over things, progressively destroying their otherness, and appropriating them in ever more thorough and universal ways. Thus, he begins with the crude act of physical seizure, a mode of taking possession that he says is "merely subjective, temporary, and extremely limited in scope" (*PR*, §55). A more thorough and stable mode of taking possession is found in giving form to a thing—for example, in cultivating a field or building a dam. The use of a thing, whereby a thing is "posited as something negative" and "exists only *for my need* and *serves* it," constitutes an even more complete and universal mode of appropriation, according to Hegel. Use, he writes, "embodies an even more universal relation, because the thing is not then recognized in its particularity, but is negated by me. The thing is reduced to a means of satisfying my need" (*PR*, §59 and A). Finally, and perhaps somewhat paradoxically, the truest and most complete mode of appropriation of a thing is found in alienating it. Hegel's argument in this regard is not very clear, relying heavily on logical triadism (*PR*, §§53, 65A). His main claim, however, that alienability necessarily belongs to property because something "is mine only in so far as I embody my will in it" (*PR*, §65), seems relatively uncontroversial.

In connection with the alienation of property, Hegel mentions the important proviso that the thing alienated must be "external in nature" (*PR*, §65). This leads him to consider certain "things" or "properties" that are inalienable and imprescriptible (i.e., incapable of being lost through disuse or the passage of time), among which he includes personality itself, the capacity to own property, ethical life, and religion. The reason Hegel gives for why these things or rights are inalienable and imprescriptible is that they "constitute my own distinct personality and the universal essence of my self-consciousness" (*PR*, §66); they are not external to my personality but, indeed, constitutive of it. As instances of the illicit alienation of personality, he lists slavery, serfdom, and restrictions on the freedom of ownership; as *the* example of the alienation of ethical life and religion, he names superstition (*PR*, §66R).

What makes Hegel's discussion of inalienable rights somewhat complicated is that he does not regard them as simply natural but, rather, as things we come to possess as property. In the important discussion of slavery in §57, he tells us that the human being begins as an "immediate existence," a "natural entity," and "it is only through the *development* of his own body and spirit, *essentially* by means of *his self-consciousness comprehending itself as free,* that he takes possession of himself and becomes his own property." What is crucial here is that the human being comes to own himself and thereby becomes incapable of enslavement once he has an awareness of his essential freedom. For Hegel, as we know, this awareness dawns with Christianity. But why is it that we cannot alienate that which we have so appropriated? The answer lies in the peculiarity of the appropriation of personality and of spiritual life. We do not own ourselves in the same way that we own a piece of land or a piece of cheese. In appropriating our personality and spiritual life, we deprive these things of the externality that allows them to be owned by others. Hegel writes: "[T]he act whereby I take possession of my personality and substantial essence and make myself a responsible being with moral and religious values and capable of holding rights removes these determinations from that very externality which alone made them capable of becoming the possessions of someone else." In short, I cannot alienate my personality or my ethical and religious life because either "I did not possess these things" in the first place, or, once I do possess them, "they exist essentially only as mine, and not as something external" (*PR,* §66R).

What are the distributive implications of Hegel's doctrine of property? According to Hegel, very few. Property is an expression or embodiment of personality, and personality is indifferent to particularity (individual needs, wants, talents, and so forth). "*What* and *how much* I possess is therefore purely contingent as far as right is concerned" (*PR,* §49). Hegel is particularly concerned to oppose the abstract demand for equality in the distribution of possessions at this point. He concedes that human beings are fundamentally equal, but only in respect of their abstract personalities. This means that human beings are essentially equal only before the law (*EPS,* §539R). For Hegel, as for Kant, such juridical equality is perfectly compatible with the utmost inequality with respect to particular possessions.[11] Hegel sums up his views on equality and property in this way:

> For while human beings are certainly equal, they are equal only as persons, that is, in relation to the source of their possessions. Accordingly, everyone ought (*müsste*) to have property. If we therefore wish to speak of equality, it is this equality we should consider. But this equality is distinct from the determination of particularity, from the question of how much I possess. In this context, it is false to maintain that justice

requires everyone's property to be equal; for it requires only that everyone should (*solle*) have property. (*PR*, §49A)

While the overall thrust of this passage seems to support economic inequality, some have focused on the sentences indicating that everyone should or must have some property. Of course, *some* property could mean the clothes on my back and the food that I consume; indeed, it could mean merely the property I have in myself. But these commentators argue that the close link Hegel draws between personality and property demands something more. Everyone should have enough property that their free personality genuinely exists and is not a mere sham.[12]

There are two things that might be said against this attempt to derive more substantial distributive implications from Hegel's doctrine of property. First, the context of Hegel's discussion of property, as we have seen, is legal personality. And legal personality is primarily concerned, as Hegel indicates in the passage above and elsewhere (see, e.g., *EPS*, §539R), with the capacity to own property rather than with what and how much is owned. Legal personality embodies itself in property, and this is why the right of property is important. But beyond that, the dependence of personality on property-ownership should not be overstressed. Second, legal personality is abstract. That considerations of particularity are excluded at the stage of abstract right does not mean that they will not play a role in the higher spheres of right. Many of the concerns that commentators seek to smuggle into Hegel's doctrine of property at the stage of abstract right—particular needs, circumstances, poverty, and so forth—are taken up in the more concrete spheres of morality and civil society.[13]

Hegel concludes his discussion of property by bringing out the underlying connection between property and recognition. Insofar as property is the existence of the will, "its existence for another can only be *for the will* of another person. This relation of will to will is the true distinctive ground in which freedom has its *existence*." This constitutes the transition from property to contract. In contract, the focus is no longer on the relation of the will to a thing but on the relation of the will to another will. In contract, "I no longer own property merely by means of a thing and my subjective will, but also by means of another will, and hence within the context of a common will" (*PR*, §71).

The "common will" (*gemeinsame Wille*) on which contract is based, however, is not to be confused with a genuinely "universal will" (*allgemeine Wille*).[14] In contract, we still have to do with "immediate" persons. This means that a contract is always based on the arbitrary wills of the contracting parties. For this reason, Hegel regards the contractual relation as utterly inapplicable to "ethical" identities such as marriage and the state. In neither marriage nor the state do we have to do with a merely common will that proceeds from the arbitrary wills of individuals. Marriage has its origin, it is true, in the arbitrary wills of the individuals, but this arbitrariness does not form the basis of the ethical bond of marriage (*PR,* §163R). In the state, the arbitrary will does not even play a role at the origin. We are all generally born members of a state. And "even if no state is yet present, reason requires that one be established." Being a member of a state is not a matter of arbitrary choice. "It is the rational destiny of human beings to live within a state" (*PR,* §75A). The argument for this final statement, which contains the crux of Hegel's departure from the individualistic social contract tradition, has, of course, yet to be fully supplied at this stage in the *Philosophy of Right.*

The breakdown of contract and the transition to "wrong" (*das Unrecht*) follows as a consequence of the mere "commonality" of the will in contract—from the fact that this common will is ultimately based on the arbitrary or particular wills of individuals. There is no guarantee that the particular wills of the contracting parties will conform with the common will that is posited in contract. Because the parties to the contract "are *immediate* persons, it is purely contingent whether their *particular* wills are in conformity with the will *which has being in itself,* and which has its existence solely through the former" (*PR,* §81). In contract, we encounter the same duality that afflicts the entire sphere of abstract right. On the one hand, we have abstract universality indifferent to particularity; on the other, we have the immediate being of the individual unaffected by universality. These two aspects of the person subsist side by side in mutual indifference. In contract, the possibility that the particular wills of the contracting parties may not conform with their common will—the possibility, in other words, that the parties may not abide by the contract—makes the transition to wrong necessary. Wrong exposes the contingency that lies at the heart of contract.

Hegel classifies wrong into three types: unintentional or civil wrong, deception, and crime. The first is, obviously, the least serious in that right—that is, property right—is still recognized as the "universal and deciding factor." Wrong occurs only in the mistaken subsumption of a particular action under this right (*PR,* §85). Deception (for example, fraud) constitutes a more serious form of wrong because, in it, right is no longer recognized in itself by the perpetrator of the wrong, although it is respected insofar as it appears to the person deceived (*PR,* §87). It is only in crime that right is not recognized in any sense, either in itself or as it appears to the victim of wrong (*PR*, §§83A, 90A). Crime constitutes a complete denial of right. It is an "an infringement of right as right" (*PR*, §§95, 99R) and therefore becomes the peculiar object of penal law or legal punishment for Hegel.

Hegel's theory of punishment is one of the frequently treated aspects of the *Philosophy of Right*.[15] Its allure as well as its significance lies in Hegel's single-minded attempt to ground punishment entirely in the idea of freedom without recourse to considerations of personal or social utility. Only Kant's theory of punishment comes close to matching this ambition of thoroughly grounding punishment in human freedom.[16] The argument takes off directly from Hegel's understanding of property-right as an existence or embodiment of freedom. To violate property-right is to violate freedom itself. Punishment is simply the violation of this violation, the "negation of the negation" of freedom that is crime (*PR*, §97A). Such negation or cancellation of crime is necessary, Hegel argues, because otherwise the crime would "be regarded as valid" (*PR*, §99). He, no less than Kant (though somewhat less colorfully), holds that no crime may go unpunished, "since the crime would then be posited as right" (*PR*, §218A).[17] Punishment overturns the crime that would assert itself as right and thus constitutes a "restoration of right" (*PR*, §99).

Hegel criticizes those theories of punishment that do not see punishment retributively as the cancellation of crime, but base themselves instead on subjective motives and inclinations: theories that interpret punishment in terms of prevention, deterrence, threat, or reform. Such theories, he argues, ultimately do not treat human beings as free. What Hegel says in this regard about the theory of punishment as threat is particularly illuminating:

> [T]o what extent is the threat compatible with right? The threat presupposes that human beings are not free, and seeks to coerce them through the representation of an evil. But right and justice must have their seat in freedom and the will, and not in that lack of freedom at which the threat is directed. To justify punishment in this way is like raising one's stick at a dog; it means treating a human being like a dog instead of respecting his honor and freedom. (*PR*, §99A)

Hegel's initial justification of punishment is couched largely in "objective" terms: crime is a negation of right (and hence of freedom), and punishment is simply the negation of this negation, the restoration of right (and hence of freedom). Punishment, on this view, is understood to be an expression of the objective or rational will of the criminal. Hegel goes on, however, to provide a slightly different justification of punishment which connects it more directly to the subjectivity or consent of the criminal. Punishment, he tells us, is not only something that is "just *in itself*," it is also "a *right for the criminal himself*, that is, a right *posited* in his *existent* will, in his action. For it is implicit in his action, as that of a *rational* being, that it is universal in character, and that, by performing it, he has set up a law which he has recognized for himself in his action, and under which he may therefore be subsumed as under *his* right" (*PR*, §100). Here Hegel justifies punishment not simply in terms of its objective rationality but in terms of the formal rationality of the criminal's will. As a formally rational being, the criminal wills that his action be universalized and thus that his crime recoil on himself. If he steals, he implicitly wills that he be stolen from; if he kills someone, he implicitly wills that he himself be killed (see *PP*, 31/244). In this way, Hegel argues, the criminal can be said to consent (*pace* Beccaria) to his punishment, even if this involves the death penalty.[18] And in this way, also, "the criminal is *honored* as a rational being," instead of being regarded as simply "a harmful animal which must be rendered harmless, or punished with a view to deterring or reforming him" (*PR*, §100R).

Hegel's theory of punishment, like Kant's, is a strongly retributive theory, and he is concerned to disentangle it from some of the more elementary confusions to which such a theory is subject. The most prominent of these confusions is the belief that retribution implies that a punishment literally fit the crime: that assault be punished by assault, robbery by robbery, and so forth. Hegel makes fun of this idea of retribution, conjuring up a picture of a society made up of one-eyed or toothless individuals. Retribution does not involve, he argues, "an *equality* in the specific character" of the crime but only "in terms of its *value*" (*PR*, §101). Thus fines and imprisonment serve as suitable equivalents for most crimes. For murder, however, the penalty must be death, since there is no comparable "value" for the life of a human being (*PR*, §101A). In general, though, Hegel exhibits a rather progressive attitude toward punishment. Even with respect to capital punishment, he praises the beneficial effects of Beccaria's efforts to abolish it: "[P]eople have begun to appreciate which crimes deserve the death penalty and which do not. The death penalty has consequently become less frequent, as indeed this ultimate form of punishment deserves to be" (*PR*, §100A). He also sees a necessary lightening of punishments as society grows stronger and crimes pose a relatively smaller danger to it (*PR*, §218; see also §96A).

Hegel's discussion of punishment in the *Philosophy of Right* takes place in the context of abstract right. It is appropriately concerned with the concept of punishment, but the conditions necessary to implement or actualize this concept—public laws, impartial judges, and so forth—are not yet present. At the stage of abstract right, we still have to do with right in its immediacy; the particular will of the individual retains its immediate or natural character and therefore remains only contingently related to the universal in the form of right. This means that punishment at this stage primarily takes the form of "revenge." It is carried out by a particular will that may or may not coincide with the universal and that may or may not be regarded as legitimate by the party punished. The particularity and contingency of such revenge leads, in a scenario similar to that found in the Lockean state of nature, to fresh infringements of right; and there is no way, within the terms of abstract right, to bring this infinite progression to an end (*PR*, §102).

To bring this Lockean state of war to an end, Hegel argues, requires "a justice freed from subjective interest and subjective shape and from the contingency of power—that is, a *punitive* rather than an *avenging justice*." This amounts to "a requirement for a will which, as a particular and *subjective* will, also wills the universal as such": the will of a disinterested and impartial judge (*PR*, §103).[19] But such a requirement cannot be fulfilled within the terms of abstract right. As we have seen repeatedly throughout this section, abstract right is the sphere of legal personality that abstracts from the particular will of the individual and remains indifferent to its particular interests, motives, and intentions. The universality of abstract right is one that does not reach to the particular will of the individual, thus leaving it in its immediate or natural state. Such an immediate or natural will is one that precisely cannot will the universal as such. The disinterested and impartial will of the judge required for the actualization of abstract right cannot be provided for within the terms of abstract right. Such a universal will can arise only within a sphere of obligation which concerns itself with the particular or subjective will of the individual. This is the sphere of morality for Hegel.

The more general point of Hegel's analysis of the breakdown of abstract right is that the legal state cannot be constructed or maintained without taking into account moral motivation and disposition. Kant's and Fichte's sharp distinction between legality and morality ultimately does not hold. A state ultimately cannot be set up by a nation of rational devils or in the absence of constancy and faith. Nor can it be maintained—to use Madison's famous formula—simply by "supplying, by opposite and rival interests, the defect of better motives."[20] For Hegel, the *Rechtstaat* that operates entirely on principles of pure legality or on motives of rational self-interest is a chimera. Moral disposition—the particular and subjective will that wills the universal as such—is ultimately a precondition for the liberal state.

MORALITY

In the section of the *Philosophy of Right* entitled "Morality," Hegel takes up that whole dimension of particularity and subjectivity from which abstract right abstracted and to which it remained indifferent. In morality, we no longer have to do with the abstract "person," which, because it is immediate and seeks to embody itself in immediate, external things, is infinite, free, and universal only "in itself"; rather, we have to do with the concrete "subject," which is infinite, free, and universal "for itself" (*PR*, §§104–5). Couched in terms of the categories of Hegel's logic, the will at the stage of morality is no longer immediate but "reflected from its external existence *into itself*" (*PR*, §33). It no longer seeks to embody itself, as it did in abstract right, "in something external"; rather, it has its existence "in itself, in something internal. It must have being for itself, as subjectivity, and be confronted with itself" (*PR*, §104A). It goes without saying that what Hegel includes under the rubric of "morality" here goes well beyond what we ordinarily associate with this term, encompassing everything that belongs to human subjectivity—particular interests, considerations of happiness, subjective motives, intentions, and convictions, and so forth. As Hegel puts it in the *Encyclopedia Philosophy of Spirit:* "The moral [*das Moralische*] must be taken in the wider sense in which it does not signify merely the morally good. . . . The moral here has the meaning of a determinacy of the will insofar as this determinacy is in the interior of the will in general; it thus includes purpose and intention, as well as moral evil" (*EPS*, §503R).

Morality is the sphere of subjective freedom, just as abstract right is the sphere of the freedom of personality. But how exactly does Hegel understand this subjective freedom? He defines it in terms of the "right of the subjective will," according to which "the will can *recognize* something or *be* something only in so far as that thing is its *own,* and in so far as the will is present to itself in it as subjectivity" (*PR*, §107). By virtue of this right, an individual can recognize and be held responsible for only that aspect of his deed which he has consciously willed. And he cannot be forced to subscribe or pay homage to anything that does not accord with his own view of things or with his convictions. According to this "infinite right of the subjective individual," as Hegel refers to it in the *Philosophy of History* (*IPH*, 25/36), "a man must possess a personal knowledge of the distinction between good and evil in general; ethical and religious determinations should not merely lay claim to him as external laws and precepts of authority to be obeyed, but should have their assent, recognition, or even justification in his heart, disposition, conscience, insight, etc." (*EPS*, §503R). Such subjective freedom is the mark of a mature human being, according to Hegel. Whereas the "uncivilized human being lets everything be dictated to him by brute force," and children "allow themselves to be determined by their parents," "the cultivated and inwardly developed human being wills that he should himself be present in everything he does" (*PR*, §107A).

For Hegel, this idea of subjective freedom, even more so than the idea of free personality, is of enormous historic importance in the self-understanding of modern Europeans. "This *subjective* or *moral* freedom," he writes, "is what a European especially calls freedom" (*EPS*, §503R). It is "an essential aspect of our time" (*IPH*, 26/37). The endowment of Christianity, it is what more than anything else differentiates the self-understanding of the modern world from that of antiquity. This appreciation of the historic significance of the idea of subjective freedom in modern self-understanding of course goes back pretty far in Hegel's development. We saw it definitively emerge toward the end of the Jena period in the *Philosophy of Spirit of 1805–6;* and it plays a crucial role in the overall structure and argument of the *Phenomenology.* But it nowhere receives clearer or more succinct expression than in the following passage from the *Philosophy of Right:*

> The right of the subject's particularity to find satisfaction, or—to put it differently—the right of *subjective freedom,* is the pivotal and focal point in the difference between *antiquity* and the *modern* age. This right, in its infinity, is expressed in Christianity, and it has become the universal and actual principle of a new form of the world. Its more specific shapes include, love, the romantic, the eternal salvation of the individual as an end, etc.; then there are morality and conscience, followed by the other forms, some of which will come into prominence below as the principle of civil society and as moments of the political constitution, while others appear within history at large, particularly in the history of art, the sciences, and philosophy. (*PR*, §124R)

As we have seen in other contexts, Hegel is not without his qualms about the unfettered expression of this right of subjective freedom. And we shall see in the *Philosophy of Right* that he ultimately criticizes it for being one-sided, subordinating it to the higher standpoints of ethical life and the state. Nevertheless, it cannot be doubted that Hegel ascribes the utmost importance to this particular determination of freedom.

In the course of the section on "Morality," the right of the subjective will undergoes development. The overall process that it pursues is one whereby the object of the subjective will—an "action"—comes to be ever more thoroughly penetrated by the self. Thus, the process begins with the rather abstract or formal recognition of self in an action in "purpose," and it ends in the thorough inwardness and disappearance of all externality—the complete being-for-self—of "conscience." Hegel also characterizes this process as one in which the subjective will progressively achieves identity with its concept, the universal will: "the process of the moral point of view" is one "whereby the subjective will further determines what it recognizes as its own in its object so that this becomes the will's true concept—i.e. becomes objective in the sense of the will's own universality" (*PR,* §107R). The culmination of this process is seen in the idea of the "good," which Hegel characterizes as the intention of an action "raised to the concept of the will" (*PR,* §114A). In his treatment of the ideas of "good" and "conscience," Hegel again returns to the critique of Kantian-Fichtean "morality" found in his earlier works. For this reason, we will carefully examine it. But before doing so, we need to look a little more closely at the moments of morality leading up to it.

The first and most formal expression of the right of the subjective will is found in the idea of "purpose" (*Vorsatz*). According to this idea, it is "the right of the will to recognize as its *action* [*Handlung*], and to accept *responsibility* for, only those aspects of its *deed* [*Tat*], which it knew to be presupposed within its end, and which were present in its *purpose*" (*PR,* §117). The will cannot be held responsible for those circumstances of its deed of which it had no knowledge and which formed no part of its purpose. Thus Oedipus, according to Hegel, cannot be accused of parricide or incest, because he did not know what he was doing. The great flaw of ancient legal codes, in contradistinction to modern ones, is that they did not pay enough attention to this subjective dimension of action. They did not grasp the distinction between "deed" and "action," between the external event and the subjective purpose informing it. Thus heroes such as Oedipus were made responsible for the "deed in its entirety," regardless of their subjective awareness (*PR,* §§117A, 118R).

The right of the subjective will extends not only to the circumstances of an action but also to its consequences. The will is responsible for only those consequences which "belong to the action as an integral part of it" (*PR,* §118). This, according to Hegel, constitutes the transition from the idea of purpose to the idea of "intention" (*Absicht*). "Intention" refers to the universal aspect of an action: not just the action as an isolated or individual existence but the action with all its necessary connections. Hegel's examples of arson and murder are helpful. The intention of the arsonist, he tells us, is not simply to set fire to an isolated piece of wood but to "the universal within it—i.e. the entire house." By the same token, the intention of the murderer is not merely to injure an isolated piece of flesh but the universal—life—enclosed within it (*PR*, §§119R, 132R). Intention, however, is not confined to what is explicitly anticipated by an individual agent. In the case of arson, for example, the fire may spread further than the arsonist wished, or it may kill people the arsonist did not realize were in the house; but Hegel still maintains that the arsonist is responsible for these unforeseen consequences, because it inheres in such an action "that it may extend to immeasurable consequences," and "by such actions, agents deliver themselves up to external circumstances" (*LNR*, §61R). To this end, he quotes the old proverb, "The stone belongs to the devil when it leaves the hand that threw it" (*PR*, §119A). As the arson example suggests, with respect to the "right of intention," Hegel is as much concerned to stress the responsibility of the individual agent as he is to vindicate his subjective freedom. Only imbeciles, lunatics, and children are relieved of the responsibility of knowing the necessary consequences of their actions. It belongs to the dignity of human beings as "thinking agents" to be aware of these consequences (*PR*, §120).

There is another aspect to intention, for Hegel. Not only does intention refer to the universal inherent in the purpose of an action; it also refers to the particular satisfaction that an agent seeks to obtain from an action and which "gives the action its subjective *value* and *interest* for me" (*PR*, §122). This aspect of intention is what we generally refer to as the "motive" of an action. In murder and arson, to return to our examples above, it is not simply the universal inherent in the purpose that is intended. There is also a particular satisfaction sought, a particular aim or motive that informs the action. Hegel writes: "Murder and arson, as universals, do not constitute my positive content as a subject. If someone has perpetrated crimes of this kind, we ask why he committed them. The murder was not committed for the sake of murder; on the contrary, some particular positive end was also present" (*PR*, §121A). The right that corresponds to this aspect of intention is no longer simply a right of knowledge, as in the previous moments of purpose and the first aspect of intention; it is "the *right* of the *subject* to find its *satisfaction* in the action" (*PR*, §121).

As for the specific content of this subjective satisfaction, Hegel tells us that, at this point, it derives solely from the natural will, consisting of needs, inclinations, passions, and so forth. The comprehensive aim of such a will is "welfare"

(*Wohl*) or "happiness" (*Glückseligkeit*). Welfare or happiness, as we have learned from the Introduction to the *Philosophy of Right*, is not simply an immediate satisfaction of our natural drives and impulses. There is an attempt, in welfare or happiness, to measure and compare our natural drives and impulses and order them into some sort of rational system. Nevertheless, the content remains "something natural and given" (*PR*, §123R), and the will does not yet have itself or freedom as its object. As we shall soon see, it is not until the will "has adopted the good as an end in itself" that it becomes "truly present for *itself*." But Hegel is not primarily concerned here to derogate the claims of natural desire and happiness to the higher claims of freedom. The natural needs, inclinations, and passions that belong to the subject as a living being have a necessary role to play and are not simply opposed to freedom. Hegel asks "whether the human being has a right to set himself ends which are not based on freedom, but solely on the fact that the subject is a living being." And his answer clearly reflects his rejection of the Kantian dualism of the rational and the passional:

> The fact that he is a living being is not contingent, however, but in accordance with reason, and to that extent he has a right to make his needs his end. There is nothing degrading about being alive, and we do not have the alternative of existing in a higher spirituality. It is only by raising what is present and given to a self-creating process that the higher sphere of the good is attained (although this distinction does not imply that the two aspects are incompatible). (*PR*, §123A)[21]

Hegel continues in this unKantian vein in the important §124, which was quoted above in relation to the crucial difference between antiquity and modernity with respect to subjective freedom. Hegel rejects the abstract view that sees the satisfaction of the subject's particularity and the objective ends of morality as mutually exclusive. He rejects the view of morality sometimes found in Kant "as a perennial and hostile struggle against one's own satisfaction, as in the injunction: 'Do with repugnance what duty commands.'" And, as he does in several other places, he castigates the "psychological view of history" that takes the presence of any sort of subjective satisfaction in an historical action as prima facie evidence that this was the sole intention of the action for which whatever was great, objective, or substantial in it was merely a means—the view, as Hegel puts it, quoting his famous *mot* from the *Phenomenology*, "of 'those psychological *valets de chambre* for whom there are no heroes, not because the latter are not heroes, but because the former are only valets de chambre'" (*PR*, §124R; compare *PS*, 404/489).[22] For Hegel, again, subjective satisfaction is not absolutely opposed to the objective ends of freedom and morality. Indeed, as his teaching about the state attempts to show, these two things—subjectivity and objectivity, particularity and universality—must ultimately work together, for "nothing great has been accomplished in the world without passion" (*IPH*, 26/38).

So far Hegel has indicated that only the welfare or happiness of the individual is the aim of the "moral" will at this point. He goes to argue, however, that it also includes the welfare or happiness of others (*PR*, §125). This move from self to others is made rather suddenly in Hegel's argument, and some have found it not very convincing.[23] The basic idea seems to be that, since subjectivity in general is the principle of the will at the stage of morality, there is a natural progression from the satisfaction of my own subjectivity to the satisfaction of the subjectivity of others. Hegel sees an analogy here to what happens in contract. Just as my personality only becomes truly objective to me when I identify it with the personality of an other in contract, so my subjectivity only becomes truly existent and objective to me when I identify it with the subjective will of others (*PR*, §112). Of course, the identification of wills that takes place at the stage of morality is more profound and concrete than that which takes place in abstract right. And this points to an important distinction between abstract right and morality for Hegel. In abstract right, the reference of the individual will to the will of others is purely negative; the legal code, as we have already seen, consists only of prohibitions not to violate the personality and property of others. In morality, on the other hand, the reference of the individual will to the will of others is positive; the individual will is enjoined not merely to refrain from violating the personality and property of others but to contribute positively to the subjective satisfaction and welfare of others (*PR*, §§112A, 113R).[24]

But regardless of whether the "moral" will adopts its own welfare or the welfare of others as its end, it remains bound up with particularity, and its actions may or may not conform to the universal, which is still understood here in terms of the conditions of abstract right (*PR*, §125). The pursuit of the general welfare can lead to the infringement of the rights of legal personality. That this ought not to be so Hegel is very clear. "My particularity," he writes "like that of others, is only a right at all in so far as I am *free*. It cannot therefore assert itself in contradiction to this substantial basis on which it rests; and an intention to promote my welfare and that of others—and in the latter case in particular it is called a *moral intention*—cannot justify an *action which is wrong*" (*PR*, §126).[25] And he goes on to heap criticism on the romantic morality of the "good heart" that sets itself against the prescriptions of right and the norms of society. This, of course, has been a favorite target of Hegel's ever since the *Phenomenology,* and here, as there, he sees it leading to nothing but a radical and standardless subjectivism. This constitutes the limitation and one-sidedness of the standpoint of welfare. Concerned only with the satisfaction of particularity, it remains indebted to abstract right for the universal, and to this universal it remains only contingently related.

But it is not just welfare—individual or general—which proves to be one-sided and nonself-sufficient in relation to abstract right. Hegel shows, in his treatment of the "right of necessity" (*Notrecht*), that abstract or formal right suffers from the same one-sidedness in relation to welfare. In the event one's life is threatened, he argues, one may claim a "right of necessity" and infringe the property-right of an other—by stealing a loaf of bread or whatever. For in such a case, one injures only "an individual and limited existence of freedom," whereas the loss of life entails a "total loss of rights" and freedom (*PR*, §127). In this case of necessity, the right of welfare trumps that of property. Hegel here shows that he, unlike Kant, does not subscribe to the proverbial saying *fiat justitia, pereat mundus.*[26] *Justitia,* understood as abstract right, has its limitations; and *mundus,* understood as "life," the totality of the ends of particularity, has it own legitimate claims.

Thus, both welfare and abstract right show themselves to be one-sided and contingent: one has particularity without universality, the other has universality without particularity. What is needed is a more comprehensive notion that somehow integrates these two standpoints without simply relating them in a contingent fashion. What is needed is a particular or subjective will that adopts the universal, freedom—as opposed to merely empirical or particular welfare—as its end. This demand is satisfied in the idea of the "good" (*das Gute*). The good, Hegel tells us, is "the unity of the *concept* of the will and the *particular* will" (*PR*, §129). In willing the good, the particular or subjective will no longer has, as it did in welfare, merely empirical or natural inclinations as its content. Rather, it now wills a content that is in accordance with its concept, namely, freedom or universality. "Within this idea [of the good], welfare has no validity as the existence of the individual and particular will, but only as the *universal* welfare and essentially as *universal in itself,* i.e. in accordance with freedom" (*PR*, §130). The good is the "substance" or "truth" of the particular will (*PR*, §§130, 131A); it is the "essence of the will in its *substantiality* and *universality*" (*PR*, §132R). In short, in willing the good, the particular or subjective will wills the free will.

Clearly, the transition to the idea of the good is one of the most important in the *Philosophy of Right*. With this idea, we have arrived, at least in principle, at a resolution of the dialectic of freedom in the book. Thus, Hegel refers to the good as "realized freedom, the absolute and ultimate end of the world" (*PR*, §129). And he soon characterizes ethical life as the "living good" (*PR*, §142). But at this point in the argument, the idea of the good remains only abstractly determined; it remains bound within the standpoint of moral subjectivity. What we have to do with here is the good in the sense of the Kantian good will. In the section "Good and Conscience," Hegel revisits his critique of Kantian morality and its extension by Fichte and some of his Romantic followers.

He begins by giving Kant his due as the discoverer of the idea of the good in contradistinction to the idea of welfare or happiness. Indeed, the very distinction between *das Gute* and *das Wohl* that Hegel uses to structure his argument in "Morality" ultimately derives from Kant.[27] It is Kant who, in his idea of duty, found a determination of the will independent of sensuous inclination and thus established the "infinite autonomy" of the will, its "pure and unconditional self-determination" (*PR*, §135R). In doing my duty for its own sake, Hegel writes, "it is in the true sense my own objectivity that I bring to fulfilment . . . In doing my duty, I am with myself [*bei mir selbst*] and free. The merit and exalted viewpoint of Kant's moral philosophy are that it has emphasized the significance of duty" (*PR*, §133A).[28]

But despite this crucial advance by Kant, he never gets beyond the abstract notion of doing one's duty for its own sake, according to Hegel. When the question is asked, What exactly is my duty? Kant has nothing to offer but the formal criterion of self-consistency or noncontradiction as expressed in the first formula of the categorical imperative, the formula of universal law. Here Hegel returns to the critique of Kantian ethics that he first developed in the *Natural Law* essay and repeated in the *Phenomenology*. The universalization test of the categorical imperative is incapable of generating any particular duties. Kant may have shown that the maxim of not returning deposits, when universalized, leads to the nonexistence of deposits, but where is the contradiction in the nonexistence of deposits? Likewise a maxim that rationalizes stealing may, when universalized, lead to the destruction of the institution of property, but where is the contradiction in the nonexistence of property? "The fact that *no property* is present is in itself no more contradictory than is the nonexistence of this or that individual people, family, etc, or the complete *absence of human life*." For there to be a contradiction, we have to assume that principles such as "property ought to exist" or "human life ought to exist" are already present. But the categorical imperative or the criterion of noncontradiction alone cannot establish these substantive principles. For this reason, according to Hegel, Kant's ethics turn out to be an "empty formalism" (*PR*, §135, R, and A).[29]

There are, as noted in my discussion of *Natural Law*, problems with Hegel's critique of the Kantian categorical imperative as it is presented here. In the first place, Hegel focuses exclusively on the first and most formalistic formulation of the categorical imperative, neglecting the second and third formulations, which go some distance toward providing the content that he claims is missing from Kant's ethics. Second, even Hegel's specific argument against the first formulation of the categorical seems somewhat flawed. Kant's point about the deposit, for example, is not that deposits must exist simply, but only that they must exist if someone is to profit by stealing one. It is in this sense alone that the maxim of gaining money by appropriating deposits is self-contradictory when universalized.

But though Hegel's critique of the Kantian categorical imperative may not be quite the tour de force he imagined it to be, there remains more than a grain of truth (again as observed in my discussion of *Natural Law*) to his charge that Kant's ethics are ultimately empty and formalistic. It is, ultimately, difficult to determine what we ought to do in any particular ethical situation, using the categorical imperative alone. As Hegel argues in other places, in any concrete and complex situation, a number of different categorical imperatives may possibly apply, thus giving rise to a conflict of duties. There is nothing in the categorical imperative itself that allows us to resolve this conflict of duties, and the choice between them becomes a matter of subjective or contingent decision. This raises the possibility that the bad man can justify his unethical conduct by picking out an aspect of it which fulfills some duty or other (see "SC," 244–46/359–62; *FK*, 183–86/425–28). As Hegel puts it now, with a certain amount of exaggeration, in the *Philosophy of Right:* "it is possible to justify any wrong or immoral mode of action" by means of the Kantian notion of formal duty (*PR*, §135R). It is perhaps the case that some of the indeterminacy of the categorical imperative may be reduced through philosophical ingenuity—and Kantians have been nothing if not ingenious in this regard—but this only serves to reinforce Hegel's point rather than to disprove it. For if reflective ingenuity is required to make the categorical imperative work, this makes it less useful for, as well as less descriptive of, ordinary moral conduct, and it also opens the door to the sort of ethical subjectivism Hegel is concerned to fight off. Over against such subjective reflection, morality is better understood—to cite the provocative formula Hegel used in *Natural Law* and which he will soon repeat in the *Philosophy of Right*—as living in accordance with the customs of one's land.

The idea of the good in its Kantian form thus proves to be abstract and incapable of generating a determinate content. To overcome this emptiness and arrive at a particular or determinate content, the moral will turns inward to the principle of "conscience" (*Gewissen*). As he did in the *Phenomenology*, Hegel here gives dialectical form to the historical move from Kant to Fichte and his Romantic successors, Novalis, Schlegel, Fries, and Schleiermacher. This move consisted essentially in the radicalization of the Kantian idea of moral auton-omy. Abandoning the Kantian notion of pure duty as too empty and external, these post-Kantian, Romantic thinkers sought to ground morality in the sub-jective and authentic conviction of the individual. In the *Phenomenology*, Hegel characterized the move from Kantian duty to Romantic conscience in this way: "Duty is no longer the universal that stands over against the self; on the contrary, it is known to have no validity when thus separated. It is now the law that exists for the sake of the self, not the self that exists for the sake of law" (*PS*, 387/469). In the *Philosophy of Right*, he gives an equally vivid description of this descent into the self that marks the culmination of the modern principle of subjectivity:

> Conscience . . . is that deepest inner solitude within oneself in which all externals and all limitation have disappeared—it is total withdrawal into the self. As con-science, the human being is no longer bound by the ends of particularity, so that conscience represents an exalted point of view, a point of view of the modern world, which has for the first time attained this consciousness, this descent into the self. Earlier and more sensuous ages have before them something external and given, whether this be religion or right; but conscience knows itself as thought, and that this thought of mine is my sole source of obligation. (*PR*, §136A)

Hegel is characteristically ambivalent about the principle of conscience. On the one hand, he sees it as an essential right of the subjective will. "*Conscience*," he writes, "expresses the absolute entitlement of subjective self-consciousness to know *in itself* and *from itself* what right and duty are, and to recognize only what it thus knows as the good" (*PR*, §137R). And in an earlier paragraph, he speaks of the "right to recognize nothing that I do not perceive as rational" or good as "the highest right of the subject" (*PR*, §132R). As the passage quoted in the previous paragraph indicates, and as we know from other contexts, Hegel identifies the "exalted point of view" of conscience with the modern world, and specifically with Protestantism. The obstinacy by which human beings "are unwilling to acknowledge in their attitudes anything which has not been justified by thought," he tells us in the Preface to the *Philosophy of Right*, "is the characteristic property of the modern age, as well as being the distinctive principle of Protestantism" (*PR*, 22/27). It is only with the Reformation that everything in the moral and spiritual world began to be submitted to the tribunal of subjective thought (see *PH*, 344/45/416–17, 416–17/496–97, 438–39/520–21). Ultimately, though, Hegel traces the principle of conscience back to Socrates, whom he refers to in the *Philosophy of History* as the "inventor of morality" (*PH*, 269/328–29). Socrates evaporated the existent and customary morality of the Greeks and for the first time sought to determine what is right and good from within himself. In doing so, Hegel suggests, Socrates was entirely justified, since "Athenian democracy had fallen into ruin," and the actual world was a "hollow, spiritless, and unsettled existence" (*PR*, §138R and A).[30]

But though Hegel ascribes the utmost importance to the principle of conscience, he ultimately sees it as being a purely formal principle that, when taken by itself, leads to a radical subjectivism. For conscience ultimately refers only to the subjective form of our knowledge, and this subjective form may or may not correspond to what is objectively rational, to what is good or universal in and for itself. For this reason, Hegel writes, "the state cannot recognize the conscience in its distinctive form, i.e. as *subjective knowledge*, any more than science can grant validity to subjective *opinion, assertion*, and the *appeal* to subjective opinion" (*PR*, §137R). He willingly concedes that "it is right to evaporate right and duty into subjectivity," but he goes on to argue that it is "wrong if this abstract foundation is not in turn developed" (*PR*, §138A). We cannot simply retreat into our subjectivity and remain there; rather, we must try to deduce from the concept of the free will itself objective determinations of right and duty. Here Hegel simply refers to the project of the *Philosophy of Right* itself. As he succinctly characterizes this project in the Preface: "In right, the human being must encounter his own reason; he must therefore consider the rationality of right, and this is the business of our science" (*PR*, 13–14A/17A). Though Hegel finds Socrates' flight from the actual world and retreat into his inner life perfectly justified owing to the hollowness and spiritlessness of that world, he clearly does not think such an attitude is warranted with respect to the modern state. The modern state is rational, the embodiment of human freedom, and the task of the philosopher is to comprehend this rationality.

The subjectivistic excesses to which the doctrine of conscience has been carried in Hegel's own time are detailed in the long Remark to §140, with which the section on "Morality" concludes. Here Hegel picks up again the polemic against romantic subjectivism with which he began in the Preface to the *Philos-*

ophy of Right. His specific concern in this Remark is with the various ways in which the "profound concept" of conscience has been used—or "twisted"—to justify evil actions and make them appear good by evaluating them purely in terms of the good intentions or subjective convictions which lie behind them. His subject may be said to be the subtle forms hypocrisy takes under the dispensation of the authentic conscience, though "hypocrisy" may not be quite the right word (as Hegel is well aware) to describe the sort of deception that is going on here. For hypocrisy generally presupposes a clear-cut distinction between good and evil, and the deception it involves is generally directed toward others. Whereas, in the perverted forms of conscience Hegel is investigating, the distinction between good and evil is blurred, and the deception involved is at least as much of the self as of others. Hegel writes:

> Nowadays, there is no longer much talk of hypocrites, partly because this accusation appears too harsh, and partly because hypocrisy in its immediate shape has more or less disappeared. This barefaced lie and cloak of goodness has now become too transparent not to be seen through, and the distinction between doing good on the one hand and evil on the other is no longer present to the same extent since increasing education has made such antithetical determinations seem less clear-cut. (*PR,* §140A)

In the most extreme versions of conscience, where "subjectivity declares itself absolute," there can no longer be any talk of hypocrisy, for here the distinction between good and evil has been completely obliterated (*PR,* §140R, pp. 177–78).

Hegel arranges the perverted forms of conscience he is studying in an ascending order according to which the subjective element becomes ever more explicit and the element of ethical objectivity ever more exiguous. He begins with the seventeenth-century Jesuit doctrine of probabilism, which holds (at least according to Hegel's caricature of it) that "an action is permissible and can be done in good conscience if the consciousness can discover *any* good reason for it" (*PR,* §140R, p. 172). Such a doctrine opens the door to ethical subjectivism. But Hegel can't have been interested in this dated doctrine for its own sake. Rather, he uses it to set up his critique of the Kantian doctrine of the good will, which resembles probabilism in that it leads to the consequence that an action is justified so long as it can be brought under some general principle or other. The Kantian good, as we have already seen, is abstract and without determinate content. It is left to the individual subject to provide the abstract good with determinate content by subsuming its action under a universal. But this process of subsumption, Hegel argues, can be carried out in the most arbitrary fashion. In any concrete action one can always find some universal content, some positive aspect, by which to justify the action. Thus, theft may be justified by being subsumed under one's duty to help the poor, and desertion in battle may be justified in terms of "one's duty to care for one's life or one's (perhaps even impoverished) family." The final result of this sort of subjective moral reflection is that "any content one pleases can be subsumed under the good" (*PR,* §140R, pp. 173–75).

In both probabilism and the Kantian good will, it is not yet explicitly acknowledged that subjectivity is the governing principle of right and duty; there is still an appeal here to objective reasons and universal principles. In the two forms of conscience Hegel takes up next, however, namely, "conviction" and "irony," "*subjective opinion* is at last expressly acknowledged as the criterion of right and duty." According to the view that takes conviction as its principle, an action is good or right insofar as my subjective conviction holds it to be so. Hegel identifies such an ethics of conviction with Jacob Fries, who was also the target of Hegel's criticisms in the Preface to the *Philosophy of Right,* and he sees in it nothing but a wholesale relativism. Here "any semblance of ethical objectivity has disappeared," and it becomes impossible to speak of hypocrisy or evil at all (*PR,* §140, pp. 176–80).[31]

It would not seem possible to go much further in the direction of absolute subjectivity, and yet there still attaches to the ethics of conviction an element of "honesty" or "authenticity" that detracts from the absolute freedom of the subject to make and unmake the law that governs it. Such an absolute freedom of subjectivity, Hegel argues, is found only in the ultraromantic doctrine of irony put forth by Friedrich Schlegel. According to this doctrine, which seems to anticipate much of what now passes under the banner of "postmodernism," the individual subject, while aware of ethical objectivity, "at the same time distances itself from it and knows *itself* as that which *wills* and *resolves in a particular way* but may *equally well* will and resolve otherwise." Such an ironic consciousness says to others:

> You in fact honestly accept a law as existing in and for itself; I do so too, but I go further than you, for I am also beyond this law and can do *this* or *that* as I please. It is not the thing which is excellent, it is I who am excellent and master of both law and thing; I *merely play* with them as will my own caprice, and in this ironic consciousness in which I let the highest of things perish, I *merely enjoy myself.* (*PR,* §140R, p. 182)

Hegel encapsulates the hubristic subjectivism of this ironic consciousness beautifully in the Addition to §140. The ironic point of view as defined by Schlegel, he writes, implies that objective goodness is merely something constructed by my conviction, sustained by me alone, and that I, as lord and master, can make it come and go [as I please]. As soon as I relate myself to something objective, it ceases to exist for me, and so I am poised above an immense void, conjuring up shapes and destroying them. This supremely subjective point of view can only arise in a highly cultivated age in which faith has lost its seriousness, its essence consisting solely in the vanity of all things.

With the intentional arbitrariness of the ironic consciousness, we have finally reached the furthest extreme of subjectivity, the point at which "subjectivity declares itself absolute." This point marks the inevitable conclusion of the dialectic of "morality" and signals its necessary going under. The moral point of view has shown itself to be as one-sided as abstract right. Whereas the latter was all objectivity without subjectivity, the former is all subjectivity without objectivity. What is required is some sort of synthesis of these two abstract moments. This Hegel claims to provide in his conception of ethical life.

ETHICAL LIFE

The transition from morality to ethical life is undoubtedly the most important in the *Philosophy of Right*. As I remarked toward the beginning of this chapter, ethical life is a crucial notion in Hegel's political philosophy, encapsulating in many ways the crux of his critique of the theoretical—largely individualistic— foundations of liberalism and of modern political philosophy in general. It is also a philosophically controversial notion for precisely the same reason. The most common criticism of Hegel's concept of ethical life is that it is a conservative or traditionalist notion that sanctifies customary morality and is hostile to individuality or any sort of moral reflection or criticism. This criticism receives particularly extreme expression in Ernst Tugendhat's contention that the "possibility of an independent and critical relation to the community or the state is not admitted by Hegel. Rather, we hear the following set of claims: the existing laws have an absolute authority; what the individual has to do is firmly established in a community; the private conscience of the individual must disappear; trust takes the place of reflection. This is what Hegel means by the overcoming of morality in ethical life."[32]

The analysis of ethical life that follows seeks to refute the sort of criticism to which Tugendhat gives voice here. The problem with all such criticisms is that they completely ignore the specific content Hegel ascribes to ethical life and focus exclusively on what he says about the substantiality of ethical life and the unreflective, customary, or habitual attitude of individuals toward this substantiality. What is not sufficiently understood is that the content of this ethical substance embraces the rights and freedoms that have been established in the preceding moments of abstract right and morality. Nor is it only Hegel's critics who fail to grasp this point but also some of his "communitarian" supporters. These latter tend to reduce Hegel's doctrine of ethical life to a doctrine about community in general and thus overlook the fact that Hegel is talking about a rather specific community, one with a rational and universal content. Such communitarian interpretations ultimately make it more difficult to defend Hegel from attacks such as Tugendhat's. I should add, though, that, while my analysis defends Hegel's concept of ethical life from the charge of historicism, it does not deny the element of unreflectiveness and custom that Hegel seems to associate with this concept. In this regard, toward the end of this section, I criticize some of Hegel's more rationalistic defenders, with whose interpretations mine otherwise shares a good deal.

Let us turn back to Hegel's text. Ethical life is the third of the three large moments which constitute the basic structure of the *Philosophy of Right*, and it is in ethical life that the one-sidednesses of the two earlier moments, abstract right and morality, are synthesized and overcome. Both formal right and morality have revealed themselves to be abstractions; the one is all objectivity without subjectivity, the other is all subjectivity without objectivity; neither can stand alone. It is only in ethical life that the objectivity or universality of abstract right is brought together with the subjectivity of morality to form a concrete whole. Hegel writes in the Introduction to the *Philosophy of Right:* "Morality and the earlier moment of formal right are both abstractions whose truth is attained only in *ethical life*. Thus, ethical life is the unity of the will in its concept and the will of the individual, that is, of the subject" (*PR*, §33A). And he elaborates in the actual transition from morality to ethical life:

> For whereas morality is the form of the will in its subjective aspect, ethical life is not just the subjective form and self-determination of the will: it also has its own concept, namely freedom, as its content. The sphere of right and that of morality cannot exist independently; they must have the ethical as their support and foundation. For right lacks the moment of subjectivity, which in turn belongs solely to morality, so that neither of the two moments has any independent actuality. (*PR*, §141A)

In addition to presenting ethical life as the synthesis of right and morality, Hegel presents it as the synthesis of the abstract moments of good and conscience. The good represents the objective pole of the antithesis to be resolved;

it is the "substantial universal of freedom," but it is abstract and lacks determination. Conscience, on the other hand, represents abstract subjectivity and lacks a universal or objective content. Thus, we have "the good lacking subjectivity and determination, and the determinant, i.e. subjectivity, lacking what has being in itself" (*PR,* §141R). Once again, the resolution to this abstract antithesis is found in ethical life: "The unity of the subjective with the objective good which has being in and for itself is *ethical life*" (*PR,* §141A).

It is, of course, the emptiness or indeterminacy of the ideas of the good and conscience against which Hegel's doctrine of ethical life chiefly takes shape. As in his critiques of the Kantian moral point of view elsewhere, Hegel characterizes this emptiness or indeterminacy here in terms of the inability of the good and conscience to get beyond the "ought" to an "is." Thus, he writes that the good and conscience are the "indeterminate which *ought* to be determined": the good "ought to be," and conscience "ought to be good" (*PR,* §141 and R). And it is in opposition to this idea of the moral "ought" that Hegel initially introduces the idea of ethical life in the *Encyclopedia Philosophy of Spirit:*

> The substance which knows itself as *free,* in which the absolute *ought* is just as much *being,* has actuality as the spirit of a *people.* The abstract diremption of this spirit is the individuation into *persons,* of whose independence it is the inner power and necessity. But the person as thinking intelligence knows that substance as his own essence; ceases in this disposition [*Gesinnung*] to be an accident of it; and looks upon it as his absolute final goal in actuality, as something both attained in the *here and now* and at the same time *brought about through his own activity,* but as something which in fact simply *is.* (*EPS,* §514)

This extraordinarily rich passage contains, in compacted form, most of the key determinations of the idea of ethical life. Let us stick for a moment, though, with what the passage says about the way in which ethical life overcomes the abstract "ought" of morality and treats it as something which just as much "is." This, as Charles Taylor has noted, is a crucial characteristic of ethical life.[33] In ethical life, our moral obligations are based on the established customs and usages (*Sitten*) of an ongoing community. In this sense they already exist, they do not have to be discovered by or spun out of the subjective rationality of the individual. For this reason they are also determinate, they do not suffer from the indeterminacy of Kantian morality. That our moral obligations already exist in this way, however, does not mean that there is nothing left for the individual subject to do. The continued existence of these norms depends on their being continuously recognized, observed, and enacted by the individuals who make up the ethical community. This is what Hegel is getting at when he speaks of the ethical substance as something that both "is" and is brought about through the subject's own activity. He elaborates on this crucial characteristic of ethical life in the Heidelberg lectures of 1817–18:

> What is living reproduces itself; it is only a game with itself, it brings forth only what already is. The rational as such, law, can be called the concept, but it has its determinate existence in the individual subject, in its intelligence. . . . [Ethical life] must have existence, must be actualized; the good must be actualized by the ethical subject. . . . The standpoint is not that the good is not present; on the contrary, substance is eternally present. All that happens is that what is already present is brought forth. (*LNR*, §69R)

In addition to bringing out how ethical life bridges the gap between the "is" and the "ought," the passage from the *Encyclopedia Philosophy of Spirit* quoted above also suggests how Hegel sees the relationship of the individual to ethical substance. Hegel distinguishes two aspects of this relationship here—this, we shall see, is a recurrent feature of his analysis of ethical life. On the one hand, he maintains that ethical substance in the form of the spirit of a people remains the "inner power and necessity" of the individual persons who comprise it. The independent existence of individuals is, in an important way, subordinate to the ethical whole; and in this respect individuals can be regarded as accidents of the ethical substance. On the other hand, Hegel tells us that "the person as thinking intelligence knows this substance as his own essence" and "ceases in this disposition to be a mere accident of it." The ethical substance is not something alien to the individual subject; rather, it is the objective expression of the individual's essence, namely, freedom, and insofar as the individual is a "thinking intelligence" he is aware of this fact. In this way, ethical life combines both objectivity and subjectivity.

As we turn to Hegel's general treatment of the concept of ethical life in §§142–56 of the *Philosophy of Right*, we see a similar but more sustained attempt to grasp ethical life as the unity of objectivity and subjectivity, of the objective (or universal or substantial) will and the subjective will. Hegel begins by characterizing ethical life as "the living good which has its knowledge and volition in self-consciousness, and its actuality through self-conscious action" (*PR*, §142). No longer do we have to do, in ethical life, with the abstract good of morality that is devoid of subjectivity and determination. The good that is the substance of ethical life is "living" because it is recognized, sustained, and "brought forth" (to borrow the phrase Hegel used in his Heidelberg lectures to describe the "living" character of ethical life) by the individual subject. But the good that is "brought forth" by the subject in ethical life is not a merely subjective content but the objective concept of the will, freedom, itself. Thus, Hegel writes that "it is in ethical being that self-consciousness has its motivating end and a foundation which has being in and for itself" (*PR*, §142). The content of ethical life is not just any content; it is a rational content; it is the good, the universal, freedom itself. Ethical life is the consummate objectification and existence of freedom toward which the *Philosophy of Right* has been developing. As Hegel puts it in the concluding sentence of §142: "Ethical life is accordingly the *concept of freedom which has developed into the existing world and the nature [Natur] of self-consciousness.*"

As indicated above, Hegel's emphasis on the rational and universal content of ethical life is generally overlooked in "communitarian" interpretations of this concept. Such communitarian interpretations tend to reduce Hegel's doctrine of ethical life to a doctrine about the importance of community in general in constituting our identities. The sort of community being talked about is left largely unspecified. This is true of Taylor's account of ethical life, still the most intelligent and nuanced of the communitarian accounts. For Taylor, Hegel's concept of ethical life is important because it grasps the dependence of our individual identities on the language and interpretive framework embedded in the larger community. "What we are as human beings," he writes, "we are only in a cultural community."[34] While this may be true, it is not what Hegel's doctrine of ethical life is primarily about. For Hegel, ethical life is important because it is the realization of our rational essence, freedom. It is not a sociological idea about the constitution of our identities but, rather, a philosophical idea about human self-realization. Nor does ethical life refer to just any community but specifically to that community which objectively realizes the rational freedom of human beings.[35]

That ethical life does not refer to just any community but only to that community which has a rational or universal content, which has freedom for its content, Hegel makes clear as he takes up the objective side of ethical life in greater detail. The substance of ethical life, he reiterates, is the good; not, of course, the abstract good of morality but the good made concrete in "laws and institutions which have being in and for themselves." These laws and institutions are determined by the concept of freedom and together they compose a rational system. "In this way," Hegel writes, "the ethical sphere is freedom, or the will which has being in and for itself as objectivity, as a circle of necessity whose moments are the *ethical powers* which govern the lives of individuals"

(*PR*, §§144–45). The "circle of necessity" that Hegel refers to here, the rational system of the objective determinations of freedom, is essentially what is developed over the course of Part Three of the *Philosophy of Right* (see *PR*, §148R). It is an articulated system that incorporates the individual rights of personality and subjectivity—for these represent, as we have seen, important determinations of the concept of freedom—but in such a way that their abstract one-sidedness is removed.

It is in the context of what he says about the objective or rational content of ethical life that Hegel's rather strong claims about the priority of ethical life to the individual have to be seen; otherwise they will seem very sinister indeed. As he did in the *Phenomenology*, Hegel claims that the laws and institutions of ethical life simply "are" in relation to individual self-consciousness, and he quotes Sophocles' *Antigone* to underline their unquestionable authority: "no one knows where the laws come from: they are eternal" (*PR*, §§144A, 146).[36] Hegel's gloss on this Sophoclean sentence is important, for once again it draws our attention to the rational content of ethical life. Antigone's words, he says, can basically be understood to mean that the determination of the laws "has being in and for itself and issues from the nature of the thing" (*PR*, §144A). In the *Philosophy of History*, he interprets the sentence in this way: "the laws of ethics are not accidental, but are the rational itself" (*IPH*, 41/56). In the face of this rationality of the laws and institutions of ethical life, the life of the individual qua individual pales in significance. It is at this point that Hegel refers in the strongest possible terms to the "accidental" character of individuals in relation to the universality and substantiality of ethical life: "Since the determinations of ethics constitute the concept of freedom, they are the substantiality or universal essence of individuals who are related to them merely as accidents. Whether the individual exists or not is a matter of indifference to objective ethical life, which alone has permanence and is the power by which the lives of individuals are governed" (*PR*, §145A).[37]

But, as he did in the *Encyclopedia Philosophy of Spirit*, Hegel points out that, insofar as the individual comes to know his universal essence in the laws and powers of ethical life, he ceases to be a mere accident of it. While from the objective point of view, the laws and powers of ethical life simply "are," possessing absolute authority over the individual, from the subjective point of view, "they are not something *alien* to the subject. On the contrary, the subject bears *spiritual witness* to them as to *its own essence*, in which it has its *self-awareness* and lives as in its element which is not distinct from itself" (*PR*, §147). In ethical life, we are not dealing with sheer substantiality but with substantiality "endowed with consciousness" (*PR*, §144A), with "self-conscious substantiality" (*PR*, §355R). The universality or substantiality of ethical life must, according to Hegel, be recognized, known, and willed by the individual subject. For this reason, he does not think that Oriental societies possessed a genuine ethical life. While such societies certainly contained substantial freedom, they had not yet attained to subjective freedom. "Where there is merely substantial freedom," Hegel writes, "commandments and laws are regarded as firmly established in and for themselves, and the individual subject adopts an attitude of complete subservience towards them. Besides, these laws need not accord with the will of the individual, and the subjects are therefore like children, who obey their parents without will or insight of their own" (*LPHI*, 197/243–44). This clearly is not how Hegel sees the relationship of the individual to ethical life in the *Philosophy of Right*. Here the individual subject does not relate to the laws and institutions of ethical life as a child does to the commands of its parents but, rather, as a self-conscious adult who recognizes the rationality of those laws and institutions. "[T]he ethical character," Hegel writes, "knows that the end which moves it is the universal which, though itself unmoved, has developed through its determinations into actual rationality, and it recognizes that its own dignity and the whole continued existence of its particular ends are based upon and actualized within this universal" (*PR*, §152).

After arguing, in §147, that the subject has its own self-awareness in ethical life and lives in it "as in its element which is not distinct from itself," Hegel adds that the relationship is one "which is immediate and closer to identity than even [a relationship of] *faith* or *trust*" (*PR*, §147). He goes on to explain in the Remark to this paragraph that, since faith and trust already involve an element of reflection and of differentiation between subject and object, they do not quite describe the "relationless identity" that characterizes the relationship of the individual subject to ethical life. An even less adequate apprehension of this relationship occurs when reflection explicitly tries to ground it on reasons or particular interests. The only "*adequate cognition* of this [relationless] identity," Hegel maintains, "belongs to the thinking concept" (*PR*, §147R).

Ludwig Siep has commented extensively on this passage and tried to show that it describes the four stages—from unreflective self-awareness to adequate cognition—through which the relationship between individual and ethical life must pass.[38] Siep's larger concern is to refute the view that Hegelian ethical life rests exclusively on unreflective habit and excludes the possibility of critical reflection on its laws and institutions—the view so clearly expressed by Tugendhat in the passage quoted at the beginning of this section.[39] While I am sympathetic to Siep's general effort to refute Tugendhat's rather crude inter-pretation of Hegel as an ultraconservative and even totalitarian thinker, I do not think his particular interpretation of the passage above can be sustained. The passage does not establish a hierarchy of ethical attitudes so much as it points to the inadequacy of the reflective understanding to grasp the "relationless iden-tity" that for Hegel authentically characterizes the relationship of the individual to ethical life. Nor do I think Siep has quite grasped Hegel's position on the role of subjective reflection in ethical life, exaggerating it to some extent and under-estimating the degree to which Hegel identifies the ethical with an unreflective attitude. To bear this out, however, we must look at what Hegel has to say about the "ethical disposition" (*sittliche Gesinnung*) in §§150–51 of the *Philosophy of Right*.

In §150, Hegel tells us that in a fully developed ethical life individual virtue takes the form of "rectitude" (*Rechtschaffenheit*), which involves "nothing more than the simple adequacy of the individual to the duties of the circumstances to which he belongs." There is nothing spectacular or heroic about rectitude; it simply involves abiding by the laws of the land and fulfilling the duties of one's station. In a properly constituted ethical life, Hegel argues, it is not difficult to know what we have to do to be virtuous; it does not require great feats of self-reflection. Indeed, as he puts it in his Heidelberg lectures of 1817–18, "an ethical disposition on the part of the subject involves setting aside reflection"; it involves a certain "self-forgetfulness." This, he says, is what "constituted the character of Roman and Greek virtue, namely, that they all did straight away what was their duty, without moral hesitation and without the presumption of knowing better—the simple consciousness that the laws exist" (*LNR*, §70 and R).[40] He makes roughly the same point in the *Philosophy of Right:* "In an ethical community, it is easy to say *what* someone must do and *what* the duties are which he has to fulfill in order to be virtuous. He must simply do what is prescribed, expressly stated, and known to him within his situation" (*PR*, §150R).

There is certainly an element of polemic in Hegel's remarks on the uncom-plicated and unreflective character of the moral life in a fully developed (i.e., modern) ethical community. He realizes that he is attacking one of the sacred cows of the modern moral consciousness, which prides itself precisely on the difficulty and strenuousness of the moral life and on the exceptional character of moral virtue. "From the point of view of morality [*Moralität*]," he writes, "rectitude can easily appear as something of a lower order, beyond which one must impose further demands on oneself and others. For the craving to be something *special* is not satisfied with the universal, with what has being in and for itself; only in the *exceptional* does it attain a consciousness of its distinctiveness" (*PR,* §150R). His undisguised contempt for this posturing of the moral consciousness and its craving to be something special above and beyond the more ordinary demands of morality is one of the most consistent features of Hegel's ethical outlook, beginning with his critique in the *Phenomenology* of the "knight of virtue" who sets himself against the "way of the world" (see *PS,* 230–35/285–91).[41] More often than not, he argues, such moral posturing represents a sophisticated attempt to wriggle out of one's duties, "which are not hard to know." Hegel makes this point in a passage from the *Philosophy of History* that also nicely sums up his attitude on the superiority of simple rectitude to the refinements and subtleties of heightened moral conscience:

> But as for the question of just what is good or not good, right or not right—in the ordinary situations of private life, that question is answered by the laws and customs of a state. There is no great difficulty in knowing what these are. Every individual has his station in life, and he knows, on the whole, what the right and honorable course of action is. To declare, in ordinary private relations, that it is so difficult to choose what is right and good; to see a superior morality in finding difficulties and raising scruples—all this rather indicates an evil and perverse will. This is a will that seeks to evade its duties, which are not hard to know; or at best we may ascribe this to an idleness of thought, a small-minded will that gives itself not much to do, and thus falls into self-indulgence and moral smugness. (*IPH,* 31–32/44)

Hegel does not see the ethical disposition of rectitude as simply a throwback to the ethical attitude that characterized premodern societies. Indeed, he ultimately sees this disposition as being more appropriate to the fully developed ethical life of modern states than to the undeveloped ethical life of ancient states. "[I]n the states of antiquity," he writes, "ethical life had not yet evolved in into [a] free system of self-sufficient development and objectivity," and therefore virtue in the exceptional sense was required to make good this deficiency (*PR,* §150R). In the same way that he sees Socrates' retreat into his inner conscience as justified in the context of the corruption of Athenian democracy, Hegel sees the appeal to heroic virtue beyond mere law-abidingness as justified in the context of the imperfect ethical life of the ancient world. In the "ethical order whose relations are fully developed and actualized," on the other hand, virtue in the heroic or exceptional sense "has its place and actuality only in extraordinary circumstances, or where the [determinate ethical] relations come into collision" (*PR,* §150R). It is not clear what Hegel is referring to in the latter part of this sentence, since he generally claims that his fully developed philosophy of the state is characterized by the absence of collisions of duty (see, e.g., *PR*, §30R). What is clear, however, from the rest of what he says is that there is no tension between the unreflective ethical disposition of rectitude and modern ethical conditions; indeed, it is only under such conditions that this simple and unquestioning attitude is completely justified.

In §151, Hegel goes even further in identifying ethical life with an unreflective ethical disposition, arguing that the universal ethical substance appears, in relation to the individual subject, as "custom" (*Sitte*), "habit" (*Gewohnheit*), a "second nature." Here Hegel returns to one of the oldest themes of his moral philosophy—again, linked with his critique of Kantian ethics—namely, the overcoming of the opposition between duty and inclination. In ethical life, the universal does not appear as something external or alien to the will of the individual; it does not supervene upon his brute desires in the form of imperious duty. Rather, it "appears as a *second nature* which takes the place of the original and purely natural will and is the all-pervading soul, significance, and actuality of individual existence" (*PR*, §151).[42] In ethical life, the particular will of the individual is in conformity with the universal in a way it was not in either abstract right or morality. The word that for Hegel sums up this unity of the particular will with the universal will in ethical life is "spirit." Ethical life in the form of custom and habit, he writes, "is *spirit* living and present as a world, and only thus does the substance of spirit begin to exist as spirit" (*PR*, §151). "Custom," he continues in the Addition, "is what right and morality have not reached, namely spirit" (*PR*, §151A). In abstract right, as we have already seen, the particular will remains an immediate or natural will only contingently related to the universal. And in morality, subjectivity is still divorced from the universal that has being in itself. It is only at the level of ethics, again, that the particular will of the individual is brought together with the universal in a truly "spiritual" unity.

The means by which the universal ethical substance becomes customary or habitual for the individual, a second nature, is education. "Education [*Pädagogik*]," Hegel writes, "is the art of making human beings ethical: it considers them as natural beings and shows them how they can be reborn, and how their original nature can be transformed into a second, spiritual nature so that this spirituality becomes *habitual* to them" (*PR*, §151A). Hegel says much more about the subject of ethical education later in the *Philosophy of Right*, especially in connection with civil society. Here it is necessary to point out only that he does not see such education as taking place individualistically, in isolation from the ethical order. He is quite critical of Rousseau's educational procedure in the *Emile* for this reason (*PR*, §153A). Ethical education, the replacement of the merely natural will of individuals with a second, spiritual nature, is a function of living in a properly constituted ethical order, of being "suckled at the breast of a universal ethical life," as Hegel put it back in the *Natural Law* essay (*NL*, 115/507). In this regard, Hegel repeats (again as he did in *Natural Law*) the advice a Pythagorean gave to a father who asked about the best way of educating his son in ethical matters: " 'Make him a *citizen of a state with good laws*' " (*PR*, §153R).

From the preceding passages, it would seem difficult to deny that Hegel identifies ethical life in an important way with an unreflective and habitual ethical disposition on the part of the individual. And yet some have tried to downplay this element of custom and habit in the ethical disposition. Allen Wood, for example, attributes what Hegel says about custom and habit in §151 to a primitive form of ethical life. When Hegel says, for example, that it is only insofar as ethical life exists as habit or custom that "the substance of spirit begins to exist as spirit," Wood contends that "this implies that spirit *also* exists in other, later, more developed forms."[43] But there is little evidence in §151 to suggest that Hegel means this passage to be understood in this developmental way. He admits that "human beings may even die as a result of habit—that is, if they have become totally habituated to life and mentally and physically blunted" (*PR*, §151A), but this clearly refers to an extreme case. And when we look beyond §151, the interpretation becomes no more persuasive. When Hegel speaks later in the *Philosophy of Right* of the political disposition of patriotism, for example, he again emphasizes its unreflective and habitual character. "This disposition," he writes, "is in general one of *trust* (which may pass over into more or less educated insight) (*PR*, §268).[44] And in the *Philosophy of History*, he states emphatically that the

> ethical life of the state is not of the moral or reflective kind, wherein one's individual conviction rules supreme. This latter is more accessible to the modern world, whereas the true ethics of antiquity is rooted in the principle of abiding by one's duty. An Athenian citizen did what was required of him as if by instinct. But if I reflect upon the object of my activity, I must have the consciousness that my will has been called upon. Ethical life, however, is duty, the substantial right, a second nature (as it has been justly called); for man's first nature is his immediate animal being. (*IPH*, 42/57)

Though the predominant emphasis in the passage above is on the unreflective character of ethical life, Hegel does add that "if I reflect upon the object of my activity, I must have the consciousness that my will has been called upon." This proviso is important. By identifying the ethical disposition with trust, habit, and custom, Hegel does not mean to deny the subjective aspect he attributed to ethical life earlier. That ethical life is a second nature does not mean that the individual relates to its laws as a child does to the commands of its parents, "without will or insight of its own." There must be some recognition or awareness on the part of the individual that these laws are in accordance with the individual's will. But Hegel does not seem to think that such recognition or awareness is incompatible with trust or habit. Thus, when he asserts that the political disposition of patriotism is "in general one of *trust*," he goes on to add, "or the consciousness that my substantial and particular interest is preserved and contained in the interest and end" of the state (*PR*, §268). And further on, he writes that the disposition of patriotism is one "which, in the normal conditions and circumstances of life, *habitually* knows that the community is the substantial basis and end" (*PR*, §268R; my emphasis). These passages suggest that Hegel does not see trust or habit as incompatible with the subjective self-consciousness or self-awareness that he regards as an essential aspect of ethical life.

But there is another difficulty that the passage from the *Philosophy of History* above seems to disclose. Hegel's appeal to the "true ethics of antiquity" in this passage—and, indeed his whole emphasis, both here and in the *Philosophy of Right,* on the unreflective character of ethical life, even in its fully developed or modern form—seems hard to reconcile with his criticisms of the naive and unreflective harmony of Greek ethical life elsewhere in his work. In the *Philosophy of History,* for example, Hegel characterizes Greek ethical life as a "merely unreflecting existence," in which subjective freedom remains undeveloped and the individual "intuitively adopts the customs and habits laid down by justice and the laws." Such a "beautiful" ethical life is "truly harmonious," but it is also "inherently unstable" and destined to fall apart "under the influence of reflection." For this reason, Hegel claims—once again indicating the normative function of the concept of ethical life—that "the aesthetic existence of Greece cannot be equated with true ethical life" (*LPHI*, 202–3/249–50).[45] The question is, How is the unreflective and customary ethical life described in the *Philosophy of Right* any different from the beautiful but inherently unstable ethical life of the Greeks?

The answer lies, once again, in the fact that modern or fully developed ethical life—"true ethical life"—incorporates subjective freedom to an extent that Greek ethical life did not. The defect of Greek ethical life, Hegel writes, is

that it "has not been reborn from the struggle through which subjective freedom is itself reborn, but remains at the earliest stage of subjective freedom; as
such, it still bears the mark of natural ethicality instead of being born anew to
the higher and purer form of universal ethical life" (*LPHI*, 203/250). But this is
not the case with modern or true ethical life. Modern ethical life has, in fact,
been reborn from the historic struggle through which subjective freedom has
developed itself. Modern ethical life precisely does incorporate the rights of
personality and moral subjectivity that are the fruit of this historic struggle. But
none of this implies that the attitude of the individual subject toward the
modern ethical order need be particularly reflective. In general, Hegel maintains, the individual "trusts" or "habitually knows" that his "substantial and
particular interest is preserved and contained in the interest and end" of the
state (*PR*, §268). The elaborate system of rights and duties which constitutes
modern ethical life and preserves our substantial and particular interests has
become a second nature for us; it is the atmosphere we breathe and the structure
upon which we unconsciously depend. Our awareness of the rationality of this
order can, of course, become more explicit through reflection; trust "may pass
over into more or less educated insight" (*PR*, §268). But such a reflective
relationship to modern ethical life is not necessary, nor does Hegel seem to
think it is typical.

In §156, Hegel concludes his discussion of the general concept of ethical life
by connecting it (as we have already seen him do in the *Encyclopedia Philosophy
of Spirit*) to the spirit of a people and the spirit of a family, as well as to the
concept of spirit in general. This important paragraph is a fitting conclusion to
our own discussion because, in it, Hegel clearly contrasts his approach to ethical
life to individualistic or atomistic approaches. "[T]here are always only two
possible viewpoints in the ethical realm," he writes: "either one starts from
substantiality, or one proceeds atomistically and moves upward from the basis
of individuality. This latter viewpoint excludes spirit, because it leads only to an
aggregation, whereas spirit is not something individual but the unity of the
individual and the universal" (*PR*, §156A). The spirit that constitutes the unity
of a family or a people cannot be understood as the mere sum of individual
wills, what Rousseau referred to as "the will of all." Rather, it must be understood as the substance or universal essence of individuals to which their individuality or particularity remains subordinate. Hegel repeats here what he said
earlier about the merely "accidental" character of individuals with respect to
ethical substance: "The spirit [of a family or a people] has actuality, and the
individuals are its accidents" (*PR*, §156A). But it is also important to remember

that, insofar as individuals know this substance as their own essence, they cease to be mere accidents of it. The spirit of a family or a people is the unity of subjectivity and objectivity.

Hegel's brief discussion of the family and the state in terms of the concept of ethical life and the concept of spirit constitutes a clear rejection of the liberal, contractual model of family and state relations. Hegel has already alluded to the inappropriateness of the model of contract to marriage and the state in his discussion of contract in abstract right (*PR*, §75R and A). In the lectures of 1817–18, he makes this rejection of the contractual model even more explicit: "In opposition to [the] relationship of a merely civil contract in the family, and in opposition to the state based on need, the contrary view has been advanced that it is universal spirit, the unity of spirit, that must constitute the [ethical] substance, not spirit as individual volition" (*LNR*, §70R). Hegel develops his alternative to the liberal, contractual understanding of family and political life in his specific discussions of these ethical spheres in the rest of the *Philosophy of Right*. It is to these specific discussions that we now turn.

Chapter 7 The Ethical Preconditions of the Rational State: Family and Civil Society

We have arrived at the standpoint of ethical life, which is distinguished from the earlier standpoints of abstract right and morality by virtue of its concreteness. Both formal right and morality have been shown to be abstract, unable to stand on their own as independent realities. Each embodies an important aspect of human freedom, but neither can stand alone because it lacks what the other possesses. Abstract right is all objectivity and universality, whereas morality is all subjectivity and particularity. A concrete standpoint is to be achieved only by uniting these two abstract points of view into a single whole. This is what is accomplished in the various forms of ethical life—the family, civil society, and the state. Each is a concrete or "spiritual" unity of objectivity and subjectivity, universality and particularity; and each, to that extent, is capable of actual existence, in contrast to either abstract right or morality. In ethical life, we no longer have to do with pure abstractions but with concrete forms of social life.

Ethical life develops from the family, through civil society, to the state. This development mirrors the movement of the logical concept from immediacy to differentiation or reflectedness to a synthesis of these two moments, identity that contains difference. Less abstractly, the family represents ethical life in its simplest form. The ethical unity of the family is an immediate one, based on the natural feeling of love. The members of a family do not relate to one another as self-sufficient personalities but as parts of a larger whole with which they immediately identify themselves. The family, however, at least in the modern world, exists in a larger context in which individuals are not bound together by the natural sentiment of love and in which they do relate to one another as self-sufficient personalities. This is civil society, the sphere largely of market or economic relationship. Here all the individuality and self-interest that remains submerged in the family is liberated. But though individuals are driven mainly by self-interest in civil society, they are also implicitly governed by the universal and invisibly led to serve one another's interests through the complex mechanism of the market. The universality that is implicit in civil society, operating as an unconscious necessity there, becomes the explicit aim or goal of individuals in the state. Here the individual once again becomes conscious of his unity with others, but no longer on the plane of immediate feeling, as in the family, but on the plane of law and reason.

In this chapter, I focus on only the first two moments in the development of ethical life—namely, the family and civil society—leaving till the next chapter Hegel's treatment of the state. These two moments do not, of course, exist simply as rungs on the ladder of ethical life, to be cast away once we've reached the goal of the state. They themselves constitute crucial elements of the modern rational state, which is distinguished precisely by the fact that it allows these subordinate moments to develop themselves freely and achieve a certain amount of independence from the state. In this regard, Hegel frequently contrasts the modern rational state with the purely substantial states of antiquity, in particular Plato's *Republic,* which seek to exclude or suppress the individuality and subjective freedom that are embodied in the family and civil society (see *PR,* §185R; *HP,* II, 109–15/124–30). But it is not simply because they embody the principle of subjective freedom that Hegel finds the family and civil society important in relation to the state. He also sees them as playing a crucial educative function, ensuring that individuals are not simply or narrowly self-interested in their relation to the state but already ethical in themselves and purged of their raw particularity. In this regard, Hegel refers to the family and the institutions of civil society as the "ethical roots" of the state (*PR,* §§201A, 255), anticipating the emphasis that would later be placed on these mediating institutions by Tocqueville as well as present-day proponents of "civil society."

Though Hegel's accounts of the family and civil society are insightful and profound, they are not without their difficulties. In the course of this chapter, I take up some of the most commonly remarked of these difficulties, having to do with Hegel's patriarchal conception of the nature and role of women, his doctrine of the social differentiation of the estates, and his treatment of the problem of poverty. Though in each of these cases, Hegel's ideas are either seriously outdated or in need of modification—in this he is no different from almost every other past thinker—none, I argue, is fatal to his political philosophy as a whole. On balance, there is far more to learn from Hegel's accounts of the family and civil society than there is to criticize.

THE FAMILY

The family in some ways represents the clearest example of what Hegel means by ethical life or ethical spirit. It is a substantial whole or universal that does not stand over against the individual but within which the individual has his or her own essential self-consciousness. The members of a family do not relate to one another as independent persons or isolated contractors but precisely as members of a larger whole within which they find their essential identity. Hegel emphasizes this nonindividualistic or substantial dimension of the family from the outset of his discussion. In the family, he writes, one has "self-consciousness of one's individuality *within this unity* as essentiality which has being in and for itself, so that one is present in it not as an independent person but as a *member*" (*PR*, §158).

Nor does such submersion of individual personality in the family constitute a regression from the individualistic standpoints of abstract right and morality, according to Hegel. It is true that in historical actuality the institution of the family preceded the institution of property and the awareness of subjective or moral freedom. But in terms of the conceptual sequence of the *Philosophy of Right*, the family represents a higher stage of development and a more concrete embodiment of freedom than either abstract right or morality (see *PR*, §32R and A). In the family, the particular will of the individual is no longer merely contingently related to the universal in the form of either abstract right or the good; rather, it wills the universal as such. In the family, we no longer have to do with the arbitrary will of the individual but with a genuinely universal will. Hegel brings out the superiority of the standpoint of the family to that of especially abstract right clearly in his Heidelberg lectures of 1817–18:

> That the free will of the person occurs as an individual will is a subordinate standpoint. The rights that are founded on the family are different from the rights we dealt

with in the case of property; their foundation is quite distinct and of another kind. Here we are dealing with substantive freedom and the foundation is a universal will, whereas the will on which property rests is of a kind remote from substantive freedom. Personality, which is at the basis of ownership or property, is here rather dissolved. The family is here founded on an identity of will. This is the truth of the will, namely that according to its concept it is a universal will. The disposition [*Gesinnung*] is here an essential moment, the moral moment, in which, however, the good itself constitutes the actual identity. (*LNR,* §73R)

But, though the family represents the substantiality of ethical spirit and embodies substantive freedom, it does so in only an immediate or natural way, in the form of "feeling" (*Empfindung*) and, more specifically, love. "The family, as the *immediate substantiality* of spirit, has as its determination the spirit's *feeling* of its own unity, which is *love*" (*PR,* §158). Love, of course, has a special significance in Hegel's philosophy. In his early writings, it was the term he used to oppose the dualism of duty and inclination in Kant's moral philosophy. And in his discussion of the concept of freedom in the Introduction to the *Philosophy of Right,* he points to love as the most immediate example of that "being with oneself in the other" that constitutes concrete freedom (*PR,* §7A). Hegel now elaborates on this latter significance of love in connection with the family, emphasizing once again the overcoming of independent personality: "Love means in general the consciousness of my unity with another, so that I am not isolated on my own, but gain my self-consciousness only through the renunciation of my independent existence and through knowing myself as the unity of myself with another and of the other with me." In love, there takes place a mutual recognition between individuals of a far more profound character than that found at the level of abstract personality or contract: in love, "I find myself in another person . . . I gain recognition in this person, who in turn gains recognition in me" (*PR,* §158A).

Again, however, the identity of self and other in the family is merely immediate, natural, based on feeling. For this reason, Hegel sharply distinguishes it from the identity or unity found in the state, which is based on reason and law. Hegel's view of the relationship between the family and the state here is rather complex. On the one hand, he sees the family and the state as importantly similar in that they are both substantial wholes or spirits in which the individual is subordinated to the universal. Neither of these substantial spirits can be understood in terms of the individualistic model of a contract. This isomorphism of the family and the state is brought out particularly well in the *Philosophy of History:* "The spirit of the family (e.g., in the Roman Penates) is as much *one* substantial entity as the spirit of a people in their state. In both, ethical life consists in the feeling, consciousness, and the will—not of the individual personality and its interests, but of the common personality and interests of all the members in general" (*IPH,* 45/60).[1] On the other hand, Hegel is concerned to distinguish the affective and merely natural solidarity of the family from the more rational and impersonal unity of the state. Thus he writes in the *Philosophy of Right:* "[L]ove is a feeling, that is, ethical life in its natural form. In the state, it is no longer present. There one is conscious of unity as law; there, the content must be rational, and I must know it" (*PR,* §158A). What exactly Hegel means here when he says that the state is based on reason and law instead of on feeling—especially given what we have already seen him say about the patriotic disposition of trust—will occupy us in the following chapter when we consider the state. For now, it is enough to observe that the communal warmth of the family, like the cold individualism of contract, ultimately proves to be an inadequate model for understanding the state.

That Hegel sees the state as resting on very different principles from the family does not mean, however, that he regards the family as irrelevant to the state. To the contrary, he sees the family as playing a crucial role in transforming individuals into something more than self-interested persons and thus in laying the ethical foundations of the state. In one place, he refers to the family as the "primary basis of the state" (*PR,* §201A); in another, as the "first *ethical* root of the state" (*PR,* §255); and in yet another, he tells us that the family is one of the institutions that provides "the firm foundation of the state and of the trust and disposition of individuals towards it" (*PR,* §265). Perhaps the clearest expression of Hegel's view of the important political role played by the family comes in the *Philosophy of History.* There he writes that the "piety of family-feeling has to be respected to the highest degree by the state. As a result of this family-feeling, the state has, as its members, individuals who are already ethical in themselves (which they would not be as self-interested persons); and as its members they bring to the state its solid foundation, because each one feels himself to be united with the totality" (*IPH,* 45/60). Hegel's view of the political function of the family here in many respects resembles that of Rousseau, who, in the *Emile,* criticizes Plato's proposal in the *Republic* to abolish the private family—"as though there were no need for a natural basis on which to form conventional ties; as though the love of one's nearest were not the principle of the love one owes the state; as though it were not by means of the small fatherland which is the family that the heart attaches itself to the large one; as though it were not the good son, the good husband, and the good father who make the good citizen."[2]

The value of the family for Hegel, however, does not consist solely in its political function. Family life on its own constitutes an important aspect of human happiness or subjective satisfaction. "According to the concept of subjective freedom," Hegel writes, "the family is just as necessary, yea, sacred to the individual as is property." In this regard, he, like Rousseau, sharply criticizes Plato's proposal in the *Republic* to abolish the private family. Such an arrangement—which Hegel fails to notice applies only to the guardian class—destroys a fundamental sphere of individual liberty and reflects the general hostility to individuality and subjective freedom that pervades Plato's entire political philosophy (*HP*, II, 111–13/126–29).[3] In Plato's purely substantial state, everything—all privacy, particularity, and individuality—is subordinated to and ultimately excluded by the universal. This is the criticism Hegel makes of Plato throughout the third part of the *Philosophy of Right*, not only with respect to the family but also, as we shall see, with respect to civil society. In contradistinction to the purely substantial character of the Platonic state, the Hegelian state will incorporate subjective freedom in the form of the private family and individual economic activity, while at the same time superseding it.

With these general considerations in mind, we may now turn to Hegel's specific analysis of the three essential aspects of family life, namely, marriage, family property, and the upbringing of children leading to the dissolution of the family. It is, of course, what Hegel has to say on the first of these heads, namely, marriage, that continues to provoke the most interest and discussion among contemporary scholars. This is partly due to Hegel's now controversial views on the respective roles of men and women, of which most contemporary scholars feel compelled to express their disapproval. But it is also due, I think, to the attractiveness of the alternative Hegel presents to the contemporary understanding of marriage, which seems to be informed by a good deal of the individualism, subjectivism, and shallow romanticism that he decries. While I do say something about the first of these issues, namely, the respective roles Hegel assigns to men and women—it is to the latter, more positive aspects of Hegel's teaching on marriage that I wish to address myself first.

Hegel states clearly the key to his entire understanding of marriage when he says that "marriage is essentially an ethical relationship" (*PR*, §161A). By this he means that marriage is a substantive unity, a unity in which the individuality of the partners is subordinated to the whole, and this substantive unity is the self-conscious goal of the partners. "The *ethical* aspect of marriage consists in the consciousness of this union as a substantial end, and hence in love, trust, and the sharing of the whole of individual existence" (*PR,* §163). Hegel's emphasis on consciousness here is important. Consciousness or self-consciousness is what distinguishes the ethical relationship of marriage from the merely natural relationship of animal generation. To be sure, marriage contains the moment of "natural vitality" in which the perpetuation of the species constitutes the universal end. But species-preservation is a merely external universal, devoid of self-consciousness. In marriage, the substantive unity of the partners becomes their self-conscious goal. "[I]n self-consciousness," Hegel writes, "the *union of the natural sexes, which was merely inward* (or had being only *in itself*) and whose existence was for this very reason merely external, is transformed into a *spiritual* union, into self-conscious love" (*PR,* §161).[4]

Hegel distinguishes his understanding of marriage as an ethical relationship from three other common (mis)understandings: the naturalistic, the contractual, and what might be called the romantic. The first of these understandings Hegel identifies with the tradition of natural law, in which marriage "was considered only in its physical aspect or natural character. It was accordingly regarded only as a sexual relationship, and its other determinations remained inaccessible" (*PR,* §161A). Hegel doesn't elaborate on this naturalistic interpretation of marriage, but at least two versions of it may be distinguished. The first version involves the claim that the chief end of marriage is the procreation of children and the reproduction of the species. We have already considered Hegel's reasons for rejecting this understanding of marriage above. There is little to add except that he consistently rejects the idea that the procreation of children constitutes the chief end of marriage; it is only amongst animals that "perpetuation of the species is the highest end" (*LNR,* §78R; also §80R). The second version of the naturalistic interpretation of marriage involves the claim that marriage exists primarily for the satisfaction of the natural sexual drive. Hegel dismisses this view, because it makes marriage indistinguishable from concubinage: "Marriage differs from *concubinage* inasmuch as the latter is chiefly concerned with the satisfaction of the natural drive, whereas this drive is made subordinate in marriage" (*PR,* §163A).

The second misunderstanding of marriage Hegel considers interprets marriage as a contractual relationship. We have already seen on several occasions that Hegel rejects this individualistic understanding of marriage, which he associates with Kant. In a contract, the parties relate to one another as self-sufficient persons. They form a common will with respect to a specific object, but they never lose their independence with respect to one another. They do not form a genuine whole or a complete unity; their independent personalities do not coalesce to form a single person. But this is exactly what is involved in marriage as an ethical relationship for Hegel. In marriage, as we have seen, the parties give up their independent personalities in order to form a genuinely universal will, a genuinely substantive identity. Hegel grants that marriage, like contract, originates in the arbitrary will of the individual person, but this does not constitute its essential basis. "For the precise nature of marriage is to begin from the point of view of contract—i.e. that of individual personality as a self-sufficient unit—*in order to supersede it.* That identification of personalities whereby the family is a *single person* and its members are its accidents . . . is the ethical spirit" (*PR,* §163R).

The third misunderstanding of marriage Hegel treats is the romantic one which "simply equates marriage with love" (*PR,* §161A). This, of course, was the understanding of marriage that had become prominent in Romantic thought toward the end of the eighteenth century, and it is an understanding of marriage that continues to have a certain vitality even in our own time. Hegel, however, like Kierkegaard after him, finds romantic love to be far too insecure a basis for marriage.[5] Love as a passion is subjective, transient, and utterly contingent; it is therefore totally at odds with the ethical or substantial character of marriage. In contradistinction to the subjectivity and contingency of romantic love, Hegel coins the phrase "rightful ethical love" (*rechtlich sittliche Liebe*) to characterize the disposition appropriate to marriage (*PR,* §161A). In this context, he also defends the public marriage ceremony "whereby the essence of [the marital] bond is expressed and *confirmed* as an ethical quality exalted above the *contingency* of feeling and *particular inclination*" against such Romantic thinkers as Friedrich von Schlegel who dismiss the marriage ceremony as an empty formality or, worse, an inauthentic ritual (*PR,* §164R and A).

It might seem that Hegel's ethical conception of marriage completely obliterates the principle of subjective freedom that he earlier said marked the decisive difference between the modern age and antiquity, but this is not the case. He insists that marriage must rest on the free consent of the individuals involved (*PR,* §162). And though he remarks that, between the scenario in which well-intentioned parents take the first step in arranging a marriage, with the mutual inclination of the marriage partners following, and the scenario in which mutual inclination comes first and the decision to marry second, the former is the "more ethical course" (*PR,* §162R), he nowhere denies that inclination in some form must be present or implies that parents can arrange the marriage without the consent of the parties. In the Addition to §162, for example, Hegel seems to associate arranged marriages with undeveloped peoples: "Among those peoples who hold the female sex in little respect, the parents arrange the marriages arbitrarily, without consulting the individuals concerned; the latter accept this arrangement, since the particularity of feeling makes no claims for itself as yet." And in his Heidelberg lectures, he makes the point against coercion and in favor of particular inclination even more forcefully: "Disposition [*Gesinnung*] is an essential feature of marriage, which rests on the voluntary consent of both parties, so that, even if the parents are opposed, the laws recognize the will of the parties as sufficient. The opposition of the parents cannot be an absolute obstacle. The more cultivated a people is, the wider the sphere assigned to the purely private disposition" (*LNR*, §80R).[6] Hegel does not dismiss particular inclination or disposition as unimportant in marriage; he only denies that it is the "only important factor" (*PR*, §162A).

Because marriage rests to a large extent on subjective disposition and feeling, it is subject to dissolution through divorce. Two people who marry cannot be compelled to stay together in the absence of love and affection. According to its ethical or substantial character, Hegel argues, marriage "ought" to be indissoluble, it is indissoluble "in itself." But because "marriage contains the moment of feeling, it is not absolute but unstable, and it has within it the possibility of dissolution" (*PR*, §163A; see also §176). By granting the right to divorce, Hegel gives the modern right of subjective freedom its due. But he does not believe this right should be exercised arbitrarily or that it gives married couples *carte blanche* to divorce one another whenever the feeling (or lack of it) moves them. Having conceded the possibility of dissolution in marriage, Hegel adds, significantly: "But all legislations must make such dissolution as difficult as possible and uphold the right of ethics against caprice" (*PR*, §163A). One can imagine that Hegel might object to the ease with which divorces are currently obtained in places like the United States and that he might side with those policy-reformers who are seeking to make divorce more difficult, especially in cases where children are involved.[7]

Hegel derives a number of other features of marriage, including that it be monogamous and that it not take place between blood relations. One might feel that Hegel stretches too far here in trying to provide philosophical reasons for otherwise conventional practices, but what he says does shed a certain light on his overall conception of marriage, especially on the relationship between marriage and free personality. Take his defense of monogamy. Marriage is essentially monogamous, Hegel argues, because it is entered into by two self-sufficient persons who then surrender their personalities in a "mutual and undivided" way (*PR*, §167). If the surrender is not mutual and undivided, the rights of one of the parties are necessarily infringed. Hegel seems to be particularly concerned about the rights of the woman. He writes in the lectures of 1817–18: "If the husband has several wives, the wife does not attain to her rights, and the marriage does not become a genuinely ethical relationship" (*LNR*, §80R). And in the lectures of 1818–19, he makes the point even more forcefully: "The woman must come into her right just as much as the man. Where [there is] polygamy, [there is] slavery of women" (*VPR* 1:301).

That marriage presupposes free personality, while at the same time transcending it, comes out in Hegel's justification of the ban on consanguineous marriages as well. Because "marriage arises out of the *free surrender* by both sexes of their personalities," he writes, "it must not be concluded within the *naturally identical* circle of people who are acquainted and familiar with each other in every detail—a circle in which the individuals do not have a distinct personality of their own in relation to one another" (*PR*, §168). Marriage does not constitute a retreat from free personality to the more primitive standpoint of merely natural existence; rather, it begins with and presupposes free personality only to supersede it. And it is precisely because marriage begins with free and distinct personalities that the unity to which it gives rise is strong and vital. In a sentence that applies as much to the state as it does to the family, Hegel writes: "All strength, all energy rests on the opposition from which unity arises" (*LNR*, §87R).

There is one final feature of Hegel's teaching concerning marriage, the most controversial, that needs to be considered: namely, what he says about the different natures and roles of the two sexes. Like most people in his time—and not a few in our own—Hegel believes there are important natural differences between men and women. For the most part, he expresses these differences in terms of the conventional dichotomies: men are active, whereas women are passive; men are objective, whereas women are subjective; men are identified with thinking, whereas women are identified with feeling; men are characterized by intellect, whereas women are characterized by emotion. Because men and women differ in these ways, they also have their own appropriate spheres. "Man . . . has his actual substantial life in the state, in science, etc., and otherwise in work and struggle with the external world and with himself." Woman, on the other hand, "has her substantial vocation in the family, and her ethical disposition consists in this [family] *piety*" (*PR*, §166).

Though Hegel certainly grants women juridical equality with men and the rights of free personality[8]—"Woman is a free being for herself" (*LNR*,

§77R)—he is emphatic that they restrict themselves to the family and not trespass into the male spheres of civil society, the state, art, and science. "A girl's vocation," he tells us, "consists essentially only in the marital relationship" (*PR,* §164A). Nor are women capable of genuine scientific or artistic activity. "There have been women who have applied themselves to the sciences," Hegel concedes, "but they never penetrated deeply or made any discoveries" (*LNR,* §77R). As he puts it in the *Philosophy of Right:* "Women may well be educated, but they are not made for the higher sciences, for philosophy and certain artistic productions which require a universal element. Women may have insights, taste, and delicacy, but they do not possess the ideal" (*PR,* §166A). Finally, he believes that women should not engage in political activity: "When women are in charge of government," Hegel writes, "the state is in danger, for their actions are based not on the demands of universality but on contingent inclination and opinion" (*PR,* §166A).

Such opinions about the nature and role of women are not likely to find much support today. Not that the question whether there are important natural differences between men and women has been resolved. It hasn't.[9] Nevertheless, there are few today who would subscribe to the way in which Hegel draws the distinction between men and women, with its emphasis on the intellectual inferiority and political incapacity of the latter. In defense of Hegel, it can be pointed out—and often is—that his views of the respective natures and roles of men and women are typical of the popular and even intelligent opinion of his time. There is, for example, more than a faint echo of Rousseau's outlook on the relationship between men and women in Hegel's treatment of this subject.[10] Also, it should be noted that Hegel does not regard women as simply inferior to men. In one passage quoted above, he indicates—again, echoing Rousseau— that women possess a certain emotional and psychological intelligence; they have "insights, taste, and delicacy." And his favorite example of female familial piety is Antigone—no mere wimp when it comes to standing up for the family in opposition to the male, albeit universal, state (see *PR,* §166R; *PS,* 267– 89/328–54).[11]

But such apologetics should not distract us from the deeper issue that lies behind Hegel's discussion of the two sexes. This deeper issue arises not so much from Hegel's belief that there are natural differences between the sexes as from his claim that these differences are somehow rational. "The *natural* determinacy of the two sexes," he writes, "acquires an *intellectual* and *ethical* significance by virtue of its rationality" (*PR,* §165). The natural difference between the two sexes is rational, according to Hegel, because it corresponds to the two fundamental moments of the concept—namely, immediate substantiality and free or thinking universality. Indeed, Hegel formulates the fundamental difference between the two sexes largely in terms of this logical opposition. Thus, he characterizes the male sex as "spirituality which divides itself up into personal self-sufficiency with being *for itself* and the knowledge and volition of *free universality*, i.e. into the self-consciousness of conceptual thought and the volition of the objective and ultimate end." And he characterizes the female sex in terms of "spirituality which maintains itself in unity as knowledge and volition of the substantial in the form of concrete *individuality* and *feeling*" (*PR*, §166).

Hegel contends, then, that the two moments represented by the sexes (and by their respective spheres, the family and the state)—namely, immediate substantiality in the form of feeling and free universality in the form of self-conscious thought, must both be explicitly present in a fully developed ethical life. And the question that initially presses itself upon us is why. It is not enough, of course, to answer that these moments correspond to the logical determinations of the concept. We need something more concrete. In the relevant paragraph from the *Philosophy of Right*, Hegel suggests that the moment of immediate substantiality that corresponds to the family and is represented by woman amounts to something like a psychic need for individuals. One cannot live one's entire life in the competitive world of civil society or in the public realm of the state with its universal demands. One needs a retreat from these strenuous occupations that involve struggle with the world and with oneself, and this retreat is provided by the private realm of the family over which the woman presides. For the man, Hegel writes, "it is only through his division that he fights his way to self-sufficient unity with himself. In the family, he has a peaceful intuition of this unity, and an emotive and subjective ethical life" (*PR*, §166). In the corresponding paragraph from his Heidelberg lectures, he makes a similar point: the man, who "must live in the state and seek to promote universal ends," finds "mental refreshment from his wife within the family so that, reinvigorated, he may rejoin the quest to further the universal" (*LNR*, §77R).

The fundamental issue raised by Hegel's argument for the rational necessity of the differences between the sexes, and specifically of the immediately substantial disposition of women, is this: the Hegelian state seems to demand a class of people who, as a matter of principle, cannot realize their freedom in the fullest possible sense, that is, in civil society or in political activity on behalf of the state. Nor is this issue confined to Hegel's treatment of women. It comes up again, as we shall soon see, in his treatment of the "substantial estate" of peasants and landowners, whose disposition is described as "that of an immediate ethical life based on the family relationship and on trust" (*PR*, §202). Again, Hegel's claim is not simply that there happen to be individuals—women, peasants—who are incapable of freedom in the fullest and most rational sense, but that a fully developed ethical life requires that there be such individuals. And it is this insistence on the rational necessity of an immediately substantial gender and an immediately substantial estate—bound up as it is with Hegel's belief that the social whole be "articulated" or differentiated—which has led a number of commentators to see Hegel's political philosophy as fundamentally incompatible with the liberal project of individual self-actualization and to attribute to him instead a more communitarian and cosmic (not to say controversial) doctrine of communal or collective self-actualization.[12]

Down this latter path we should hesitate to go. The doctrine of communal (as opposed to individual) self-actualization that is being imputed to Hegel is neither attractive on its own nor particularly descriptive of the intentions of his overall political philosophy. Hegel certainly believes that there are degrees of individual self-actualization, but the subject of self-actualization remains the individual and does not migrate to the community or to some cosmic subject. We are still left, however, with his arguments for the rational necessity of an immediately substantial gender and an immediately substantial estate. These arguments no doubt stem from an important concern on Hegel's part with the unsettling effects of modern individualism and its corrosive reflective mentality. But they are also reinforced by certain transitory beliefs and social realities of Hegel's time which have nothing to do with the fundamental categories of his political philosophy. To confine ourselves to his discussion of women, leaving until later his treatment of peasants, Hegel argues that there must be an immediately substantial gender at least partly because he believes there exists such a gender. His argument does not rest primarily on the philosophically controversial notion that women actualize themselves as communal beings in some substantial organic sense; rather, it rests on the now exploded belief that women are inherently limited in their ability to fully and rationally actualize themselves as individuals. Though Hegel is undoubtedly wrong in holding this latter belief, he is no different in this regard from most other philosophers prior to the mid-nineteenth century; and the basis of his political philosophy need not be seen as collapsing simply on the account of this erroneous belief.

But what about Hegel's insistence on the necessary articulation or differentiation of the social whole? Surely this cannot be viewed as an incidental aspect of his political philosophy. Without denying Hegel's point about the necessary articulation or differentiation of the social whole, we might still question whether this differentiation must take place at the level of individuals instead of simply taking place at the level of institutions or ethical spheres. For Hegel, the requirement that there be a private familial sphere differentiated and sheltered from the public spheres of civil society and the state seems to involve the requirement that there be a human type or character—namely, woman—who embodies and is exclusively devoted to this sphere. But does the former require-ment necessarily depend on the latter? We may agree with most of what Hegel says about the necessary role of the family and yet reject that this implies anything about the nature and role of women or men. We might argue that the immediate domestic sphere could be looked after by either the man or the woman, or that the burden (or joy) could be shared by both. Hegel, for his part, though, might respond that such mixing and mingling of roles may lead to their not being well or fully performed and also to a certain confusion among the spheres themselves; for example, the individualism and self-interest charac-teristic of civil society might begin to infiltrate the atmosphere of immediate love and trust that should envelop the family. This raises a legitimate issue, but one which, while stemming from an Hegelian perspective, can no longer be resolved simply in terms of the traditional and outdated conception of women found in Hegel's political philosophy.

Let us briefly turn now to the other two aspects of family life that Hegel discusses—namely, family property and the upbringing of children. With respect to the first, Hegel's argument is pretty straightforward. Because the family constitutes a single person over and above the personalities of its individ-ual members, it gives itself existence in property. This property does not belong to any single member of the family but to all members in common, though the husband or father as head of the household controls and administers it. From this latter circumstance arises the possibility of a "collision" or "conflict" in which the husband fails to fulfill his "ethical duty to preserve and increase the family property," using it instead to satisfy his own private desires. Hegel appears to be quite concerned about this possibility and defends marriage settlements and even state intervention to avert it (*PR*, §§169–72).[13] He is particularly critical of the arbitrariness that reigns in wills and matters of inheritance and exists in clear tension with the substantial and common inter-ests of the family (*PR*, §§178–80).

A more spiritual, less thing-like objectification of the unity of the family— and specifically of the parents—comes into being with the children. Children, according to Hegel, are the genuine existence or objectification of the love between the parents (*PR*, §173). The principal duty of parents with respect to their children—or right of the children with respect to their parents—has to do with their upbringing or education (*Erziehung*). Here Hegel introduces a theme that occupies him throughout his treatment of the various articulations of ethical life, especially civil society. Education is necessary because "human beings do not arrive by instinct at what they are destined to become; on the contrary they must attain this by their own efforts" (*PR*, §174A).[14] The goal of the education that takes place in the family is to raise "the children out of the natural immediacy in which they originally exist to self-sufficiency and freedom of personality" (*PR*, §175). With respect to achieving this goal, Hegel characteristically emphasizes the role of discipline: "One of the chief moments in a child's upbringing is discipline, the purpose of which is to break the child's self-will in order to eradicate the merely sensuous and natural" (*PR*, §174A). He also displays little sympathy with Rousseau-inspired pedagogical methods that seek to educate children through play, treating "childishness itself as already inherently valuable" and worth prolonging. Against Rousseau's exhortation to "love childhood and its games,"[15] Hegel argues that education in the family should have the effect of making children dissatisfied with the way they are and creating in them "a longing to grow up" (*PR*, §§174A, 175R).[16]

For all his Teutonic emphasis on discipline and authority, however, Hegel recognizes the limits of the education that takes place in the family with respect to raising children out of their natural immediacy. For the family remains the sphere of immediate feeling, and the predominant character of the relationship between parents and children remains love and trust (*PR*, §175 and A). In his Heidelberg lectures, Hegel considers the immediate love of parents for their children to be of such importance that he says "it is dangerous to remove children even from parents who have a bad influence on them, for even bad parents love their children, and in this feeling the children must necessarily grow stronger" (*LNR*, §86R). And in some of his scattered remarks on education, he indicates that school plays a much greater role in raising children out of their natural immediacy than does the family. "Life in the family," he writes, "which precedes life in the school, is a personal relationship, a relationship of feeling, of love, of natural faith and trust." School, on the other hand, "is the intermediate sphere which leads man out of the family circle into the world, out of the natural relations of feeling and inclination into the element of things [*Sache*]" (*Werke* 4:349). In the *Encyclopedia Philosophy of Spirit*, Hegel characterizes school as the transitional phase between the family and civil society:

In the [family], the child counts in his immediate individuality, is loved whether its behavior is good or bad. In school, on the other hand, the immediacy of the child loses its validity; here the child is respected only insofar as it has worth and achieves something; here the child is no longer merely loved but, rather, criticized and guided in accordance with universal principles, molded by instruction according to fixed rules, and in general subjected to a universal order which forbids many things innocent in themselves because everyone cannot be permitted to do them. Thus school forms the transition from the family into civil society. (*EPS*, §396A, p. 61; see also §395A, pp. 51–52)

Once again, the goal of the education children receive in the family, in conjunction with the education that they receive in school, is to raise them up to be free and self-sufficient personalities. The achievement of this goal marks the dissolution of the family and the transition to civil society (*PR*, §177), to which we now turn our attention.

THE IDEA OF CIVIL SOCIETY

For Hegel, civil society (*bürgerliche Gesellschaft*) is the sphere of private, social, primarily economic, relationship situated between the family and the state. This idea of a separate social sphere beyond the patriarchal ties of the family and below the universal claims of the state is, of course, one that is quite familiar to us now. But at the time Hegel was writing, it was still an emergent reality, especially in Germany. Hegel was by no means the first to theorize this rich, nonpolitical sphere of social-economic activity. In this he was preceded by a number of eighteenth-century thinkers, in particular those associated with the Scottish Enlightenment—Smith, Ferguson, and Steuart, among others— upon whom he draws for his account of civil society.[17] Hegel was, nevertheless, the first to use the expression "civil society" to refer exclusively to this nonpolitical, social-economic realm.[18] As Manfred Riedel has shown, in the tradition of European political thought prior to Hegel, "civil society" (*societas civilis*) was used interchangeably with "political society" to designate the condition human beings entered upon leaving the state of nature. A classic example of this is the title to chapter 7 of Locke's *Second Treatise,* "Of Political or Civil Society." Hegel was the first to clearly distinguish "civil society" from political society or the state, and in doing so he gave conceptual clarity to this singular achievement of the modern world.[19]

Civil society has, of course, become a hot topic in contemporary social and political discourse. In Central and Eastern Europe, the term has been used to designate that sphere of intermediate institutions and associations—churches, neighborhoods, unions, and political parties—which communism suppressed and which many intellectuals now regard as indispensable to creating vibrant new democracies. In the West, the rich associational life of civil society—again comprising churches, neighborhoods, clubs, charities, and so forth—has been invoked for a slightly different purpose: less as a bulwark against totalitarianism than as a means of overcoming the individualism that threatens to rend the social fabric upon which liberal democracy depends. Here, of course, the master thinker is Tocqueville, who saw in the "art of association" the means of transforming narrowly self-interested individuals into public-spirited citizens.[20]

Although Hegel is an important forerunner of the current preoccupation with civil society, it is worth pointing out that his use of this term tends to be somewhat narrower than that of contemporary neo-Tocquevilleans. For him, "civil society" does not refer primarily to the vast array of associations and groups that fill the space between the intimate family and the impersonal state; rather, it refers primarily to the individualistic sphere of self-interested economic activity: the system of needs, the legal structure necessary to support it, and the regulatory and welfare functions of the state with respect to the free market. It is only when he talks about the estates and corporations that Hegel's discussion of civil society begins to have the associational resonance of contemporary discussions of civil society. In this respect, Marx's use of the term "civil society" to refer almost exclusively to the realm of economic or market relationship is not all that far from Hegel's.[21] On the other hand, against the Marxist critique of civil society, Hegel's account does point forward to the positive ethico-political role envisaged for this intermediary sphere by contemporary theorists.

What is the significance of civil society in the argument of the *Philosophy of Right* as a whole? As usual, Hegel's attitude is complex. On the one hand, civil society represents the most dramatic expression of the principle of particular or subjective freedom which Hegel introduced in connection with "morality" and which he regards as the distinguishing feature of the modern European world. On the other hand, civil society represents only an incomplete actualization of human freedom and one that needs to be distinguished from and ultimately subordinated to the full actualization of human freedom in the state. Thus, Hegel's account of civil society contains both a recognition of liberal individuality, on the one hand, and a critique of a certain type of liberal individualism, on the other. Let us take up each of these aspects of his account in a little more detail, before going through the specific features of civil society.

First, civil society constitutes the liberation of the moment of self-sufficient personality and particularity that remained undeveloped and tightly bound within the immediate ethical unity of the family. In civil society, in contrast with the family, "each individual is his own end, and all else means nothing to him" (*PR*, §182A). Here everyone pursues his or her own self-interest, and all ethical identity "appears to be lost" (*PR*, §181A). While in terms of the conceptual scheme of the *Philosophy of Right* the individualistic sphere of civil society follows immediately upon the dissolution of the family and precedes the more concrete formation of the state, Hegel is clear that in actuality it comes after the state and, indeed, depends upon it. The full development of civil society, he writes, "occurs later than that of the state; for as difference, it presupposes the state, which it must have before it as a self sufficient entity in order to subsist itself" (*PR*, §182A); "only within the state does the family first develop into civil society" (*PR*, §256R). The emergence of an autonomous sphere of self-interested, individual activity, free of the patriarchal claims of the family and the universal claims of the state, constitutes a rather late development in the history of European civilization: "the creation of civil society belongs to the modern world, which for the first time allows all the determinations of the Idea to attain their rights" (*PR*, §182A).

In §185, Hegel graphically evokes the subjective and particular freedom that receives consummate expression in civil society, referring to "particularity for itself . . . indulging itself in all directions as it satisfies its needs, contingent arbitrariness, and subjective caprice." Here, too, he repeats that it is this recognition of subjective or particular freedom that decisively differentiates the modern world from the ancient. In this connection, he elaborates his well-known interpretation of Plato's *Republic,* alluded to at various points in the *Philosophy of Right,* as the embodiment of ancient substantiality devoid of subjective freedom. The *Republic,* Hegel argues, is no mere ideal but, rather, a defense of the substantiality of Greek ethical life against what Plato saw as the corrupting and destructive force of the principle of subjective freedom: "The principle of the *self-sufficient and inherently infinite personality* of the individual, the principle of subjective freedom, which arose in an inward form in the *Christian* religion and in an external form (which was therefore connected with abstract universality) in the *Roman* world, is denied its right in that merely substantial form of the actual spirit [in Plato's *Republic*]" (*PR*, §185R; see also Preface, 20). It is against Plato's purely substantial state in the *Republic* that Hegel defines his position throughout his account of civil society in the *Philosophy of Right.*[22]

Though particularity is the determining principle of the individual in civil society, this stage of ethical life is not without its own universality, according to Hegel. Though the individual in civil society pursues his own self-interest "without reference to others," he necessarily stands in relation to other particular individuals and finds that he cannot gain satisfaction without "simultaneously satisfying the welfare of others." In this way, the particular individual, along with his particular ends, takes on the "form of universality" (*PR*, §182 and A). Here, and throughout his account of civil society, Hegel avails himself of the Smithian "invisible hand" argument by which the pursuit of private self-interest leads to the general welfare of all. The universal is not the conscious object of individuals, but it remains operative behind their backs, binding them together in a complex system of interdependence. For this reason, Hegel insists that ethical life at the stage of civil society only "appears to be lost." It is not actually lost because, while I believe I am only pursuing my own selfish goals, I am really "serving the universal which in fact retains ultimate power over me" (*PR*, §181A; see also §§182–84).

The universality that belongs to civil society is, however, only a formal or abstract universality. It is a universality that is ultimately in the service of particularity. The universal here does not form the conscious object of individuals; it is not willed for its own sake but, rather, as a means to individual existence. "[H]ere we do not yet have life within the universal *for* the universal. Here the purpose is the subsistence and right of the individual. The universality that is in question here is only abstract universality, a universality that is only a means" (*LNR*, §89R). By the same token, the unity belonging to civil society is, like the unity belonging to contract, only "commonality" (*Gemeinsamkeit*), in which the arbitrary will of the individual retains its primacy (*PR*, §182A; see also §71A). Such commonality is not to be confused with the genuine universality of the state, in which the universal is willed for its own sake. To underline this distinction between civil society and the state, Hegel refers to civil society as the "external state, the state based on need [*Notstaat*] and as the understanding envisages it [*Verstandesstaat*]" (*PR*, §183).

This brings us to the second, more critical aspect of Hegel's attitude toward civil society. While civil society gives existence to the important principle of subjective freedom that distinguishes the modern world from the ancient, by itself it represents only an incomplete actualization of human freedom and one that needs to be distinguished from and subordinated to the full actualization of human freedom in the state. Though this aspect of Hegel's attitude toward civil society becomes explicit only when he makes the transition to the state, it is implicit throughout his discussion of civil society, not only when he refers to it as the "state based on need or as the understanding envisages it" but also when he observes that in civil society "the burghers [*Bürgernen*] are *bourgeois,* not *citoyens*" (*LNR,* §89; see also §72 and *PR,* §190R). This distinction between *bourgeois* and *citoyen,* which can be found in some of Hegel's earlier writings as well (see *HHS,* 158/261; *PP,* 48/266), inevitably recalls Rousseau and the problem he meant to call attention to with it: namely, the problem of the relationship between commerce and citizenship.[23] Rousseau lamented the fact that in the modern world there were no longer citizens in the genuine sense, only *bourgeoisie;* that, whereas "ancient politicians spoke incessantly about mores and virtue, ours speak only of commerce and money."[24] Although Hegel's tone in the section of the *Philosophy of Right* devoted to civil society is far from lamentational, his treatment of this sphere of activity shows an acute awareness of Rousseau's problem.[25]

Of course, Hegel's concern with this problem of the relationship between commerce and citizenship goes back to his earliest writings, especially those at Jena. There, as we have seen, Hegel took enormous pains to differentiate "absolute ethical life," which is centered around politics, from "relative ethical life," which revolves around economic acquisition. In keeping with his early civic republicanism, he identified the political sphere with freedom and the economic sphere with necessity, and he was particularly concerned to prevent the latter from infecting or overwhelming the former (see *NL,* 92–94/480–83, 99–104/489–95; *SEL,* 147–56/57–68). In these writings, Hegel also provided some of his most vivid descriptions of the destructive inequality produced by the free market and of the dehumanization and dislocation arising from the division of labor. He insisted that the government must bring the blind and unconscious necessity that characterizes the economic system of needs under the control of the universal: the "monstrous system of community" created by the system of needs "requires strict dominance and taming like a wild beast" (see *SEL,* 167–73/80–86; *FPS,* 247–49/321–24). His proposals in this latter regard, however, were only vaguely sketched, focusing mainly on regulation and taxation (see *SEL,* 171–73/84–86; *HHS,* 140–41/244–45).

By the time Hegel writes the *Philosophy of Right,* his discussion of the economic sphere in relation to the political sphere has lost almost all of the archaic qualities observed in his Jena writings. No longer are the features of a modern capitalistic economy blended with institutions of the ancient polis to form a kind of anachronistic hybrid. Here Hegel's discussion is up to date and grounded in the most advanced analyses of modern political economy—those of Smith, Say, and Ricardo (see *PR*, §189R). Nevertheless, Hegel retains from his early writings a certain suspicion of unfettered economic activity and a desire to subordinate it to the higher, more universal aims of the state. This is evident not only in the distinction between civil society and state, *bourgeois* and *citoyen*, which frames Hegel's entire discussion of civil society in the *Philosophy of Right*. It is also evident quite early in his discussion, where Hegel notices— again, as he did in his earlier writings (see *SEL*, 170–71/83–84; *HHS*, 140/244)—that the great wealth produced by modern economic conditions also produces great poverty. "[C]ivil society," he writes, "affords a spectacle of extravagance and misery as well as of the physical and ethical corruption common to both" (*PR*, §185). In civil society, both extravagance and depriva- tion and want are "boundless," and "this confused situation can be restored to harmony only through the forcible intervention of the state" (*PR*, §185A).

For all his sensitivity to the Rousseauan worry about the corrupting effect of modern commercial civilization on civic virtue, however, Hegel sees the rela- tionship between civil society and political citizenship very differently from Rousseau. Indeed, one might say that Hegel uses the Rousseauan worry to frame a defense of civil society against Rousseau's anti-commercial critique. This is made clear in what Hegel says about the educative role of civil society. Civil society is not simply a realm of selfish individualism opposed to the universality of the state. Rather, in an important way, civil society educates the individual to universality. Because individuals in civil society can attain their selfish ends only by simultaneously satisfying the ends of others, they are forced to surrender some of their natural or immediate particularity and to adopt in ever increasing ways the form of universality. Civil society does not mark a corruption of the original simplicity and immediacy of the state of nature, as Rousseau would have it, but, rather, a necessary overcoming of it. In civil society, individuals must put aside their personal idiosyncrasies and engage in the "*hard work* of opposing mere subjectivity of conduct, of opposing the immediacy of desire as well as the subjective vanity of feeling and the arbitrari- ness of caprice" (*PR*, §187R). This is what education (*Bildung*) consists in for Hegel, as we have seen from his remarks on school in relation to the family above. "By educated people," he writes, "we may understand in the first place those who do everything as others do it and who do not flaunt their particular characteristics . . . education irons out particularity to make it act in accor- dance with the nature of the thing" (*PR*, §187A).[26]

This rather conformist image of the education that takes place in civil society may strike modern readers as an unappealing prospect. In what one commentator has referred to as the "most chilling of analogies," Hegel encapsulates this image of education by comparing educated human beings to "coins which have circulated for a long time" (*VPR* 1:310).[27] Nietzsche later uses this same analogy to an opposite effect, when he writes that modern education is designed to "rear the most 'current' men possible, 'current' in the sense the word is used of coins of the realm."[28] Though our sympathies may now lie more with Nietzsche's individualistic protest against the leveling conformism of modern society than with Hegel's apparent embrace of it, I think it is misleading to characterize the latter's position as "chilling" unless we are willing to apply this adjective to the whole of his philosophical outlook. For it is certain that what Hegel says here about education in relation to civil society represents a deep strain in his ethical thought, ultimately going to his fundamental conception of rational freedom. In an important passage considered earlier, Hegel writes that the "rational is the high road where no one stands out from the rest." He then applies this insight to the realm of art, arguing that the greatest works of art are those in which "the artist's particularity has completely disappeared and no *mannerism* is apparent in it" (*PR*, §15A; see also §187A). No passage captures the rationalism of Hegel's overall project as sharply as this one, and none perhaps suggests as persuasively that the universalizing and educative role he attributes to civil society need not be seen as simply leveling or stultifying.

THE SYSTEM OF NEEDS AND THE ADMINISTRATION OF JUSTICE

We now turn to the first two of the three specific foci of Hegel's analysis of civil society, namely, the system of needs and the administration of justice, leaving till the next section his treatment of the police and the corporations. Let us begin with the system of needs, which in many respects provides the clearest illustration of the educative aspect of civil society we have just discussed. What most impresses Hegel about the nature of human needs is their nonnatural and nonnecessitous character. Whereas the needs of animals and their means of satisfying them are given and limited, the needs of human beings and their means of satisfying them are capable of almost infinite multiplication and refinement. Human needs, unlike those of animals, are never merely natural; rather, they are mediated by our opinion of what our needs are and by judgments of taste and utility. "In the end," Hegel writes, "it is no longer need but opinion which has to be satisfied" (*PR*, §190A); for example, "what the English call 'comfortable' is something utterly inexhaustible" (*PR*, §191A). Apart from this "spiritual" character of human needs, Hegel also points to the universal or social character of human needs and their means of satisfaction. Because I depend on others to satisfy my needs, I must accept to some extent their opinions as to what my needs are. By the same token, because I must produce means whereby the needs of others can be satisfied, I must pay heed to their opinions of what their needs are. The generation and satisfaction of human needs takes place within an element of universal "recognition," which forces people to fit in with one another and adapt their activity to the form of universality (*PR*, §192 and A).

In the eyes of some, the multiplication, refinement, and socialization of human needs that Hegel describes here may not be seen as a blessing. One thinks of Rousseau and his attack on the way in which society, through its tyranny of opinion, creates in human beings all sorts of artificial needs and distracts them from their "real" needs. Hegel, in fact, alludes to Rousseau's view that human beings were somehow freer in the state of nature, subjected as they were to only their natural needs, but he rejects this view as incompatible with a proper understanding of human freedom. A condition such as Rousseau envisages "in which natural needs as such were immediately satisfied would merely be one in which spirituality was immersed in nature, and hence a condition of savagery and unfreedom; whereas freedom consists solely in the reflection of the spiritual into itself, its distinction from the natural, and its reflection upon the latter" (*PR*, §194R). For Hegel, the social character of human needs does not entail human dependence and unfreedom; on the contrary, it "contains the aspect of *liberation*, because the strict natural necessity of need is concealed and man's relation is to *his own opinion*, which is universal, and to a necessity imposed by himself alone" (*PR*, §194).

The socialization and universalization that Hegel attributes to human needs and their satisfaction he also discerns in human work. In this regard, he focuses primarily on the division of labor. It will be remembered that in some of his earlier writings, particularly those at Jena, Hegel was quite sensitive to the dehumanizing effects of the division of labor. Thus, in the *Philosophy of Spirit of 1803–4*, after illustrating the division of labor by way of Smith's example of the pin factory, he commented that "the consciousness of the factory laborer is impoverished to the last extreme of dullness" (*FPS*, 248/323–24). And in the *Philosophy of Spirit of 1805–6*, he wrote that, through the division of labor, the individual becomes "more mechanical, duller, spiritless" (*HHS*, 139/243). What is most surprising about Hegel's discussion of the division of labor in the *Philosophy of Right* is how laconic it is on this dehumanizing aspect of the

division of labor. After indicating how the division of labor leads to the simplification and abstraction of human labor and to a greater interdependence
between human beings, Hegel concludes simply that the division of labor
"makes work increasingly *mechanical,* so that the human being is eventually
able to step aside and let a *machine* take his place" (*PR,* §198). In his earlier
Heidelberg lectures, Hegel expands a bit more on his analysis of the division of
labor but ends up offering the same optimistic conclusion: human work under
the division of labor becomes increasingly mechanical, but this eventually
opens the way for it to be replaced by machines. "A factory presents a sad
picture of the deadening of human beings," he writes. "But once factory work
has reached a certain degree of perfection, of simplification, mechanical human
labor can be replaced by the work of machines . . . In this way, through the
consummation of this mechanical progress, human freedom is restored" (*LNR,*
§101R).

It would be a mistake, however, to exaggerate the optimism that is implied in
these passages. On the one hand, Hegel clearly believes that the division of
labor and the introduction of machinery make work easier and thus emancipate the worker to some extent. On the other hand, he is aware of the negative
effects of the division of labor. In the passage from the Heidelberg lectures
above, he speaks of the "deadening" effect of factory work on individuals. And
later in the *Philosophy of Right,* he observes that, as "the *specialization* and
limitation of particular work . . . increase," so do "the *dependence* and *want* of
the class which is tied to such work; this in turn leads to an inability to feel and
enjoy the wider freedoms, and particularly the spiritual advantages, of civil
society" (*PR,* §243). In his initial discussion of the system of needs, Hegel dwells
mainly on the positive aspects of—the universalization brought about by—
modern economic conditions. It is only later on, primarily in his discussion of
poverty, that a more hardheaded analysis of the impact of modern economic
and industrial conditions is to be found.

Hegel concludes his analysis of the system of needs by considering its distributive implications and its impact on the organization of society. With respect to
the first, he insists on the necessary inequality of civil society. One's share of the
"universal resources" of civil society is conditional on the capital assets one
begins with as well as on one's skills; and the latter are conditional on the former
as well as on unequal natural aptitudes and other contingent circumstances.
Inequality is part and parcel of the arbitrariness and particularity that are
liberated by and lie at the basis of civil society. As he did earlier in relation to
property, Hegel dismisses the demand for equality in the distribution of wealth

or resources as abstract and "characteristic of the empty understanding." Such a demand, he argues, ultimately fails to give the right of particularity which is enshrined in civil society its due (*PR*, §200 and R; also §49R).

But the system of needs does not simply differentiate individuals according to their particular skills, aptitudes, and resources; it also knits them together into social groups or "estates" based on common forms of work, means of satisfaction, and types of education. This marks an important transition in the development of Hegel's argument about civil society, for with the gathering of individuals into estates the atomism of civil society begins to be transcended. The estates serve a similar integrative function to the family, linking the individual to something larger and more universal than their private self-interest. The universality involved here is not simply that of the invisible hand of the market but entails a more substantial and explicit identification of the individual with others. For this reason, Hegel writes that, "while the family is the primary basis of the state, the estates are the second. The latter are of special importance, because private persons, despite their selfishness, find it necessary to have recourse to others. This is accordingly the root which links selfishness with the universal, i.e. with the state, which must take care to ensure that the connection is a firm and solid one" (*PR*, §201A).

Hegel distinguishes three estates—later he will add a fourth—each corresponding to a moment of the concept. Thus, there is the substantial or immediate estate, made up of agricultural workers and landholders; the formal or reflective estate, made up of tradesmen, manufacturers, and businessmen; and finally, the universal estate, made up of civil servants and public officials who engage in the universal business of the state. This social scheme is pretty much the one Hegel laid out in the *Philosophy of Spirit of 1805–6* (see *HHS*, 162–72/266–77)—the only real difference being that Hegel now includes the landed aristocracy in the agricultural estate—and what interests us most is the way in which he characterizes the differences between the first two estates, the substantial estate of agricultural workers and landholders and the reflective estate of tradesmen and businessmen. The former he characterizes in terms of the same substantial disposition he earlier attributed to women. It is marked by immediate feeling, the absence of reflection, and a generally accepting attitude toward what is given by nature. In this substantial estate, "reflection and the will of the individual play a lesser role, and thus its substantial disposition in general is that of an immediate ethical life based on the family and trust" (*PR*, §203). In the estate of trade and industry, an opposite spirit reigns. Not content merely to accept the gifts of nature but, rather, regarding them as raw materials to be transformed, this spirit is marked by the reflectiveness, will, and self-reliance that is missing from the substantial estate. It is in the estate of trade and industry, Hegel tells us, that the "sense of freedom" first arose, whereas the substantial estate of agricultural workers and landholders is "more inclined to subservience" (*PR*, §204A).

The way in which Hegel draws the distinction between the estates here raises some obvious problems, many of which we have already encountered in his discussion of the differences between men and women. Peasants and land-holders, like women, seem to be incapable of realizing their freedom and rationality in the fullest possible sense. There is an important difference be-tween women and the members of the substantial or agricultural estate: the latter are accorded a political role in the state which is denied to the former (see *PR*, §§305–7). Nevertheless, there remains something radically incomplete about the members of the agricultural estate: they are simple, unreflective, dependent, and ultimately inclined to subservience. That Hegel's conception of society seems to require the existence of such an inferior and substantial estate seems to violate, as one commentator put it, "the basic liberal view of citizens as morally equally individuals."[29] And it raises the suspicion, once again, that Hegel's political philosophy rests on an organicism in which collective or communal self-actualization takes precedence over individual self-actualization.

Before addressing this criticism, we should remind ourselves of the reasons why Hegel finds the presence of a substantial element to be so important to society. As was pointed out earlier, he is clearly anxious about the destabilizing effects on society of the commercial and industrial spirit. Such a spirit is constantly changing, constantly innovating. It dissolves all that is customary or sacred in reflection, and it regards everything that is given by nature as mere raw material to be transformed. No one has described the unconservative nature of this bourgeois spirit more eloquently than Marx:

> Constant revolutionizing of production, uninterrupted disturbance of all social conditions, everlasting uncertainty and agitation distinguish the bourgeois epoch from all earlier ones. All fixed, fast-frozen relations, with their train of ancient and venerable prejudices and opinions, are swept away, all new-formed ones become antiquated before they can ossify. All that is solid melts into air, all that is holy is profaned.[30]

For Hegel, the conservative, trusting, substantial disposition found in the agricultural estate, as well as in the family, serves to counteract the instability and uncertainty that flow from the innovative and individualistic spirit of the bourgeoisie. In this respect, Hegel attributes to the members of the agricultural estate a role in society not dissimilar to that which Burke ascribes to hereditary wealth in England: they are "the ballast in the vessel of the commonwealth."[31]

The problem Hegel is addressing here is not a false or imaginary one. We are all familiar with the way in which the reflective and innovative spirit of modern commerce dissolves all that is traditional, authoritative, and sacred. The difficulty with Hegel's solution to this problem, however, is that it invokes a social condition that has almost completely disappeared from the modern world and, indeed, was already beginning to disappear at the time Hegel was writing. Hegel himself shows some awareness of this. He remarks in one of the additions to the *Philosophy of Right:* "In our times, the [agricultural] economy, too, is run in a reflective manner, like a factory, and it accordingly takes on a character like that of the second estate and opposed to its own character of naturalness." But he adds that, despite this, the "first estate will always retain the patriarchal way of life and the substantial disposition associated with it" (*PR*, §203A).[32] Here Hegel obviously lets the desirabilities of his political philosophy overwhelm his otherwise acute observation of emergent social realities. This does not detract, however, from his accurate insight into what remains a serious problem in modern commercial society.

Let us now take up the larger philosophical issue of whether Hegel's articulation of the social whole into different estates implies that he sees the collective or the community or (most metaphysically) cosmic spirit as the true subject of self-realization in his political philosophy instead of the individual. Here again I urge caution in attributing such a metaphysically controversial view to Hegel. While it is true that the substantial disposition of the agricultural estate lacks the reflectiveness and self-will that are the hallmark of modern subjective freedom, it remains the case that the members of the agricultural estate know and will the universality of the state no less than any other estate, and in this lies their rational freedom. In other words, the substantiality of the agricultural estate affects only the form of the will of its members and not its substantial or universal content (see *PR*, §203R). All this is confirmed by the fact that Hegel gives the agricultural estate a political role in the state and, indeed, considers this estate to be better equipped for political service than the estate of trade and industry (see *PR*, §306). Hegel's organic conception of the social whole is not of the traditional sort in which the individuals or parts are mere tools of the self-realization of the larger community. The substantial freedom embodied by the state is not devoid of subjective insight; it is known and willed by all the members of the community, including those who belong to the agricultural estate; and in this willing and knowing consists their own self-realization as free and rational beings. Individuals, for Hegel, are not mere vehicles of some collective or cosmic spirit.[33] Indeed, it is truer to say that the state is the vehicle of the self-realization of individuals as free and rational beings, though such an understanding of the state must not be confused with the typical liberal view of the state as a mere instrument for the particular will and private satisfaction of the individual.

This, undoubtedly, takes us beyond the present context of Hegel's argument. In his treatment of the estates in civil society, he is not much concerned with the issue of individual versus collective self-realization. He is concerned, however, to distinguish his doctrine of the differentiation of the social whole into estates from traditional doctrines in which such differentiation is brought about in an objective or compulsory way independent of the subjective or arbitrary will of the individual. Here, besides the Indian caste-system, Hegel once again mentions Plato's *Republic* as failing to embody the modern principle of subjective particularity in giving to the guardians the responsibility of allocating individuals to specific estates. For Hegel, the choice of which estate to belong to ultimately rests with the individual and is determined by his arbitrary will. In this way, the modern principle of subjective particularity is given full recognition. "The recognition and right according to which all that is rationally necessary in civil society and in the state should at the same time come into effect *through the mediation of the arbitrary will*," Hegel writes, "is the more precise definition of what is primarily meant by the general idea [*allgemeinen Vorstellung*] of *freedom*" (*PR*, §206 and R).

Of course, it might be objected that, by forcing individuals to commit themselves to a single estate, Hegel is limiting the subjective or particular freedom he claims to be preserving. But such an objection rests on what Hegel regards as a completely abstract or negative conception of freedom that sees commitment to any determinate content in the finite world as a limitation (see *PR*, §5R). Such an attitude Hegel associates particularly with youth and, as we have seen before, is fond of quoting against it Goethe's dictum that "whoever aspires to great things must be able to limit himself" (see *PR*, §13A).[34] For Hegel, the individual attains actuality only by committing himself to a particular estate, and such actuality is always higher than abstract possibility. It is only by attaching himself to a particular estate that the individual "gains *recognition* in his own eyes and in the eyes of others" and becomes "somebody" (*etwas*) (*PR*, §207 and A). Finally, it is only within a particular estate that individual morality begins to take on determinate existence. In contrast to the emptiness of Kantian morality, membership in an estate provides "the real content for duty" and "imposes determinate duties that can be known to everyone" (*LNR,* §107R). The ethical disposition here is that of "rectitude," which consists simply in fulfilling the determinate duties prescribed by one's station (*PR,* §207). Hegel is well aware, as we have already seen, that such rectitude will appear to be something lower and more pedestrian than the strenuous ideal of moral virtue enshrined in the moral point of view. Nevertheless, he sees rectitude as giving a determinacy to our moral duties which the moral point of view, with its talk of duty for its own sake, is incapable of supplying (see *PR,* §150 and R).

Hegel's discussion of the estates concludes his analysis of the system of needs, from which he moves on to consider the second major component of civil society, namely, the administration of justice (*die Rechtspflege*). The universality implicit in the system of needs becomes explicit, "for itself," in the administration of justice. The justice or right that is being administered here is abstract right or property-right. When Hegel originally considered property-right in the first part of the *Philosophy of Right,* it was merely abstract, without existence or actuality in the particular or subjective will of the individual. It is only now that property-right takes on such concrete existence or actuality, ceasing to be merely "in itself" and becoming "for itself." It is only after the particular or subjective will has shed its immediacy and been educated to universality through the system of needs that abstract right takes on "an *existence* in which it is *universally recognized, known, and willed*" (*PR,* §209). Abstract right, Hegel tells us, "comes into existence only because it is useful in relation to needs" and only after the particular will has thinkingly adapted itself to the form of universality through the system of needs (*PR,* §209A). At this point, the particular or subjective will no longer stands alongside the abstract universality of property-right, only contingently related to it; in the administration of justice, the particular or subjective will explicitly wills the universal in the form of property-right.

It is precisely because abstract right at this stage is "recognized, known, and willed" that it must be "posited" (*gesetzt*) and exist as "law" (*Gesetz*). By "posited" here Hegel does not mean primarily willed or commanded, as Hobbes would have it in his "positive" conception of law; rather, he means brought to consciousness, thought, or recognized. "To posit something as *universal*—i.e. to bring it to the consciousness as a universal—is, as everyone knows, *to think*" (*PR,* §211A).[35] What more than anything else Hegel means to draw attention to with his emphasis on the posited character of law is the conscious way in which human beings subscribe to laws in contradistinction to the unconscious way in which animals and other natural things are governed by laws. "The sun and the planets," he writes, echoing Kant, "also have their laws, but they are unaware of them" (*PR,* §211A).[36] The laws that govern the stars and cattle are laws that "are only internally in these objects, not *for them,* not as *posited* laws; whereas it is man's privilege to *know* his law" (*EPS,* §529R).

From this understanding of the posited and known character of law, Hegel goes on to defend codification of the law against those Romantic and historicist critics, such as von Savigny, who argue in favor of customary law. For Hegel, the distinction between laws and customs is not absolute; both contain the aspect of being thought or known: "Since only animals have their law as instinct, whereas human beings have theirs as custom [*Gewohnheit*], *customary rights* contain the moment of being *thoughts* and of being *known.*" The only difference between customary rights and written laws is that the former "are known in a subjective and contingent manner, so that they are less determinate for themselves and the universality of thought is more obscure" (*PR,* §211R). Codifying the laws simply develops the element of thought and universality that is implicit but undeveloped in customary rights. Nor does such codification destroy the "living" quality of customs, as defenders of customary right assert. Indeed, Hegel insists that "the valid laws of the nation do not cease to be its customs [*Gewohnheiten*] merely because they have been written down" (*PR,* §211R); they, too, continue to rest on the identity of subject and objective determination (*PR,* §211A). The principal problem with customary right is that it creates enormous confusion in the administration of justice and makes right the privileged preserve of a few judges and experts. Hegel's favorite example of the juridical chaos and inequality created by the failure to codify the law is the common law of England (see *PR,* §211R and A).[37]

What is the relationship between posited or positive right and what is right in itself, what Hegel sometimes refers to as "natural" or "philosophical" right? In the Introduction to the *Philosophy of Right,* Hegel claimed that "natural right or philosophical right is different from positive right, but it would be a grave misunderstanding to distort this difference into an opposition or antagonism" (*PR,* §3R). Here, in his treatment of positive right, he essentially repeats this understanding of positive right as different from but not opposed to what is right in itself. On the one hand, it is only by being posited that what is right in itself gains existence; and thus positive right is "the source of cognition of what is *right*" (*PR,* §212R). On the other hand, the positing of right brings in its train all sorts of contingent factors, and therefore "what is law may differ in content from what is right in itself" (*PR*, §212). For this latter reason, Hegel sharply distinguishes, again as he did in the Introduction, between the positive— largely historical—science of right and the philosophical science of right. Whereas the former is concerned to "deduce in every detail from its positive data both the historical development and the applications and ramifications of the given determinations of right," only the latter is capable of ascertaining whether a given determination of right is rational in and for itself (*PR*, §212R).

For Hegel, then, the posited character of law does not imply, as it did for Hobbes, that it contains an authoritative element that is utterly opaque to speculative reason.[38] Positive right contains both rational and contingent elements, and it is the task of the philosophical science of right to penetrate beneath its bright and manifold surface and, in the famous words of the Preface, "to recognize in the semblance of the temporal and transient the substance which is immanent and the eternal which is present" (*PR*, 20). Nevertheless, Hegel does recognize a "purely positive" aspect of the law that does resist being penetrated by speculative reason and that cannot be derived from the philosophical concept. This aspect concerns the quantitative determinations involved in the application of the universal concept to individual cases: the amount of a fine, the term of an imprisonment, and so forth. These determinations are ineluctably contingent and arbitrary; they cannot be deduced from speculative reason. Indeed, "it is reason itself which recognizes that contingency, contradiction, and semblance have their (*albeit limited*) sphere and right" (*PR*, §214 and R). Such recognition of a purely positive aspect of law is salutary, according to Hegel, because it keeps philosophy from getting tangled up in all sorts of contingent considerations with which it has no concern (see *PR*, 21) and because it protects us from the illusion of a perfectly rational code of law and the "futile perfectionism" that goes along with it (*EPS*, §529R).

Most of the institutions and practices Hegel discusses in connection with the administration of justice relate to the requirement that the law be "recognized, known, and willed" by individuals. This requirement itself flows from the right of subjective insight or self-consciousness that Hegel deduced in his discussion of morality. There, it will be remembered, Hegel was careful to restrict this right of subjective self-consciousness to insight into what is generally "*recognized* as right," to "*cognizance* in the sense of *familiarity* with what is legal and to that extent obligatory," differentiating it from the more general and ultimately impracticable right to recognize as valid only what conforms to one's own subjective reason or conviction (*PR*, §132R). Now he spells out what this right of subjective self-consciousness demands with respect to the administration of justice.

Reducing Hegel's detailed discussion to its essentials, the right of subjective self-consciousness demands, among other things, that "the laws be made *universally known*" (*PR*, §215), that their application in particular cases be revealed through the publicity of legal proceedings (*PR*, §224), and that the verdict of guilt or innocence in a criminal trial be pronounced by a jury of one's peers (*PR*, §227, R, and A). Though Hegel here seems to be defending procedures and practices that we now take for granted, it is important to notice that they were not widely available at the time he was writing. In the Prussia of his day, for example, trials were not held in public, nor were they by jury. Throughout his discussion of the administration of justice, Hegel seems most concerned about the possibility of its becoming the exclusive preserve of a professional class of lawyers and judges, thus alienating ordinary individuals from right. When knowledge of right becomes "the *property* of a class," he writes, the "members of civil society . . . remain *alienated* not only from their own most personal interests but also from the substantial and rational basis of these, namely *right*, and they are reduced to a condition of *tutelage*, or even a kind of serfdom, in relation to the class in question" (*PR*, §228R; see also §215A). For all his emphasis on the rationalization of law, Hegel is unwilling to trade the sacred right of subjective self-consciousness for the increased efficiency deriving from the professionalization of the administration of justice.

POLICE, POVERTY, AND THE CORPORATIONS

The transition from the administration of justice to the police and the corporations essentially recapitulates at the level of ethical life the transition from abstract right to welfare that Hegel educed earlier in the *Philosophy of Right*. Just as in that earlier transition abstract right was found wanting because it related only to the abstract personality of individuals and did not reach to their subjective particularity, so the administration of justice is now found to be incomplete insofar as it is concerned only with annulling infringements of abstract right—infringements of property and personality—leaving to contingency the livelihood and welfare of individuals. It is true that in the administration of justice the universal determinations of abstract right are made actual in the subjective consciousness of the individual; this is what renders it more concrete than the original standpoint of abstract right. Nevertheless, the universal in the administration of justice remains that of abstract right and abstract personality, and it does not encompass the subjective particularity and welfare of the individual. "[T]he universal, which in the first instance is merely right," Hegel argues,

> has to be extended over the whole field of particularity. Justice is a major factor in civil society: good laws will cause the state to flourish, and free ownership is a fundamental condition of its success. But since I am completely involved in particularity, I have a right to demand that, within this context, my particular welfare should also be promoted. Account should be taken of my welfare, of my particularity, and this is the task of the police and the corporation. (*PR,* §229A)

In Hegel's time, of course, the term "police" (*Polizei*) denoted much more than the maintenance of public order and the enforcement of law, comprising a wide field of government activity in the free market. For Hegel, it includes the regulation of commerce and industry, the provision of public goods such as streetlights and bridges, and finally the provision of necessities for the poor. It also includes "policing" in the narrower sense of preventing crimes (and other harms) and apprehending criminals. This latter activity is to be distinguished from what goes on in the administration of justice: whereas the "role of the legal system is to annul infringements of right, that of the police is to prevent them" (*LNR,* §92R; see also §119R).

With respect to policing in this narrower sense, Hegel argues that there can be no fixed determinations or boundaries. What counts as harmful or suspicious in some circumstances—war, for example—may not be so in others. In general, the scope of police activity in this narrower sense "will depend on custom, the spirit of the rest of the constitution, prevailing conditions, current emergencies, etc." (*PR,* §234). In refusing to draw absolute boundaries here, Hegel does not mean to give the police free reign to search, detain, and otherwise harass individuals. "[P]olice supervision," he writes, "must go no further than is necessary, though it is for the most part not possible to determine where necessity begins" (*LNR,* §119R). And he is particularly critical of Fichte's state "centered on the police," in which no one is allowed to remain unknown to the police and everyone is required to carry their identity papers with them. Such a state, he writes, "becomes a world of galley slaves, where each is supposed to keep his fellow under constant supervision" (*LNR,* §119R).[39] But, despite his sympathy for the general desirability of keeping police supervision to a minimum, Hegel's appreciation for circumstances prevents him from fixing this minimum in an abstract principle or definition.

As I have already indicated, police-activity for Hegel extends well beyond the narrow function of preventing crime and apprehending criminals. One of its chief functions pertains to the provision and oversight of "arrangements of public utility": government regulation of commerce and industry, the inspection of commodities, the building and maintaining of public works, the provision of public services, and so forth. Hegel gives a good idea of what he has in mind here when he says that the "police should provide for street-lighting, bridge-building, the pricing of daily necessities, and public health" (*PR*, §236A). Government intervention in the market is necessary to make sure that common necessities such as bread are not priced too highly. And governmental supervision and direction of the market have become especially important in recent times as "large branches of industry" have become "dependent on external circumstances and remote combinations whose full implications cannot be grasped by the individuals who are tied to these spheres by their occupation" (*PR*, §236; *LNR*, §120R). Policing in a modern civil society, in other words, involves having some sort of industrial policy.

One of the great questions of modern politics is how much the government should involve itself in the everyday workings of the economy. Hegel tells us that "two main views are prevalent on this subject. One maintains that the police should have oversight over everything, and the other maintains that the police should have no say in such matters" (*PR*, §236A). It is clear that Hegel himself means to steer a middle course between these two views. He clearly rejects the arguments for total laissez-faire. There are many arrangements in the public interest that individuals cannot be expected to provide for on their own as they pursue their private interests. But Hegel is also aware of the danger of too much police, too much government intervention and regulation. Here again he seems to have the Fichtean police-state in mind (see *VPR₁₉*, 190–91). Hegel's concern about excessive governmental regulation and intrusion into civil society is evident in his Heidelberg lectures, where he remarks on the importance of civil freedom and (anticipating Tocqueville) of political freedom in promoting a vibrant and prosperous civil society (*LNR*, §120R).[40] It is also evident in some of his earlier writings, where he criticizes what he calls the "machine state" (which, again, he identifies with Fichte, as well as with Jacobin France and Frederician Prussia) in which everything in society is regulated from the top down by the supreme public authority. Again anticipating Tocqueville, Hegel decries the effect such administrative centralization has on the private initiative and public spirit of citizens: "How dull and spiritless a life is engendered in a modern state where everything is regulated from the top downwards, where nothing with any general implications is left to the management and execution of interested parties of the people" (*GC,* 163–64/484).[41]

The third function Hegel attributes to the state in its police capacity is to guarantee individuals a share in the universal resources of civil society by educating them, giving them skills, and, in the event they cannot earn their own living, providing them with the necessities of existence. The basis of this duty on the part of civil society toward individuals is that civil society deprives individuals of their "natural means of acquisition" (*PR,* §241)—namely, agriculture—and displaces the natural social structure which originally provides for their particular welfare, namely, the family: "civil society tears the individual away from family ties . . . substitutes its own soil for the external inorganic nature and paternal soil from which the individual gained his livelihood, and subjects the existence of the whole family itself to dependence on civil society and to contingency" (*PR,* §238). "Civil society . . . is the immense power which draws people to itself and requires them to work for it, to owe everything to it, and to do everything by its means" (*PR,* §238A). Because civil society replaces the family in this way, the individual becomes a "son of civil society" (*PR,* §238), and civil society itself assumes the role of "universal family" with respect to the individual, with all the attendant rights and duties. Among the latter is included the right and duty to educate children so that they can become productive members of civil society (*PR,* §239). But most importantly, civil society assumes the duty to provide for those who cannot provide for themselves—that is, to provide for the poor (*PR,* §241).[42]

Hegel's discussion of poverty in the *Philosophy of Right* is one of the most frequently commented upon sections of the book. It is a discussion marked by considerable sociological acuity, especially in its recognition that modern poverty is not simply the result of individual laziness or incapacity but a necessary consequence of modern economic conditions. It also reflects an appreciation of the seriousness of the problems posed by modern poverty and of the fact that there are no easy solutions to these problems. This latter, realistic aspect of Hegel's analysis of poverty is reflected in such oft-quoted sentences as: "The important question of how poverty can be remedied is one which agitates and torments modern societies especially" (*PR,* §244A); and "[D]espite an *excess of wealth,* civil society is *not wealthy enough* . . . to prevent an excess of poverty and the formation of a rabble" (*PR,* §245). These sentences disclose a pessimism that contrasts sharply with the more optimistic and reconciliationist tenor of Hegel's general philosophical outlook, and a number of commentators have celebrated them for precisely that reason. Shlomo Avineri, for example, praises

Hegel for his "basic intellectual honesty" in his treatment of modern poverty and for admitting that it is a problem to which he, for once, does not have a definitive solution.[43]

There are some difficulties with a view such as Avineri's. In the first place, despite some gloomy asides, Hegel does seem to put forward some solutions to the problem of poverty: namely, colonization and the corporations. At the very least, he doesn't simply throw up his hands and leave the problem of poverty as an unsolved and insoluble problem.[44] But even if he did, or even if his proposed solutions turned out to be nonsolutions, we would still have to ask ourselves what the impact of this is on Hegel's general project of grasping the state as the embodiment of reason and the actualization of freedom. Does the intractability of the problem of poverty pose a serious challenge to Hegel's grand claims for the rationality of the modern state?[45] Or does it possibly suggest Hegel's own recognition of the irrationality of the modern state as it is currently constituted and of the need for more radical solutions to the current organization of civil society?[46]

The latter suggestion is not a very plausible one. Nowhere in the *Philosophy of Right* does Hegel indicate that the modern state that includes civil society as one of its moments is anything less than the embodiment of reason and the actualization of freedom. Proponents of the radical interpretation of Hegel's views on civil society often point to the earlier lectures on the philosophy of right—the Heidelberg lectures of 1817–18 and the Berlin lectures of 1819–20—as containing a sharper critique of civil society than that found in the *Philosophy of Right,* but it is not clear that this is so.[47] For the most part, the account of poverty in the *Philosophy of Right* is not substantially different from the accounts in the earlier lectures. This leaves us with the first question raised above, namely, whether Hegel's treatment of poverty does not pose a serious challenge to his claims for the rationality and freedom of the modern state. I take up this important question below, but first we need to go through Hegel's analysis of poverty in more detail.

The first thing to notice about Hegel's analysis of poverty is its thoroughgoing modernity.[48] By this I mean that Hegel takes the modern view that poverty is not simply the result of personal vice or inadequacy but, rather, arises from factors that are largely beyond the control of the individual. In the first place, whether one is poor has a great deal to do with the amount of capital resources one begins with (*PR,* §§200, 241). And beyond this, modern poverty is a necessary consequence of modern capitalistic economic conditions, the inevitable counterpart of modern wealth. Hegel states this point most clearly in his

Berlin lectures of 1819–20: "The emergence of poverty is in general a consequence of civil society, and on the whole it arises necessarily out of it" (*VPR₁₉*, 193). But this insight also runs through his analysis in the *Philosophy of Right*, where he is constantly pointing out that with the infinite increase in extravagance and wealth in civil society there also comes an infinite increase in deprivation and want (*PR*, §§185A, 195, 243). Hegel succinctly puts it in a later lecture-note: "where there is wealth there is poverty" (*VPR* 4:495). This insight into the correlativity of modern wealth and modern poverty, or "great wealth" and "great poverty," can also be found in a number of Hegel's early writings (see *SEL*, 170/83–84; *HHS*, 140/244).

Why is it that great wealth and great poverty necessarily go hand in hand? Hegel doesn't go into much detail in the *Philosophy of Right* with respect to the inner connection between these two things, sometimes giving the impression that the distribution of wealth in civil society is a zero-sum game. In §243, however, he suggests that the correlativity of wealth and poverty in modern civil society has to do with the division and ultimately the mechanization of labor. The universalization of labor through division and mechanization leads to greater profits and wealth for the owners of factories and machines; but it also leads to "the *specialization* and *limitation* of particular work" and to "the *dependence* and *want* of the class which is tied to such work; this in turn leads to an inability to feel and enjoy the wider freedoms, and particularly the spiritual advantages, of civil society" (*PR*, §243; see also §253R). The connection between modern industrial wealth and poverty that Hegel suggests here is more clearly brought out in his Berlin lectures of 1819–20. There he explains, with particular reference to England, how modern industrial conditions produce, on the one hand, great wealth, and on the other, "poverty, need, and misery." "In England, the work of many hundreds of thousands of men is accomplished by machines," leading to greater unemployment and lower wages. At the same time, the internationalization of business exposes individual branches of industry to greater contingency and possibility of accidents, again leading to loss of work for large sectors of the population and, inevitably, poverty (*VPR₁₉*, 193–94).⁴⁹

Of course, it is not poverty per se that Hegel is most concerned about here but, rather, the emergence of what he calls a "rabble" (*Pöbel*). A rabble emerges when the "feeling of right, integrity, and honor which comes from supporting oneself by one's activity and work is lost" (*PR*, §244). Such a rabble is characterized not simply by its objective poverty but by a certain subjective disposition associated with it: "by inward rebellion [*innere Empörung*] against the rich, against society, the government, etc." Without a stake in society, and without the sense of honor or pride that comes from supporting themselves, the members of a rabble become ever more shameless "frivolous and lazy." They no longer even try to support themselves through work but, rather, demand that they be supported by society, on which they blame their impoverished condition. It is in the context of this insightful and all too familiar portrait of the culture of poverty that Hegel utters the quote above that the "important question of how poverty can be remedied is one which agitates and torments modern societies especially." And yet it is important to point out that he does not see the rabble-mentality as a necessary consequence of poverty. "Poverty in itself," he argues, "does not reduce people to a rabble." And he cites England—somewhat anomolously, because England generally appears as a negative example in Hegel's discussions of poverty (see *PR*, §245R; *LNR*, §118R; *VPR$_{19}$*, 197)—as a place where "even the poorest man believes he has rights" (*PR*, §244A). Clearly, the task of modern societies is to prevent the poverty that inevitably arises from modern industrial conditions from reaching a scale where a large number of people feel they no longer have any rights and therefore any duties.[50]

Hegel's most graphic and sympathetic depiction of the rabble-mentality appears in the Berlin lectures of 1819–20 (in contrast with the lectures of 1817–18, where it is mentioned only briefly). Here Hegel once again speaks of the "inward rebellion" or "indignation"—*Empörung* has both meanings—of the poor man whose external existence no longer corresponds to his consciousness of himself as "an infinite, free being." What particularly arouses the indignation of the poor man is that his freedom is opposed and thwarted not simply by nature but by the arbitrary will of another. In the end, "self-consciousness appears driven to the point where it no longer has any rights, where freedom has no existence" (*VPR$_{19}$*, 195). One interesting aspect of this passage from the lectures of 1819–20 is that, in it, Hegel argues that the rabble-mentality can also characterize the rich as well as the poor: "The rich man thinks that he can buy anything," and thus "wealth can lead to the same mockery and shamelessness that we find in the poor rabble" (*VPR$_{19}$*, 196). Hegel's point here recalls his analysis of the "disrupted consciousness" in the *Phenomenology*. There the "arrogance" of the rich man, who views everything as a "plaything of [his] whims, an accident of [his] caprice," was seen as the necessary counterpart of the "inner rebellion" of the alienated poor man (*PS*, 315/383–84).

Commentators who see Hegel's treatment of the problem of poverty as containing a covert indictment of the bourgeois state and an argument for the right to rebel against it draw their strongest support from this passage from the lectures of 1819–20.[51] Dieter Henrich finds particularly significant Hegel's invocation of the "right of necessity" (discussed in §127 of the *Philosophy of Right*) in this context:

> Earlier we considered the right of necessity as something referring to a momentary need. Here necessity no longer has this momentary character. In the emergence of poverty, the power of particularity comes into existence in opposition to the reality of freedom. That can produce the negatively infinite judgment of the criminal (*VPR$_{19}$*, 196).

Henrich sees in this passage unambiguous evidence that Hegel believes the poor have a right to rebel.[52] It is, however, somewhat slender evidence for such a large conclusion. And it receives little echo in the rest of Hegel's oeuvre. Hegel certainly does seem to "justify" in the passage the poor man's criminal non-recognition of right, but he nowhere suggests that this criminal nonrecognition issues in political action or that it is directed against the very structure of society except in the general sense that all crime is a denial of right as right (see *PR*, §95). Beyond that, though, it is not clear what a right to rebel might mean here. Poverty is not the result of a contingent abuse of power on the part of the rulers but an inevitable consequence of the capitalist structure of civil society. And Hegel is certainly not suggesting that the whole bourgeois system of civil society needs to be overthrown and replaced with something different.[53] In the lectures of 1819–20, as in the text of the *Philosophy of Right* itself, he goes on to discuss how the problem of poverty might be rectified and the emergence of a rabble prevented without overthrowing the entire structure of civil society. His concern is to modify civil society from within, not to replace it with it something altogether different.

Hegel's understanding of what might count as a solution to the problem of poverty is very much determined by his concern to prevent the emergence of a rabble. Thus, he quickly rejects the idea that the poor should be directly supported by taxing the rich. Such direct support violates the principle of civil society, which requires that the satisfaction of needs be mediated by work, and destroys "the feeling of self-sufficiency and honor" among the poor (*PR*, §245). In the lectures of 1819–20, Hegel makes this point even more emphatically. The direct support of the poor by the rich brings about the "complete degeneration" of the former, destroying the "self-feeling" by which they seek to live through their own industry and work, and inspiring the kind of "shamelessness that we see in England" (*VPR$_{19}$*, 197).[54] The paternalistic poor laws of England, which were to be swept away by the reforms of 1834, seem to be at the forefront of Hegel's mind as he criticizes various schemes to support the poor without requiring them to work. Again in the lectures of 1819–20, he states that in those places in England where there are no poor-rates "the poor are always better-mannered and more inclined to work" (*VPR₁₉*, 197). And in the *Philosophy of Right,* he commends the policy of Scotland (again, where the poor-rates were not operative), which "leaves the poor to their fate and directs them to beg from the public" (*PR,* §245R). The latter, rather harsh method of dealing with poverty does not, of course, represent Hegel's favored solution to the problem; it recommends itself to him only in comparison with the paternalistic system of the English poor laws.

Given his opposition to direct support of the poor through welfare payments, one might presume that Hegel would favor a solution to the problem of poverty that requires them to work. But he quickly dismisses this proposal as well. Providing the poor with the opportunity to work would lead only to an overproduction of goods and exacerbate the condition that led to the creation of a large class of impoverished and unemployed individuals in the first place (*PR,* §245). This does not seem to have always been Hegel's view. In the Heidelberg lectures of 1817–18, for example, he says that, in an effort "to combat the idleness and malevolence that poverty usually brings in its train," "civil society must keep the poor working; in this way there awakens in them the feeling of standing on their own feet, which is the best counter to malevolence" (*LNR,* §118R). But by the time he delivers the lectures of 1819–20, the concern with overproduction resulting from putting the poor to work is firmly in place (*VPR₁₉*, 197). Neither providing direct support to the poor without the mediation of work nor providing them with the opportunity to earn their living through the mediation of work—neither welfare nor workfare, in the current jargon—offers an adequate solution to the problem of modern poverty. It is in this context that Hegel draws the pessimistic conclusion quoted above: "despite an *excess of wealth,* civil society is *not wealthy enough*—i.e. its own distinct resources are not sufficient—to prevent an excess of poverty and the formation of a rabble" (*PR,* §245).

But, as has already been pointed out, Hegel does not leave it at this pessimistic conclusion. He finds in civil society itself certain resources with which it can deal with the problem of poverty it has created. The first of these involves seeking markets in foreign countries to absorb the surplus of goods produced by a particular civil society (*PR,* §246). This solution is perfected through the establishment of colonies, which provide not only a market for surplus goods

but also the means of subsistence for surplus workers (*PR*, §248).[55] The inhabitants of such colonies, Hegel argues, are not to have fewer rights than the
inhabitants of the mother country, and therefore he supports their attempts to
gain independence: "The liberation of colonies itself proves to be of the greatest
advantage to the mother state, just as the emancipation of slaves is of the
greatest advantage to the master" (*PR*, §248A). There are, of course, definite
limitations to this colonial solution to the problem of poverty in civil society.
While Hegel accurately envisages the strategies industrializing European econ-
omies would adopt in the nineteenth century to handle their excess productivity, it is clear that colonial adventure in no way constitutes a permanent solution
to the problem of poverty created by modern civil society.

The more important solution to the problem of modern poverty Hegel finds
in the "corporations." The corporations are civil bodies that are formed by
members of the estate of trade and industry who share a certain skill, trade, or
occupation. They serve as a "second family" for their members, educating them
for membership, looking after their interests, and protecting them against
particular contingencies (*PR*, §§250–52).[56] For Hegel, the corporations are
able to provide for the poor in a way that avoids the problems he associates with
the rabble-mentality. "Within the corporation," he writes, "the help which
poverty receives loses its contingent and unjustly humiliating character, and
wealth, in fulfilling the duty it owes to its association, loses the ability to
provoke arrogance in its possessor and envy in others" (*PR*, §253R). One might
ask why the help provided to the poor by a particular corporation is any less
paternalistic or productive of a dependent disposition than that provided by
society at large. Hegel's answer seems to be that such corporate aid occurs
always within the context of an occupation and thereby loses the character of a
simple transfer payment from the rich to the poor. One might also ask whether,
in assuming that the poor already belong to corporations, Hegel has not made
his problem somewhat easier and contradicted his understanding of the poor as
"deprived of all the advantages of society" (*PR*, §241).[57] It is not clear what
Hegel's answer to this question would be except to say that every member of
civil society who does not belong to the agricultural or universal estates should
be urged to join a corporation.

This concludes Hegel's treatment of the problem of poverty, and we now
return to our earlier question as to whether it undermines the claim of the
modern state to be the actualization of freedom and the embodiment of rationality. It is difficult to give a definitive answer because Hegel's discussion of
poverty, contrary to the aims of his philosophical method, remains so full of

empirical considerations. Within the terms of his own argument, poverty does not pose an insurmountable challenge to the freedom and rationality of the modern state. Contrary to Avineri's contention, Hegel does not simply throw up his hands at the problem of poverty but proposes two solutions—namely, colonization and the corporations—by which its worst effects can be counteracted. Whether these proposed solutions constitute genuine or complete solutions to the problem of modern poverty is, of course, another question.[58] I suggested above that there is some reason to doubt that they do. On the other hand, it is not clear that some solutions Hegel rejects—private charity, taxation of the wealthy, job-creation and training, and so forth—are as inefficacious as he makes them out to be. It may be that the effective management of the problem of modern poverty requires a complex blend of these strategies. This suggests, though, that poverty does not necessarily pose an insurmountable challenge to the claim of the modern state to be the actualization of freedom and the embodiment of rationality. While Hegel may not have come up with the definitive solution to the problem of modern poverty—it would have been remarkable if he had—the great virtue of his discussion is that it candidly recognizes poverty as a distinctive problem of modern civil society and correctly identifies the criteria to be applied and many of the pitfalls to be avoided in the pursuit of a solution.

Hegel concludes his elaborate analysis of civil society with a discussion of the corporation. We have already discussed the role the corporations play in Hegel's treatment of the problem of poverty. But they have an even more general and fundamental significance with respect to the development of civil society as a whole. The central significance of the corporations for Hegel is that, in them, individuals begin to go beyond the individualism and selfishness that characterize civil society and make the universal, a common good, their explicit purpose. Universality has, of course, been the implicit goal and nisus of civil society, from the system of needs on. But this universalization and integration of individuals has taken place largely behind their backs, in the manner of Smith's invisible hand. It is only at the level of the corporation that individuals begin to work consciously for others and make universality their explicit purpose. Hegel writes: "We saw earlier that, in providing for himself, the individual in civil society is also acting for others. But this unconscious necessity is not enough; only in the corporation does it become a knowing and thinking [part of] ethical life" (*PR*, §255A).

Why is it important that individuals adopt the universal as their explicit, and not merely implicit, end or purpose? Why is the unconscious universality of the earlier stages of civil society "not enough"? Two slightly different considerations appear to be at work in Hegel's response to this question. The first has to do with his concept of rational freedom. An individual is rationally or truly free only if he is actively engaged in promoting a universal end above and beyond his merely private or particular ends. "[I]t is necessary," Hegel writes, "to provide ethical man with a universal activity in addition to his private end." In the ancient polis, this universal activity was provided through direct participation by the citizens in public or political life. But in the modern state, *pace* Rousseau, this is no longer possible: "In our modern states, the citizens have only a limited share in the universal business of the state . . . [The] universal [activity] which the modern state does not always offer [ethical man] can be found in the corporation" (*PR*, §255A). It is mainly through the corporations that most people—those outside the universal or political estate—have the direct experience of subordinating their private, selfish interest to a common or universal interest which transcends it.

The second reason why the corporations are important for Hegel is that they serve as a crucial bridge from the individualism and atomism of civil society to the universal life of the state. It is not enough that individuals be linked to one another and to the universal through the invisible hand of the system of needs. The stability of the state demands that they begin to adopt the universal as their explicit purpose: "The whole, the state, only achieves inner stability when what is universal, what is implicit, is also recognized as universal" (*LNR*, §121R). In the corporation, analogous to what happens in the family, the individual learns to subordinate his self-interest to the whole; and this gives the state its firm foundation. For this reason, Hegel refers to the corporation as the "second ethical root" of the state: "The *family* is the first *ethical* root of the state; the *corporation* is the second, and it is based in civil society" (*PR*, §255). The family and the corporation—to some extent also the estates (see *PR*, §201A)—are the two fundamental institutions by which the atomism of civil society is counteracted and individuals begin to orient themselves to a whole that transcends their merely private self-interest: "The sanctity of marriage and the honor attaching to the corporation are the two moments round which the disorganization of civil society revolves" (*PR*, §255R).

The role Hegel envisages for the corporations here is similar to the role Tocqueville envisages for associations in a democracy, as many commentators have observed.[59] Like Tocqueville—and like his contemporary heirs who sing the praises of "civil society"—Hegel is very much concerned with the atomism that is produced by modern civil society.[60] Out of such atomized individuals, bent on their own self-interest and heedless of the common interest, a free state cannot be constructed or long maintained. The atomism of modern civil society must be combatted, but—again like Tocqueville—Hegel sees the cure as arising from within civil society in the form of the corporations, not as having to be imposed from without. The corporation joins the family as one of the key institutions that educates the individual to universality and to ethical life. Together the corporation and the family form the crucial ethical preconditions of the modern rational state. It is to the latter comprehensive entity, the apex of Hegel's political philosophy, that we now turn.

Chapter 8 The Rational State

The argument of the *Philosophy of Right*, and of Hegel's political philosophy in general, culminates in his teaching about the state. The state is the substantial ground or basis of all the rights and institutions whose development we have followed up to this point—the rights of property, contract, welfare, and conscience, as well as the institutions of the family and civil society. At the same time, the state marks the telos of the dialectic of human freedom pursued in the *Philosophy of Right* insofar as it is in the state that individuals finally make the universal their explicit aim and purpose. In this latter regard, Hegel argues that the state is to be sharply distinguished from civil society. Whereas in civil society—with the important but ultimately incomplete exception of the corporations—the universal is an unintentional byproduct of the pursuit of individual self-interest and thus appears as an "unconscious necessity," in the state it becomes an end that citizens knowingly and willingly acknowledge.

Hegel, of course, rests much weight on this distinction between the state and civil society. The contractarian tradition of modern political philosophy—the tradition of Hobbes, Locke, Rousseau, Kant, and

Fichte—ultimately founders precisely because it fails to draw this distinction, confusing the state with civil society. Nevertheless, it must be admitted that the grounds for this distinction between civil society and the state are not always clear from Hegel's argument. Many critics have found the relationship between civil society and the state in the *Philosophy of Right* to be deeply obscure. Why is the move to the state necessary, and what exactly does the state add that is not already available in civil society? Beyond this, what exactly is the relationship of the individual to the state? On the one hand, Hegel tells us that the movement from civil society to the state is necessary because "the destiny of individuals is to lead a universal life" (*PR*, §258R). On the other, he indicates that, in "our modern states, the citizens have only a limited share in the universal business of the state" (*PR*, §255A). How exactly are the majority of members of the Hegelian state to be regarded, as *citoyens* or as mere *bourgeois*?

These two related issues provide the thematic thread of this chapter. The first issue of the relationship between civil society and the state I take up most fully in the first section. There I make clearer just how Hegel draws this distinction and the modification of the modern tradition of political philosophy he thereby effects. The second issue of the relationship of the individual to the state comes up at various points in the chapter but receives its most sustained treatment in the section devoted to the rational constitution. There I show that, while Hegel certainly envisages that individuals participate in varying degrees in the universality of the state, with the universal or political class participating most fully, he nevertheless delineates a number of ways in which ordinary citizens can transcend their merely bourgeois existence and begin to fulfill their destiny of leading a universal life. In connection with this latter issue, I also consider the question of how self-consciously or reflectively the ordinary citizen apprehends the universality embodied in the state, especially in the light of what Hegel says about the patriotic disposition and religion.

FROM CIVIL SOCIETY TO THE STATE

Next to the transition from morality to ethical life, the transition from civil society to the state is the most important in the *Philosophy of Right*. At first, one may wonder why this step from civil society to the state is necessary. Civil society would seem to have everything it needs to be a self-complete entity: a system of justice to regulate the interactions between individuals as they pursue their economic self-interest, a police force to maintain public order, a public authority to regulate the market and provide for the poor, and finally corporations to lift individuals out of their narrow self-interest and lead them to identify with a more universal purpose. Why is this not enough? "How is it," as one commentator asks, "that [civil] society is not the last category of social philosophy? Why does it lack something, so that Hegel thinks he has to move on to the *state?*"[1]

Hegel's answer to this question is a mixture of both mundane and speculative considerations. The mundane considerations revolve around the need for a unifying or sovereign power above and beyond the particularistic institutions of civil society. The specific transition from civil society to the state is out of the corporations, the particular interests of which, Hegel argues, need to be subordinated to something higher and more universal. Though the corporations possess a relative universality, their ends remain "limited and finite" (*PR*, §256; see also §288). It is only in the state that the universal as such, the genuinely common good, is willed. "That the universal as such is willed," Hegel writes in the lectures of 1819–20, "characterizes the state as such," in contradistinction to the particularism of the corporations (*VPR$_{19}$*, 207).[2] The corporations "must come under the higher supervision of the state, for [they] would otherwise become ossified and set in [their] ways, and decline into a miserable guild system" (*PR*, §255A).[3] The point Hegel makes here about the need for an overarching authority to coordinate and supervise the corporations can be extended to other activities that characterize the state as well: political deliberation, war, and so forth. All these activities demand a commitment to the whole, the common good, the universal as such, which is simply not available within the individualistic terms of civil society.

Besides these mundane concerns with the integrity of the social whole, however, Hegel has other, more speculative reasons for making the move from civil society to the state. These more speculative reasons, which nowhere receive separate or specific treatment but instead pervade the whole of Hegel's argument, once again have to do with his doctrine of rational freedom. In civil society individuals enjoy only their particular or subjective freedom, whereas in the state they will the universal, they lead a universal life, and are thus positively or affirmatively or substantially free. "[I]t is only through being a member of the state," Hegel writes, "that the individual himself has objectivity, truth, and ethical life. *Union* as such is itself the true content and end, and the destiny of individuals is to lead a universal life" (*PR*, §258R). The distinction Hegel draws here between the merely particular freedom of civil society and the substantial freedom of the state of course recalls some of the civic republican themes of his earliest writings—the primacy of the political to the economic, of the public to the private—and this civic republican aspect of his teaching is clearly evinced when he invokes the Rousseauan distinction between *bourgeois* and *citoyen* to characterize the ascent from civil society to the state: whereas in civil society the individual is merely a *bourgeois,* in the state he "exists for universal life as a public person" and "is a *citoyen*" (*LNR,* §72R).

There are things to be observed in connection with this second, more speculative line of argument for the necessity of moving from civil society to the state. The first is that it does not strictly demonstrate the necessity for the transition from civil society to the state except in the most external fashion. The rational freedom Hegel attributes to the state may in fact be something eminently desirable, but it does not emerge as a necessary result of some internal failure or breakdown of civil society. The "necessity" spoken of here stems more from the telos of Hegel's philosophy of human freedom than from an immanent critique of civil society itself.[4] The second thing to be observed with respect to this line of argument is that it remains unclear who is to enjoy the rational freedom which Hegel identifies with the state. Hegel tells us that it is the "destiny of individuals to lead a universal life" as *citoyens,* but it remains unclear how many individuals actually fulfill this destiny in the Hegelian state. We have already seen him say, in connection with the corporations, that "in our modern states, the citizens have only a limited share in the universal business of the state" (*PR,* §255A); and this observation about the limited political role of citizens will be confirmed later in what he says about the constitution of the state. How can this restriction on political participation be reconciled with the requirement to lead a universal life?[5]

This, of course, is one of the fundamental questions raised by Hegel's doctrine of the rational state. Before it can be satisfactorily answered, however, we must go through Hegel's entire argument concerning the state, beginning with his elaboration of the basic concept of the state in §§257–70 of the *Philosophy of Right.* These fourteen paragraphs are among the most important in the *Philosophy of Right,* not only further specifying the *differentia* of the state vis-à-vis civil society but also laying bare Hegel's differences with social-contract teaching and with the liberal tradition in general.

Hegel gives his most essential definition of the state in §257: "The state is the actuality of the ethical Idea—the ethical spirit as substantial will, *manifest* and clear to itself, which thinks and knows itself and implements what it knows in so far as it knows it." Two things stand out in this definition. First, the state is a form of ethical life; that is, it is a substantial whole or universal in which individuals do not relate to one another as independent or self-interested persons but as members of a larger whole in which they find their essential self-consciousness. In this respect, the state resembles the family and fundamentally differs from civil society. In both the state and the family, "ethical life consists in the feeling, the consciousness, and the will, not of the individual personality and its interests, but of the common personality and interests of all the members in general" (*IPH*, 45/60). But unlike in the family, in the state the individual's sense of unity with others and with the substantial whole does not take the form of immediate "feeling" but, rather, of "thought," "knowing," and conscious will. This is the second point contained in the definition of the state quoted above, reflected in the words that the substantial will of the state is one that is "*manifest* and clear to itself, which thinks and knows itself and implements what it knows in so far as it knows it." Hegel elaborates on this thinking, knowing, willing character of the ethical life of the state in the Remark to §257, where he contrasts it with the "piety" which characterizes the ethical life of the family: "The *Penates* are the inner and *lower* gods, while the *spirit of the nation* (Athene) is the divine which *knows* and *wills* itself. *Piety* is feeling and ethical life governed by feeling, and *political virtue* is the willing of that thought-end which has being in and for itself."[6]

This distinction between the thinking and known character of the state and the feeling character of the family is one we encountered earlier in Hegel's initial characterization of the family (see *PR*, §158A); and it runs through his analysis of the basic concept of the state (see *PR*, §§260, 263A, 270). In §270, for example, he repeats the point that the state "*knows* what it wills, and knows it in its *universality* as something *thought.*" Nevertheless, it is not always clear what Hegel means by this thinking and knowing character of the state. To some it seems to suggest a more reflective relationship between the individual and the state.[7] But such a view is rendered problematic by Hegel's references to custom, habit, and trust in the political disposition (see *PR*, §268). Indeed, in the definition of the state found in the Heidelberg lectures of 1817–18 that parallels the one found in the *Philosophy of Right*, "custom" (*Sitte*) is mentioned alongside the thinking and knowing character of the state without apparent sense of contradiction: "The state is the actuality of the ethical spirit as the manifest, self-transparent universal will, achieving knowledge and fulfillment in custom as it exists immediately in the individual self-consciousness" (*LNR*, §123). And though Hegel makes more of a distinction between custom and the knowing or thinking character of the state in the *Philosophy of Right*, he still does not see them as mutually opposed but, rather, as complementary aspects of the state: "[The state] has its immediate existence in *custom* and its mediate existence in the *self-consciousness* of the individual, in the individual's knowledge and activity" (*PR,* §257).

What exactly, then, does Hegel mean when he refers to the thinking and knowing character of the state? What he primarily seems to mean is not that the individual has a reflective or utterly transparent relationship to the state, but that the individual is governed in the state by known laws that exist for or are "posited" in his consciousness, instead of being governed by instinct or feeling. As we have seen, thinking and knowing belong to law insofar as it "posited" (see *PR,* §209–11). And it is in terms of its determination by law that Hegel frequently distinguishes the state from the family: whereas in the family one is conscious of one's unity with another in the form of feeling, in the state "one is conscious of unity as law; there, the content must be rational, and I must know it" (*PR,* §158A). It must be admitted that Hegel also suggests that the state is characterized by knowledge and thought in another and perhaps more substantial way, one that does not extend to every citizen in the state but only to the members of the political or universal estate, but we will deal with this aspect more fully below when we consider §270.

From the definition of the state as the "actuality of the ethical idea," Hegel goes on in §258 to define it further as "the actuality of the substantial will." With this typically abstract phrase, Hegel indicates the essential relationship between the state and freedom. The state is the actuality of freedom—but of freedom understood, not in terms of the particular or arbitrary will of the individual, but in terms of the individual's substantial or rational will. The state is not simply a means to the satisfaction of the individual in his or her own particularity; rather, it is the objective embodiment of that universality or rationality that represents the deepest essence of human beings. This substantial freedom that is realized in the state is not something utterly divorced from the subjective awareness of individuals. Thus, Hegel writes that the actuality of the state is one "which it possesses in the particular *self-consciousness* when this has been raised to its universality; as such, it is the *rational* in and for itself" (*PR,* §258). But the emphasis in §258 remains on the objective character of the freedom realized in the state, on its substantiality and rationality, not on the individual's subjective willing of it. This emphasis is reflected in a previously quoted sentence from the Addition: "Any discussion of freedom must begin not with individuality or the individual self-consciousness, but only with the essence of self-consciousness; for whether human beings know it or not, this essence realizes itself as a self-sufficient power of which individuals are only moments" (*PR,* §258A).

The priority of the substantial end of the state to the individual articulated in this sentence forms the basis of what Hegel says about the right of the state in relation to individuals: the substantial end of the state "possesses the highest right in relation to individuals, whose *highest duty* is to be members of the state" (*PR*, §258). Here we have clearly left the world of the social contract. A contract is something grounded in the arbitrary wills of individuals and at their option. But for Hegel, membership in the state cannot be an optional matter. Again, the state represents the actualization of the universal and rational essence of human beings. Therefore, there is an obligation to belong to it; it is the "highest duty" of individuals to belong to it. As Hegel put it earlier in the *Philosophy of Right* when commenting on the inappropriateness of the model of the contract for understanding the state: "It is the rational destiny of human beings to live within the state, and even if no state is yet present, reason requires that one be established" (*PR*, §75A). Against the contractual model of the state, Hegel here returns to the Aristotelian understanding of humans as by nature political animals. Indeed, in the passage of the lectures of 1819–20 where he speaks of the "absolute right" of the state over against individuals and of the "absolute duty" of individuals to belong to it, he refers to Aristotle's famous dictum that the man who is capable of being solitary and self-sufficient would be either a beast or a god (*VPR₁₉*, 210).

Of course, it is not just the social contract that Hegel is rejecting here but the whole classical liberal understanding of the state for which the social contract serves as the chief theoretical construct. According to classical liberal doctrine, as definitively expressed by Locke, the end or purpose of the state is to secure the life, liberty, and property of the individual. Hegel, however, identifies this individualistic understanding of the state with the standpoint of civil society; it is the state, as we have already seen him say, merely as the understanding conceives it, "the external state, the state based on need" (*PR*, §183). In the oft-quoted Remark to §258, he clearly states his reasons for rejecting this liberal understanding of the state:

> If the state is confused with civil society and its determination is equated with the security and protection of property and personal freedom, *the interest of individuals as such* becomes the ultimate end for which they are united; it also follows from this that membership of the state is an optional matter. But the relationship of the state to the individual is of a quite different kind. Since the state is objective spirit, it is only through being a member of the state that the individual himself has objectivity, truth, and ethical life. *Union* as such is itself the true content and end, and the destiny of individuals is to lead a universal life. (*PR*, §258R, p. 276)

This passage encapsulates almost all of Hegel's critique of the classical liberal conception of the state. According to this liberal conception, the individual qua individual is of supreme value. The state serves merely as a means by which the individual can more safely and securely pursue his or her own particular ends or purposes. But Hegel rejects this understanding of the relationship of the state to the individual. As we have seen, the state is not simply a means to the satisfaction of the individual in his or her own particularity; rather, it is the actualization of that universality that represents the destiny and deepest essence of human beings. For this reason, too, it is a mistake to view the state as being based on a contract. The state is not something grounded in the arbitrary wills of individuals and at their option; rather, it is the realization of their substantial or rational wills. From this it follows, as we have seen, that there is an obligation or duty to belong to it.

With respect to the "Idea" of the state Hegel is presenting here—namely, as the actualization of the substantial will or rational freedom of the individual—the historical origin of the state "makes no difference" (*PR*, §258R, p. 276). The fact that the state has arisen from patriarchal conditions or been founded through force or fear in no way detracts from its authority or right. From early on, Hegel recognized that states have generally been established, not through voluntary agreement, but through "the noble force of great men," a Theseus or a Robespierre (*HHS*, 154–57/257–60). And in the Heidelberg lectures of 1817–18, he even defends the "right of coercion" on the part of the founders of states (*LNR*, §124 and R).[8] Again, none of this counts against the right or ultimate legitimacy of the state; and philosophy generally ought not to concern itself with the purely contingent question of historical origins. Instead, the "philosophical approach deals only with the internal aspect of all this, with the thinking concept" (*PR*, §258R, p. 276). That is to say, philosophy is concerned with grounding the state in the concept of human freedom; it is concerned with the state, not insofar as it arises from the free choice of individuals, but insofar as it corresponds to and actualizes their substantial or rational wills.

With respect to this philosophical enterprise of grounding the state in the concept of human freedom, it is Rousseau who marks the crucial turning point, according to Hegel. "[I]t was the achievement of Rousseau," he writes, in a passage which we have quoted several times, "to put forward the *will* as the principle of the state, a principle which has *thought* not only as its form (as with the social instinct, for example, or divine authority) but also as its content, and which is in fact *thinking* itself" (*PR*, §258R, p. 277). Why is it that Hegel attributes this crucial innovation of making will the basis of the state to Rousseau instead of to Hobbes or any of the other thinkers who seek to ground political authority in individual consent? To answer this question, we have to unpack what Hegel is trying to say in his idiosyncratic way about "thought" in this passage.

For Hegel, "thought" essentially refers to the universalizing and idealizing activity of the self or subject, the activity by which the self or subject penetrates objects and deprives them of their externality and independence. "Thought" in this sense is the distinguishing principle of the modern world, exhibiting itself in modern natural science and above all in the Reformation (see *PH,* 344–45/417, 416–17/496–97, 438–42/520–24). It also finds expression in modern natural right teachings, where "right and ethical life came to be looked upon as having their foundation in the present will of men," instead of in the external commands of God or the purely positive rights found in "old parchments." In these modern natural right teachings, the source of civil and political right was sought in principles internal to human beings, for example, "the social instinct" and "the principle of security for the person and property of the citizens" (*PH,* 440–41/522). It is Hobbes in particular whom Hegel credits with having made "thought" in this sense the basis of political right. Before Hobbes, "ideals were set before us, or Holy Scripture or positive law was quoted as authoritative. Hobbes, on the contrary, sought to derive the bond which holds the state together and the nature of state-power from principles which lie within us and which we recognize as our own." He traced political authority back to "natural necessities and wants" (*HP,* III, 316/226, 317/227).

As momentous as this theoretical innovation was, Hegel argues, the principles invoked as the basis of the state by Hobbes and other social-contract theorists still had thought only as their form and not as their content. Though Hobbes and Locke did ultimately ground political authority in the will of the individual, they did not demand that the state should directly correspond to or emanate from the self-conscious will of the individual. It is this distinctive and democratic demand for identity between the will of the individual and the state that Hegel associates with Rousseau; and it is this demand which he has in mind when he asserts that Rousseau was the first to adduce a principle for the state which has thought as both its form and its content. Whereas Hobbes and Locke made self-preservation or property-protection the principle of the state, Rousseau made free will itself the principle of the state. It is only with Rousseau, Hegel maintains in his *Lectures on the History of Philosophy,* that freedom was recognized as "the distinguishing feature of man"; that there came "into consciousness as content the sense that man has liberty in his spirit as the altogether

absolute, that free will is the notion of man" (*HP,* III, 401–2/306–7).⁹ Hegel
sums up the distinctive turn given to political philosophy by Rousseau vis-à-vis
his predecessors in the following passage from the *Philosophy of History:*

> An *intellectual principle* [*Gedankenprinzip*] was thus discovered to serve as a basis for
> the state—one which does not, like previous principles, belong to the sphere of
> opinion, such as the social instinct, the desire of security for property, etc., nor to
> religious piety, such as the divine appointment of the governing power—but the
> principle of certainty, which is identity with my self-consciousness . . . This is a vast
> discovery in regard to the profoundest depths of being and freedom. (*PH,* 445–
> 46/527)

Despite Rousseau's great achievement in making will the basis of the state,
Hegel argues (as we saw in chapter 1) that he completely undermined this
achievement by understanding the will in the wrong way, taking it as the
individual will instead of as the rational will: "Rousseau considered the will
only in the determinate form of the *individual* will (as Fichte subsequently also
did) and regarded the universal will not as the will's rationality in and for itself,
but only as the *common element* arising out of this individual will *as a conscious
will*" (*PR,* §258R, p. 277).¹⁰ Once again, it might be objected that Hegel's
interpretation of Rousseau's notion of the general will here is one-sidedly
individualistic. After all, Rousseau does take some trouble to distinguish the
general will from what he calls "the will of all." Nevertheless, Rousseau's
doctrine of the general will is notoriously ambiguous, and Hegel's interpretation of it does capture certain individualistic elements that creep into it: for
example, Rousseau's contention that, in joining civil society and submitting to
the general will, each "nevertheless obeys only himself and remains as free as
before"; his insistence that the general will cannot be represented and demands
some sort of directly democratic arrangement; and so forth.¹¹

At any rate, Hegel sees the individualism implicit in Rousseau's democratic
doctrine of the general will as having disastrous consequences for our understanding of the state, consequences that were realized in the destructive events
of the French Revolution. When the universal will is misunderstood as merely
the common element arising out of everybody's individual will,

> the union of individuals within the state becomes a *contract,* which is accordingly
> based on their arbitrary will and opinions, and on their express consent given at their
> own discretion; and the further consequences which follow from this, and which
> relate merely to the understanding, destroy the divine [element] which has being in
> and for itself and its absolute authority and majesty. Consequently, when these

abstractions were invested with power, they afforded the tremendous spectacle, for the first time we know of in human history, of the overthrow of all existing and given conditions within an actual major state and the revision of its constitution from first principles and purely in terms of *thought*. (*PR,* §258R, p. 277)

The connection Hegel draws here between Rousseau's doctrine of the general will and the terrible events of the French Revolution of course goes back to his famous discussion of the French Revolution in the *Phenomenology*. What is worth attending to in the passage above is Hegel's contention that Rousseau's individualistic interpretation of the universal will and his contractual understanding of the state "destroy the divine [element] which has being in and for itself and its absolute authority and majesty." The divine character of the state receives even more explicit expression in the famous (or infamous) sentence from the Addition: "The state consists in the march of God in the world" (*PR,* §258A). Avineri translates the German sentence "*Es ist der Gang Gottes in der Welt, dass der Staat ist*" in a somewhat less authoritarian way: "It is the way of God in the world, that there should be [literally: is] the state."[12] However one translates it, the central point remains: for Hegel, the state is not merely a human artifact but at some level an expression of the divine. It is equally important to emphasize, however, that Hegel does not, in reactionary fashion, interpret the divine character of the state as somehow opposed to human will and rationality. Rather, he sees both points of view, taken by themselves, as one-sided; a true view of the state can only be achieved by synthesizing them. Thus he writes in his Berlin lectures of 1819–20: "It has been said on the one side that the state subsists through divine authority, and the governmental powers are appointed by God. On the other side [represented chiefly by Rousseau] it has been said that the state is the product of human will. Both are one-sided. The Idea of the state unites both principles in itself" (*VPR₁₉,* 211).

That he does not mean to endorse any sort of reactionary divine-right theory of political authority Hegel makes clear in his acerbic comments on Karl Ludwig von Haller in the Remark to §258. In his *Restoration of Political Science,* published between 1816 and 1820, Haller provided the theoretical justification for the restoration of the conservative patrimonial state in Prussia. This justification consisted essentially in a critique of social-contract theory and a defense of the natural-divine (the two being equated) order based on inequality and the relationship of domination and dependence. Political authority, for Haller, was emphatically "not a human creation" but, rather, "rooted in nature" as "an expression of the will of God."[13] Haller thus lies at the opposite extreme from

Rousseau, taking natural domination as the basis of political authority instead of "thought" or human freedom. Hegel makes it clear that he finds Haller's "naturalism" far less philosophically compelling than Rousseau's "intellectualism." By "*banishing thought* from the apprehension of [the state's] inner nature," Haller has produced a work that is thoroughly "thoughtless" (*PR*, §258R, p. 278). While Rousseau may have insufficiently understood his great principle that free will is the basis of the state, Haller does not even attain this essential philosophical starting-point.

I will say more about Hegel's complex understanding of the relationship between religion and the state in the following section. Now we must conclude our consideration of his critique of Rousseau in the Remark to §258. The crux of this critique is that Rousseau misinterprets the general or universal will in terms of the individual will. In opposition to Rousseau, Hegel interprets the universal will in terms of the rational will. Unlike the individual will, the rational will does not derive its content from something other than itself— from our inclinations, fancies, or desires. Rather, the rational will derives its content from the concept of will, freedom, itself. The rational will is simply the will that wills freedom—in the form of the objective rights and institutions developed over the course of the *Philosophy of Right*—and hence wills itself. While for the individual will it is the mere fact that the individual chooses that is important, for the rational will it is *what is chosen* that is decisive. It is the rationality of the content of the rational will, whether that content is chosen by individuals or not, that Hegel emphasizes in his critique of Rousseau's notion of the general will in the Remark to §258:

> In opposition to the principle of the individual will, we should remember the fundamental concept according to which the objective will is rational in itself, i.e. in its *concept*, whether or not it is recognized by individuals and willed by them at their discretion—and that its opposite, knowledge and volition, the subjectivity of freedom (which is the *sole* content of the principle of the individual will) embodies only *one* (consequently one-sided) moment of the *Idea of the rational* will, which is rational solely because it has being both *in itself* and *for itself*. (*PR*, §258R, p. 277)

Hegel's subordination of the subjective, "for itself" character of the individual will to the objective, "in itself" rationality of the genuinely free will in this passage clearly encapsulates his departure from the conventional liberal understanding of freedom and from the liberal idea of the state which is ultimately based on it. Nevertheless, though "the subjectivity of freedom" is clearly subordinated to the objectivity of the rational will in this passage, it is not altogether ignored. Hegel does say that this subjectivity of freedom constitutes one moment of the Idea of the rational will. And this point is echoed throughout the structure of the *Philosophy of Right* in the recognition subjective freedom receives in abstract right, morality, and especially civil society. In the ensuing paragraphs (§§260–68), the importance of this subjective aspect of freedom— the aspect beloved by liberalism—in Hegel's overall conception of the rational state is clearly brought out.

Paragraph 260 makes the fundamental point in this regard:

> The state is the actuality of concrete freedom. But *concrete freedom* requires that personal individuality and its particular interests should reach their full *development* and gain *recognition of their right* for itself (within the system of the family and of civil society), and also that they should, on the one hand, *pass over* of their own accord into the interest of the universal, and on the other, knowingly and willingly acknowledge this universal interest even as their own *substantial spirit*, and *actively pursue it* as their *ultimate end. (PR*, §260)

This passage is of interest not only because of its recognition of the essential role of subjective freedom in making the state and its universality concrete but also because of the way in which it conceives of the relationship between the particular interests of individuality and the universal interest of the state. Hegel indicates that there are two aspects to this relationship. On the one hand, the particular interests of individuality "*pass over* of their own accord into the interest of the universal." This process of "passing over" is perhaps best exemplified in the dialectic of civil society whereby the purely self-interested quest to satisfy personal needs leads inevitably and unconsciously to the promotion of the universal. On the other hand, "this unconscious necessity is not enough" (*PR*, §255A). It must ultimately be accompanied by a more self-conscious, less instrumental relationship to the universal; otherwise there would be nothing to the categorial distinction between the state and civil society which Hegel insists upon elsewhere. For this reason, Hegel adds that the personal interests of individuality must also "knowingly and willingly acknowledge [the] universal interest even as their own *substantial spirit*, and *actively pursue it* as their *ultimate end.*" Thus, in sharp contrast with civil society, "individuals do not live as private persons merely for these particular interests without at the same time directing their will to a universal end and acting in conscious awareness of it" (*PR*, §260).

What exactly Hegel means by "conscious awareness" of the universal here— how self-conscious or reflective he envisages the individual's awareness of the universality of the state to be—is a question we have already discussed and will consider further. For now, we need to define more precisely the unity of particular interest and universal interest that Hegel sees as taking place in the state. This unity, he tells us, can also be expressed in terms of the identity of right and duty. In his conception of the state, Hegel wants to get away from the abstract notion of duty as somehow opposed to particular interests or individual rights. "[I]n the process of fulfilling his duty," he writes, "the individual must somehow attain his own interest and satisfaction . . . Particular interests should certainly not be set aside, let alone suppressed; on the contrary, they should be harmonized with the universal, so that both they themselves and the universal are preserved." It is through fulfilling his duties as a citizen that the individual finds that his rights—of person, property, welfare, and so forth—are preserved (*PR*, §261R). Here, in his understanding of the harmony of particular and universal, right and duty, in the state, we are once again reminded of Hegel's rejection of the opposition of duty and inclination in Kant's moral philosophy. His difference with the Kantian notion of duty for duty's sake comes through particularly clearly in the lectures of 1817–18, where he writes:

> People take no share in the universal unless it is in their own self-interest. The universal must occur necessarily, and the moral will can be disregarded here; instead, since the universal must occur, the individuality of each as such must reside in the universal. The universal must be accomplished and in such a way that the individual, in accomplishing the universal is working for himself. The particularity of the individual must be maintained in the universal will. (*LNR*, §132R)

Why is it so important that subjective freedom be recognized and allowed to develop fully in the rational state? Earlier in the *Philosophy of Right*, Hegel emphasized the fact that the right of subjective freedom represents the "higher principle" of modernity versus the purely substantial principle of antiquity. Largely the endowment of Christianity, subjective freedom is something modern people have learned not only to manage and come to enjoy but also to expect and demand to be satisfied. Such a demand the modern state cannot ignore (see esp. *PR*, §§124R and 185R). Now, in connection with the constitution of the state, Hegel also emphasizes the tremendous practical advantage accruing to the state from its incorporation of subjectivity and particularity. If the state can somehow link its universal interest to the particular interest of the individual, it will be internally strong and stable. If, on the other hand, the individual does not find the satisfaction of his particularity in the state, the state will be weak; its universality will remain abstract, without actuality. "What matters most is that the law of reason should merge with the law of freedom, and that my particular end should become identical with the universal; otherwise, the state must hang in the air. It is the self-awareness of individuals which constitutes the actuality of the state, and its stability consists in the identity of the two aspects in question" (*PR*, §265A). In contradistinction to the substantialistic states of antiquity, the modern state is strong and stable, according to Hegel, precisely because it allows for the satisfaction of subjective freedom and shows itself to be "the sole precondition of the attainment of particular ends and welfare" (*PR*, §261). "The principle of modern states has enormous strength and depth because it allows the principle of subjectivity to attain fulfillment in the *self-sufficient extreme* of personal particularity, while at the same time *bringing it back to substantial unity* and so preserving this unity in the principle of subjectivity itself" (*PR*, §260).

Hegel's point here about the need for the individual to find his particular interests—his person, his property, his particular welfare—protected and secured in the state in order for the latter to be strong and stable may seem to blur the point we saw him make repeatedly above about the state's not being a mere means to the protection of life, liberty, and property of the individual. Indeed, he says at one point that "it has often been said that the end of the state is the happiness of the citizens. This is certainly true, for if their welfare is deficient, if their subjective ends are not satisfied, and if they do not find that the state as such is the means to this satisfaction, the state itself stands on an insecure footing" (*PR*, §265A). We must be careful not to misconstrue what Hegel says here, however. He does not say that the ultimate end of the state is to promote the subjective freedom or particular interests of individuals. He says only that individuals must find their subjective ends satisfied in the state and that they must see the state as somehow instrumental to this satisfaction; otherwise the state will stand "on an insecure footing." Again, his point is a practical one. It is not about the ultimate end of the state but about what is necessary to make that end—the universal, rational freedom—actual and concrete.

Hegel never tires of stressing the importance of the unity of particular and universal, subjective will and rational will, in the state. He says in one place: "Everything depends on the unity of the universal and the particular within the state" (*PR*, §261A). And in another, he asserts that it is "a proposition of the highest intrinsic importance" that "a state is well-constituted and strong if the private interest of citizens is united with the universal goal of the state, so that each finds its fulfillment and realization in the other" (*IPH*, 27/39). In the first instance, this unification of the particular and the universal takes place in the prepolitical institutions of marriage and the corporations. As Hegel reiterates here, in marriage and the corporations, the interest of the individual is linked to a universal or common interest. For this reason they constitute "the firm foundation of the state and of the trust and disposition of individuals towards it. They are the pillars on which public freedom rests" (*PR*, §265).

Despite their ethical character, however, marriage and the corporations only imperfectly unify the particular and the universal. It is true that in these institutions the individual transcends his individuality and subordinates it to a larger whole. But the whole or universal in these institutions itself remains something particular—the particular family or the particular corporation. The universal as such is not willed in marriage or the corporations, and for this reason Hegel writes that "the union of freedom and necessity is present" only "*in itself* within these institutions" (*PR*, §265). It is only in the "political constitution" and the "political disposition" corresponding to it that the said unity of freedom and necessity becomes "for itself." Here "substantial universality becomes *its own object* and end, with the result that the necessity in question similarly becomes its own object and end in the *shape* of freedom" (*PR*, §§266–67).

For the moment, we will confine ourselves to what Hegel says about the "political disposition" (*politische Gesinnung*) or "patriotism." Speaking generally, in the political or patriotic disposition, the individual identifies himself with the universality of state. But it is the peculiar form this patriotic identification takes in the modern, rational state that interests Hegel here. In particular, he wants to distinguish the political or patriotic disposition appropriate to the modern, rational state from the image of extraordinary deeds and heroic self-sacrifice that he associates with the patriotic disposition of the Greeks and that he himself embraced in some of his earliest writings. Against the idea of self-sacrifice, Hegel emphasizes the satisfaction of particular interests in the patriotic disposition. And against the idea of extraordinary deeds, he emphasizes the mundane and even habitual character of rational patriotism. Let us take up each of these interrelated aspects of Hegel's conception of the modern political or patriotic disposition separately.

The satisfaction of individual interests, both particular and substantial, is prominent in Hegel's initial description of the political or patriotic disposition. "This disposition," he writes, "is in general one of *trust* (which may pass over into more or less educated insight), or the consciousness that my substantial and particular interest is preserved and contained in the interest and end of an other (in this case, the state), and in the latter's relation to me as an individual. As a result, this other ceases to be an other for me, and in my consciousness of this, I am free" (*PR*, §268). The emphasis on the satisfaction of particular interests in this passage can also be found in parallel passages on the patriotic disposition from the lectures. In the lectures of 1819–20, for example, Hegel claims that the "patriotic disposition has more precisely the determination that the individual knows that the ends of his particularity can only be satisfied through the universal. English patriotism displays this character particularly often" (*VPR₁₉*, 227).[14] The reference to English patriotism here is interesting. In some ways English patriotism, with its emphasis on the satisfaction of the individual instead of on self-sacrifice, represents the countermodel to the civic spirit of the Greeks for Hegel. "The English have a corporate spirit," he writes in one place, "because they know all individuals receive their right, and the state, as universal will, is their will, the people's own will" (*LNR*, §129R). Hegel's distinction here between ancient and modern patriotism in many ways parallels the one later drawn by Tocqueville between the instinctive patriotism characteristic of aristocracies and the more rational and self-interested patriotism characteristic of well-ordered democracies.[15]

The other feature Hegel underlines with respect to the political or patriotic disposition in the modern, rational state is its habitual character. The political disposition consists in "a volition which has become *habitual*" (*PR*, §268). In contrast to the common understanding of patriotism as "a willingness to perform *extraordinary* sacrifices and actions," the patriotic disposition is one "which, in the normal conditions and circumstances of life, habitually knows that the community is the substantial basis and end" (*PR*, §268R). Hegel does not deny that extraordinary or heroic actions will sometimes be required of citizens, especially in times of war (see *PR*, §324). But he argues that it is the habitual confidence in the state evinced in the ordinary circumstances of life "which underlies the willingness to make extraordinary efforts" (*PR*, §268R). The point Hegel makes here with respect to the habitual and thoroughly mundane character of the political disposition resembles in many ways the point he made earlier about "rectitude" in the ethical disposition (*PR*, §150). And as he did there, he here complains about the hypocrisy of the moral "craving to be something special" or "exceptional": "[J]ust as human beings often prefer to be guided by magnanimity instead of right, so also do they readily convince themselves that they possess this extraordinary patriotism in order to exempt themselves from the genuine disposition, or to excuse their lack of it" (*PR*, §268R). Hegel goes on to say that, even when people criticize the state, they continue to be informed by an underlying trust or confidence in it:

> Thus people's apparent political disposition should be distinguished from what they genuinely will; for inwardly, they in fact will the thing [*Sache*], but they fasten on to details and delight in the vanity of claiming superior insight. They *trust* that the state will continue to exist and that particular interests can be fulfilled within it alone; but *habit* blinds us to the basis of our entire existence. It does not occur to someone who walks the streets in safety at night that this might be otherwise, for this *habit* of [living in] safety has become *second nature,* and we scarcely stop to think that it is solely the effect of particular institutions. Representational thought often imagines that the state is held together by force; but what holds it together is simply the basic sense of order which everyone possesses. (*PR,* §268A, emphasis added)

Some commentators have seen Hegel's emphasis on trust and habit in the political disposition as fundamentally in tension with his general emphasis on the knowing and self-conscious character of the state.[16] But such a view imports an unduly reflective meaning into Hegel's references to the knowing and thinking character of the state. When Hegel says that, in the state, "the universal does not attain validity or fulfillment without the interest, knowledge, and volition of the particular" (*PR,* §260), he does not imply that the interest, knowledge, or volition involved is necessarily of a reflective sort. The individual must have some awareness that his particular interests are preserved in the state and that it is thereby in accordance with his will. But this awareness need not be particularly reflective; it may be habitual, more akin to trust, although Hegel also holds out the possibility that it "may pass over into more or less educated insight." In a passage from the *Philosophy of History* that I quoted earlier in connection with his discussion of the habitual and unreflective character of the ethical disposition, Hegel writes that "the ethical life of the state is not of the moral or reflective kind, wherein one's individual conviction rules supreme." But he adds that "if I reflect upon the object of my activity, I must have the consciousness that my will has been called upon" (*IPH,* 42/57). By identifying the political disposition with unreflective trust and habit, Hegel does not mean to deny the knowing, thinking, and willing character of the state. That the ethical life of the state is a second nature does not mean that the individual relates to its laws as a child does to the commands of its parents, "without will or insight of its own" (*LPHI,* 197/243–44). Again, there must be some awareness on the part of the individual that these laws are in accordance with the individual's will. But this awareness is not incompatible with trust or habit. The

unreflective character of the political or patriotic disposition is thus not inconsistent with Hegel's general emphasis on the knowing and self-conscious character of the state.

Hegel's discussion of the political or patriotic disposition leads directly to the
consideration of the political constitution, since this disposition "takes its
particularly determined *content* from the various aspects of the organism of the
state" (*PR*, §269). The patriotic disposition of citizens in the modern state is
not, like the republican virtue of the ancient Greeks, undifferentiated. It receives its particular content from the specific sphere of action or estate to which
the individual belongs (*LNR*, §132R). Hegel therefore turns his attention to the
organism of the state or the political constitution. But before doing so, he
inserts a lengthy aside on the relationship between religion and the state.

RELIGION AND THE STATE

In the Remark to §270 of the *Philosophy of Right*, Hegel addresses himself to the
issue of the relationship between religion and the state. This issue—what
Spinoza referred to as the theologico-political problem—of course has a central
place in the origins of modern political philosophy. And it plays no small role in
Hegel's own political philosophical outlook. Indeed, George Kelly has said of
Hegel's discussion of the relationship between church and state in §270 of the
Philosophy of Right that it "is a strategic hinge of that whole work."[17] At the very
least, the discussion encapsulates much of what is most distinctive in Hegel's
political philosophical outlook. Hegel's attitude toward the relationship between religion and the state is typically complex. On the one hand, he rejects
the Enlightenment liberal idea that church and state should be kept strictly
separate. On the other hand, he wants nothing to do with theocracy. As he
succinctly puts it in his lectures of 1819–20: "Only in despotisms are state and
church one" (*VPR₁₉*, 225).

It will be remembered that the issue of the relationship between religion and
the state was one that occupied the young Hegel greatly. The writings from the
1790s, as we saw, disclose an ambivalent attitude on this issue. On the one hand,
in many of these writings, Hegel draws a sharp line between church and state,
relying heavily on the Kantian distinction between morality and legality. The
civil sphere of legality, insofar as it is a sphere of coercion, must not be allowed
to infringe on the freedom which is the essence of both morality and religion.
Moral and religious obligations cannot be made into civil obligations (see
"PC," 86–87/124–25, 95–129/134–58; "BF," 74–75/66, 78–80/70–72). On the

other hand, Hegel also holds up the ideal of a more integrated relationship between religion and political life. This is most clearly seen in his celebration of the unity of religion and politics in the Greek polis, against the unworldly and nonpolitical character of Christianity (see "TE," 499/33, 504–7/41–44; "SC," 301/418). This Hellenic aspect of Hegel's understanding of the relationship between church and state receives its most succinct expression in a fragment from the late 1790s: "If the principle of the state is a complete whole, then church and state cannot possibly be distinct. . . . The whole of the church is thus only a fragment if men are totally smashed into particular state-men and particular church-men" (*Werke* 1:444).

In his discussion of the relationship between religion and the state in the *Philosophy of Right,* Hegel convincingly reconciles the two positions that he seems to hold somewhat inconsistently in his early writings. Before turning to that discussion, however, we must examine the context in which it appears in the argument of the *Philosophy of Right.* Paragraph 270, to which Hegel's discussion of religion and the state is appended, actually says nothing about religion. Instead, it brings out once again the knowing and thinking character that distinguishes the state. The substantiality of the state, Hegel writes, is animated by

> the spirit which knows and wills itself as having *passed through the form of education.* The state therefore *knows* what it wills, and knows it in its *universality* as something *thought.* Consequently, it acts and functions in accordance with known ends and recognized principles, and with laws which are laws not only *in themselves* but also for consciousness; and it likewise acts in determinate knowledge of existing circumstances and relations in so far as its actions have relevance to these. (*PR,* §270)

As was pointed out above in connection with §257, what Hegel primarily has in mind when he thus characterizes the state in terms of knowing and thinking is that, in the state, the individual is governed by known laws which exist for or are "posited" in his consciousness, instead of being governed by subjective instinct or feeling. To be governed by "known" and "posited" laws presupposes that the individual has "passed through the form of education"; which is to say that he has emancipated himself from the subjectivity of mere feeling and learned how to "think" or "adapt the form of universality to objects" (*PR,* §209A; §§209–11 in general). In thus being determined by posited and known law, the ethical life of the state is distinguished from the more immediate ethical life of the family.

But is something more implied in this passage? It has been suggested that when Hegel says that the "state therefore knows what it wills," he is referring only to the enlightened consciousness of the bearers of state power, the members of the political or universal estate who hold some sort of political or bureaucratic office. Such knowing is incompatible with the patriotic disposition of ordinary citizens, which consists mainly of "trust."[18] Some of the things Hegel says in the *Philosophy of Right* admittedly support this interpretation. For example, when he says later that "the people" refers "to that category of citizens *who do not know their own will*" (*PR*, §301R), it would seem that he excludes "the people" from the knowing character of the state. Nevertheless, the aspect of being governed by posited and known law mentioned above, in which everyone would seem to participate, cannot be ignored. While the members of the political or universal class may participate more completely in the knowing character of the state, "the people" are not entirely excluded from it. The latter do not relate to the state simply in the form of feeling, as in the family; rather, they are "conscious of unity as law," where "the content must be rational, and I must know it" (*PR*, §158A; see also §§257R, 263A).

What does all this have to do with religion? Religion, like family life, Hegel associates with the sphere of immediate and subjective feeling. While religion has the same content as the state, namely, absolute truth, its consciousness of this substantial content is in the form of subjective feeling or faith rather than determinate thought and knowledge. A good deal of what Hegel says about the relationship between religion and the state in the Remark to §270 revolves around this difference in their respective forms and its implications. While he does not ignore the important unity between religion and the state, the context of his discussion determines that the emphasis will fall on the difference between these two forms of spiritual existence. Thus, Hegel begins by complaining about Romantic and reactionary thinkers—both being in agreement on this subject—who maintain that "religion is the foundation of the state" (*PR*, §270R, p. 291) or that "the state should grow out of religion" (*PR*, §270A, p. 302). Hegel's emphasis does not always fall on the divergence between the state and religion as much as it does in the *Philosophy of Right;* therefore, after considering his discussion there, I will consider some of his other discussions in which the aspect of unity is more prominent.

Recognition of the essential unity of religion and the state is not altogether absent from Hegel's discussion in the *Philosophy of Right.* He tells us that the content of religion, like that of the state, is absolute truth (*PR*, §270R, p. 292). "It is philosophical insight which recognizes that church and state are not opposed to each other as far as their *content* is concerned, which is truth and rationality, but merely differ in form" (*PR*, §270R, p. 299). Because the content of religion is absolute truth, Hegel goes on to argue, it is "associated with a disposition of the most exalted kind." And this disposition is of supreme importance to the state—a point we will see Hegel make even more emphatically in some of his other writings. It is from religion that "the state, laws, and duties all receive their highest confirmation as far as the consciousness is concerned, and become supremely binding upon it." It is in this sense, but only in this sense, that religion can be said to be the "foundation" of the state (*PR*, §270R, p. 292).

Hegel is particularly concerned that this legitimate understanding of religion as the foundation of the state not be confused with another, very different view. Some have argued that religion is the foundation of state in that religion represents the infinite, the spiritual in general, whereas the state is a merely finite and unspiritual entity. Here religion is viewed as an end in itself, while the state is regarded "purely as a *means*." Such an understanding of the state, however, completely deprives the state of the ethical and spiritual character that has been the burden of Hegel's political philosophy to establish. The view that the state is a mere means whose "sole function is to protect and secure the life, property, and arbitrary will of everyone, in so far as the latter does not infringe the life, property, and will of others" is the view of the state which belongs to civil society; it is the state as the understanding conceives it, a mere need-state (*Notstaat*) (*PR*, §270R and A, pp. 297–98, 302–3). This is not Hegel's ethical understanding of the state. Hegel grants that "the state may have need of religion and faith" in order to inculcate a disposition of respect and reverence for the state in people (*PR*, §270A, p. 303). But this confirmation that the state receives from religion must not be understood as the external provision of a spiritual and ethical content which is utterly missing in the state.

Though religion shares with the state the same absolute content, its relation to this content is completely different from that of the state. The state, Hegel tells us, "is the divine will as present spirit *unfolding* as the actual shape and *organization of a world*." The state is an articulated, differentiated organism consisting of objective determinations and distinctions in the form of laws and institutions. Religion, on the other hand, "is the relation to the absolute *in the form of feeling, representational thought, and faith*." In religious feeling, everything that is objective and determinate dissolves into mere subjectivity and undifferentiated inwardness. Religion gives us such precepts as " 'Be pious, and you may otherwise do as you please,' " or (to take the Augustinian rule that governed the conduct of the members of Rabelais's Abbaye de Thélème) "Love and do what you will."[19] And when this subjective attitude seeks to impose itself on the objective world of the state, "it leads to religious *fanaticism*," the destruction of the determinate laws and institutions which comprise the articulated edifice of the state. "Those who 'seek the Lord,'" Hegel writes, "and assure themselves, in their uneducated opinion, that they possess everything *immediately* instead of undertaking the work of raising their subjectivity to cognition of the truth and knowledge of objective right and duty, can produce nothing but folly, outrage, and the destruction of all ethical relations" (*PR*, §270R, pp. 292–94). For this reason he warns that "religion as such should not hold the reins of government" (*PR*, §270A, p. 304).

Having sketched in general terms just where religion and the state overlap with each other and where they diverge, Hegel defines more specifically and practically the attitude the state ought to take with respect to the church. He begins by arguing that the state's attitude toward the church will not be simply a neutral one. Because, as has been pointed out, "religion is that moment which integrates the state at the deepest level of the disposition," the state must give "the [religious] community every assistance and protection in the pursuit of its religious end." Indeed, Hegel goes so far as to say that "the state ought even to require all its citizens to belong to such a community" (*PR*, §270R, p. 295). In other words, like Locke, who did not extend toleration to the atheist, as well as many of the American founders and Tocqueville, Hegel is not neutral with respect to the question of religion versus irreligion.[20] Nevertheless, he does not believe that the state can compel citizens to belong to a particular religious community. The decision to belong to a particular religious community must be left up to the individual, and the state should exercise tolerance with respect to these individual choices to the widest extent possible: "A state which is strong because its organization is fully developed can adopt a more liberal attitude in this respect, and may completely overlook individual matters which might affect it, or even tolerate communities whose religion does not recognize even their direct duties towards the state (although this naturally depends on the numbers concerned)" (*PR*, §270, p. 295). In this regard, Hegel argues—against not only contemporary reactionaries but also "progressive" thinkers such as Fries—for the complete extension of civil rights to the Jews. He does so, however, not simply out of pluralistic respect for Jewish identity, but because such civil recognition prevents the Jews from remaining "in that isolation with which they have been reproached" and brings about their "desired assimilation in terms of attitude and disposition" (*PR*, §270R, pp. 295–96n.).[21]

Though the external actions and property of a religious community rightly come under the jurisdiction of the state, according to Hegel, internal matters of conscience and belief generally don't. But this distinction between internal and external is by no means absolute for Hegel, as is evidenced in what he says about the supervision the state may exercise over church doctrine. Though the state in general will respect the sphere of inwardness to which religious doctrine belongs, it cannot be completely indifferent to the beliefs its citizens hold. Since, as we have already seen, the state is not a spiritless mechanism but "the rational life of self-conscious freedom and the system of the ethical world," it must concern itself with the disposition of its citizens and the beliefs in which that disposition is expressed. Hegel does not see the state as exercising its censoring authority very vigorously or intrusively. Insofar as the state is internally strong, its attitude toward subjective religious opinion will generally be one of "infinite indifference." But should these opinions "give themselves a universal existence which undermines actuality, the state must protect objective truth and the principles of ethical life." The state may also exercise its censoring authority with respect to the pretensions of science, though Hegel generally believes the conflicts between science and the state will be fewer because they share the same knowing and thinking form (*PR*, §270, pp. 296–301).

Hegel concludes his discussion of the relationship between church and state in the *Philosophy of Right* by once again criticizing the overemphasis on their unity by Romantic writers such as Novalis, Friedrich Schlegel, and Adam Müller. Though church and state are one in having the absolute truth as their content, the forms of their consciousness of this absolute content are different; and this difference Hegel believes "should attain *particular existence.*" Once again he declares that "that unity of church and state which has so often been wished for is to be found [only] in oriental despotism—but in this case, there is no state in the sense of that self-conscious configuration of right, of free ethical life, and of organic development which is alone worthy of the spirit (*PR*, §270R, p. 301). Hegel's emphasis on the difference between church and state here is in keeping with the main thrust of his discussion in the *Philosophy of Right*. This is not, however, where his emphasis always falls when discussing the relationship between religion and the state. In some of his other writings, he places greater stress on the unity of church and state. We need now to look at these other writings, in order to round out our picture of Hegel's complex understanding of this important subject.

Let us turn first to the *Lectures on the Philosophy of History*. There are two substantial discussions of the relationship between religion and the state in this work. The first occurs in the introduction, where Hegel argues that "the state rests upon religion" in the sense that secular reality, being "merely temporal" and "motivated by individual interests," needs to be absolutely justified "by being recognized as the manifestation of the essence of God." This at first seems to be a little at odds with the discussion in the *Philosophy of Right*, where Hegel insists that the state is not to be seen as a merely secular and mechanical entity in need of external spiritual justification by religion. But the inconsistency is only apparent, for Hegel goes on to reject as incorrect the view that assumes "that the state is already there, and that in order to maintain the state, religion must be brought in—in buckets and bushels—to be impressed on people's minds." The state is not to be regarded as a spiritless mechanism that needs to be covered by the "decent drapery" (to borrow Burke's phrase) of religion but, rather, as something that partakes of the same spiritual element as religion and whose principles are "acknowledged to be determinations of the divine nature itself." Hegel's view of the relationship between religion and the state has nothing in common with the crudely utilitarian view of religion as providing external sanctification to that which is inherently without spiritual significance. He dismisses the belief that religion can be used simply to shore up the state and protect it from dissolution: "[R]eligion is not at all such an instrument; its self-production goes far deeper" (*IPH,* 53–54/70–71).

Hegel goes on to criticize a "foolishness we meet with in our own time" opposite to the one which tries to crudely import religion into the state: namely, "that of trying to invent and institute types of government without taking account of religion." Here one might suppose that Hegel has in mind the Enlightenment project of establishing the state on a purely secular foundation. But in fact his immediate concern is with Catholicism and its inability to recognize the state as a spiritual and ethical formation in its own right. Catholicism "does not concede to the state the inherent justice and ethical status that follows from the inwardness of the Protestant principle"; it "does not recognize law and the ethical as independent, as substantial" (*IPH,* 54–55/71–72). As a result, church and state, the spiritual and the temporal, remain opposed to one another, and the state is deprived of that spiritual confirmation which is essential to its existence. As we will see, this incompatibility of Catholicism with the modern, rational state is a feature of all of Hegel's discussions of the relationship between church and state, outside of his discussion in the *Philosophy of Right*.[22] And, like his discussion of the Jews, it clearly demarcates the limits of his pluralism. Despite the tolerance it extends toward most religions, the Hegelian state clearly privileges a certain type of Protestant religiosity.[23]

The second major discussion of the relationship between religion and the state in the *Philosophy of History* appears in Hegel's analysis of the French Revolution. One of the reasons the French Revolution took the violent course that it did, Hegel argues, is that "disposition [*Gesinnung*] and religion were not taken into account." The French Revolution based itself entirely on the modern principle of the individual free will, leaving "no guarantee that the will in question has that right disposition which is essential to the stability of the state." Hegel insists on the importance of disposition—"the sentiment [*Gesinnung*] that the laws and the constitution are on the whole firm and that it is the highest duty of individuals to subject their particular wills to them"—as a stabilizing element in the state. And he sees religion as the key to nourishing such a stabilizing disposition. Here Hegel reiterates his understanding of the unity and separation of religion and the state, but with the emphasis now more on unity: "To be sure it is considered a maxim of the profoundest wisdom to separate the laws and constitution of the state entirely from religion, since bigotry and hypocrisy are to be feared as the results of a state religion. But though religion and the state are different in relation to the content, they are one at the root; and the laws receive their highest confirmation in religion" (*PH*, 449/531).

Here again Hegel points to the incompatibility of Catholicism with the rational state: "Here it must be frankly stated that with the Catholic religion no rational constitution is possible; for government and people must mutually share that final guarantee of disposition, and they can share it only in a religion that is not opposed to a rational political constitution" (*PH*, 449/531). In Catholicism, unlike in Protestantism, the religious conscience remains separate from and to a large extent opposed to the sphere of secular right, and this can serve only to undermine the stability of the latter. We have seen that one of the reasons the French Revolution took the violent course that it did was because "disposition and religion were not taken into account." But in France disposition and religion could not be taken into account because they remained under the aegis of a Catholicism that opposed itself to the sphere of secular right and to the modern principle of individual free will. The latter were therefore forced to take on the abstract and atomistic form that led to the fury and destruction Hegel generally associates with the French Revolution (*PH*, 444–45/526–27, 449/531, 456/539). A similar fate awaited other Catholic nations to which the principles of the Revolution spread. Liberalism remained an abstraction, without the stabilizing disposition nourished by religion. "The abstraction of liberalism, emanating from France, traversed the Roman world, but religious slavery held that world in the fetters of political servitude. For it is a false principle that the fetters which bind right and freedom can be broken without the emancipation of conscience—that there can be a revolution without a reformation" (*PH*, 453/535).

Many of the same points that he makes in the *Philosophy of History* appear in the lengthy paragraph Hegel devotes to the relationship between religion and the state in the *Encyclopedia Philosophy of Spirit*. Here again the emphasis falls on the inseparability of religion and the state: "the state rests on ethical disposition, and the latter on the religious" (*EPS*, §552, p. 283). In this regard, Hegel rails against "the monstrous blunder of our times" which "tries to see these inseparables as separable from one another and even as mutually indifferent." This blunder has taken the form either of regarding religion instrumentally as something extra to be brought in to strengthen the state or of dismissing religion altogether as unnecessary to the state (*EPS*, §552, p. 284). Hegel spends the bulk of the paragraph considering the harmful effects of the separation of church and state that takes place in Catholicism as opposed to Protestantism, repeating the points he made in the *Philosophy of History* that a "free state and a slavish religion are incompatible" (in Wallace's rather free translation) and that it is impossible "to make a revolution without having made a reformation" (*EPS*, §552, p. 287).

Hegel's final discussion of the relationship between religion and the state appears in the 1831 version of the *Lectures on the Philosophy of Religion*. Here again the focus is on the unity of religion and the state rather than on their separation. And in this connection, Hegel makes the by now familiar point that, in the modern world where the state is based on freedom, Protestantism supports this unity, whereas Catholicism thwarts it (*R*, I, 452–58/237–44). But the most interesting aspect of this discussion concerns what Hegel says about the role of disposition in modern constitutional government. Again he stresses the importance of disposition in upholding the state and the role of religion in sustaining the proper disposition. And he dismisses as one-sided the modern view which holds that the formal constitution can be self-sustaining, a machine that goes of itself, without need of disposition or religion. Hegel illustrates the one-sidedness of this view with an example that recalls the transition from abstract right to morality in the *Philosophy of Right*. Laws do not apply themselves but have to be administered by judges who possess a certain subjective disposition; "everything depends upon their integrity as well as upon their insight, for it is not the law that rules human beings but human beings who are to make it rule." Hegel adds that exclusive reliance on disposition can also be one-sided. This is the "deficiency from which Plato's *Republic* suffers," in which everything is made to depend on "education and cultivation." Such a view fails to take account of the modern demand to be governed by known, posited, and universal law (*R*, I, 458–59/244–45).[24]

As with his emphasis on habit and trust in the patriotic disposition, commentators have seen Hegel's emphasis on the role of religion in upholding the state as in tension with his conception of the knowing and self-conscious character of the state.[25] In the *Philosophy of Right*, the state's reliance on religion is sometimes downplayed. For example, Hegel says in one place that the best way of inculcating respect for the state in people is "through philosophical insight into its essence. But if this insight is lacking, the religious disposition may lead to the same result" (*PR*, §270A, p. 303). In the *Lectures on the Philosophy of Religion*, however, the primary role of religion in inculcating respect for the state in the general populace is clearly brought out:

> Disposition does not necessarily take the form of religion; it can in large measure remain in an undefined condition. But in what we refer to as "the people" the ultimate truth does not have the form of thoughts and principles, for what is to count as right for the people can only be so esteemed to the extent that it is something determinate and particular. For the people this determinate character of right and ethical life has its ultimate verification only in the form of an extant religion. (*R*, I, 460/245–46)

Such an emphasis on the role of religion in upholding the state does not necessarily conflict with the knowing and thinking character of the latter. That the respectful disposition of citizens toward the state receives its deepest nourishment from religion, and that the laws of the state receive their highest confirmation from it, in no way detracts from the fact that the citizens of the state are governed by known and posited laws which exist for determinate thought and not for indeterminate feeling. As we saw with the patriotic disposition, the knowing and self-conscious character of the state does not presuppose that the citizens' relationship to it is of purely reflective or transparent sort. Religion in its proper place is perfectly compatible with and, indeed, necessary for the rational state.

Hegel's reflections on the relationship between religion and the state represent one of the profoundest parts of his political philosophy. In them, he manages to steer a path between liberal secularism, on the one hand, and theocracy, on the other. In this respect, his outlook resembles Tocqueville's.[26] While Hegel recognizes that religion can play an important role in sanctifying the state and cultivating the appropriate disposition in citizens, he also recognizes that in the modern world church and state must be kept separate. The state must not be identified with religion, but neither should it be indifferent to it. Of course, the balance Hegel tries to strike here ultimately rests, as we have seen, on a certain, Protestant understanding of religion. While the modern state can tolerate most religions—Judaism and Catholicism, for example—it ultimately privileges that religious outlook identified by Hegel with Protestantism whose distinctive principle, like that of the modern state, is subjective freedom. For this reason, Hegel, for all of his insight into the relationship between religion and the modern state, remains a somewhat imperfect guide to the theologico-political problem in our own, increasingly pluralistic time.

THE RATIONAL CONSTITUTION

Perhaps no other aspect of Hegel's theory of the state has been as severely questioned as his views on the constitution of the state. His defense of monarchy, his faith in bureaucracy, his fears of democracy along with his resort to antiquated corporate institutions to contain it—all have come in for heavy criticism from a wide variety of points of view. While I show in this section that many of these criticisms rest on misunderstandings, it is nevertheless difficult to deny that Hegel's constitutional outlook has an air of unreality about it. In its announcement that constitutional monarchy is the achievement toward which the modern world has been developing (*PR*, §273R), it seems to belong to a world quite remote from the democratic one that we currently inhabit and that Tocqueville, not too many years after Hegel, saw clearly on the horizon.

That Hegel should have insufficiently appreciated the future world-historical significance of democracy should not altogether surprise us. After all, modern mass democracy was something hardly intimated in the constitutional struggles of Hegel's own time in Germany. During the tumultuous decades following the French Revolution—"possibly the richest that world history has had," Hegel once remarked ("PEAW," 282/507)—the fundamental constitutional conflict in Germany was not so much between monarchists and democrats as it was between reformers like Stein and Hardenberg who advocated a central, sovereign state which guaranteed the social and economic freedom of individuals and traditionalists who defended decentralized political authority and the local privileges of aristocrats.[27] Hegel clearly belongs to the former, progressive camp, and it is in this context that his defense of a constitutional monarchy run largely by bureaucratic officials—the *Beamtenstaat* or bureaucratic state—must be seen.

Despite the relatively time-bound character of Hegel's reflections on the rational constitution, there is still much in them that remains of permanent interest and from which we can still learn. His "organic" theory of the division of powers in the state marks an important step beyond the overly formalistic and mechanical doctrine of the separation of powers belonging to the eighteenth century. Also, his conception of executive power shows a remarkable sensitivity to the deadening effect of excessive bureaucratic control operating from the top down—what Tocqueville would refer to a few years later as "administrative centralization." For all that Hegel defends the *Beamtenstaat*, it must never be forgotten that he does not conceive of it as a spiritless "machine-state." Finally, while Hegel no doubt offers a rather cramped conception of popular political participation, his insights into the atomizing and alienating effects of mass democracy and the frequently worthless character of public opinion are not without merit. Hegel may not have appreciated as much as Tocqueville did the extent to which we are "fated" to democracy, but he certainly possessed as robust a skepticism about democracy's worst inclinations and propensities as Tocqueville possessed.

It is appropriate to begin our analysis of Hegel's specific argument concerning the rational constitution by pointing out that Hegel in no way regards his enterprise as one of ideal constitution-making. For the most part, he regards questions such as, Which is the best form of government? or, Who is to make up the constitution? as utterly nonsensical. Such questions falsely assume that the constitution a people has rests purely on a "theoretical decision," that it is merely "a matter of free choice determined by reflection" (*IPH*, 47–48/63).[28] But this is not at all what is involved in the adoption of a constitution. A constitution, Hegel tells us, echoing Montesquieu, "is not simply made"; it is the product of the specific historical spirit of a people or *Volksgeist*. "Each nation accordingly has the constitution appropriate and proper to it." To try to impose a constitution on a people a priori is thus a misguided and ultimately futile endeavor. Hegel's favorite example of such a priori constitutional imposition is Napoleon's giving of a constitution to Spain: "What Napoleon gave to the Spanish was more rational than what they had before, and yet they rejected it as something alien, because they were not yet sufficiently cultivated. The constitution of a nation must embody the nation's feeling for its rights and [present] condition; otherwise it will have no meaning or value" (*PR*, §274, R, and A).[29]

As the preceding quote suggests, though Hegel recognizes the historical element in all constitutional arrangements, he does not relativistically assume that all constitutions are equal or equally rational. The constitution that

Napoleon gave to the Spanish was certainly more rational than the one they had before, they simply were not "sufficiently cultivated" or rational to receive it. The constitution of a people, Hegel writes, ultimately depends "on the stage attained by its self-consciousness in regard to freedom, on its spiritual development in general" (*LNR*, §136).[30] The more cultivated or developed a people is with respect to its awareness of human freedom, the more rational is the constitution that is appropriate to it.

The constitution corresponding to the highest stage of historical development with respect to the idea of freedom—and therefore the most rational constitution—is, according to Hegel, constitutional monarchy. To try to define what Hegel means by constitutional monarchy here would involve nothing less than a full elaboration of his entire argument concerning the constitution of the rational state. Provisionally we may say that constitutional monarchy refers to a state in which the legislative, executive, and "princely" powers are differentiated but ultimately united under the head of a monarch who rules in accordance with the constitution and the decisions of his ministers (*PR*, §§273, 275). Such a constitution represents the peak of constitutional development, according to Hegel, because it alone is able to reflect and accommodate the subjective freedom that constitutes the great achievement of the modern world. "The development of the state to constitutional monarchy," he writes, "is the achievement of the modern world, in which the substantial Idea has attained infinite form" (*PR*, §273R). Constitutional monarchy alone corresponds to the modern principle of subjective freedom, "according to which all essential aspects present in the spiritual totality develop and enter into their own right" (*PR*, §273A). Hegel brings out the correlativity of constitutional monarchy and the modern principle of subjective freedom perhaps most clearly in the lectures of 1817–18: "For a people that has developed to civil society, or in general to consciousness of the infinitude of the free ego in its determinate existence, in its needs, its freedom of choice, and its conscience, *constitutional monarchy* alone is possible" (*LNR*, §137).

Why does Hegel see constitutional monarchy as corresponding to the modern principle of subjective freedom rather than democracy? Here Hegel's argument, as he himself acknowledges, is heavily indebted to Montesquieu. Like Montesquieu, he believes that virtue, "the continuous preference of the public interest over one's own," is the principle of democracy.[31] Democracy depends on citizens having a virtuous disposition by which they subordinate their own particular interests to the universal interest of the state. Once this virtuous or public-spirited disposition is lost and the powers of particularity unleashed in a democracy, the regime is destroyed (*PR*, §273R). This, of course, is what happened in Athens (*LNR*, §137R). "The principle of particularity," Hegel writes in the lectures of 1817–18, "is not contained in democracy, and if it comes on the scene, it has an annihilating effect on it" (*LNR*, §135R). For this reason, democracy is incompatible with the modern principle of subjective freedom. It is also incompatible with the size of modern states. The virtue or public spiritedness required by democracy, Hegel argues (again following Montesquieu), can flourish only in small states. In large modern states, this virtuous disposition is necessarily attenuated (*LNR*, §§136R, 141R, 156R).

Monarchy, in contrast with democracy, does not presuppose a virtuous disposition on the part of its citizens. It operates largely through law rather than disposition; and it does not require that citizens subordinate their particular interests to the universal interest of the state but, rather, leads the individual to the universal *through* his particular interests. Once again summarizing Montesquieu, as well as echoing the invisible hand argument of Smith, Hegel writes: "In monarchy the place of all virtues is taken by the laws, although the motivation is honor. Each contributes to the common welfare, believing that he is seeing to his own interest, and that by each making himself his own end the interweaving [of individual ends] gives rise to the whole" (*LNR*, §135R). Hegel is careful to point out, however—and here he differs somewhat from Montesquieu, who sometimes stresses the nonmoral character of monarchy[32]—that we must not suppose that monarchy can do completely without virtue or that it can be totally indifferent to the disposition of its citizens. Such a view would go against much of what we have already seen Hegel say about the inadequacy of the purely legalistic model of the state and the importance of disposition in the state. "[W]e must avoid imagining," he writes, "that, since the disposition of virtue is the substantial form in a democratic republic, this disposition thereby becomes superfluous, or may even be totally absent, in a monarchy; and still less should we imagine that virtue and the *legally determined* activity of an *articulated* organization are mutually opposed and incompatible" (*PR*, §273R).

It must be added, however, that Hegel is not always consistent in his rejection of the Montesquieuan image of monarchy as resting purely on honor and ambition to the exclusion of virtue. In the lectures of 1817–18, he argues that, whereas in small states "there can be republican constitutions, where the main consideration is moral rectitude, in large states it is not possible to have regard to moral and religious motivations." In large states, ambition becomes the primary virtue: "[W]hat we mean by virtue in the state is that what one person proposes partly from ambition others find to be concordant with the universal"

(*LNR*, §156R). It is difficult to square this passage from the lectures with the comment from the *Philosophy of Right* quoted above where Hegel denies that virtue can be completely disregarded in a monarchy. It may be that in the passage from the lectures the sharp contrast Hegel wishes to draw between small, republican states and large, monarchical ones leads him to exaggerate the absence of moral motivation in the latter. Nevertheless, the passage is important in that it suggests how close Hegel's constitutional thinking can sometimes come to the mechanistic model of such eighteenth-century constitutionalists as Montesquieu and his great American disciple Madison. This is not the only occasion on which we will observe such a similarity between Hegel and his supposedly more realistic eighteenth-century predecessors.

One area in which Hegel clearly seems to depart from his liberal eighteenth-century predecessors, however, is in what he says about the division of powers. As we have seen, Hegel argues that the political state is divided into three powers, the legislative, the executive, and the princely. These powers correspond to the three moments of the logical concept, namely, universality, particularity, and individuality. Properly understood, the division of powers in the state may be regarded as "the guarantee of public freedom" (*PR*, §272R). This means understanding the different powers not as completely independent and self-sufficient entities related to one another in terms of mutual fear and hostility but, rather, as members of an organic whole or as moments of a single concept. Hegel repudiates the negative and mechanical doctrine of the separation of powers most famously articulated by Montesquieu in *The Spirit of the Laws* and adapted to the democratic circumstances of the United States by Madison; the doctrine of checks and balances in which "power must check power by the arrangement of things"[33] and "ambition must be made to counteract ambition."[34] Such a view, Hegel writes,

> attributes to the principle [of the division of powers] the false determination of the *absolute self-sufficiency* of each power in relation to the others, and on the other hand, it one-sidedly interprets the relation of these powers to one another as negative, as one of mutual *limitation*. In this view, the reaction of each power to the others is one of hostility and fear, as if to an evil, and their determination is such that they oppose one another and produce, by means of this counterpoise, a general equilibrium rather than a living unity. (*PR*, §272R)

Nor is this abstract and merely negative doctrine of the separation of powers confined to Montesquieu and Madison; it can also be found in Hegel's more immediate predecessors, Rousseau, Kant, and Fichte. Hegel criticizes what seems to be the Rousseauan understanding of the separation of powers—though he does not mention Rousseau by name—in the *Encyclopedia Philosophy of Spirit*. According to this understanding, legislative power and executive power are sharply distinguished, with the former, in which all citizens have a part, being supreme and the latter being merely dependent. This Rousseauan understanding of the separation of powers differs slightly from the classic checks and balances model in that there is a clear subordination of one power to another, but Hegel still finds it devoid of spiritual unity (*EPS*, §541).[35] Kant's understanding of the division of powers is in many respects close to Rousseau's, but Hegel tends to interpret it along the lines of the checks and balances model in which "each of the three powers retains the ultimate power of decision," no power "is subordinate to the others," and "the whole is not an organic whole" (*LNR*, §131R).[36] Finally, there is Fichte's institution of the ephorate to serve as a check on the executive power and insure that it hews to the general will of the people. As early as the *Natural Law* essay, Hegel criticized this Fichtean notion of the ephorate on the basis that there is, ultimately, no way to settle the issue should a dispute arise between the executive and the ephorate regarding the interpretation of the general will (*NL*, 85–89/471–76). In his mature political philosophy, Hegel's criticism remains roughly the same. The "hollowness" of Fichte's notion of an ephorate that checks the executive is "apparent from the facts that two self-subsistent powers are opposed to each other and that the executive can easily send the whole ephorate into exile" (*LNR*, §133R).[37]

Hegel clearly rejects the overly formalistic and mechanical doctrine of separation of powers and checks and balances found in such thinkers as Montesquieu, Madison, Kant, and Fichte, favoring instead a more organic conception of the division of powers in the state. Nevertheless, it would be a mistake to assume that Hegel simply abandons the whole notion of one governmental power checking another or of building in safeguards against the abuse of power by the various branches of government. We will see below, when we consider the various powers of government individually, that Hegel is very much concerned with the problem of the abuse of power and that he builds in numerous safeguards by which one branch of government monitors and checks another. Thus, the power of the monarch will be checked by the constitution and the advice of his ministers, the ministers will be checked through their accountability to the Estates, the class of civil servants will be checked from above by the monarch and from below by the corporations, and the legislative power of the Estates will be organized and checked through the combined influence of all of the above institutions. Some have seen a tremendous tension between what might be called this Madisonian aspect of Hegel's constitutional thought and his organic conception of the state,[38] but the copresence of these two elements need not be viewed in this way. That Hegel finds the eighteenth-century doctrine of the rigid separation of powers overly formalistic and mechanistic does not mean he is indifferent to the real problems of power to which the doctrine was originally addressed. It means only that he doubts whether the strict application of this doctrine represents an effective or concrete manner of governing at all.

Apropos of this, a general comment about the "realistic" element in Hegel's constitutional thought is perhaps in order. Hegel's organic understanding of the division of powers is not meant to be a kind of utopian reflection on government, far removed from the hard-edged realism of Madisonian or Montesquieuan checks and balances; indeed, quite the contrary. His numerous comments—especially in the lectures of 1817–18—to the effect that the state must be internally organized in such a way that "what is rational, the universal will, should happen as a necessity" (*LNR*, §122R), that "the universal must occur necessarily" (*LNR*, §132R), that "the rational must happen" (*LNR*, §140R),[39] all suggest that Hegel is very concerned to elaborate a realistic constitutional scheme in which reliance on virtue is reduced to a minimum and the actualization of the right order is guaranteed. In this vein, in a tone that recalls Machiavelli's famous repudiation of classical idealism in *The Prince*, he criticizes Plato and Aristotle for leaving the actualization of the best regime to chance: "To say that the best constitution is the one where the best people rule is to say something very trivial, since the question whether the constitution is to be good cannot be made dependent on contingency. Plato and Aristotle regard it as divine good fortune if government is in the hands of the best, and believe that necessity is to be found when they are at the helm" (*LNR*, §130R).[40] The constitution must be arranged in such a way that what is rational or universal happens necessarily, regardless of whether virtuous and enlightened statesmen are at the helm. Hegel sums up this consummately realistic position on constitutional matters in his article on the Württemberg Estates: "A political institution cannot be content with the mere demand that something ought to happen, with the hope that it will happen, with barring certain factors which might impede its happening. It deserves its name only when it is so organized that what ought to happen does happen" ("PEAW," 262/485–86).

Now to Hegel's more in-depth treatment of each of the three powers of government, beginning with his discussion of the "princely power" (*die fürstliche Gewalt*).[41] The first question we must ask ourselves is why Hegel begins with the princely power, especially since the logical sequence would seem to demand that he begin with the universal moment embodied in the legislative power? K.-H. Ilting has made much of Hegel's inversion of the dialectical order here, arguing that it ultimately destroys the internal coherence of Hegel's theory of the state and the democratic thrust of his whole political philosophy. The aberration can only be explained, he contends, as a concession on Hegel's part to the conservative forces of the restoration after the Carlsbad Decrees.[42] Such an explanation hardly makes sense, though, given that Hegel was already treating the princely power first in the lectures of 1817–18, long before the Carlsbad Decrees. By treating the princely power first, Hegel is not contradicting the essential thrust of his theory of the state, regardless of whether he is diverting from the rigid logical schema in which universality is followed by particularity which is followed by individuality. More than anything else, the Hegelian state is characterized by unity, a unity which is not to be understood in terms of contract or as the product of merely particular wills. This unity of the state is most directly embodied in the princely power, and even more specifically in the person of the monarch.

Another term for the unity of the state is sovereignty. Accordingly, it is to this central concept of modern political thought that Hegel turns first in his treatment of the princely power, defining it—not much differently from the mainstream of modern reflection on this concept since Bodin and Hobbes[43]—in terms of the supremacy of the central state vis-à-vis all the particular powers and functions that comprise it. The peculiar expression Hegel uses to describe this sovereign character of the state is the "ideality" of its moments or constituent parts. The moments or constituent parts of the state are "ideal" in the sense that none is self-sufficient or completely independent of the whole. In other words, the constituent parts of the state are "ideal" in the same sense that the state itself is an "organic" whole and not a mere aggregate of independent and self-subsistent parts (*PR*, §§276–78). Sovereignty understood in this way Hegel sees as the distinctive attribute of the modern state in contradistinction to feudal monarchy, in which "the particular functions and powers of the state and civil society were vested in independent corporations and communities" and "were the private property of individuals, so that what the latter had to do in relation to the whole was left to their opinion and discretion" (*PR*, §277R).[44] Of course, the historic consolidation of the authority previously dispersed and held by private individuals in medieval constitutions had long been achieved in states such as England and France by the time Hegel was writing, but in Germany it remained a process in the making, the forces of *Herrschaft* only slowly giving way to the forces of *Verwaltung*.[45] In his concept of sovereignty, Hegel once again shows himself to be firmly in the latter, progressive camp.

The sovereignty of the state is not to be identified with any single element in the state, according to Hegel; it is an attribute of the ensemble that includes the legislative and executive as well as the princely powers. Nevertheless, it is the person of the monarch which is uniquely suited to express the radical unity and ideality with which Hegel identifies the sovereignty of the state. The state ultimately has to act as an individual, as a unified "personality" whose "simple self supersedes all particularities, cuts short the weighing of arguments and counter-arguments (between which vacillations in either direction are always possible) and *resolves* them by its 'I will,' thereby initiating all activity and actuality." But, Hegel argues, "personality . . . has its *truth* . . . simply and solely as a person. . . . The personality of the state has actuality only as a *person*, as *the monarch*" (*PR*, §279R).

This last step in Hegel's argument has caused the most difficulty. It is not clear why the "personality" of state must ultimately be embodied in a single person. Nor is it clear why the state's manifest need to act as a unit requires that an actual individual pronounce the "I will" that resolves and concludes all political deliberation. Modern democracies seem to get along very well without this element of monarchical decision; they do not fall apart or show themselves incapable of unified action in the absence of a single person's pronouncing the "I will." Hegel, however, would dismiss such an objection as a mere piece of ratiocination or reflective thinking that "stops short at isolated determinations, and consequently knows only [individual] reasons, finite viewpoints, and *deduction* from such reasons" (*PR*, §279R). In his analysis of monarchy, he continually reminds us that "all considerations of mere utility, externality, and the like must be . . . excluded from a philosophical treatment [of this subject]." He realizes that "representational thought can easily comprehend that the state is the self-determining and completely sovereign will, the ultimate source of decisions. But it is more difficult to grasp this 'I will' as a person" (*PR*, §279A).

How, then, are we to understand the role of the monarch in Hegel's constitutional scheme, if not in terms of utility or some other finite necessity? Hegel seems to understand the role of the monarch as primarily symbolic, which is not to say that he views it as "merely symbolic."[46] "The state," he writes, "must be regarded as a great architectonic edifice, a hieroglyph of reason which becomes manifest in actuality" (*PR*, §279A). As part of this "architectonic edifice," the monarch seems to symbolize at least two different things. In the first place, it symbolizes the moment of subjective will which remains submerged in the substantial states of antiquity and only receives complete recognition in the modern state. In the ancient world, the ultimate decision on major issues had to be attributed to forces beyond human beings, external phenomena such as oracles, the entrails of animals, and so forth. It is only in the modern world that this power of ultimate decision is attributed to a human being. "This 'I will' constitutes the great difference between ancient and modern worlds, so that it must have its own distinct existence in the great edifice of the state" (*PR*, §279A; see also §§279R, 356). This argument is only partly successful. While it perhaps suggests a plausible rationale for monarchy vis-à-vis ancient naturalism, it remains unclear why the modern principle of subjective will is any better represented by reposing the power of ultimate decision in a single human being rather than in a group of human beings.

The second thing monarchy symbolizes—here Hegel seems to be on somewhat stronger ground—is the substantial unity of the state. This aspect of the state, which Hegel earlier argued is what differentiates the state from civil society (*PR*, §258R), can be only imperfectly captured by any sort of democratic arrangement. The symbolic role the monarch plays with respect to the substantial unity of the state is perhaps most clearly revealed in what Hegel has to say about the "majesty" of the monarch. The majesty of the monarch derives not only from the fact that his power of ultimate decision is ungrounded, rests on nothing more than his subjective "I will," but also from the fact that his right to rule is equally ungrounded insofar as it rests on birth or hereditary succession. Hereditary monarchy reflects, as elective monarchy cannot, the substantial unity of the state that stands beyond the subjective caprices and arbitrary wills of individuals—the latter belonging to the sphere of civil society. Hegel grants that "*elective monarchy* may well seem the most *natural* idea, i.e. the one most obvious to superficial thinking; for since it is the concerns and interests of the people that the monarch must look after, it can be argued that the people must be left to choose whom they wish to entrust their welfare to, and that it is from this trust alone that the right to rule arises." Nevertheless, he goes on to argue,

> this view, like the ideas of the monarch as the first servant of the state, of a contractual relationship between monarch and people, etc., bases itself on the will in the sense of *caprice*, opinion, and arbitrariness *of the many*—a determination which, as we noticed some time ago, is of primary importance in civil society . . . but is not the principle of the family, let alone of the state, and is completely opposed to the Idea of ethical life. (*PR*, §281R)

Only hereditary monarchy gives adequate symbolic expression to the substantiality of the ethical life of the state.

Although what Hegel is arguing for here is remote from current constitutional beliefs, he does have a point. Modern democracies are singularly incapable of manifesting the majesty and substantiality that are absolutely essential to the Hegelian notion of the state. There is nothing in the democratic state that escapes entirely the bargaining and calculus of interests which Hegel associates with civil society. Even the office of president in modern democracies, which sometimes borrows the trappings of monarchy, remains bound to the compromises, coalitions, particular interests, and arbitrary wills that make up the mutable world of democratic politics. Of course, one might object that there is nothing wrong with this, but to do so involves not simply the rejection of an incidental part of Hegel's political philosophy but the denial of his central point about the substantiality of state and the necessity for this substantiality to be represented in the edifice of the state. I do not wish to be misunderstood here. I am not arguing for the anachronistic revival of hereditary monarchy in today's world; for, as Michael Oakeshott has observed, "the authority of an office of rule remains always a delicate matter of current belief."[47] I am merely suggesting that Hegel's philosophical justification of hereditary monarchy plausibly connects an unquestionably fundamental feature of his political philosophy to a still existing institution of his time.

So far I have considered only why Hegel thinks the monarch is a necessary part of the rational constitution; I have said nothing about what he thinks the monarch actually does. Hegel's position on this latter score has been frequently remarked upon and is fairly straightforward. In a well-organized state, the monarch is bound by the laws and the constitution as well as by the objective advice of his ministers; therefore, "he often has nothing more to do than sign his name" (*PR*, §279A). To the frequent objection that hereditary monarchy exposes the state to contingency, since the monarch may be unequipped to rule, Hegel replies that the actual role of the monarch is so circumscribed that his particular character is of practically no consequence: "In a fully organized state, it is only a question of the highest instance of formal decision, and all that is required in a monarch is someone to say 'yes' and dot the 'i'; for the supreme office of rule should be such that the particular character of its occupant is of no significance" (*PR*, §280A).[48] Negligible as it is, Hegel does not argue that the role of the monarch is completely nil. He sometimes criticizes the English constitution for reducing the monarch "virtually to a cipher" (*LNR*, §133R).[49] The monarch retains the power to appoint and dismiss his highest ministers

(*PR*, §283), though Hegel believes the arbitrary exercise of this power may be limited through certain features of the constitution. The monarch also has the right to intervene in cases where executive officials have abused their power (*PR*, §295R). Finally, in conjunction with his cabinet of ministers, the monarch has supreme command over the army and is in charge of the conduct of foreign policy (*PR*, §329).

I have said that the Hegelian monarch remains bound by the laws and the constitution and by the objective advice of his ministers (see *PR*, §§275, 283–85). The role of the latter is of particular importance in Hegel's constitutional scheme. The ministers advise the monarch on all matters of state but most importantly on the "bills to be laid before the legislature" (*LNR*, §140R). (In the Hegelian scheme, legislative initiative rests with the princely power under the supervision of the ministers.) (*LNR*, §149R). The monarch, of course, retains the power to appoint and dismiss his highest ministers according to his "unrestricted arbitrary will" (*PR*, §283). But because these ministers remain accountable to the parliament, Hegel argues that the monarch will be forced to appoint competent individuals instead of his cronies:

> The main guarantee of the competence of ministers is their answerability to parliament, to which they have to indicate clearly what they intend. So a minister's position is the most dangerous in the state, for he has to defend himself against the monarch, against his colleagues, against public opinion, and against parliament. The French and English ministers are necessarily our examples here. Men who maintain their position as ministers, and show themselves good at the job, merit the highest respect. (*LNR*, §140R)[50]

Hegel regards the answerability of the ministers to parliament as the most important "check" on their power, and he cannot withhold his admiration when this essential task is performed well. In the debates of the parliamentary assembly,

> ministers can be questioned on anything; here they can show their talent, skill, and presence of mind, since they are under constant attack from the assembly, which stands over against their ministry, and since the assembly's proceedings must always be public. And this is the most vexatious thing about being a minister, for here he often has to spend six to eight hours thinking and speaking about what are in part unexpected questions. This check on the executive is the best guarantee for having ministers who are competent and whose attitude is governed by right. It is an outstanding spectacle to see such matters examined by ministers and Estates. (*LNR*, §149R)[51]

Hegel's comments here on the accountability of ministers are very much in keeping with the fundamental aspiration of reformers such as Stein and Hardenberg "to replace the arbitrary and irresponsible rule of royal cronies with orderly and responsible ministerial government." Making the king's ministers accountable was a crucial step in the historic process by which—in Otto Hintze's famous phrase—"the absolute monarchy was transformed into a bureaucratic monarchy."[52]

So much, then, for the princely power. Let us turn now to the second of the three elements of the rational constitution, the executive power (*die Regierungsgewalt*). This power, consisting of the judiciary and the police, has the task of applying the universal decisions of the princely power to the particular spheres of civil society and to individual cases, of subsuming the particular under the universal (*PR*, §§273, 287). The language of "application" and "subsumption," however, is misleading here, for it suggests that everything in the executive operates from the top down. But Hegel is quite concerned to avoid such a model of executive power in which everything in society is regulated from the top down by a centralized bureaucracy. Early in his career, in *The German Constitution*, he criticized what he called the "machine state" for its destructive effect on the public spirit of citizens: "How dull and spiritless a life is engendered in a modern state where everything is regulated from the top downwards, where nothing with any general implications is left to the management and execution of interested parties of the people" (*GC*, 163–64/484). This same Tocquevillean apprehension about administrative centralization permeates Hegel's treatment of the executive power in the *Philosophy of Right*.

The key to Hegel's avoidance of the tyranny of the universal that he associates with the machine state or the pure *Beamtenstaat* once again lies in the corporations. In the corporations, the particular interests of civil society are already mixed with universal interests and have become to a certain extent ethical. The key is to nurture and not destroy this natural link between the particular and the universal. To this end, Hegel insists that the corporations be at least partly self-governing. Of course, the corporations "must be subordinated to the higher interests of the state"; and therefore the administrators charged with overseeing the interests of the corporations should be chosen through a "mixture of popular election by the interested parties and confirmation and determination by a higher authority" (*PR*, §288).

Over these corporate administrators exists a layer of "executive civil servants" charged with "*upholding*, within the particular rights [of the corporations], *legality* and the *universal interest of the state*" and with "bringing these rights back to the universal" (*PR,* §289). Following the reforms of Stein, Hegel argues that these officials should be organized into functionally defined departments dealing with particular policy areas such as finance, foreign affairs, education, and so forth.[53] But he again expresses concern that this mode of organization not lead to everything being regulated from the top down so that civil life is no longer governed "in a *concrete* manner from below" (*PR,* §290). This is what has happened in the highly centralized government of France, a country that also "lacks corporations and communal associations—that is, circles in which particular and universal interests come together" (*PR,* §290A).[54] Hegel concludes by again emphasizing the importance to the state of these corporations and communal associations in which "the individual finds protection for the exercise of his rights, so that his particular interest is bound up with the preservation of the whole":

> For some time now, organization has always been directed from above, and efforts have been devoted for the most part to this kind of organization, despite the fact that the lower level of the masses as a whole can easily be left in a more or less disorganized state. Yet it is extremely important that the masses should be organized, because only then do they constitute a power or force; otherwise, they are merely an aggregate, a collection of scattered atoms. (*PR,* §290A)

Hegel goes on to sketch the essential features of the civil servants who comprise the "universal estate," his account in many ways anticipating Weber's classic portrait of the bureaucratic official who performs his duty *sine ira et studio.*[55] Entrance into the universal estate of civil servants is in principle open to everyone regardless of birth or status, the sole qualification being one's objective ability as demonstrated through examinations (*PR,* §291; *LNR,* §144R). Though appointment to the civil service is to some extent contingent on the arbitrary will of the monarch—there generally being more qualified candidates than there are posts—officials are protected against arbitrary dismissal by the monarch (*PR,* §292–93).[56] Finally, the civil servant is paid a salary. This reflects that his services are not simply discretionary, and it also removes from him the temptation "to seek the means of satisfying [his particular needs] at the expense of his official activities and duty" (*PR,* §294 and R).

Hegel also believes that there must be safeguards against the potential abuse of power by bureaucratic officials. Such safeguards are found in the answerability of civil servants to their superiors in the bureaucratic chain of command—in the last resort, to the monarch himself—as well as in the legal recognition accorded to the corporations and other communal associations

(*PR,* §295 and R). Protection against the abuse of power by officials also depends on their having certain ethical qualities—dispassionateness, integrity, politeness—qualities that Hegel believes can be fostered through "direct education in ethics and thought." Such an education "provides a spiritual counterweight to the mechanical exercises and the like which are inherent in learning the so-called sciences appropriate to these [administrative] spheres." In a quasi-Madisonian argument, Hegel even suggests that the size of the state can have an important effect on the ethical character of officials, reducing "the burden of family ties and other family commitments" and blunting the passions of revenge and hatred (*PR,* §296).

Particularly interesting with respect to this issue of bureaucratic abuse of power is what Hegel says about the danger of the middle class's becoming a kind of aristocracy with interests remote from those of the general citizenry. Hegel realizes that the middle class as "the most conspicuously educated class" is absolutely crucial to the kind of *Beamtenstaat* he is advocating. But he also realizes that this class can develop into a bureaucratic elite that uses its superior knowledge and education as a means of exploiting the rest of the populace (*PR,* §297 and A). Such a class "may become remote and alien, and, by its skill and education and use of official authority, may provide a channel for the caprice and oppression of citizens" (*LNR,* §145). Echoing a point made earlier in the *Philosophy of Right,* Hegel also highlights the danger that the administration of justice may be "transformed into an instrument of profit and domination" when it comes to be controlled by a single class wielding its technical mastery of the law in a manner alien to the understanding of the ordinary citizen (*PR,* §297R; see also §228R). As checks on this sort of bureaucratic abuse of power, Hegel again points to the action of the monarch from above and the rights of the corporations from below (*PR,* §297). In the lectures of 1817–18, he adds a further safeguard in the Estates assembly, which would be empowered to receive and examine complaints about officials by citizens (*LNR,* §§145, 147). More important than his particular solutions, however, is the fact that Hegel clearly recognizes the problem for which, later, Marx most famously would take him to task: namely, that the bureaucracy can develop into a mandarin class with a corporate interest of its own different from the general interest.[57] Hegel far from exhibits the uncritical faith in bureaucracy that he is often accused of.

Finally, we come to the third moment of the rational constitution, the legislative power (*die gesetzgebende Gewalt*). Hegel suggests, at least at first, that this power is not radically creative; it is concerned more with modifying already existent laws than with creating altogether new ones.[58] "The *legislative power,*" he writes, "has to do with the laws as such, in so far as they are in need of new and further determination" (*PR*, §298). And in some places, he intimates that the reach of this power is quite circumscribed: "In a civilized state . . . legislation can only be a further modification of existing laws, and so-called new laws can only deal with minutiae of detail and particularities" (*EPS*, §544R). Beyond this, legislative activity is conditioned by the constitution—the basic institutional structure of the state—of which it is a part. Hegel does not, however, conceive the constitution as something fixed and immutable or as something completely unaffected by legislative activity: "the constitution does undergo further development through the further evolution of the laws" (*PR*, §298). His conception of constitutional evolution has a distinctly Burkean quality to it. Constitutional change "takes place imperceptibly and without possessing the form of change." As the incremental modifications to a constitution slowly accumulate, it is finally transformed into something completely different: "conditions evolve in an apparently peaceful and imperceptible manner, with the result that a constitution completely changes its character over a long period of time" (*PR*, §298A). If the constitution does not keep pace with the development of the spirit of a nation, it opens the state up to discontent and ultimately to the possibility of revolution (*LNR*, §146 and R). Here Hegel echoes a point he made in one of his earliest writings: "How blind they are who may hope that institutions, constitutions, laws which no longer correspond to human manners, needs, and opinions, and from which the spirit has flown, can subsist any longer; or that forms in which intellect and feeling now take no interest are powerful enough to be any longer the bond of a nation" ("RDA," 244/269).

As far as what legislation is about, Hegel distinguishes two broad areas of activity. The first is concerned with determining the benefits the state enables citizens to enjoy: rights of property, corporations, and so forth. The second has to do with determining the services the state may demand from citizens. With respect to the latter, Hegel maintains that, with the exception of military service, the state can only extract services in the form of money or taxes. In earlier times, the state demanded particular services from citizens—the fulfilling of certain offices, the performance of certain tasks. But such allotment of concrete tasks and jobs is inconsistent with the modern principle of subjective freedom. Only services in the abstract form of money or taxes which leave the individual's choice of substantive occupation free are consistent with the modern demand "that all of an individual's actions should be mediated by his own will" (*PR*, §299, R, and A).

Hegel also rejects the idea that legislation only has to do with general or universal matters, leaving everything that belongs to implementation or the particular to administrative bodies. This idea of course derives from Rousseau's sharp distinction between the legislative and executive powers, the sovereign general will and government.[59] While Hegel believes there may be a limited validity to the distinction between universal legislation and particular administration, he ultimately thinks the line between the two can become quite blurry. To avoid being hopelessly general, a law must include within itself a determinate content. But the more determinate and empirical a law becomes, the less it fulfills its character as a pure law (*PR*, §299R). Hegel's prime example of the hybrid character of much legislation is the annual granting of the government's budget. Such measures are wholly taken up with particulars, and the fact that they cover only a single year hardly qualifies them as general laws in the pure or proper sense. In an actual state, the distinction between legislation and administration is no more ironclad than the distinction between the legislative and executive powers (*EPS*, §544R).

Consonant with the latter point, Hegel argues against the view, arising from the negative doctrine of the separation of powers he has already rejected, which holds that "members of the executive should be excluded from the legislative bodies." In keeping with his organic understanding of the division of powers, he insists that the legislative power does not simply consist of the Estates but includes the monarch and the executive as well (*PR*, §300 and A).[60] Hegel doesn't draw a clear picture of the legislative process in the *Philosophy of Right*, but in the lectures and elsewhere he indicates that the king's ministers, who occupy the highest rung of the executive ladder, are charged with introducing legislation into the Estates assembly. They do not have the right to vote on legislation but only to introduce, explain, and defend it in the manner we saw above (*LNR*, §156R). Though the ministers have only an ex officio role in the Estates assembly, Hegel sometimes suggests that lower officials in the executive branch can actually be members of the assembly. To exclude these officials from being members of the Estates assembly would be a mistake, since "they are for the most part the best educated, who were at universities, and bring with them into the assembly this mentality trained for office" (*LNR*, §156R). In his article on the Württemberg Estates, Hegel argues vehemently against the provision that seeks to exclude bureaucratic officials from being representatives to the assembly. Only these officials possess the requisite "political sense" (*Sinne des Staates*) that is "principally acquired through habitual preoccupation with public affairs" ("PEAW," 257/475–76). One of the things Hegel most admires about the English parliamentary system is that, despite its corruption, "it introduces a majority of men into parliament who are statesmen, who from their very youth have devoted themselves to political business and have worked and lived in it" (*PH,* 455/538).

Though the Estates constitute only one element of the legislative power, it is the most distinctive element belonging to that power; accordingly, Hegel devotes the rest of his discussion to it. He is aware that the issue of popular political participation is in many respects *the* issue that preoccupies his contemporaries and that will no doubt agitate the next generation, and therefore he is particularly concerned to dispel the manifold misconceptions which swirl around it. The most prominent of these is the belief that the desirability of popular political participation lies in the superior wisdom of the people, the belief that "delegates of the people, or indeed the people themselves, *must know best* what is in their own best interest, and that their own will is undoubtedly the one best equipped to pursue the latter." Such a democratic faith can be associated with a kind of vulgar Rousseauism,[61] and it is in connection with it that Hegel utters some of his most acerbic comments. With respect to the belief that the people know best what is in their own best interest, he writes that

> the reverse is in fact the case, for if the term "the people" denotes a particular category of members of the state, it refers to that category of citizens *who do not know their own will.* To know what one wills, and even more, to know what the will which has being in and for itself—i.e. reason—wills is the fruit of profound cognition and insight, and this is the very thing which "the people" lack. (*PR,* §301R)[62]

Hegel puts this anti-democratic point even more succinctly in the lectures on the *Philosophy of History:* "[I]t is a false and dangerous assumption that *only* the people possess reason and insight and know what is right. . . . [W]hat really constitutes a state is a matter of trained intelligence, not a matter of 'the people'" (*IPH,* 46/61).

Though skeptical about the alleged wisdom of the people, Hegel nevertheless sees popular political participation in the form of the Estates as playing an important, if restricted, role in the rational constitution. It is through the Estates that the moment of subjective or formal freedom "attains its right in relation to those members of civil society who have no share in government" (*PR,* §314). The distinctive contribution of the Estates has nothing to do with the extra insight they bring to bear on issues of the state. Rather, the "proper conceptual definition of the Estates should . . . be sought in the fact that, in them, the subjective moment of universal freedom—the personal insight and will of that sphere which has been described in this work as civil society—comes *into existence in relation to the state*" (*PR,* §301R).

But what exactly does this mean? In what way does the moment of subjective or formal freedom "attain its right" through the Estates? In what way does the personal will and insight of individuals come "into existence in relation to the state"? It becomes clear fairly quickly that Hegel does not see the Estates, and hence the personal will and insight of individuals, as playing a creative or constitutive role with respect to the universal interest of the state. Rather, he sees the Estates as insuring that the universal interest, which is most clearly grasped by "those who know," the ministers and officials of the executive power, is not simply imposed on ordinary citizens but is somehow mediated by their own activity and understanding. It is in this rather attenuated sense that the moment of subjective freedom attains its right through the Estates. Through the Estates, the universal interest, which could otherwise be efficiently pursued by the trained officials of the bureaucracy, comes to be endowed with the subjective self-consciousness of all (*LNR,* §147R). Or, in good Hegelese, the universal interest that previously existed only "in itself" now comes to exist "for itself" (*PR,* §301).

But the significance of the Estates does not simply consist in endowing the universal interest of the state with self-consciousness so that it exists not merely "in itself" but also "for itself." It also consists in the fact that subjective self-consciousness comes to be endowed with universality. This is perhaps the deepest significance of the Estates. As Hegel writes: "The proper significance of the Estates is that it is through them that the state enters into the subjective consciousness of the people" (*PR,* §301R). Early on in his discussion of the state, Hegel asserted that "the destiny of individuals is to lead a universal life" (*PR,* §258R). We now see that the Estates play an essential role in the fulfillment of this destiny.

So far, Hegel has been concerned with what he calls the "conceptual definition" of the Estates. And he characteristically observes that this conceptual definition "should not be confused with *external necessities* and *utilities.*" Nevertheless, he does go on to point out that the Estates perform an important checking function with respect to the executive power. In the first place, the delegates to the Estates are better able to monitor "those officials who are less visible to their superiors"; and they also have a better sense of the "more urgent and specialized needs and deficiencies" of the communities and corporations they represent than do most public officials. Second, the possibility of criticism and censure by the Estates keeps public officials honest: "the expectation of criticism, indeed of public criticism, at the hands of the many" compels "officials to apply their best insights, even before they start, to their functions and to the plans they intend to submit, and to put these into effect only in accordance with the purest of motives (*PR*, §301R). In the lectures, this checking function of the Estates receives even greater emphasis (see *LNR*, §§145, 147).

In the Estates, then, the people come to be represented in the state. But the Estates do not simply represent the people; they articulate them into a rational organization based on the existing circles and corporations of civil life. In this way, the Estates "ensure that individuals do not present themselves as a *crowd* or *aggregate*, unorganized in their opinions and volition, and do not become a massive power in opposition to the organic state" (*PR*, §302). This turns out to be a major preoccupation throughout Hegel's discussion of the Estates. The people must not be allowed to appear in the state as an unorganized crowd or aggregate, a condition Hegel melodramatically describes in the *Encyclopedia Philosophy of Spirit* as one of "lawlessness, unethicalness [*Unsittlichkeit*], irrationality," in which "the people would only be a shapeless, wild, blind force, like that of the stormy, elemental sea" (*EPS*, §544R). Such a condition is promoted by the prevalent atomistic view which holds that individuals should participate and be represented in the political sphere as individuals. Hegel criticized this atomistic view of political participation, which he then associated with Rousseau, as far back as the *Phenomenology* (see *PS*, 357/432–33), and he is no kindlier disposed toward it in the *Philosophy of Right*. Political life must be grounded in the circles and associations of civil life, otherwise its universality will lack concreteness. Sever political life from the meaningful differentiation of civil life and it will be left "hanging, so to speak, in the air; for its basis is then merely the abstract individuality of arbitrary will and opinion, and is thus grounded only on contingency rather than on a foundation which is *stable* and *legitimate* in and for itself" (*PR*, §302R).

Following from his view that the political Estates must be grounded in the estates of civil society, Hegel proposes that the Estates assembly be divided into two houses or chambers based on the two estates of civil society, the substantial estate and the estate of trade and industry (*PR*, §303, 312). With respect to the substantial estate—specifically the wealthy and educated landowning class within it—Hegel argues that it is particularly "equipped for its political role" by virtue of its independence. Possessing permanent property that is independent of both the state and the "uncertainty of trade," this landowning estate lends an essential stability to the state; it serves, to invoke Burke's lapidary phrase once again, as "the ballast in the vessel of the commonwealth."[63] To insure the perpetuation of the landowning estate, its members do not enjoy the same civil rights as other citizens: they are restricted from disposing of their property freely, and inheritance is governed by the institution of primogeniture. And though the landowning estate acts as a kind of "hereditary nobility" in the rational state, Hegel insists that it does not enjoy feudal rights or privileges. Indeed, its members "have more duties than privileges" and are expected to make "stringent sacrifices for the *political end*" (*PR*, §§306 and A, 307; *LNR*, §152 and R).

The second chamber of the Estates is filled with deputies who come from the estate of trade and industry. Again in opposition to atomistic notions of representation, Hegel argues that these deputies are not elected by isolated individuals in one-man-one-vote fashion but by the various corporations into which the members of the estate of trade and industry are organized. In this way, "society acts *as what it is*," and again the people do not appear on the political scene as an unarticulated crowd or aggregate (*PR*, §308 and R). The deputies themselves represent not simply individuals but the "major interests" of society (commerce, manufacturing, and so forth), with whose "special needs, frustrations, and particular interests" they are expected to be familiar and sympathetic. Through such corporate representation Hegel believes that the problem which particularly afflicts large states, the problem of indifference to the franchise on part of the electorate due to the comparative insignificance of individual votes, can to some extent be avoided (*PR*, §311, R).[64]

The picture Hegel draws above of the deputies directly representing the major interests of society is somewhat clouded when he goes on to say that the "deputies are elected to deliberate and decide on matters of *universal* concern," and that they "will not subordinate the universal interest to the particular interest of a community or corporation." In this connection, he makes the Burkean point that the deputies are not to be regarded as "commissioned or mandated agents" (*PR*, §309).[65] But this image of the deputy as disinterestedly deliberating with a view only to the common good immediately gives way once again to a more interest-based notion of representation. The deputy is said to be qualified for political office not so much because he possesses superior insight into the universal interest as distinguished from the particular interests of civil society but because he is more enlightened about those particular interests themselves and how to further them. Here Hegel says the deputy must have "sufficient insight to treat my cause as if it were his own, and to deal with it in the light of his own best knowledge and conscience"; and he must give the voter a guarantee that he will promote the latter's interests "in an assembly which deals with universal issues" (*PR*, §309R). It must be pointed out that Burke displays a similar ambivalence on this question of representation, sometimes arguing that a representative's duty is to uphold the one national interest, at other times arguing that it is to maintain the true interests of his constituents as opposed to their merely ephemeral opinions.[66] As in the case of Burke, though, Hegel's views on representation here need not be seen as inconsistent. The universal interest is not completely different from the particular interests of the various corporations and associations which make up civil society; rather, it is composed of them. The universal interest emerges from a process of rational deliberation in which all the objective interests of society are represented and adjusted to one another.

As far as the specific qualifications of deputies are concerned, Hegel highlights—in contrast to the independence characterizing the substantial section of the Estates—the practical knowledge and skill that deputies possess by virtue of having engaged in business and occupied positions of authority (*PR*, §310). He also gives a qualified defense—somewhat in contrast to the view he expresses in other places (see *LNR*, §153)—of property qualifications for deputies. Though such qualifications no doubt have the appearance of merely external conditions, they serve some purpose if the deputies do not receive a salary (*PR*, §310R). On the subject of property qualifications for voters Hegel is silent in the *Philosophy of Right*. In other places, however, he expresses his opposition to such qualifications for voters (*LNR*, §153R; "PEAW," 262/481–82). The only relevant qualification for a voter is that he belong to a corporation or association. This leads Hegel to a certain inconsistency. On the one hand, he says that "no one in the state must be allowed not to be a member of an association." On the other, somewhat akin to the exclusions on voting Kant draws, he remarks that "it goes without saying that day laborers, servants, etc., are not [allowed to vote, but] are excluded as not being members of an association" (*LNR*, §153R).[67]

The rationale for dividing the Estates assembly into two houses is, as we have seen, that the two estates of which the two houses are composed bring very different qualities to the table: the landowners bring independence, permanence, and stability; the deputies from the estate of trade and industry bring energy and a knowledge of the manifold workings of civil society. To this rationale Hegel adds one further, practical reason for dividing the Estates assembly into two houses. Such an arrangement "ensures that the Estates are less likely to come into direct opposition to the government." The presence of three actors—the government and the two houses—eliminates the possibility of a stand-off between any two of them. The substantial or upper house generally plays the mediating role, either backing up the government's initiative or lending weight to the more democratic lower house's opposition (*PR*, §313; *LNR*, §151). Here again Hegel's concern that the executive power not be regarded as simply opposed to the legislative power is apparent.

The final point Hegel makes with respect to the Estates is that their proceedings should be conducted in public. The whole justification of the Estates, as we saw at the beginning of Hegel's discussion, is that they mediate the universal interest of the state to the subjective consciousness of the ordinary citizen; they give this interest an existence in the self-consciousness of the people. This task cannot be fully accomplished if the proceedings of the Estates are conducted in private (*PR*, §314). Most important of all, the publicity of the proceedings of the Estates serves as a means of educating ordinary citizens about the universal interest of the state, "permitting *public opinion* to arrive for the first time at *true thoughts* and *insights* with regard to the condition and concept of the state and its affairs, thereby *enabling it to form more rational judgments on the latter*" (*PR*, §315). Here Hegel speaks glowingly of the "great spectacle of outstanding educational value to the citizens," in which ministers "armed with wit and eloquence" defend their policies and "one ingenious idea devours another" (*PR*, §315A). Perhaps nowhere else does the essentially cognitive, nonvoluntaristic, character of Hegel's model of political participation reveal itself more clearly than in this paragraph. Political participation is important for Hegel not because it brings the subjective wills of individuals to bear on the universal interest of the state but because it allows the universal interest of the state to enter into the subjective consciousness of individuals. By attending to the public proceedings of the Estates, ordinary citizens are educated up to the universal and thereby enabled to fulfill their destiny of leading a universal life.

Having shown how public opinion can be formed to arrive at "true thoughts and insight," Hegel goes on to say a bit more about this most important phenomenon of modern democratic politics. He realizes that public opinion plays an increasingly important role in politics because it reflects the modern demand that "whatever is to be recognized by everyone must be seen by everyone as entitled to such recognition" (*PR*, §317A; see also §316A). Nevertheless, he is dubious about the substantive worth of most public opinion. He rejects the naive optimism of predecessors such as Kant who see the public use of reason as absolutely essential to public enlightenment[68] and takes what might be called a more modern and skeptical view of the matter. For the most part, he regards public opinion as a congeries of unformed subjective opinions and erroneous judgments. And as such, he argues that it deserves to be despised (*PR*, §§317–18).

But Hegel adds that public opinion "deserves to be *respected* as well as *despised*" (*PR*, §318). Public opinion does not simply contain subjective opinions and arbitrary fancies; it also embodies "the eternal and substantial principles of justice," generally in the form of "common sense" (*des gesunden Menschenverstandes*) and unreflective "prejudices." Contingency and error begin to creep in only when the wisdom latent in common sense and prejudices comes to be expressed in more reflective and ratiocinative form (*PR*, §317; compare §268A). Public opinion thus contains two aspects: a deep, substantial aspect and a more superficial, subjective aspect. It is the latter which Hegel says the great man must be indifferent to if he is to achieve anything great. But the great man must not ignore public opinion altogether; rather, he must "discover the truth within it," the so-called real will of the citizens: "He who expresses the will of his age, tells it what its will is, and accomplishes this will, is the great man of the age. What he does is the essence and inner content of the age, and he gives the latter actuality" (*PR*, §318A).

Despite this concession, Hegel's attitude toward public opinion in the reflective form most familiar to us remains largely negative. And this negativity is reflected in his remarks on the freedom of the press. Here again we do not find Hegel arguing, like Kant, that freedom of the pen is the key to public enlightenment or "the only safeguard of the rights of the people."[69] Nor do we find him, like Fichte—or Milton and Mill, for that matter—defending freedom of communication on the basis that it is absolutely indispensable to discovering "the truth."[70] Rather, his greatest concern seems to be with what renders the freedom to express one's subjective opinions in writing innocuous. In this regard, he mentions again the publicity of the proceedings of the Estates assembly, in which "sound and educated insights concerning the interests of the state" are given expression, "leaving little of significance for others to say, and above all denying them the opinion that what they have to say is of distinctive importance and effectiveness." He also points to "the rationality of the constitution and the stability of government" as important factors which render the freedom of the press innocuous (*PR*, §319).[71] Because the modern state is internally strong, it can tolerate a fair amount of subjective prattling. Finally, Hegel mentions laws against slander, libel, and incendiary speech as serving to check the abuses of freedom of the press. He argues, however, that such laws have little application to the sciences, because the sciences do not belong to the "sphere of opinion and subjective views" and therefore "do not come under the category of public opinion" (*PR*, §319R). Contrary to what he suggests in the Preface (*PR*, 18–20), Hegel here clearly condemns the censorship to which the *Philosophy of Right* was subject under the Carlsbad Decrees.

Hegel's views on public opinion and freedom of the press display the same fear of irrational subjectivism and atomism that runs through his entire analysis of the democratic institutions of the modern state. And though there is per-haps, as one commentator noted, "something almost laughable" to the English or American mind about Hegel's "nervous solicitude" toward popular political participation in the *Philosophy of Right*, [72] there is also something depressingly true. The problem to which Hegel points—the problem that the democratic will is rarely a rational will—has not been resolved and, if anything, under the impact of advertising and mass media, has gotten worse. Hegel's solutions to this problem—giving a landed quasi-aristocracy a checking role, corporate voting, publicity of parliamentary proceedings, and so forth—no doubt strike us as quaint today. But Hegel was only trying to find in institutions that still had some vitality in his own social-political world—though they were soon to be swept away—forces to combat the democratic individualism and atomism he saw looming on the horizon. It is incumbent on us to make the same effort in our very different social-political circumstances.

WAR AND INTERNATIONAL RELATIONS

Like his views on the rational constitution, Hegel's views on war and interna-tional relations with which he concludes the *Philosophy of Right* have had their share of criticism. To many liberal interpreters, Hegel's defense of war and his denial of the efficacy of international law confirm that he is some sort of militaristic nationalist and totalitarian.[73] While there is little to support such extreme charges (and few who currently subscribe to them), it remains true that Hegel's views on war and international relations depart fairly sharply from conventional liberal orthodoxy on these matters. This departure mirrors (and brings home) Hegel's more general difference with liberal political philosophy and its individualistic conception of the state as based on a social contract. In what follows, I am particularly concerned with this more general implication of Hegel's views on war and international relations. At the same time, I bring out the relative strengths and weaknesses of his specific views vis-à-vis the liberal, and especially the Kantian, model of international relations.

Hegel's views on war and international relations are, of course, ultimately grounded in his understanding of the sovereignty of the state. As we have seen,

Hegel defines the sovereignty of the state in terms of the "ideality" of its moments or constituent parts. With respect to the internal constitution, this means that no particular power or function within the state is completely self-sufficient or independent of the whole. This unity of the state, or the ideality of every particular authority within it, achieves consummate expression in the relationship of the state as a unit or individual in relation to other states. Here, in its "external sovereignty" vis-à-vis other states, the state attains its "*own* highest moment—its actual infinity as the ideality of everything finite within it. It is that aspect whereby the substance, as the state's absolute power over everything individual or particular, over life, property, and the latter's rights, and over the wider circles within it, gives the nullity of such things an existence and makes it present to consciousness" (*PR,* §323).

It is in war that the "ideality of everything finite within the state" spoken of above becomes actual. This constitutes what Hegel calls—in a purposely paradoxical phrase—the "ethical moment of war." This ethical significance of war cannot be grasped if one equates the state with civil society and sees its highest purpose as the preservation of the life and property of individuals. Indeed, such a liberal or contractarian view has a great deal of difficulty justifying to the individual why he should in any circumstance sacrifice his life for the state. As Hegel writes: "It is a grave miscalculation if the state, when it requires this sacrifice, is simply equated with civil society, and if its ultimate end is seen merely as the *security of the life and property of individuals.* For this security cannot be achieved by the sacrifice of what is supposed to be *secured*—on the contrary." Not in the security of life and property but precisely in the positing of these finite things as non-necessary, contingent, and transient lies the true significance of war. "War," Hegel writes, "is that condition in which the vanity of temporal goods—which tends at other times to be merely a pious phrase— takes on a serious significance, and it is accordingly the moment in which the ideality of *the particular attains its right* and becomes actuality." To cap his point, he quotes the provocative passage on war from the early *Natural Law* essay:

> The higher significance of war is that, through its agency (as I have put it on another occasion), "the ethical health of nations is preserved in their indifference towards the permanence of finite determinacies, just as the movement of the winds preserves the sea from stagnation which a lasting calm would produce—a stagnation which a lasting, not to say perpetual, peace would also produce among nations. (*PR,* §324R)

Some commentators claim that, in passages such as the one above, Hegel does not necessarily glorify war but simply recognizes its inevitability and treats it as an "unavoidable evil."[74] But this is to go too far in an apologetic direction. There is no getting around the fact that Hegel sees war as serving a positive function. In peace, individualism is promoted at the expense of citizens' commitment to the universal or the whole, and civil society threatens to overwhelm the state. "In peace," Hegel writes, "the bounds of civil life are extended, all its spheres become firmly established, and in the long run, people become stuck in their ways. Their particular characteristics become increasingly rigid and ossified." War is necessary to shake people out of their comfortable privacy and rigid particularity and reconnect them to the universal. As a result of such shaking up, peoples emerge stronger and, if "troubled by civil dissension," often "gain internal peace." For these reasons, as the passage above suggests, Hegel sees the Kantian notion of perpetual peace as ultimately nonsensical. Perpetual peace could lead only to stagnation and ultimately death in the organism of the state. In an interesting twist, Hegel suggests that even if something like a Kantian federation of states could be realized, it would still have to "generate opposition and create an enemy." The unity of the state depends to some extent on its defining itself in opposition to an other (*PR*, §324A). It should be pointed out that Kant himself sometimes recognizes the point that Hegel is making here. In the *Critique of Judgment*, for example, Kant writes that "even war has something sublime about it if it is carried on in an orderly way and with respect for the sanctity of citizens' rights. . . . A prolonged peace, on the other hand, tends to make prevalent a merely commercial spirit, and along with it base selfishness, cowardice, and softness, and to debase the way of thinking of that people."[75]

As the quote from the *Natural Law* essay suggests, the view about war that Hegel articulates in the *Philosophy of Right* goes back to his earliest writings on politics; it constitutes one of the most consistent tenets of his political philosophy. In *The German Constitution*, for example, he writes that the "health of a state is generally revealed not so much in the calm of peace as in the stir of war" (*GC*, 143–44/462). And in the *Philosophy of Spirit of 1806–7*, he states that war "shakes up . . . the all-embracing systems of right, of personal security and property" and makes them "vanish in the power of the universal" (*HHS*, 171/276). Finally, and perhaps most famously, he declares in the *Phenomenology* that,

> in order not to let [the systems of personal independence and property] become rooted and set in this isolation, thereby breaking up the whole and letting the [communal] spirit evaporate, government has from time to time to shake them to their core by war. By this means the government upsets their right to independence, while the individuals who, absorbed in their own way of life, break loose from the

whole and strive after the inviolable independence and security of the person, are made to feel in the task laid on them their lord and master, death. (*PS*, 272–72/335)

All of these passages reflect the civic republican strand in Hegel's early political thought. War is credited with clearly revealing the primacy of the political or ethical whole over the particular interests comprising the state. Insofar as this view is essentially restated in the *Philosophy of Right*, one might argue that Hegel never really abandons his early civic republican outlook. Such an interpretation, however, fails to take into account the significantly reduced role that war plays in Hegel's overall argument in the *Philosophy of Right* as compared with his earlier writings. In the *Natural Law* essay, for example, war is adduced at the outset as the defining principle of ethical life and is made the basis of the radical distinction between state and civil society, ethical life and economic life, the free, political class and the unfree, bourgeois class, which runs through that work. In the *Philosophy of Right*, on the other hand, war comes in only at the end of the book and occupies a rather minor place in the enormous edifice of mediations by which the individual comes to participate in the universal. While war brings out, to a degree no other moment can, the difference between state and civil society and the primacy of the universal to the particular, it must also be remembered that Hegel does not generally identify patriotism with making heroic sacrifices on behalf of the state but with "that disposition which, in the normal conditions and circumstances of life, habitually knows that the community is the substantial basis and end" (*PR*, §268R).

Though every citizen has a duty to defend the state if its independence is at risk, there is also a special estate, the estate of courage or valor, which is permanently dedicated to this purpose (*PR*, §§325–26). But just as virtue in the rational state takes the prosaic form of rectitude (*PR*, §150), so valor loses its personal and heroic character and takes on a more universal form. The "true valor" of the military estate is not the same thing as the courage of a robber, a murderer, or even of a knight, Hegel argues; rather, it consists in "readiness for sacrifice in the service of the state, so that the individual merely counts as one among many. Not personal courage but integration with the universal is the important factor here" (*PR*, §327A). This more impersonal and mechanical valor also does not direct itself "against individual persons, but against a hostile whole in general." From this modification of valor by the modern principle of "thought and the universal" Hegel ingeniously, if implausibly, deduces the invention of the gun. "[T]his invention," he writes, "which did not come about by chance, has turned the purely personal form of valor into a more abstract form" (*PR,* §328R).[76]

Hegel's rather optimistic assessment of the role of the gun in modern warfare highlights a common and legitimate criticism of his whole philosophical justification of war: no matter how valid that justification may have been in the circumstances of warfare at the beginning of the nineteenth century, it certainly does not seem to have much relevance to the totalistic conditions of warfare in the twentieth century.[77] Hegel believes that modern wars will be waged in a limited and humane manner (*PR,* §338). But already in Hegel's own time Napoleon had rendered such a belief about the limited nature of modern warfare old-fashioned. The observation that Hegel's conception of the civic role of war is no longer applicable in modern circumstances of warfare, however, does not so much solve a problem as leave us with another: namely, how to generate a patriotic identification with the universal in citizens and prevent their becoming completely absorbed in bourgeois comfort and particularity when war becomes prohibitively costly. A similar question arises if we project an "end of history" in which the homogenization of humanity and its agreement on the fundamental (essentially bourgeois) aims of life render war unnecessary. I will have more to say about the notion of the "end of history" in a moment. But it is clear from what has been said so far about Hegel's attitude toward war that this particular conception of it forms no part of his philosophical outlook.[78]

That Hegel sees war as not only unavoidable but also salutary does not mean that he entirely rejects the idea of international law in the relations between states. Indeed, he devotes the penultimate section of the *Philosophy of Right* to precisely this idea. And though he ultimately shows that international law does not form a completely stable or authoritative set of norms, being based on a moral "ought" rather than actual power, he still believes it plays some role in the relations between states.

In treating international law, Hegel returns to some of the earliest categories of his political philosophy, namely, the categories of abstract right. He begins by grounding international law in the desire for recognition on the part of states. As we have seen, the state is an individual, "a sovereign and independent entity," in relation to other states. But this sovereignty and independence of the state does not have actual existence unless it is recognized by other states. "Without relations with other states," Hegel writes, "the state can no more be an actual individual than an individual can be an actual person without a relationship to other persons" (*PR,* §331 and R). Such recognition rests on many factors. In the lectures of 1817–18, echoing one of the principal themes of his accounts of the struggle for recognition, Hegel argues that recognition partly depends on a state's willingness to risk its life: a state gains recognition only "by demonstrating that its life is a matter of indifference to it; and this existence of what is free can be shown only in war" (*LNR*, §161R). But, in addition to this, recognition also "requires a guarantee that the state will likewise recognize those other states which are supposed to recognize it, i.e. that it will respect their independence" (*PR*, §331R). Such mutual recognition provides the basis for international law.

The problem with international law is that the agreements, treaties, and obligations that flow from the reciprocal recognition between states "possess the formal nature of *contracts* in general." Recurring to his analysis of the contractual relationship in abstract right, Hegel argues that any agreement between states is ultimately "determined by the independent arbitrary wills of both parties" (*PR*, §332). There is no guarantee that the particular wills of the contracting parties will be in conformity with the common will that is posited in any agreement. Thus, abiding by such agreements in accordance with international law remains a mere moral "ought," contingent and without actuality (*PR*, §333). Of course, in civil relations this defect of contract is remedied by the institution of judges and a system of justice to enforce contracts. But such a solution is not available in the international realm, according to Hegel. Here "there is no praetor to adjudicate between states, but at most arbitrators and mediators, and even the presence of these will be contingent, i.e. determined by particular wills." Hegel again dismisses "Kant's idea of a perpetual peace guaranteed by a federation of states"; for such a federation rests on an agreement between states which is itself "dependent on particular sovereign wills" and therefore "tainted with contingency" (*PR*, §333R).

But why, it might be wondered, does the development of international law have to be arrested at the level of contract? Why can't the logic that Hegel deploys in the first part of the *Philosophy of Right* with respect to individuals— the logic that leads from contract to ethical community via "wrong"—also be applied to sovereign states in their mutual relations? In which case, not the breakdown of international law but its fulfillment in some sort of international community would be the conclusion of Hegel's argument. Hegel himself may have been prevented from drawing such a conclusion because no such international community existed at the time he was writing. But this constitutes only a factual, and not a logical, reason for arresting his argument in this way.[79]

This is an interesting point and worthy of consideration. Perhaps the first thing to notice is that this objection seems to imply, if the parallel with the earlier development of the *Philosophy of Right* is to be completely followed, not simply that there must be a federation of states (along the lines suggested by Kant) but something like a world-state with overarching authority. If this is the case, then the real question is whether such a world-state could generate the identification and sense of commonality that is of the essence of Hegel's conception of the ethical life of the state. Or would such a world-state degenerate into a "soulless despotism," to borrow a phrase from Kant, who, despite his commitment to international peace, seems to have had real doubts about the advantageousness of a world-state.[80] Beyond this, the objection does not seem to take sufficient account of the ethical significance Hegel ascribes to war. Nor does it reflect sufficient appreciation of the fact that the idea of an international community it espouses remains as much of a will-o'-the-wisp in our own time as it was in Hegel's. Whether we are talking about the League of Nations, the United Nations, or the World Court, none seems to escape the contingency Hegel believes all international law is afflicted by.

When the contingency inherent in international law becomes actual, that is, when the particular wills of the parties to an agreement or a treaty assert themselves, there is no recourse but war. The circumstances that might justify one state's going to war with another Hegel believes are "inherently indeterminable." It is impossible to specify a priori just which injury suffered by a state will be regarded as an affront to its essential honor or recognition such that it must go to war (*PR*, §334). Nor can a state simply wait for an injury to take place but must sometimes anticipate dangers and preemptively respond (*PR*, §335). The state must be concerned above all with its own preservation; its particular "welfare is the supreme law for a state in its relations with others" (*PR*, §336). For this reason, Hegel rejects the idea that there is an opposition between morality and politics, along with the Kantian "demand that the latter should conform to the former." There is no higher morality to which the preservation or welfare of the state is subordinate. The suggestion that there is rests on "superficial notions of morality, the nature of the state, and the state's relation to the moral point of view" (*PR*, §337).[81]

But though Hegel denies that there are efficacious norms to prevent the outbreak of war, he still believes there are certain norms that govern the conduct of war. Wars are waged not for their own sakes but for the purpose of recognition. Therefore, any act of war that destroys the possibility of future mutual recognition and peace—for example, the killing of ambassadors or of the civilian population—constitutes a breach of international law (*PR*, §338). Here

Hegel seems to accept Kant's preliminary article of perpetual peace that "no state at war with another shall permit such acts of hostility as would make mutual confidence impossible during a future time of peace,"[82] though he also recognizes, at least in the lectures, that such a norm remains "by and large only an 'ought' " and that the line between what belongs to war and what doesn't can be very fluid (*LNR*, §163R). Beyond this fundamental limitation on the conduct of war, Hegel argues, the behavior of states toward one another in wartime will be determined by "national customs" (*PR*, §339). In this regard, he sees a certain consensus on conventions in war emerging among European nations: "The European nations form a family with respect to the universal principle of their legislation, customs, and culture, so that their conduct in terms of international law is modified accordingly in a situation which is otherwise dominated by the mutual infliction of evils" (*PR*, §339A).

THE END OF HISTORY

This brings us to the final transition in the *Philosophy of Right*. Though the "relations between states are unstable, and there is no praetor to settle disputes," there still exists a "higher praetor" in the form of the "world spirit" who passes judgment on the finite spirits of nations in the "court of judgment" (*Weltgericht*) of world history (*PR*, §§339A, 340). From here, Hegel sketches his familiar dialectic of world history that begins with the purely substantial Oriental world, proceeds through the Greek and Roman worlds, and culminates with the Germanic (i.e. modern European) world in which the substantial will of the state is completely mediated by the subjective freedom of the individual (*PR*, §§352–60).[83] I do not intend to give a detailed account of this dialectic of world history here, since to do so would take us far beyond the scope of this chapter. Besides, we have already encountered a version of this dialectic in the *Phenomenology of Spirit*, and it is never very far in the background of Hegel's argument throughout the *Philosophy of Right*. Instead, I will confine myself to a few concluding remarks about the controversial and much-discussed notion of the "end of history" that Hegel's dialectic of world history seems to imply.

The notion of the "end of history"—or at least the phrase—of course originates with Alexandre Kojève's idiosyncratic reading of Hegel,[84] and it has been revived and applied to the end of the cold war by Francis Fukuyama.[85] That Hegel believes history has an end or goal, and that he identifies this end or goal of history with the modern, rational state described in the *Philosophy of Right*, would seem to be indisputable. The dialectic of world history with which the *Philosophy of Right* concludes clearly culminates in the modern European state, which is described in the final sentences of the book as the "image and actuality of reason" in which "self-consciousness finds the actuality of its substantial knowledge and volition in organic development" (*PR*, §360). The *Lectures on the Philosophy of History* conclude in roughly the same way. Nevertheless, it remains a question just what it means to speak of history as having or coming to an end in this way. And the phrase "the end of history" has an air of paradox about it which not only makes it endlessly fascinating to undergraduates but also invites all sorts of irrelevant notions. Some clarification of Hegel's meaning is therefore necessary before we can fairly evaluate this final aspect of his political philosophy.

Let us begin by rejecting the crudest misunderstanding of Hegel's conception of the end of history: namely, that it represents a condition of things that has "proved" itself historically simply by triumphing over and outlasting all other competitors.[86] Thus (on this view), it might be argued that, with the fall of communism in Eastern Europe and the Soviet Union at the end of the twentieth century, liberal democracy has revealed itself to be the definitive end of history. Hegel's repeated invocation of the formula that *die Weltgeschichte ist das Weltgericht* might seem to suggest that he holds some such pragmatic or historicist understanding of the dialectic of world history (see *PR*, §340; *LNR*, §164R); but the entire argument of the *Philosophy of Right* serves as a standing refutation of the view that history alone is the final arbiter of the rationality or ethicality of any political order or institutional arrangement. This brings us back to some of the issues raised in chapter 4 in connection with Hegel's assertion of the rationality of the actual. And I repeat here what I argued there: namely, that the rationality of the actual and, by extension, of history cannot be determined by anything in the historical process itself but only by the philosophical concept. The ultimate justification of the modern, rational state is not that it is the political order which emerges victorious at the end of the historical process, but that it is the political order which most fully and deeply actualizes human freedom. It is true that Hegel sees the empirical course of world history as reflecting or confirming this philosophical justification—this is his faith— but it does not have independent verifying power. To grasp the rationality of history—to know what counts as "progress" or "success" in the dialectic of world history—one must ultimately go to history armed with the philosophical concept (see *EL*, §16R).

Connected with this point, Hegel's identification of the modern European state with the end or goal of history does not preclude the possibility of a decline from this peak in the future. Again, the end of history is not to be equated simply with what comes last or with what succeeds in displacing previous historical constellations. Hegel has nothing to do with the "deification of success" or "idolatry of the factual" of which Nietzsche accused his vulgar and historicistic followers.[87] Indeed, toward the end of his life, in the wake of the July Revolution of 1830 in France, Hegel seems to have been filled with gloomy forebodings about the future of the modern European state and of the higher cultural spheres conjoined with it. In December 1830, for example, he laments that "at present the immense interest in politics has drowned all others. It is a crisis in which everything that was formerly valid appears to be made problematic" (L, 544/3:323). And in a letter to his sister from January of 1831, he writes: "But these are still anxious times, in which everything that previously was taken to be solid and secure seems to totter" (L, 422/3:329). Hegel's faith in the providential course of world history does not seem to have prevented him from worrying about whether the supreme achievement of the rational state might not be overwhelmed by irrational forces in the future.

But the principal objection to Hegel's claim that the modern European state represents the end or goal of history does not stem from the worry that it denies the possibility of decline in the future. Rather, the principal objection has to do with what seems to be the implicit denial in Hegel's claim of the possibility of further progress in the future. This, of course, is an objection that surfaced early in the reception of Hegel's philosophy—most prominently among the "left" or "young" Hegelians—and many of his closest followers were eager to refute it.[88] To what extent is it true? To what extent does Hegel's conception of the end of history deny the possibility of significant progress or new developments in the future?

Many contemporary apologists for Hegel's philosophy point to a passage from the *Philosophy of History* in which Hegel refers to America as "the land of the future" as evidence that his philosophy does not represent a closed system that forecloses the possibility of new discoveries and developments in the future. The passage reads in full:

America is therefore the land of the future. In the time to come, the center of world-historical importance will be revealed there—perhaps in a conflict between North and South America. It is the land of longing for all those weary of the historic arsenal that is old Europe. Napoleon is reported to have said, "*Cette vieille Europe m'ennuie.*" America has to separate itself from the ground upon which the world's history has taken place until now. What has taken place in America so far is a mere echo of the Old World, and the expression of an alien vitality. As a land of the future it does not concern us here: for in the historical perspective we are concerned with what has been and with what is; and in regard to philosophy our concern is neither with what was nor with what is yet to be, but with what *is* as eternal reason—and that is enough to keep us occupied. (*IPH,* 90/114)

It is difficult to know what to make of this passage. It does not find an echo in anything else that Hegel wrote; and, indeed, it exists in considerable tension with his numerous assertions that the Germanic (or European) world constitutes the complete actualization of the idea of freedom, the perfect reconciliation of substantive freedom with subjective freedom.[89] The passage itself also seems to contain an ambiguity. Hegel depreciates the importance of anticipating future developments, since the fundamental concern of philosophy is "with what *is* as eternal reason." The implication seems to be that no matter what happens in America in the future, it will not affect the essential reality of eternal reason that has already disclosed itself in the modern European state.

Going beyond this isolated passage, though, it is difficult to imagine how one *could* go beyond what Hegel conceives to be the end of history, at least given the general way in which he characterizes this end. In the Orient—so goes the most general and famous of Hegel's accounts of history in terms of the idea of human freedom—only one man was free; in the Greek and Roman worlds only a few men were free; it is only in the modern European and Christian world that all men are recognized to be free in their essence and treated accordingly (see *IPH,* 22/31, 93/134). Given this triadic account of the history of human freedom—from one, to some, to all—it is difficult to see how or where one could go beyond the final term. This goes for Hegel's other general account of the dialectical course of world history in terms of the reconciliation of substantial freedom with subjective freedom as well. According to this account, as we have seen, the human spirit proceeds dialectically from the purely substantial Oriental world, through the Greek and Roman worlds, and achieves complete satisfaction only in the Germanic world in which the substantial will of the state is completely mediated by the subjective freedom of the individual (see *PR,* §§352–60; *IPH,* 92–98/133–41). Again, it is difficult to see how one could advance beyond the sort of reconciliation of substantial freedom with subjective freedom that Hegel here attributes to the modern European state.

But even if it is unimaginable how one might progress beyond Hegel's general conception of the end of history in terms of the freedom of all human beings and the reconciliation of substantial freedom with subjective freedom, one still might question the connection he draws between this general end of history and the specific institutions of the modern state. Can it be maintained that the bourgeois family, the market economy, the differentiation of society into separate estates, and constitutional monarchy are *the* institutions that realize most fully the rational freedom of individuals and that therefore cannot be essentially improved upon or superseded by future developments? It is this grand claim that most critics have in mind when they question Hegel's conception of the end of history. It is important to point out, however, that the objection here has at least as much to do with Hegel's specific doctrine of the state as it does with his general philosophy of history. The question that it raises is to what extent the institutions Hegel describes in the *Philosophy of Right* actually realize the rational freedom that it is the aim of world history to bring about.

With respect to this question, I have argued in this chapter and the previous one that Hegel's analysis of the role played by the family, civil society, religion, and the political constitution in the actualization of rational freedom in the modern world represents a remarkable achievement and that his specific arguments for these institutions are not as flawed as they are frequently supposed to be. Nevertheless, it would be difficult to deny that some of the specific arrangements that he defends—the sharp differentiation of gender-roles in the family, the idea of distinct social and political estates, constitutional monarchy and the restricted role of democracy—reflect contingent features of Hegel's world that no longer apply to our own and that fall far short of the requirements of eternal reason. To what extent does this fact discredit Hegel's entire project and call into question the relevance of his political philosophy to today's world? In my view, not a great deal. A more detailed explanation and defense follows in the epilogue.

Epilogue

Every interpreter of Hegel's philosophy, it seems, is inevitably driven to ask the Crocean question: What is dead and what is still living in it? Although I do not depart from this venerable tradition here, I do modify Croce's question somewhat to avoid misleading implications. I do not, for example, wish to break up Hegel's philosophy into separate parts and consign some of them—the social or political philosophy, for example—to the living and the rest—the speculative logic and metaphysics, for example—to the dead. I have given my reasons for rejecting this piecemeal approach to Hegel's philosophy above. I will, however, confine myself in this epilogue (as I have for the most part in the rest of the book) to Hegel's political philosophy. And the simple question I ask of it is, Why is Hegel's political philosophy still important to us today?

The answer that has been developed over the preceding pages is Hegel's political philosophy represents the most profound and systematic attempt in the modern world to understand the state as the realization of human freedom. Freedom is the central idea around which the whole of modern political philosophy revolves. In Hobbes and Locke and all of their classical liberal progeny, freedom was largely conceived in "negative" terms as the capacity to pursue one's empirical wants and desires in an unobstructed fashion. With Rousseau, however, a more profound and "positive" conception of freedom entered the bloodstream of modern political philosophy. Freedom was now no longer conceived simply in terms of the unimpeded pursuit of one's empirical desires but in terms of rational self-direction, radical self-determination and self-dependence, autonomy. This idea of freedom as radical self-determination or autonomy was, of course, taken over and developed by Kant and Fichte, but for the most part they identified it with morality and viewed politics or the state as merely providing an external framework within which the individual's moral and subjective quest for autonomy might take place. It is only with Hegel that the state and the social institutions comprising it are no longer viewed as merely establishing the negative or external conditions for the quest for human autonomy but as directly promoting and cultivating such autonomy. It is true that this more direct linking of human autonomy and rational self-direction to social and political institutions had already been intimated in Rousseau's political philosophy. But Rousseau was able to effect this link only by appealing to the civic republican ideal of the ancient polis, whereas Hegel effects it completely on the plane of the modern state and the institutions of modern civil society.

Hegel's specific analyses of the institutions that make up the modern state and progressively actualize human freedom are not, as has already been observed, without their difficulties. His conception of the family is patriarchal and rests on a differentiation of the sexes that few would accept today. His division of society into sharply defined estates and corporations is redolent of a social world that we have long since lost. And his strictures on democracy severely underestimate the extent to which the claims of modern subjective freedom demand expression in the realm of politics. But these shortcomings in Hegel's analysis of modern society and the state must not be allowed to overshadow its more important achievements. It is true that Hegel is a little too eager to translate the contingent features of his own social-political world into the edicts of eternal reason. But while he fails to anticipate a number of important developments in the modern social and political landscape, what is perhaps more noteworthy is just how much he gets right. Thus, while his differentiation of the roles of men and women may be excessively traditional, his emphasis on the family as a crucial ethical precondition of the rational state remains a valuable insight. By the same token, while his division of society into separate estates and corporations may not be directly applicable to current social reality, the underlying insight that a vital liberal democracy requires local organizations and associations to mediate between the individual and the state is one that is currently being rediscovered by proponents of "civil society." Finally, while his conception of democracy is no doubt cramped by today's standards, his concern that "the people" in a democracy somehow be meaningfully articulated and not appear as an atomized and unorganized mass continues to be a vexing concern today.

In describing Hegel's achievement above, I have found it difficult to avoid the term "liberalism." This is not altogether surprising, since liberalism, too, purports to be the political philosophy of freedom. What exactly is the relationship between Hegel's political philosophy of freedom and liberalism? Two broad conclusions have emerged from our analysis in the foregoing chapters. First, in its incorporation of subjective freedom, the Hegelian state is able to account for almost all the rights and freedoms we ordinarily associate with the liberal state. Second, though Hegel is able to provide for these liberal rights and freedoms in his state, his ultimate justification for them is not the typical liberal one. Subjective or particular freedom is not the end or purpose of the Hegelian state, as it is of the liberal state. The end or purpose of the Hegelian state is rational freedom, the willing of the universal that corresponds to the universality of the human essence, or, less metaphysically, the willing of a content that corresponds to the self-determining nature of the human will. It is only through its connection to this rational freedom that subjective freedom receives its ultimate justification as the activating and self-conscious element. The rational freedom that is realized in the Hegelian state is not inimical to subjective freedom—indeed, it derives its greatest strength and depth from being conjoined to subjective freedom—but neither is it simply identical or reducible to subjective freedom. It is in this notion of the state as the realization of rational freedom that Hegel most radically departs from the instrumentalist conception of the state that predominates in liberal theory.

The question with which I would like to close this book is that of the relevance of Hegel's ideal of the rational state to our understanding of contemporary liberalism and its discontents. Of what use is Hegel's peculiar blend of liberal and nonliberal ideas—his placement of liberal political ideals in the larger context of a nonliberal theoretical justification—to the understanding and/or defense of liberalism as we near the end of the twentieth century? This, of course, is a rather large question. And in the following paragraphs, I offer only a few sketchy—but hopefully suggestive—ideas. Nevertheless, it is a question to which any thoughtful student of Hegel's political philosophy is inevitably driven, dwelling as we do in the intact but strangely insecure edifice of liberalism in the post-Marxian and (to use the current jargon) postmodern era.

As to what Hegel positively has to contribute to contemporary reflection on liberalism, we do not have to search far. Our attention is immediately drawn to his critique of liberal individualism. Hegel offers a way out of the atomism and narrow self-interest of traditional liberal theory. He offers a conception of the social good that is more exalted and inspiring than mere security of life and property. And, as pointed out above, he delineates a complex network of institutions and associations that mediate between the particular interest of the individual and the universal interest of the state. Moreover, he does all this without sacrificing the individual rights and liberties that constitute the central political ideals of liberalism. With respect to these liberal rights and freedoms, Hegel sets them in a larger context that endows them with a meaning and purpose beyond the one ordinarily given them in traditional liberal theory. Subjective freedom, particularity, and even arbitrariness are not seen as ends in themselves but, rather, as essential elements in a much grander conception of the nature and overall destiny of human beings.

It is, of course, this critique of liberal individualism that contemporary communitarians have fixed upon in their appropriation of Hegel's political philosophy. As indicated in the Preface to this book, there is much in the communitarian interpretation of Hegel to be commended. Above all, I am sympathetic to the communitarian attempt to find in Hegel an alternative to traditional and much contemporary liberal theory. Nevertheless, my interpretation moves in a slightly different direction. Whereas communitarians have tended to emphasize Hegel's break with Enlightenment rationalism and his affinity with such romantic themes as belonging, personal wholeness, and communal solidarity, I have stressed Hegel's doctrine of rational freedom and self-determination—a doctrine that descends from the Kantian doctrine of rational autonomy and that, far from being antithetical to Enlightenment aspirations, in some ways represents their highest fulfillment. My interpretation cuts not only against the communitarians' positive appropriation of Hegel but also against those critics of communitarianism who see Hegel as an early and antiliberal exponent of "political romanticism."[1]

For all the attractiveness of Hegel's critique of liberal individualism, however, his ideal of the rational state is not without its difficulties as an instrument for understanding and defending contemporary liberalism. In some ways these difficulties are simply the other side of the virtues of Hegel's theory of the state.

What is attractive about Hegel's theory of the state, as we have seen, is that it preserves most of the individual rights and freedoms liberals prize, while at the same time placing them in a theoretical context that links them to something higher than mere self-interest, security, and arbitrariness; that links them to a more exalted conception of the rational and self-determining nature and destiny of human beings. But the question arises, Is the purpose that Hegel here attributes to the state too exalted, too grand, for our current circumstances? Does his conception of the state as the actualization of rational freedom correspond, in the end, to what most people in liberal democracies currently understand the state as providing?

The answer is obviously not an easy one to give. Nor is it clear that Hegel would see the deliverances of ordinary or unreflective consciousness on this issue as decisive, although he frequently invokes the agreement between philosophy and ingenuous consciousness as proof against the sophistries of the sophisticated consciousness. Nevertheless, if I had to venture a guess, I would say that the vast majority of the denizens of modern liberal democracies do not view the state as Hegel viewed it, as the realization of their rational freedom, but, rather, in precisely the instrumental way he found inadequate, namely, as a vehicle for pursuing their own self-chosen ends, a necessary condition for the widest exercise of their arbitrary will.

In this regard, Hobbes and Locke continue to come much closer to the self-understanding of most members of liberal democracies than does Hegel. And perhaps even better than Hobbes and Locke is John Stuart Mill. Mill manages to combine the instrumental conception of the state typical of earlier liberalism with a more highly developed doctrine of individual self-actualization. It is this combination of a utilitarian conception of the state with a romantic conception of individuality that forms the deepest core of the ordinary citizen's belief in contemporary liberalism. The state is understood as a means to the greatest possible personal freedom, which is itself seen as a means to the greatest possible individuality and diversity. There is, of course, a great deal more to Mill than this—the belief in rational progress and so forth—but this constitutes his most enduring legacy to the contemporary self-understanding of liberalism.

A contemporary variation on this Millean and not very Hegelian theme of a limited state designed to promote the widest possible individuality is provided by Michael Oakeshott. Oakeshott may not seem the most likely thinker to bring up in connection with Mill and in opposition to Hegel. The references to Mill in his writings are at best equivocal, whereas the treatment of Hegel is generally quite positive. Indeed, a deep Hegelian strain runs through most of

Oakeshott's writings. But Oakeshott's Hegelianism is largely confined to his critique of rationalism and the reflective model of practical rationality which belongs to it. When it comes to his liberal ideal of civil association, it is the influence of Hobbes, not of Hegel, that dominates—though Oakeshott tries valiantly to provide an interpretation of Hegel that makes him compatible with Hobbes.[2] Civil association, for Oakeshott, is the mode of political association that best corresponds to the historic disposition of individuality, the disposition on the part of individuals "to make choices for themselves and to find happiness in doing so."[3] No one, not even Mill, has evoked this disposition of individuality more subtly and beautifully than Oakeshott. And he has argued that the most satisfying liberal theory need not involve anything more than the recognition of the currency of this disposition and of the governmental arrangements appropriate to it. What is not needed are "unnecessary hypotheses" concerning human nature or "metaphysical theories of personality"[4]—in short, just the sort of thing that Hegel's conception of the state as the realization of rational freedom seems to invoke.

Oakeshott's nonmetaphysical and individualistic conception of the liberal state, like Mill's (or Rawls's or Rorty's, for that matter),[5] no doubt comes closer to capturing what most people today find valuable about liberal institutions than does Hegel's grandiose vision. This suggests that it may be more useful not only for understanding liberalism at the end of the twentieth century but also for defending it against antiliberal competitors. But we should not draw this conclusion too quickly. For Oakeshott's skeptical and nonmetaphysical liberalism, like a great many other contemporary liberalisms, ultimately seems to lack the moral dignity with which Hegel (and Kant and Fichte) sought to endow liberal institutions. And the largely negative conception of freedom that it invokes seems to only partially capture the aspiration to radical self-determination and autonomy that forms such a central part of the modern moral consciousness. Beyond this, it is not clear that the purely instrumental role Oakeshott envisages for the liberal state is capable of generating the sort of allegiance and identification that is necessary to sustain it. And the individualism such a skeptical understanding of liberalism promotes seems to provide only the most exiguous basis for communal solidarity and common purpose. For all of these reasons, we may find ourselves groping for the something more provided by perfectionist theories such as Hegel's, which seek to embed liberal freedoms and institutions in a larger and more exalted conception of the self-determining nature and destiny of human beings.

Let us be clear about what Hegel has to offer here. It is not that he provides a "philosophical foundation" for liberalism by grounding it in the sort of meta-physical theory of personality which Oakeshott refers to above. Although Hegel does ultimately ground his conception of freedom as rational self-determination in a metaphysical doctrine about human nature, I have argued that the value of that conception does not stand or fall with his metaphysical justification of it. Regardless of whether we follow Hegel in thinking that freedom as he understands it is the essence of human beings, we can still grant that his positive conception of freedom as rational self-determination brings out more clearly than other—especially negative—conceptions just what we understand by freedom and why we find it valuable. Our deepest intuitions about freedom suggest that it does not involve simply doing what we please but, rather, self-mastery, self-coherence, cultivation of capacities, and fulfillment of significant purposes. It involves willing not just any content but one that expresses or mirrors the self-determining nature of the human will. It is this self-realizing and self-determining dimension of freedom that Hegel captures with his positive conception of freedom. It may be that the disposition to cultivate and not suppress the capacity for self-determination is a contingent and historic disposition—as Oakeshott would put it—but Hegel provides us with an account of this disposition and what it involves that, for its penetration and subtlety, surpasses most metaphysically more parsimonious contemporary theories.

It is, of course, Hegel's account of freedom as rational self-determination that enables him to conceive of the liberal state in other than the instrumental way that it has been conceived by liberal theorists from Locke to Mill and Oakeshott. For Hegel, as we have seen, liberal institutions are not simply and externally instrumental to individual freedom; rather, they are the very realization and embodiment of that freedom understood as rational self-determination; they are (to borrow a word beloved by communitarians) "constitutive" of human freedom. By conceiving of the political community in this positive, one might say Aristotelian way, Hegel endows it with a moral dignity that is otherwise missing from typical liberal accounts and thus generates the sort of allegiance and identification that is necessary to sustain it. In this regard, he even surpasses his predecessors Kant and Fichte, who, while sharing Hegel's conception of freedom as radical self-dependence or autonomy, nevertheless continued to view the state largely in the instrumentalist terms that have predominated in the liberal tradition.

For all its attractiveness, though, we come back to the observation that Hegel's understanding of the state does not seem to correspond to what most people today understand by and value about the liberal state. For the moment, it seems that liberalism in the sense Hegel, if not despised, at least found radically incomplete has triumphed. What does this imply that the Hegelian attitude toward the existing social order should be? Does it suggest that Hegel's political philosophy of freedom can be used as a standard by which to criticize the existing social order, that it can serve as an instrument of radical criticism and reform?[6] Though we have seen that Hegel's philosophical theory of the state does not represent a conservative apology for the status quo and that his defense of the rationality of the actual does not amount to a sanctification of everything that exists, to turn his philosophy too far in a "left Hegelian" direction threatens to undermine what is perhaps its deepest insight: namely, "to recognize reason as the rose in the cross of the present and thereby to delight in the present—this rational insight is the *reconciliation* with actuality which philosophy grants to those who have received the inner call *to comprehend*" (*PR*, 22). Hegel recognized that ours is an age that is only too happy to occupy itself with "negative fault-finding" and to eschew the much more difficult task of detecting the "affirmative aspect" that lies beneath the motley and disfigured surface of things (*PR*, §258A; *PH*, 38–39/52–53). His political philosophy struggles valiantly against this reflexive impulse of our age. It offers an image of ourselves and of our political arrangements that is not so much an alternative to the modern, liberal social order as it is the inner core from which that social order derives its deepest meaning and justification.

Notes

PREFACE

1. See Robert Pippin, *Hegel's Idealism: The Satisfactions of Self-Consciousness* (Cambridge: Cambridge University Press, 1989); *Modernism as a Philosophical Problem: On the Dissatisfactions of European High Culture* (Oxford: Basil Blackwell, 1991); and several of the essays in *Idealism as Modernism: Hegelian Variations* (Cambridge: Cambridge University Press, 1997).
2. Alan Ryan, "Professor Hegel Goes to Washington," *New York Review of Books,* 26 March 1992, 8.

CHAPTER 1 AUTONOMY AND POLITICS: ROUSSEAU, KANT, AND FICHTE

1. For this understanding of the context of the masterpiece of political philosophy, see Michael Oakeshott, Introduction to Hobbes's *Leviathan* (Oxford: Basil Blackwell, 1946), viii–xiii. For a similar approach to Hegel's political philosophy, see Manfred Riedel, *Between Tradition and Revolution: The Hegelian Transformation of Political Philosophy* (Cambridge: Cambridge University Press, 1984), vii.
2. M. B. Foster, *The Political Philosophies of Plato and Hegel* (Oxford: Clarendon Press, 1935), 72.
3. Isaiah Berlin, "Two Concepts of Liberty," in *Four Essays on Liberty* (Oxford: Oxford University Press, 1969).

4. Hobbes, *Leviathan,* chap. 14.
5. For helpful synoptic discussions of this tradition of reflection on human freedom that runs from Rousseau through Hegel, see Charles Taylor, *Hegel* (Cambridge: Cambridge University Press, 1975), 367–78; "Kant's Theory of Freedom," in *Philosophy and the Human Sciences: Philosophical Papers* 2 (Cambridge: Cambridge University Press, 1985), 318–25; Riedel, *Between Tradition and Revolution,* chap. 3; Pippin, "Hegel, Ethical Reasons, Kantian Rejoinders," in *Idealism as Modernism,* 92–104; Allen Wood, *Hegel's Ethical Thought* (Cambridge: Cambridge University Press, 1990), chap. 2. George Armstrong Kelly's *Idealism, Politics, and History: Sources of Hegelian Thought* (Cambridge: Cambridge University Press, 1969) remains a useful and illuminating survey of the idealist tradition of political philosophy that runs from Rousseau through Kant and Fichte to Hegel.
6. Rousseau, *Emile,* trans. Allan Bloom (New York: Basic Books, 1979), 40. On the problem of the "bourgeois" in Rousseau's political thought, see Bloom's introduction to the *Emile,* 4–6; also "Rousseau's Critique of Liberal Constitutionalism," in *The Legacy of Rousseau,* ed. Clifford Orwin and Nathan Tarcov (Chicago: University of Chicago Press, 1997), 146–47.
7. Rousseau, *Discourse on the Origins of Inequality,* in *The Basic Political Writings,* trans. Donald Cress (Indianapolis: Hackett, 1987), 57.
8. Rousseau, *Discourse on the Origins of Inequality,* 67–68.
9. Rousseau, *Discourse on the Origins of Inequality,* 80–81.
10. See Rousseau, *Discourse on the Origins of Inequality,* note 9, 94–95; *Emile,* 193, 214–15, 255, 444–45, 473; *Social Contract,* in *The Basic Political Writings,* I, 8.
11. Rousseau, *Emile,* 205; see also 255, 406.
12. Rousseau, *Emile,* 84.
13. Rousseau, *Emile,* 48, 64–69.
14. On the centrality of sex in Books IV–V of the *Emile,* see Bloom's introduction, 16; also *Love and Friendship* (New York: Simon and Schuster, 1993), 67.
15. See the famous autobiographical passage in the *Remarks to the Observations on the Feeling of the Beautiful and the Sublime* (1764–65), in which Kant records the impact of Rousseau on his conception of the vocation philosophy. From Rousseau, Kant writes, "I learned to honor men, and I would consider myself more useless than the common laborer if I did not believe that this view could give worth to all others to establish the rights of mankind" (*Gesammelte Schriften,* ed. Preussischen Akademie der Wissenschaften [Berlin: Walter de Gruyter, 1902-], vol. 20, 44). For a thorough analysis of the *Remarks* and of the influence of Rousseau on Kant's mature philosophy, see Richard L. Velkley, *Freedom and the End of Reason: On the Moral Foundations of Kant's Critical Philosophy* (Chicago: University of Chicago Press, 1989).
16. Rousseau, *Emile,* 444–45.
17. Though the *Emile* concludes with a summary of the argument of the *Social Contract,* Emile still seems to lack the civic virtue that marks the citizens of the latter work.
18. Rousseau, *Emile,* 39–40. Note, however, that Rousseau goes on to refer to the "double object" of natural education and suggests that raising a man entirely for himself can be

reconciled with raising him for others (41). Whether this amounts to making him a citizen in the strong sense is another question.

19. Rousseau, *Emile,* 40.

20. Rousseau, *Social Contract,* I, 8.

21. Rousseau, *Social Contract,* II, 9; III, 15.

22. Montesquieu, *The Spirit of the Laws,* trans. Anne Cohler, Basia Miller, and Harold Stone (Cambridge: Cambridge University Press, 1989), XI, 6; XIX, 27.

23. Rousseau, *Social Contract,* III, 15.

24. Rousseau, *Social Contract,* II, 3.

25. Rousseau, *Social Contract,* II, 4.

26. Rousseau, *Social Contract,* II, 3.

27. Rousseau, *Social Contract,* II, 7. See also II, 12 on the "most important" part of the law which deals with "mores, customs, and especially of opinion, a part of the law unknown to our political theorists but one on which depends the success of all the others; a part which the legislator secretly occupies himself, though he seems to confine himself to the particular regulations that are merely the arching of the vault, whereas mores, slower to arise, form in the end its immovable keystone."

28. Rousseau, *Social Contract,* I, 8.

29. See also *PR,* §29R; *HP,* III, 401–2/306–7.

30. Rousseau, *Emile,* 40.

31. See Bloom's insightful remark that Kant and Hegel give "an account of moral dignity in freedom based on Rousseau while using it to reinterpret and sublimate bourgeois society" ("Rousseau's Critique of Liberal Constitutionalism," 164).

32. See Taylor, "Kant's Theory of Freedom," 319–25.

33. Kant, *The Metaphysics of Morals,* trans. Mary Gregor (Cambridge: Cambridge University Press, 1991), 42, 45–47, 51, 56, 57.

34. Kant, *Religion Within the Limits of Reason Alone,* trans. T. M. Greene and H. H. Hudson (New York: Harper & Row, 1960), 87.

35. For Kant's distinction between negative and positive freedom, see *The Metaphysics of Morals,* 42; also *Foundations of the Metaphysics of Morals,* trans. Lewis White Beck (Indianapolis: Bobbs-Merrill, 1959), 64–65.

36. Kant, "On the Common Saying: 'This May Be True in Theory, But It Does Not Apply in Practice'" (hereafter cited "Theory and Practice"), in *Kant's Political Writings,* ed. Hans Reiss (Cambridge: Cambridge University Press, 1970), 73.

37. Kant, *Metaphysics of Morals,* 56.

38. Kant, "Theory and Practice," 74.

39. Kant, "Perpetual Peace," in *Kant's Political Writings,* 112–13.

40. Taylor, *Hegel,* 372. In "Kant's Theory of Freedom," Taylor makes a greater effort to bring out the inner relationship between Kant's moral theory and his political theory.

41. Kant, "Perpetual Peace," 125.

42. For insightful discussions of the relationship between Kant's moral philosophy and his political philosophy, see Patrick Riley, *Kant's Political Philosophy* (Totowa, N.J.: Rowman and Littlefield, 1983); Taylor, "Kant's Theory of Freedom"; Robert Pippin, "On the Moral Foundations of Kant's *Rechtslehre,*" in *Idealism as Modernism.*

43. Kant, *Metaphysics of Morals*, 121.
44. Kant, *Metaphysics of Morals*, 123–24.
45. Kant, "Theory and Practice," 73.
46. Kant, *Metaphysics of Morals*, 127; compare Rousseau, *Social Contract*, I, 8.
47. Kant, "Perpetual Peace," 121n; see also 113; "Idea for a Universal History from a Cosmopolitan Point of View," in *Kant's Political Writings*, 45–46. Kant seems to take a somewhat different view, however, in "The Contest of the Faculties," where he argues that the progressive movement toward a just constitution based on the natural rights of man will not result in "an ever increasing quantity of *morality* in [mankind's] attitudes. Instead, the *legality* of its attitudes will produce an increasing number of actions governed by duty, whatever the particular motive behind these actions may be." Though men will become less violent and more law-abiding and trustworthy, "such developments do not mean that the basic moral capacity of mankind will increase in the slightest, for this would require a kind of new creation or supernatural influence" ("Contest of the Faculties," in *Kant's Political Writings*, 187–88). Riley interprets this passage more compatibly with Kant's view of public legal justice as being instrumental to morality; see *Kant's Political Philosophy*, 14, 80–81.
48. See Pippin's thorough and nuanced discussion of this issue in "The Moral Foundations of Kant's *Rechtslehre*."
49. Kant, *Foundations*, 47.
50. Kant, *Foundations*, 48.
51. Kant's vehement opposition to the right of revolution has struck many commentators as deeply inconsistent with his ardent defense of the rights of man. His reasons for rejecting the right of revolution, however, are similar to his reasons for arguing that we have a duty to leave the state of nature and enter the civil condition. The state represents the indispensable condition for the enjoyment of all of our other rights and for being treated as ends instead of as means. When the people overthrow the government, "the state of anarchy supervenes, with all the terrors it may bring with it" ("Theory and Practice," 83n.); resisting the government is tantamount to "abolishing the entire legal constitution" (*Metaphysics of Morals*, 131). Though he dismissed the right of revolution as self-contradictory, Kant always seems to have approved of the French Revolution (see especially "The Contest of the Faculties," 182).
52. Kant, "Theory and Practice," 74.
53. Kant, "Theory and Practice," 77.
54. Kant, "Perpetual Peace," 99n.
55. Kant, *Metaphysics of Morals*, 125.
56. Kant, *Metaphysics of Morals*, 152.
57. See "Theory and Practice," 77–78; *Metaphysics of Morals*, 126.
58. Kant, "Theory and Practice," 79.
59. Kant, *Metaphysics of Morals*, 149; see also "Perpetual Peace," 100–2.
60. Kant, "Contest of the Faculties," 187; see also 184.
61. This formulation comes from Howard Williams, *Kant's Political Philosophy* (Oxford: Basil Blackwell, 1983). For helpful comparisons of Kant's and Hegel's political philosophies, see also 58–59, 162–65, 191–93.

62. For a good overview of Fichte's philosophical project and its significance, see Allen Wood, "Fichte's Philosophical Revolution," *Philosophical Topics* 19 (1991): 1–28.

63. Fichte, *Briefe* (Stuttgart-Bad Cannstatt: Frommann, 1968), quoted by Luc Ferry in *Political Philosophy 2: The System of Philosophies of History,* trans. Franklin Phillip (Chicago: University of Chicago Press, 1992), 99.

64. Fichte, *Some Lectures Concerning the Vocation of the Scholar,* in *Fichte: Early Philosophical Writings,* trans. Daniel Breazeale (Ithaca: Cornell University Press, 1988), 147, 149.

65. Fichte, *Vocation of the Scholar,* 149.

66. Fichte, *Vocation of the Scholar,* 155.

67. Fichte, *Science of Ethics as Based on the Science of Knowledge,* trans. A. E. Kroeger (London: Kegan Paul, Trench, Trübner, 1897), 33, 37, 44, 47, 53; *Sämmtliche Werke,* ed. I. H. Fichte (Berlin: Walter de Gruyter, 1971) (hereafter *SW*) 4:28, 32, 39, 42, 49. Because Kroeger's translation of the *Sittenlehre* is not reliable, I have frequently modified it and provided references to the German text.

68. Fichte, *Science of Ethics,* 33; *SW* 4:28.

69. See also *IPH,* 20/30; *PR,* §23.

70. Fichte, *Science of Ethics,* 155; *SW* 4:147.

71. Fichte, *Science of Ethics,* 148–49; *SW* 4:142.

72. See Kant, *Foundations,* 51–54; *Religion Within the Limits of Reason Alone,* 86–93.

73. Fichte, *Vocation of the Scholar,* 156.

74. Fichte, *Science of Ethics,* 247; *SW* 4:235.

75. Fichte, *Vocation of the Scholar,* 160–61.

76. Fichte, *Vocation of the Scholar,* 156.

77. Fichte, *Science of Ethics,* 250; *SW* 4:237–38.

78. Fichte, *Vocation of the Scholar,* 156.

79. Fichte, *Science of Ethics,* 266; *SW* 4:253.

80. Fichte, *Vocation of the Scholar,* 157n.

81. Fichte, *Foundations of Natural Right* (*Grundlage des Naturrechts*), translated by A. E. Kroeger as *The Science of Rights* (London: Routledge & Kegan Paul, 1970), 78; see also 19, 20, 131, 161, 172, etc.; *SW* 3:52; see also 3:9, 10, 89, 112, 120, etc. Again, since Kroeger's translation is not reliable, I have modified it where necessary and provided references to the German text.

82. Fichte, *Foundations of Natural Right,* 80–81; see also 19–21; *SW* 3:54; see also 3:10–12.

83. Hegel's major discussions of Fichte's political philosophy as it is articulated in the *Foundations of Natural Right* appear in *DFS,* 142–49/79–87; *NL,* 83–92/469–82; *HP,* III, 503–4/412–13.

84. For a useful summary of the argument of Fichte's *Foundations of Natural Right,* see Susan Shell, "'A Determined Stand': Freedom and Security in Fichte's *Science of Right, Polity* 25 (1992): 95–121. For an interesting discussion of Fichte's understanding of the relationship between right and morality in the *Foundations of Natural Right,* see Frederick Neuhouser, "Fichte and the Relationship between Right and Morality," in *Fichte: Historical Contexts: Contemporary Controversies* (Atlantic Highlands, N.J.: Humanities Press, 1994): 158–80; though I think Neuhouser ultimately underestimates the degree to which politics is instrumental to morality for Fichte.

85. Fichte, *Foundations of Natural Right*, 67–68; see also 50–51; *SW* 3:44; see also 3:31.

86. Fichte, *Science of Ethics*, 230; *SW* 4:219.

87. Fichte, *Foundations of Natural Right*, 52; *SW* 3:32–33.

88. Fichte, *Foundations of Natural Right*, 56–57; *SW* 3:35–36.

89. Fichte, *Foundations of Natural Right*, 60–61; *SW* 3:39.

90. Fichte, *Foundations of Natural Right*, 62–79; *SW* 3:41–53.

91. Fichte, *Foundations of Natural Right*, 139; *SW* 3:94.

92. Fichte, *Science of Ethics*, 138–45; *SW* 4:132–39. This distinction between formal and material freedom is comparable to Kant's distinction between negative and positive freedom; see *Metaphysics of Morals*, 42; *Foundations*, 64–65.

93. Fichte, *Foundations of Natural Right*, 169; *SW* 3:119.

94. Fichte, *Foundations of Natural Right*, 255; *SW* 3:168.

95. Fichte, *Foundations of Natural Right*, 140–49, 189–201; *SW* 3:94–101, 137–48.

96. Fichte, *Foundations of Natural Right*, 326; *SW* 3:244.

97. Fichte, *Foundations of Natural Right*, 237–74; *SW* 3:154–187. Later in his career, in the *Rechtslehre* of 1812, Fichte rejects the idea of the ephorate as impracticable, given that one cannot guarantee the incorruptibility of the ephores; see translator's note, *Foundations of Natural Right*, 284–85.

98. In his lectures on *Morality and Politics in Modern Europe* (New Haven: Yale University Press, 1993), 64, Michael Oakeshott counts Fichte among the greatest of the philosophical exponents of the political theory of individualism, matched only by Spinoza, Hobbes, and Kant. In *On Human Conduct* (Oxford: Clarendon Press, 1975), 251–52, he adds Bodin and Hegel to this select list of philosophical theorists of civil association.

99. Fichte, *Foundations of Natural Right*, 165–66, 289–343; *SW* 3:115–16, 210–59. For Fichte's nonliberal views on political economy, see also *Der geschlossene Handelsstaat*, in *SW* 3.

100. Fichte, *Foundations of Natural Right*, 378–79, 386; *SW* 3:295–96, 302.

101. See also *FK*, 182–83/425. On the "machine-state," see *GC*, 161–63/479–81.

102. Fichte, *Foundations of Natural Right*, 228; *SW* 3:204. In this context, Fichte refers to Rousseau's statement that, in entering the social contract, each individual gives himself entirely to the community (*Social Contract*, I, 6); see *Gesamtausgabe der Bayerischen Akademie der Wissenschaften*, ed. R. Lauth and H. Jacob (Stuttgart-Bad Cannstatt: Frommann, 1965), I, 4:15.

103. Fichte, *Foundations of Natural Right*, 229; *SW* 3:206.

104. On Hegel's nickname of "the old man," see H. S. Harris, *Hegel's Development: Toward the Sunlight, 1770–1801* (Oxford: Clarendon Press, 1972), 68, 71, 72n.

105. See Bernard Yack, *The Longing for Total Revolution: Philosophic Sources of Social Discontent from Rousseau to Marx and Nietzsche* (Princeton: Princeton University Press, 1986), 209–23, for such an interpretation of Hegel's mature philosophical outlook.

CHAPTER 2 HEGEL'S DEVELOPMENT TO 1806

1. Most importantly, see H. S. Harris, *Hegel's Development: Toward the Sunlight, 1770–1801; Hegel's Development: Night Thoughts (Jena 1801–1806)* (Oxford: Clarendon Press, 1983); "Hegel's Intellectual Development to 1807," in *The Cambridge Companion to Hegel*, ed.

F. Beiser (Cambridge: Cambridge University Press, 1993), 25–51. See also Raymond Plant, *Hegel: An Introduction,* 2nd ed. (Oxford: Basil Blackwell, 1983), chaps. 1–5; Shlomo Avineri, *Hegel's Theory of the Modern State* (Cambridge: Cambridge University Press, 1972), chaps 1–3; Laurence Dickey, *Hegel: Religion, Economics, and the Politics of Spirit, 1770–1807* (Cambridge: Cambridge University Press, 1987); Steven Smith, *Hegel's Critique of Liberalism: Rights in Context* (Chicago: University of Chicago Press, 1989), chap. 2; Charles Taylor, *Hegel,* chap. 2; Bernard Cullen, *Hegel's Social and Political Thought* (New York: St. Martin's, 1979), chaps. 1–4; Georg Lukàcs, *The Young Hegel,* trans. R. Livingstone (Cambridge, Mass.: MIT Press, 1976). James Schmidt has written two excellent surveys of the literature dealing with Hegel's development up through the *Phenomenology:* "Recent Hegel Literature: General Surveys and the Young Hegel," *Telos* 46 (Winter 1980–81): 113–47; "Recent Hegel Literature: The Jena Period and the *Phenomenology of Spirit,*" *Telos* 48 (Summer 1981): 114–41.

2. As I think happens in Plant, Avineri, and Cullen.

3. Stanley Rosen, *G. W. F. Hegel: An Introduction to the Science of Wisdom* (New Haven: Yale University Press, 1974), 3n.1.

4. Something like this view can be found in Yack's chapter on Hegel in *The Longing for Total Revolution* (chap. 5).

5. Fred Dallmayr, in his *G. W. F. Hegel: Modernity and Politics* (Newbury Park, Calif.: Sage Publications, 1993), 35, also rejects this dichotomy between a youthful romanticism and a mature rationalism or realism in Hegel's career, though he criticizes it from an opposite angle, stressing the romantic, erotic element running through Hegel's work. Though I agree with Dallmayr's general point, I think he exaggerates when he characterizes Hegel as "basically an *erotic* philosopher, in tune with the legacy deriving from Socrates and Plato."

6. On Hegel as *Volkserzieher,* see Harris, *Toward the Sunlight.*

7. See Friedrich Schiller, *On the Aesthetic Education of Man,* trans. E. M. Wilkinson and L. A. Willoughby (Oxford: Clarendon Press, 1967); "On Grace and Dignity," in *Schiller's Works* (Chicago: Belford, Clarke, 1880), esp. 202–10. For Kant's response to the criticism Schiller makes in "On Grace and Dignity" of the opposition between duty and inclination in his moral philosophy, see *Religion Within the Limits of Reason Alone,* 18–19n.

8. Rousseau, *Emile,* 321, 323. On Rousseau's influence on the young Hegel, see Harris, *Toward the Sunlight,* 66, 85.

9. For a good discussion of Hegel's views on Judaism, see Steven Smith, *Spinoza, Liberalism, and the Question of Jewish Identity* (New Haven: Yale University Press, 1997), 185–96; also Emil Fackenheim, *Encounters Between Judaism and Modern Philosophy* (New York: Basic Books, 1973), 81–134. Both Smith and Fackenheim see Hegel's outlook on Judaism as undergoing considerable change from his early writings to his mature writings.

10. See also "PC," 86–87/124–25, 95–129/134–58 in general.

11. "TE," 499, 504–7; *Werke* 1:33, 41–44.

12. Rousseau, *Social Contract,* IV, 8.

13. See also "BF," 80–81/66–67.

14. See also "BF," 101–2/99–101.

15. See Machiavelli, *Discourses,* trans. H. Mansfield and N. Tarcov (Chicago: University of Chicago Press, 1996), II, 2; Rousseau, *Social Contract,* IV, 8.

16. On the Kantian revolution, see Hegel's letter to Schelling of 16 April 1795 quoted above, in *L,* 35–36/1:23–24. For Hegel's disenchantment with the direction taken by the French Revolution under the Jacobins, see his letter to Schelling of 12 December 1794, in *L,* 29/1:12.

17. Plant, *Hegel,* 58.

18. On the increasing importance of religion in Hegel's thought as reflected in "SC," see T. M. Knox, "Hegel's Attitude to Kant's Ethics," *Kant-Studien* 49 (1957–58), 76–81.

19. Hegel's concern with conflicts of duty is evident as early as "TE," 497–98/31–32. On Hegel's treatment of collisions of duty in "SC," see Harris's helpful discussion in *Toward the Sunlight,* 337–41.

20. Plant, *Hegel,* 71–73, and Smith, *Hegel's Critique of Liberalism,* 49, 55. For criticism of Plant's argument, see Schmidt, "Recent Hegel Literature: General Surveys and the Young Hegel," 136–45.

21. On Hegel's early political studies, see Harris, *Toward the Sunlight,* 416–34.

22. On the genesis of the manuscript, see Harris, *Toward the Sunlight,* 434–48.

23. On this feature of scholarly interpretation of *The German Constitution,* see Schmidt, "Recent Hegel Literature: General Surveys and the Young Hegel," 141.

24. Schmidt, "Recent Hegel Literature: General Surveys and the Young Hegel," 144.

25. On the collapse of the Holy Roman Empire between 1789 and 1806, see James J. Sheehan, *German History: 1770–1866* (Oxford: Clarendon Press, 1989), 235–50. On the nature of the Holy Roman Empire and the erosion of its power in the eighteenth century, see 9–71.

26. On this alleged shift in Hegel's thought at this time, see Plant, *Hegel,* chap. 3 and p. 130.

27. See Avineri, *Hegel's Theory of the Modern State,* 39–40.

28. See in particular Hegel's comments around the time of the battle of Jena in 1806; for example, his final lecture at Jena on 18 September 1806, in *Dokumente zu Hegels Entwicklung,* ed. J. Hoffmeister (Stuttgart: Frommann, 1936), 352; letter to Zellman, 23 January 1807, in *L,* 122–23/1:137–38.

29. See Avineri, *Hegel's Theory of the Modern State,* 40–41.

30. On the divisive effect of religion when combined with politics in Germany, see also *GC,* 189–95/516–23. Hegel's point about religion here need not be seen as a repudiation of his earlier views on the unity of church and state, since his concern is with religion as it has actually operated in Christian Europe, not with a genuine folk religion.

31. On this, see Avineri, *Hegel's Theory of the Modern State,* 45–46.

32. For Tocqueville's views on the importance of "administrative decentralization," see *Democracy in America,* trans. George Lawrence and ed. J. P. Mayer (New York: Harper & Row, 1966), vol. 1, pt. 1, chap. 5.

33. Here I differ from Schmidt, "Recent Hegel Literature: General Surveys and the Young Hegel," 142–43, who states that the concept of the state found in *The German Constitution* "is hardly indicative of Hegel's views on the essential structures of political life"; see also Harris, *Toward the Sunlight,* 465–73.

34. See also *HP,* III, 494–503/403–12. For Fichte, see *The Science of Knowledge,* trans. P.

Heath and J. Lachs (Cambridge: Cambridge University Press, 1970); also Allen Wood, "Fichte's Philosophical Revolution," 6–8, 12–16.

35. See also *HP,* III, 515/422–23, 516–18/424–26, 534–36/443–45, 542/453–54.

36. See Harris's introduction to *DFS,* 5–7; also Pippin, *Hegel's Idealism,* 60–66.

37. See Riedel, *Between Tradition and Revolution,* 76–87.

38. The strengths and weaknesses of empirical natural law theories to which Hegel draws our attention here are more clearly explained in *PH,* 440–41/522, 445–46/527 and in the section on Hobbes in *HP,* III, 316–17/226–27.

39. Kant, *Foundations,* 39.

40. F. H. Bradley, *Ethical Studies,* 2nd ed. (Oxford: Oxford University Press, 1927), 155.

41. Kant, *Foundations,* 47.

42. See Allen Wood's discussion of the emptiness charge, *Hegel's Ethical Thought,* 154–60. For various attempts to defend Kant from the emptiness charge, see Onora Nell (O'Neill), *Acting on Principle* (New York: Columbia University Press, 1975), esp. chap. 5; Ping-cheung Lo, "A Critical Reevaluation of the Alleged 'Empty Formalism' of Kantian Ethics," *Ethics* 91 (January 1981): 181–201; Riley, *Kant's Political Philosophy,* chap. 3; Christine Korsgaard, "Kant's Formula of Universal Law," *Pacific Philosophical Quarterly* 66 (1985): 24–47; Sally Sedgewick, "On the Relation of Pure Reason to Content: A Reply to Hegel's Critique of Formalism in Kant's Ethics," *Philosophy and Phenomenological Research* 49 (1988–89): 59–80.

43. Bradley, *Ethical Studies,* 193–99.

44. Hans-Georg Gadamer, *Philosophical Hermeneutics,* trans. and ed. D. Linge (Berkeley: University of California Press, 1976), 112–13.

45. H. B. Acton's introduction to *NL,* 32–34, is helpful on this difficult passage. For the specific passage in Fichte that Hegel seems to be reacting to, see *The Foundations of Natural Right,* 194–98; *SW* 3:142–45.

46. This phrase comes from Jean Hyppolite, *Genesis and Structure of Hegel's Phenomenology of Spirit,* trans. S. Cherniak and J. Heckman (Evanston: Northwestern University Press, 1974), 331. Dallmayr is far too generous when he argues that, in *NL,* Hegel shows himself to be "keenly aware of the impossibility of a simple return to the classical tradition" (*Modernity and Politics,* 47).

47. See Riedel, *Between Tradition and Revolution,* 76–87.

48. For two helpful discussions of the struggle for recognition in Hegel's Jena writings, see Ludwig Siep, "Der Kampf um Anerkennung: Zu Hegels Auseinandersetzung mit Hobbes in den Jenaer Schriften," *Hegel Studien* 9 (1974): 155–207; and H. S. Harris, "The Concept of Recognition in Hegel's Jena Manuscripts," *Hegel-Studien Beiheft* 20 (1980): 229–48.

49. Riedel, *Between Tradition and Revolution,* 88–97.

50. Dickey, *Hegel,* chaps. 6–7, contains an interesting discussion of *NL* and *SEL,* the connections between them, and their relation to themes found in other eighteenth-century writers such as Ferguson, Rousseau, and Schiller.

51. Harris, introduction to *FPS,* 197–98. On Hegel's departure from Hobbes in this regard (contra Leo Strauss's suggestion of their affinity), see Siep, "Der Kampf um Anerkennung."

52. Reported in Karl Rosenkranz, *Georg Wilhelm Friedrich Hegels Leben* (Berlin, 1844; reprinted Darmstadt, 1963), 86; see also Harris, *Hegel's Development,* 434–36; Joachim Ritter, *Hegel and the French Revolution: Essays on the Philosophy of Right,* trans. R. D. Winfield (Cambridge, Mass.: MIT Press, 1982), 68; Avineri, *Hegel's Theory of the Modern State,* 4–5. Much has been written on Hegel's discovery of political economy and its impact on his thought; see, for example, Paul Chamley, *Economie politique et philosophie chez Steuart et Hegel* (Paris, 1963); "Les Origines de la pensée économique de Hegel," *Hegel-Studien* 3 (1965): 225–61; Plant, *Hegel,* chap. 3; Dickey, *Hegel,* chap. 5; Norbert Waszek, *The Scottish Enlightenment and Hegel's Account of 'Civil Society'* (Dordrecht: Kluwer Academic Publishers, 1988).

53. See, for example, Avineri, *Hegel's Theory of the Modern State,* 94.

54. Hyppolite, *Genesis and Structure of Hegel's Phenomenology of Spirit,* 331.

55. On this shift in Hegel's outlook, see Harris, "Hegel's Intellectual Development to 1807," 38–41.

56. Compare the section on "Abstract Right" in *PR.*

57. This reference to the "inner indignation" (*innere Empörung*) of the worker recurs in Hegel's later discussions of civil society; see *PR,* §244A and *VPR$_{19}$,* 195.

58. Riedel, *Between Tradition and Revolution,* 95–96; see also Yack, *The Longing for Total Revolution,* 204–5.

59. Siep makes a similar point in "Der Kampf um Anerkennung," 188–92.

CHAPTER 3 THE MORAL AND POLITICAL IDEAS OF THE *PHENOMENOLOGY OF SPIRIT*

1. In trying to make sense of the many obscure passages of the *Phenomenology,* I have consulted a number of commentaries. The most useful and drawn upon in what follows is Hyppolite's classic *Genesis and Structure of Hegel's Phenomenology of Spirit.* Also helpful, though somewhat freer, is Taylor's commentary in *Hegel.* The commentary whose focus is closest to my own, Judith Shklar's *Freedom and Independence: A Study of the Political Ideas of Hegel's 'Phenomenology of Mind'* (Cambridge: Cambridge University Press, 1976), is also the least reliable. Though containing some good insights, its overall view of the *Phenomenology* as an "elegy for Hellas" seriously distorts Hegel's intention in the book. Terry Pinkard's *Hegel's Phenomenology: The Sociality of Reason* (Cambridge: Cambridge University Press, 1994) provides a challenging nonmetaphysical account of the *Phenomenology,* though sometimes his claims in the latter regard go too far in downplaying the metaphysical aspects of Hegel's argument. Michael Forster's recent *Hegel's Idea of a Phenomenology of Spirit* (Chicago: University of Chicago Press, 1998) appeared too late for me to make use of in this chapter.

2. Hegel first makes this connection between critical philosophy and romantic intuition-ism or subjectivism in *Faith and Knowledge;* see also *EL,* 5–6/15–16 and §§61–63.

3. See also Hegel's letter to Voss, May 1805, where he criticizes the formalism and esoteri-cism of current philosophy and expresses the wish to "try to teach philosophy to speak German" (*L,* 104–8/1:95–101).

4. For an influential reading of Hegel in terms of the romantic and untenable metaphysics of "cosmic spirit," see Taylor, *Hegel.* For a slightly different but no less extreme meta-

physical reading, see Michael Inwood, *Hegel* (Routledge & Kegan Paul, 1983). In general, I draw upon in what follows, without arguing for at any length, the philosophically more attractive "nonmetaphysical" reading of Hegel of Klaus Hartmann, Terry Pinkard, Robert Pippin, and others. For a brief guide to the various nonmetaphysical readings of Hegel, see Pippin, *Hegel's Idealism*, 262n.10.

5. Pippin, *Hegel's Idealism*, 39.

6. Here I disagree with Pinkard's claim that Hegel's underlying premise that dialectic is not something optional for us does not rest on any assumptions about the distinctive nature of human beings (see *Hegel's Phenomenology*, 13). Hegel invokes the distinction between human beings and animals in another famous passage from the *Phenomenology*: "[I]t is the nature of humanity to press onward to agreement with others; human nature only really exists in an achieved community of minds. The anti-human, the merely animal, consists in staying within the sphere of feeling, and being able to communicate only at that level" (*PS*, 43/65).

7. Needless to say, Hegel's conception of dialectic has little to do with the formula of thesis-antithesis-synthesis with which it has generally come to be identified in textbooks and simplified introductions to Hegel's thought. On this, see G. E. Mueller, "The Legend of 'Thesis-Antithesis-Synthesis'," *Journal of the History of Ideas* 19 (1958): 411–14.

8. For a good brief discussion of the scholarly controversy over this question, see Schmidt, "Recent Hegel Literature: The Jena Period and the *Phenomenology of Spirit*," 131–34.

9. J. N. Findlay, Foreword to the *Phenomenology of Spirit*, trans. A.V. Miller, v–vi; Plant, *Hegel*, 129–38. See also Taylor, *Hegel*, 95–100, 129–35, 216–25, who attributes to Hegel a very strong notion of "ontological" necessity in the first three chapters of the *Phenomenology* and the *Logic* and a looser "interpretive" or "hermeneutical" dialectical necessity in the more historical portions of the *Phenomenology*. For Taylor, of course, it is on the former, "ontological" necessity, required by the system as a whole, that Hegel's philosophy founders.

10. See Pippin, *Hegel's Idealism*, 108.

11. Rudolf Haym, *Hegel und seine Zeit: Vorlesungen über Entstehung und Entwicklung, Wesen und Wert der Hegelschen Philosophie* (Berlin: R. Gaertner, 1857), 243. On the scholarly debate over this question of the coherence of the *Phenomenology*, see Pippin, "You Can't Get There from Here," in *The Cambridge Companion to Hegel*, 52–58; Schmidt, "Recent Hegel Literature: The Jena Period and the *Phenomenology of Spirit*," 125–30; Otto Pöggeler, "Zur Deutung der Phänomenologie des Geistes," in *Hegels Idee einer Phänomenologie des Geistes* (Freiburg/Munich: Karl Alber, 1973): 170–230.

12. See *EL*, §25R and the reduction of the "Phenomenology" to a moment in *EPS*, §§413–39.

13. See Pippin, "You Can't Get There from Here," 57.

14. Alexandre Kojève, *Introduction to the Reading of Hegel: Lectures on the Phenomenology of Spirit*, trans. J. H. Nichols (Ithaca: Cornell University Press, 1980).

15. See Pippin, *Hegel's Idealism*, chap. 7; "You Can't Get There from Here," 63–71; Joseph Flay, *Hegel's Quest for Certainty* (Albany: SUNY, 1984), chap. 4.

16. For criticism of Kojève on this score, see George Armstrong Kelly, "Hegel's Lordship and Bondage," in *Retreat from Eleusis: Studies in Political Thought* (Princeton: Princeton

University Press, 1978): 31–32; P. Riley, "Introduction to the Reading of Alexandre Kojève," *Political Theory* 9 (February 1991), 25; *Will and Political Legitimacy: A Critical Exposition of Social Contract Theory in Hobbes, Locke, Rousseau, Kant, and Hegel* (Cambridge, Mass.: Harvard University Press, 1982), 189–90.

17. See Leo Strauss, *The Political Philosophy of Hobbes* (Chicago: University of Chicago Press, 1952), 57–58.

18. On the different role the fear of death plays in Hegel's account of the struggle for recognition in the *Phenomenology* from that in Hobbes, see Siep, "Der Kampf um Anerkennung," 198.

19. See Kelly, "Hegel's Lordship and Bondage," 31–32, 51–52; Riley, "Introduction to the Reading of Alexandre Kojève," 25; *Will and Political Legitimacy,* 189–90; Smith, *Hegel's Critique of Liberalism,* 121.

20. Shklar, *Freedom and Independence,* chap. 3.

21. This use of "spirit" is brought out particularly well in the early essay "The Life of Jesus," where Hegel opposes Jesus' concern with the spirit of the law to the Pharisees' mechanical observance of the letter of the law (see especially 108–11/79–83).

22. Judith Shklar, "Hegel's 'Phenomenology': An Elegy for Hellas," in *Hegel's Political Philosophy: Problems and Perspectives,* ed. Z. A. Pelczynski (Cambridge: Cambridge University Press, 1971), 74. This distorting understanding of the *Phenomenology* as an elegy or "lament" for Hellas thoroughly informs Shklar's book, *Freedom and Independence;* see especially pp. 69–95. Patrick Riley seems to follow Shklar in understanding the *Phenomenology* as an assault on modern subjectivity and individualism; see *Will and Political Legitimacy,* 164, 176–89, 190–91, 197–98.

23. Schmidt, "Recent Hegel Literature: The Jena Period and the Phenomenology of Spirit," 141.

24. Emil Fackenheim, *The Religious Dimension in Hegel's Thought* (Chicago: University of Chicago Press, 1967), 50n.

25. See also *PH,* 278–79/339–40, 314–17/380–85.

26. Shklar completely misses the positive significance of the section on *Bildung* in the *Phenomenology,* the way in which Hegel sees modern culture as genuinely educating the individual through alienation; see *Freedom and Independence,* 44–45, 151–52.

27. Lionel Trilling provides an interesting discussion of this section of the *Phenomenology* in relation to the development of modern European moral consciousness in *Sincerity and Authenticity* (Cambridge, Mass.: Harvard University Press, 1971), 33–47.

28. Taylor, *Hegel,* 403. There are numerous accounts of Hegel's relation to the French Revolution. The classic account is Joachim Ritter's "Hegel and the French Revolution," in *Hegel and the French Revolution,* though it deals mainly with the *Philosophy of Right.* See also H. S. Harris, "Hegel and the French Revolution," *Clio* 7 (1977): 5–18.

29. See Hegel's letter to Schelling, 12 December 1794, in *L,* 29/12.

30. Victor Cousin, the French philosopher and liberal whom Hegel met in 1824, reported that Hegel was "impregnated with the modern spirit. He considered the French Revolution to be the greatest step taken by the human race since Christianity, and he never ceased to inquire about the affairs and men of this great era" (quoted in *L,* 667).

31. Rousseau, *The Social Contract,* I, 6; III, 12–15.

32. See, e.g., *PR*, §§29R, 258R. For a more sympathetic view of Rousseau's concept of the general will, however, see the *EL*, §163AI.

33. Taylor devotes some good pages to the connection between absolute freedom, or the modern ideal of total and universal political participation, and the homogenization of society, the elimination of any meaningful social differentiation, in *Hegel*, 403–21.

34. Again, Shklar's melodramatic perspective on the *Phenomenology* as an elegy for Hellas and unremitting critique of the subjectivity of modernity prevents her from appreciating the positive significance of "morality"; see *Freedom and Independence*, chap. 5.

35. These postulates are based loosely on those set forth by Kant in *The Critique of Practical Reason*, trans. L. W. Beck (New York: Macmillan, 1956), 114–53.

36. Hyppolite, 491–528, is particularly helpful in filling out the literary and philosophical background of this section on conscience.

37. The figure of the "beautiful soul" can be found in, among other places, Rousseau's *La Nouvelle Heloise*, Schiller's essay "Uber Anmut und Würde" ("On Grace and Dignity"), and Goethe's *Wilhelm Meister's Lehrjahre*. Novalis, however, remains the *locus classicus* of this type for Hegel (see *PH*, III, 510/418; *A*, I, 159–60/211).

38. See also *PR*, §124R; *IPH*, 34/48; *EL*, §140A.

39. Rosenzweig's argument, set forth in *Hegel und der Staat* (Munich/Berlin: Oldenburg, 1920), is discussed by Hyppolite on pp. 326–31 of his commentary.

40. I do not think it even fair to say that, in the *Phenomenology*, there is "an unresolved tension in Hegel's ethical thought" between the "*systematic* superiority of ethical life," on the one hand, and the "*historical* superiority of morality," on the other; a tension that was not to be resolved until Hegel's return to university teaching a decade after the *Phenomenology* (see Wood, *Hegel's Ethical Thought*, 133). Already in the *Philosophy of Spirit of 1805–6* Hegel had sketched a modern *Sittlichkeit* that took full account of the "higher principle" of modernity embodied in moral consciousness.

41. On religion as the supreme self-intuition of the political community, see also *NL*, 116/508; *SEL*, 144/54–55.

42. Shklar's brief remarks on the relationship between the *Phenomenology* and the *Philosophy of Right*—to the effect that, whereas the former lovingly elegizes the Greek polis, the latter asks us simply to forget it and "accept the rules such as they are"—are highly misleading (see *Freedom and Independence*, 205–8).

CHAPTER 4 HEGEL'S IDEA OF POLITICAL PHILOSOPHY

1. Avineri provides a good account of Hegel's political views from 1806–15, from the battle of Jena to the battle of Waterloo, in *Hegel's Theory of the Modern State*, 62–72.

2. Sheehan, *German History, 1770–1866*, 296–310.

3. See also letter to Zellmann of 23 January 1807 (*L*, 122–23/1:137–39) and letter to von Knebel of 30 August 1807 (*L*, 143/1:187); also Hegel's final lecture at Jena, delivered on 18 September 1806, in *Dokumente zu Hegels Entwicklung*, 352.

4. See *L*, 296–300/6–16. See also Hegel's scathing attack on German nationalism in his letter to Paulus of 30 July 1814 (*L*, 311–12/2:41–44).

5. Sheehan, *German History, 1770–1866*, 402–409; Wood's editorial notes to *PR*, 382–89.

6. See *L*, 444–56, 461.

7. Avineri writes: "[I]t can unequivocally be stated that these original and early lectures . . . bear out that Hegel's original philosophy of right was a much more liberal and open-ended system than the volume which he eventually published" ("The Discovery of Hegel's Early Lectures on the Philosophy of Right," *The Owl of Minerva* 16 [1984–85], 201). Ilting has a full discussion of Hegel's political views between 1817 and 1820 in his introduction to the first volume of *VPR* (pp. 25–126). Based on the lecture notes, he argues that Hegel's real political sympathies lay with the liberal reformers in Prussia but that he had to conceal his liberal sympathies in the 1821 edition of the *Philosophy of Right*; see also Ilting's article, "Hegel's Concept of the State and Marx's Early Critique," in *The State and Civil Society: Studies in Hegel's Political Philosophy*, ed. Z. A. Pelczynski (Cambridge: Cambridge University Press, 1984): 93–113. For a questioning of Ilting's thesis that Hegel's political views changed dramatically between the unpublished lecture notes and the published version of the *Philosophy of Right*, see Klaus Hartmann's review of the lecture notes in *Modern Law and Society* 9 (1976): 21–27; and R.-P. Horstmann's review in *Hegel-Studien* 11 (1976): 273–77. Dieter Henrich, in his introduction to *VPR₁₉*, and the translators of *LNR* seem to follow Ilting's and Avineri's line of interpretation.

8. Hegel was, of course, fully aware of how provocative his Preface would appear. In his letter of 9 May 1821 to the Heidelberg professor, Karl Daub, he writes of his attack in the Preface on the Jacobian philosophy of subjective feeling epitomized by Schleiermacher and Fries: "With my Preface and the explosive statements in it I have of course, as you will have seen, tried to strike a blow at this indigent though arrogant sect. I have sought to hit the calf in the eye, as the Swabians say" (*L*, 460/2:263).

9. See Haym, *Hegel und seine Zeit*, especially 365–68; also the contributions by Carritt and Hook in *Hegel's Political Philosophy*, ed. W. Kaufmann (New York: Atherton Press, 1970). A more recent and nuanced version of this charge can be found in Ernst Tugendhat, *Self-Consciousness and Self-Determination*, trans. P. Stern (Cambridge, Mass.: MIT Press, 1986), 317–23.

10. This has long become the consensus view of Hegel's political philosophy, shared, as Allen Wood notes, by "virtually every responsible scholar in the past generation" (editor's Introduction to *PR*, xxxi n.10; see also ix–x). See contributions by Knox, Avineri, Pelczynski, and Kaufmann in *Hegel's Political Philosophy*, ed. Kaufmann; also Ritter, "Hegel and the French Revolution"; Avineri, *Hegel's Theory of the Modern State*, chap. 6; Jacques d'Hondt, *Hegel in His Time: Berlin, 1818–1831*, trans. J. Burbidge (Lewiston, N.Y.: Broadview Press, 1988); K. -H. Ilting's introductions to vols. 1 and 4 of *VPR*; Adriaan Peperzak, *Philosophy and Politics: A Commentary on the Preface to Hegel's Philosophy of Right* (Dordrecht: Martinus Nijhoff, 1987), 15–31.

11. See also Hegel's letter to Hardenberg of October 1820, in which he writes that the principal aim of the *Philosophy of Right* "is scientific treatment and theoretical form" (*L*, 459/2:241).

12. See also the Prefaces to the second and third editions of *EL*. A good, brief statement of Hegel's understanding of the relationship between philosophy and prephilosophical experience appears in *EL*, §22A: "The business of philosophy consists in bringing into consciousness explicitly what people have held to be valid about thought from time

immemorial. Thus, philosophy establishes nothing new; what we have brought forth by our reflection here is what everyone already takes for granted without reflection."

13. Edmund Burke, *Reflections on the French Revolution,* ed. C. C. O'Brien (Harmondsworth: Penguin, 1968), 122.

14. See Kant, *Foundations,* 29.

15. See Wood's introduction to *PR,* ix–x , and editorial notes 6, 11, and 12 to the Preface; also Knox, "Hegel and Prussianism," in *Hegel's Political Philosophy,* ed. Kaufmann, 13–21; Avineri, *Hegel's Theory of the Modern State,* 115–22; d'Hondt, *Hegel in His Time;* Ilting, Introduction to *VPR* 1; and Peperzak, *Philosophy and Politics,* 15–31.

16. Compare *PR,* §§273R, 274.

17. Avineri seems to be reading more into this passage than is there when he says that it suggests that what is rational "will eventually triumph. Far from being an apotheosis of the existing historical conditions, the immediate context clearly points to Hegel's contention that reason triumphs over mere historicity, antiquated tradition and the irrational remnants of the past" ("The Discovery of Hegel's Early Lectures on the Philosophy of Right," 201). I suppose it depends on how much work the word "mere" is doing here.

18. See Henrich's Introduction to *VPR$_{19}$,* 13–17; Avineri, "The Discovery of Hegel's Early Lectures on the Philosophy of Right," 204; Wood, *Hegel's Ethical Thought,* 13; translators' note to *LNR,* §122R.

19. As does Michael Hardimon, *Hegel's Social Philosophy: The Project of Reconciliation* (Cambridge: Cambridge University Press, 1994), 65. Hardimon's discussion of the *Doppelsatz* in this book (52–83) is, on the whole, quite good.

20. Hegel notes this affinity between his notion of "actuality" and Aristotle's notion of *energeia* in *EL,* §142A.

21. For a good analysis of the relationship between the two halves of the *Doppelsatz* in *PR,* see Avineri, *Hegel's Theory of the Modern State,* 126–27.

22. See Fackenheim, *The Religious Dimension in Hegel's Thought,* 207–8n.; Avineri, *Hegel's Theory of the Modern State,* 127; Hardimon, *Hegel's Social Philosophy,* 55–56.

23. The Introduction to *VPR$_{19}$* also contains a discussion of Plato's *Republic* (47–48).

24. Machiavelli, *The Prince,* trans. Harvey Mansfield (Chicago: University of Chicago Press, 1985), chap. 15.

25. It seems that Smith is only half right when he states that "presumably the only way we have of knowing whether a social institution or belief is fully in accord with reason is its ability to adapt and survive over time. If it proves to be unable to adapt to changing circumstances, then it cannot be fully rational" (*Hegel's Critique of Liberalism,* 225). While the second sentence is unobjectionable, the first seems to push Hegel too far in a pragmatic and historicist direction. Kojève goes even further in attributing to Hegel a radically pragmatic conception of rationality and truth; see what he says about the "method of historical verification" in Leo Strauss, *On Tyranny,* revised and expanded edition, ed. Victor Gourevitch and Michael S. Roth (New York: Free Press, 1991), 152–76, esp. 167–68.

26. These phrases come from Nietzsche's essay "The Advantages and Disadvantages of History for Life," in *Untimely Meditations,* trans. R. J. Hollingdale (Cambridge: Cambridge University Press, 1983), 105, 114.

27. See also *LNR*, §§1–2 on this distinction. There Hegel argues that "the term 'natural right' [*Naturrecht*] ought to be abandoned and replaced by the term 'philosophical doctrine of right' [*philosophische Rechtslehre*]," owing to the ambiguity of the word "nature," which can refer to the concept of a thing but also to immediate nature, as in the "state of nature" (§2R). On the ambiguity of the term *Naturrecht*, see also *EPS*, §502R.

28. Many what might be called "left" Hegelian theorists exaggerate this critical dimension of Hegel's thought, most recently Pinkard, *Hegel's Phenomenology*, 339–43.

29. See also the *IPH*, 75–82/96–105.

30. Smith, *Hegel's Critique of Liberalism*, 222–23.

31. Avineri, *Hegel's Theory of the Modern State*, 129–30.

32. See Taylor, *Hegel and Modern Society* (Cambridge: Cambridge University Press, 1979), 66–69, 135. For similar views, see Z. A. Pelczynski's introduction to *Hegel's Political Writings*, 135–36; Anthony Quinton, "Spreading Hegel's Wings," *New York Review of Books*, 12 June 1975, 42.

33. Wood, *Hegel's Ethical Thought*, 5.

34. See, for example, David Kolb, *The Critique of Pure Modernity: Hegel, Heidegger, and After* (Chicago: University of Chicago Press, 1986), chaps. 2–6; Peter Steinberger, *Logic and Politics: Hegel's Philosophy of Right* (New Haven: Yale University Press, 1988); Terry Pinkard, *Hegel's Dialectic* (Philadelphia: Temple University Press, 1988).

35. See, for example, *EL*, §25 and the subordinate role of the "Phenomenology" in the *Encyclopedia* as a whole.

36. See also *EL*, §22A.

37. Again, see Taylor, *Hegel and Modern Society*, 66–69, 135; also *Hegel* in general. See also Inwood, *Hegel*.

38. On this, see Pippin, *Hegel's Idealism*, 8–9, 24–41.

39. For this understanding of Hegel's project in the *Logic* vis-à-vis Kant's critical philosophy, I am drawing heavily on Pippin's analysis in *Hegel's Idealism;* see especially 7–9, 37–38, 204, 208–9, 222.

40. On the dialectical method, see also *SL*, I, 53–57/48–53; *PR*, §31R.

41. For Hegel's most sustained defense of starting the *Logic* with the immediate thought of "being," see the section entitled "With What Must the Science Begin," in *SL*, I, 67–78/65–79. See also Hegel's letter to Sinclair from 1813, where he writes that "however much trouble one is justifiably used to taking in philosophy about the beginning, in another respect one ought not to make so much fuss over it. The nonphilosophers in particular foolishly demand a beginning which is absolute and against which they cannot immediately quibble—an incontrovertible first principle. . . . But it would show little cleverness for a philosopher to let himself be tricked or misled into honestly wishing to make such a beginning. For the beginning, precisely because it is the beginning, is imperfect. . . . [The philosopher's] entire philosophy is nothing but a struggle against the beginning, a refutation and annihilation of his starting-point" (*L*, 293/2:3–4).

42. For the ontologicization of Hegel's dialectic of "quality" in this way, see Taylor, *Hegel*, 232–39. For a criticism of such ontologicization, see Pippin, *Hegel's Idealism*, 188–94.

43. Pippin, *Hegel's Idealism,* 247.
44. Pippin, *Hegel's Idealism,* 246–47.

CHAPTER 5 HEGEL'S CONCEPT OF FREEDOM

1. For this formulation of the difference between ancient and modern political philosophy, again see Foster, *The Political Philosophies of Plato and Hegel,* 72; also Oakeshott, Introduction to Hobbes's *Leviathan,* xi–xii.
2. For similar defenses of Hegel's belonging to the voluntaristic tradition of modern political philosophy, see Riedel, *Between Tradition and Revolution,* chaps. 3–4; George Armstrong Kelly, *Hegel's Retreat from Eleusis* (Princeton: Princeton University Press, 1978), 113; Donald Maletz, "The Meaning of 'Will' in Hegel's *Philosophy of Right,*" *Interpretation* 13 (1985): 195–97; "Hegel on Right " as Actualized Will," *Political Theory* 17 (1989): 34–35.
3. See Foster, *The Political Philosophies of Plato and Hegel,* chaps. 3–6; Riley, *Will and Political Legitimacy,* chap. 6.
4. E. F. Carritt, "Reply," in *Hegel's Political Philosophy,* ed. W. Kaufmann, 38. Ernst Tugendhat provides a more recent example of this sort of criticism. Commenting on Hegel's identification of freedom with duty to the state in §514 of *EPS,* he writes: "This reversal of freedom into something that is normally considered its opposite means that the individual is to feel free precisely by fulfilling the duties originating from the power of the existing order . . . With this reversal, a level of perversity is reached that even Hegel cannot surpass" (*Self-Consciousness and Self-Determination,* 316).
5. See Berlin, "Two Concepts of Liberty."
6. See, for example, Gilbert Ryle, *The Concept of Mind* (London: Hutchinson, 1949), chap. 3. On the emergence of the concept of will, especially under the impact of Christian ideas and the reflective effort of St. Augustine, see Hannah Arendt, *The Life of the Mind: Willing* (New York: Harcourt Brace Jovanovich, 1978), 3, 55–110; Riley, *Will and Political Legitimacy,* 3–8; Albrecht Dihle, *The Theory of Will in Classical Antiquity* (Berkeley: University of California Press, 1982), chaps. 1, 4–6.
7. See also *EPS,* §§445, 468A.
8. See also *EPS,* §381A.
9. Again, see also *EPS,* §381A.
10. See also *EPS,* §443.
11. See also *EPS,* §468A. In the Introduction to the *Philosophy of History,* Hegel argues that the human being, as a thinking being, represents his impulses to himself before they are satisfied, interposes "the ideal, the realm of thought," between his impulses and their satisfaction, and this enables him ultimately to control his impulses. The animal, on the other hand, "cannot interpose anything between its impulse and the satisfaction of its impulse; it has no will, and cannot even attempt to control itself. . . . Man, however, is not independent because he is the initiator of his own movement, but because he can restrain this movement and thereby master his spontaneity and natural constitution" (*LPHI,* 49–50/57). On this distinction between the freedom that belongs to human conduct and the purely instinctive character of animal behavior, compare Rousseau,

Discourse on the Origin of Inequality: "Nature commands every animal, and beasts obey. Man feels the same impetus, but he knows that he is free to go along or to resist and it is above all in the awareness of this freedom that the spirituality of his soul is made manifest" (*Basic Political Writings,* 45).

12. Kant and Fichte also distinguish between "formal" or "negative" freedom and "material" or "positive" freedom; see Kant, *Foundations,* 64–65, and *Metaphysics of Morals,* 42; Fichte, *Science of Ethics,* 138–45 (*SW* 4:132–39). For a more recent version of this distinction between freedom as a formal condition intrinsic to agency and freedom as substantive self-direction, see Oakeshott, *On Human Conduct,* 36–37.

13. In his treatment of the struggle for recognition in the *Philosophical Propaedeutic,* Hegel explicitly distinguishes between "purely negative freedom, which consists in the abstraction from natural existence" and the positive concept of freedom, which consists in "selfsameness in otherness, that is, in part the beholding of oneself in another self and in part freedom not *from* existence but *in* existence, a freedom which itself has an existence" (*PP,* 62–63/120–21).

14. See Berlin, "Two Concepts of Liberty," 121–23.

15. On this idea of negative or indeterminate freedom in Kant, see *HP,* III, 459–60/367.

16. On this idea of freedom as "being with oneself in an other," see Wood's subtle discussion in *Hegel's Ethical Thought,* 44–49.

17. On the superiority of the actual to the possible, see also Soren Kierkegaard, *Concluding Unscientific Postscript to "Philosophical Fragments,"* trans. Howard and Edna Hong (Princeton: Princeton University Press, 1992), 320; also his critique of the "aesthetic" point of view, which values possibility above actuality, in *Either/Or,* trans. David and Lillian Swenson (Princeton: Princeton University Press, 1959).

18. See also *EPS,* §§476–77. Mark Tunick, in *Hegel's Political Philosophy: Interpreting the Practice of Legal Punishment* (Princeton: Princeton University Press, 1992), 57n.92, criticizes a number of commentators for blurring the distinction between the "natural will" and the "reflective" or "arbitrary" will. While there is something to this criticism, Tunick I think exaggerates the difference between the natural will and the arbitrary will. The arbitrary will represents an aspect and implication of the natural will insofar as its content remains tied to our natural drives and inclinations.

19. See Michael Sandel, *Liberalism and the Limits of Justice* (Cambridge: Cambridge University Press, 1982).

20. Kant, *Foundations,* 64–65; *Metaphysics of Morals,* 42. Again compare parallel distinction between "formal freedom" and "material freedom" in Fichte, *Science of Ethics,* 138–45 (*SW* 4:132–39).

21. Hegel deploys this analogy of art in connection with the discussion of freedom of the will as early as 1810, in *PP,* 16/224–25. On the difference between genuine artistic originality—which Hegel associates preeminently with Homer, Sophocles, Raphael, and Shakespeare—and mere mannerism, the expression of the particular idiosyncrasies of the artist, see *A,* I, 291–98/376–85.

22. Quoted in Sheehan, *German History: 1770–1866,* 332.

23. For Kant's "counsels of prudence," see *Foundations,* 36; also Wood's editorial note to §17 of *PR.*

24. Wood, *Hegel's Ethical Thought,* 53. My discussion of happiness that follows owes much to Wood's instructive chapter on this subject.

25. See Kant, *Foundations,* 35–36.

26. See also *EPS,* §469; *PH,* 442–43/524. In the Berlin lectures of 1818–19 on the philosophy of right, Hegel relates his notion of the genuinely free will to Fichte's notion of absolute self-activity: "I must equal I, as Fichte says. Self-consciousness [comes into being] in becoming the free will that has being in and for itself. The will determines itself, invests itself in an object, but this object is itself; in its object it is at home with itself [*bei sich*]. This is the absolutely real will" (*LNR,* p. 325/274).

27. Richard Schacht captures well the centrality of the idea of self-determination to Hegel's concept of freedom in his essay, "Hegel on Freedom," in *Hegel: A Collection of Essays,* ed. Alasdair MacIntyre (New York: Doubleday, 1972): 289–328.

28. See also *EPS,* §469.

29. See also *EPS,* §482. Hegel sees the Reformation as having given this Christian insight that human beings are by nature free its decisive impetus in the modern world (see *PH,* 344–45/416–17, 416–17/496–97).

30. See also *EL,* §§24A2, 172A, 213A.

31. See also *EPS,* §486.

32. Compare *PR,* §49A.

33. In his 1817–18 Heidelberg lectures on the philosophy of right, Hegel writes: "*Right* expresses in general a relation which is constituted by freedom of the will and its realization. *Duty* is one such a relation insofar as I regard it as essential and have to recognize it, respect it, or bring it about" (*LNR,* §8).

34. Rousseau, *Social Contract,* I, 7.

35. For example, when Rousseau says that, in joining civil society and submitting to the general will, each "nevertheless obeys only himself and remains as free as before" (*Social Contract,* I, 6). Or when he argues that the general will cannot be represented and therefore demands some sort of directly democratic arrangement (*Social Contract,* III, 12–15). Hegel provides a more sympathetic view of Rousseau's concept of the general will in *EL,* §163A1.

36. Spinoza, *The Ethics,* trans. S. Shirley (Indianapolis: Hackett, 1982), pt. I, def. 7, p. 31.

37. On the development of this idea of freedom as self-determination or self-dependence and Hegel's relation to it, see Schacht, "Hegel on Freedom," 291–300; Wood, *Hegel's Ethical Thought,* 42–45. Charles Taylor's attempt to see Hegel's doctrine of freedom as a rejection of the modern idea of freedom as self-dependence in favor of the notion of "situated freedom" seems to me somewhat problematic; see *Hegel,* 560–62, 568–69.

38. See Hobbes, *Leviathan,* chap. 14; Bentham, *Of Laws in General,* ed. H. L. A. Hart (London: Athlone Press, 1970), 54–55.

39. Locke, *Second Treatise,* ed. Peter Laslett (Cambridge: Cambridge University Press, 1988), §§22, 57.

40. John Stuart Mill, *On Liberty,* ed. E. Rapaport (Indianapolis: Hackett, 1978), 12.

41. See Berlin, "Two Concepts of Liberty," 123n., 148.

42. Locke, *Second Treatise,* §57. See also Wood's discussion of how the Hobbesian-

Benthamite idea of law as a restriction of freedom does not accord with ordinary usage (*Hegel's Ethical Thought*, 40–41).

43. Berlin, "Two Concepts of Liberty," 134.
44. Berlin, "Two Concepts of Liberty," 142.
45. Berlin, "Two Concepts of Liberty," 143.
46. See G. H. R. Parkinson, "Hegel's Concept of Freedom," in *Hegel*, ed. M. Inwood (Oxford: Oxford University Press, 1985), 171.
47. Berlin, "Two Concepts of Liberty," 145.
48. Berlin, "Two Concepts of Liberty," 152.
49. Berlin, "Two Concepts of Liberty," 169.
50. Wood, *Hegel's Ethical Thought*, 42.
51. Foster, *The Political Philosophies of Plato and Hegel*, 72.
52. Foster, *The Political Philosophies of Plato and Hegel*, 131.
53. Foster, *The Political Philosophies of Plato and Hegel*, 179; in general, see chaps. 3–6, esp. 125–41, 167–79, 180–204.
54. Riley, *Will and Political Legitimacy*, 1–9.
55. Riley, *Will and Political Legitimacy*, 166–67, 192–93, 199. In keeping with this assessment of Hegel's political philosophy, Riley agrees with Shklar's interpretation of the *Phenomenology* as a "massive assault upon the 'subjectivity' of individualism" (see *Will and Political Legitimacy*, 165, 176–90)—an interpretation that I rejected in chap. 3.
56. See Riley's discussion of freedom in terms of "undetermined choice," *Will and Political Legitimacy*, 12.
57. On this difference between the classical ideal of rational self-realization and the Kantian-Hegelian ideal of rational self-determination or autonomy, see Pippin, *Modernism as a Philosophical Problem*, 12–14. This book powerfully argues for the centrality of the Kantian (and Hegelian) idea of autonomy or self-determination to the self-understanding of modernity.
58. Pippin, *Modernism as a Philosophical Problem*, 13–14.
59. See, for example, Pinkard, *Hegel's Phenomenology*, 13, 272–74, 296–97, 336. Pinkard admits that Hegel sometimes speaks of freedom as the essence or nature of human beings, but he argues that Hegel's language in these instances is "misleading" (see 418n.4).
60. Charles Taylor, "What's Wrong With Negative Liberty," in *Philosophy and the Human Sciences*, 219. This essay presents a cogent contemporary defense of the move from a simple-minded negative conception of freedom to a more positive conception.

CHAPTER 6 THE BASIC STRUCTURE OF THE *PHILOSOPHY OF RIGHT*

1. For similar structural approaches, see K. H. Ilting, "The Structure of Hegel's *Philosophy of Right*," in *Hegel's Political Philosophy*, ed. Pelczynski, 90–110; Kenneth Westphal, "The Basic Context and Structure of Hegel's *Philosophy of Right*," in *The Cambridge Companion to Hegel*, 234–69.
2. For a similar approach, see Wood, *Hegel's Ethical Thought*, especially chaps. 11–12; Pippin, "Hegel's Ethical Rationalism," in *Idealism as Modernism*.

3. See also *LNR*, §8R.

4. For a questioning of Hegel's philosophical procedure in the *Philosophy of Right* and specifically of his claim to have "deduced" or immanently developed the content of the book out of the concept of freedom, see K. -H. Ilting, "The Dialectic of Civil Society," in *State and Civil Society*.

5. On this double significance of Hegel's treatment of abstract right, see also Ilting, "The Structure of Hegel's *Philosophy of Right*"; Peter Stillman, "Hegel's Critique of Liberal Theories of Rights," *American Political Science Review* 68 (1974): 1086–92.

6. See also *LNR*, §12R.

7. For a good discussion of the relationship between recognition and abstract right, see Wood, *Hegel's Ethical Thought*, chap. 4.

8. See also *LNR*, §13; *PP,* 24/234–35.

9. See Fichte, *Foundations of Natural Right*, 22–23, 80–81; *SW* 3:13, 54.

10. See Jeremy Waldron, *The Right to Private Property* (Oxford: Clarendon Press, 1988), 373.

11. See Kant, "Theory and Practice," 74–76.

12. See Waldron, 4, 343, 350, 377–386; Wood, *Hegel's Ethical Thought*, 107. Waldron, in particular, puts a great deal of weight on this passage from *PR*, §49A, but his argument for the expansive distributive implications of it go well beyond the considerations of abstract right and personality, and this introduces a certain amount of confusion into his interpretation.

13. Again, see Waldron, especially 377–86.

14. On the difference between genuine universality and mere commonality, see *EL*, §163A1.

15. See David Cooper, "Hegel's Theory of Punishment," in *Hegel's Political Philosophy*, ed. Pelczynski, 151–67; Peter Stillman, "Hegel's Idea of Punishment," *Journal of the History of Philosophy* 14 (1976): 169–83; Steinberger, *Logic and Politics*, chap. 3; Wood, *Hegel's Ethical Thought*, chap. 6.

16. See Kant, *Metaphysics of Morals*, 140–45.

17. According to Kant, "Even if a civil society were to be dissolved by the consent of all its members (e.g., if a people inhabiting an island decided to separate and disperse throughout the world), the last murderer remaining in prison would first have to be executed, so that each has done to him what his deeds deserve and blood guilt does not cling to the people for not having insisted upon this punishment; for otherwise the people can be regarded as collaborators in this public violation of justice" (*Metaphysics of Morals*, 142).

18. Compare Kant's rejection of Beccaria's contractarian argument against capital punishment in *Metaphysics of Morals*, 143–44.

19. See also *LNR*, §§40, 48.

20. Hamilton, Madison, and Jay, *Federalist Papers*, ed. Clinton Rossiter (New York: Mentor, 1961), #51.

21. Compare *PP,* 43/261.

22. See also *IPH*, 34–35/47–48; *EL*, §10A.

23. See Ludwig Siep, "The 'Aufhebung' of Morality in Ethical Life," in *Hegel's Philosophy of Action*, ed. L. Stepelevich and D. Lamb (Atlantic Highlands, N.J.: Humanities Press, 1983), 140.

24. See also *PP,* 37/253.

25. See also *LNR,* §62; *PP,* 19/228, 37/252.

26. Kant defends this proverb in "Perpetual Peace," 123. For Kant's treatment of the right of necessity, see *Metaphysics of Morals,* 60.

27. On the distinction between *das Gute* and *das Wohl,* see Kant's *Critique of Practical Reason,* 61–65.

28. Hegel characterizes Kant's great achievement in this way in the *History of Philosophy:* "It is a great determination of the highest importance in the Kantian philosophy that what is to count for self-consciousness as essence, law, the in-itself has been traced back to itself. . . . It is a great advance when the principle is established that freedom is the last hinge on which man turns, the ultimate point which allows nothing to be imposed on it, so that man allows nothing, no authority, to count for him insofar as it goes against his freedom" (*HP,* III, 459/367).

29. See also *NL,* 76–79/461–64; *PS,* 256–60/316–20.

30. This latter judgment seems to sit uneasily with Hegel's earlier contention that Plato was justified in suppressing the principle of subjective freedom in the *Republic* because it could appear in the context of Greek ethical life only as a "destructive force" (*PR,* 20/24).

31. On Fries' ethics of conviction and Hegel's somewhat mistaken criticism of it, see Wood, *Hegel's Ethical Thought,* 178–87.

32. Tugendhat, *Self-Consciousness and Self-Determination,* 315–16.

33. Taylor, *Hegel,* 376.

34. Taylor, *Hegel,* 380–81.

35. On the rational and "ideal" character of ethical life, see Adriaan Peperzak, "Hegels Plichten- und Tugendlehre," *Hegel-Studien* 17 (1982): 101, 102. Peperzak insists that everything Hegel says about the institutions of ethical life in §§142–56 of *PR* applies "only if the institutions are in fact the adequate objectification of spirit and also truly rational" (101). On the difference between Hegel's notion of ethical life and communitarian invocations of it, see Wood, *Hegel's Ethical Thought,* 202–3, though strangely he does not mention Taylor.

36. See also *PS,* 261/321–22.

37. On this relationship of the individual to the universal substance, compare *PP,* 47/266.

38. See Siep, "The 'Aufhebung' of Morality in Ethical Life," 146–47. Wood largely follows Siep's interpretation of this passage (see *Hegel's Ethical Thought,* 217–18).

39. Siep himself quotes the passage from Tugendhat, "The 'Aufhebung' of Morality in Ethical Life," 137.

40. In the lectures of 1817–18, however, unlike in the *Philosophy of Right,* Hegel identifies rectitude exclusively with the ethical disposition belonging to the estates in civil society. For this reason, he writes that rectitude, the disposition to "maintain oneself in the chosen estate and carry out the corresponding duties . . . is not yet ethical life [as such], because human beings must have still higher aims" (*LNR,* §107R).

41. See also *PP,* 37/252.

42. Contrast Kant on the role of habit in the moral life: "So we cannot define *virtue* as *acquired aptitude* [or habit] for free and lawful actions; for then it would be a mere mechanism in the exercise of our forces. Virtue is, rather, *moral strength* in pursuing our

duty, which never becomes habit but should always spring forth, quite new and original, from our way of thinking" (*Anthropology from a Pragmatic Point of View,* trans. Mary Gregor [The Hague: Martinus Nijhoff, 1974], 26–27).

43. Wood, *Hegel's Ethical Thought,* 198; see also 217–18. Steinberger offers a particularly unconvincing interpretation of this passage, arguing that "habitual obedience should not be understood in the usual sense as something unreflective or automatic" but, rather, as something like self-disciplined action," even as "rational and self-conscious" action (*Logic and Politics,* 158). It is true that Hegel does not identify habitual conduct with unconscious or purely instinctual conduct. Thus, he writes that "since only animals have their law as instinct, whereas only human beings have theirs as custom or habit [*Gewohnheit*], *customary rights* [*Gewohnheitsrechte*] contain the moments of being *thoughts* and of being *known*" (*PR,* §211R). But this is a far cry from the reflectiveness and self-conscious rationality Steinberger wishes to import into Hegel's notion of habit.

44. See Siep on this passage, "The 'Aufhebung' of Morality in Ethical Life," 149–50.

45. See also *PS,* 279–89/342–54; *PH,* 250–53/306–9, 268–70/327–30.

CHAPTER 7 THE ETHICAL PRECONDITIONS OF THE RATIONAL STATE: FAMILY AND CIVIL SOCIETY

1. On the isomorphism of the family and the state, see Merold Westphal, "Hegel's Radical Idealism: Family and State as Ethical Communities," in *The State and Civil Society,* 77–92.

2. Rousseau, *Emile,* 363.

3. See also *PR,* §185R.

4. See also *LNR,* §76R.

5. See Kierkegaard, *Either/Or,* "The Aesthetic Validity of Marriage," vol. II, 5–157.

6. See also *HP,* II, 112/127.

7. See Mary Ann Glendon, *Abortion and Divorce in Western Law* (Cambridge, Mass.: Harvard University Press, 1987), 91–103; William Galston, *Liberal Purposes: Goods, Virtues, and Diversity in the Liberal State* (Cambridge: Cambridge University Press, 1991), 283–88; "A Liberal-Democratic Case for the Two-Parent Family," *The Responsive Community* 1 (1990–91): 14–26; Jean Bethke Elshtain, William Galston, Enola Aird, and Amitai Etzioni, "A Communitarian Position on the Family," *National Civic Review* (1993): 25–35; Barbara Dafoe Whitehead, "Dan Quayle Was Right," *The Atlantic Monthly* 271 (April 1993): 47–84.

8. Contrary to what Susan Okin suggests in *Women in Western Political Thought* (Princeton: Princeton University Press, 1979), 285.

9. For some recent attempts to articulate the natural differences between the sexes, see Nancy Chodorow, *The Reproduction of Mothering: Psychoanalysis and the Sociology of Gender* (Berkeley: University of California Press, 1978); Carol Gilligan, *In a Different Voice: Psychological Theory and Women's Development* (Cambridge, Mass.: Harvard University Press, 1992); Camille Paglia, *Sexual Personae: Art and Decadence From Nefertiti to Emily Dickinson* (New Haven: Yale University Press, 1990).

10. See Rousseau, *Emile,* Book V, "Sophie," 357–405; see also Fichte's rather elaborate

discussion of marriage and the relations between the sexes in the *Foundations of Natural Right*, 391–451. Some twenty years after Hegel wrote the *Philosophy of Right*, Rousseau's greatest student, Tocqueville, also defended the differentiation of roles between men and women; see especially *Democracy in America*, vol. 2, pt. 3, chap. 12, "How the American Views the Equality of the Sexes."

11. For the point that Hegel's feminine ideal is not wholly negative or characterized by weakness, see Wood, *Hegel's Ethical Thought*, 245; Hardimon, *Hegel's Social Philosophy*, 184–85.

12. See Hardimon, *Hegel's Social Philosophy*, 186–89; also Frederick Neuhouser, review of *Hegel's Ethical Thought*, by Allen Wood, *Journal of Philosophy* 89 (1992), 319–20.

13. See also *LNR,* §83.

14. As Michael Oakeshott pithily puts this point: "A man is what he learns to become: this is the human condition" ("A Place of Learning," in *The Voice of Liberal Learning*, ed. Timothy Fuller [New Haven: Yale University Press, 1989], 17n.; see also 21).

15. Rousseau, *Emile,* 79.

16. See also *EPS,* §396A, pp. 59–60.

17. For an exhaustive account of Hegel's relationship to the figures of the Scottish Enlightenment, see Waszek, *The Scottish Enlightenment and Hegel's Account of 'Civil Society'.*

18. Hegel first uses the expression "civil society" in this distinctive sense in his 1817–18 Heidelberg lectures on the philosophy of right.

19. Riedel, *Between Tradition and Revolution,* chap. 6.

20. Some recent discussions of "civil society" and its importance for contemporary democratic life include: Michael Walzer, "The Idea of Civil Society: A Path to Social Reconstruction," *Dissent* 38 (1991): 293–304; Ernest Gellner, *Conditions of Liberty: Civil Society and Its Rivals* (New York: Penguin, 1994); Jean Bethke Elshtain, *Democracy On Trial* (New York: Basic Books, 1995); Charles Taylor, "Invoking Civil Society," in *Philosophical Arguments* (Cambridge: Harvard University Press, 1995).

21. Contrary to what Hardimon suggests in *Hegel's Social Philosophy*, 190.

22. Foster's *The Political Philosophies of Plato and Hegel* remains one of the most thought-provoking discussions of Hegel's critique of Plato in this regard; see especially chap. 3.

23. For this formulation of the problem to which Hegel's account of civil society addresses itself, see James Schmidt, "A *Paideia* for the *'Bürger als Bourgeois':* The concept of 'Civil Society' in Hegel's Political Thought," *History of Political Thought* 2 (1981–82): 474–79.

24. Rousseau, *Discourse on the Sciences and Arts,* in *The Basic Political Writings,* 12; see also *Social Contract,* I, 6, n.4; *Emile,* 40, 337n.

25. Of course, it was not only Rousseau's problem but a general concern of eighteenth-century political and economic thinkers such as Montesquieu, Steuart, and Ferguson. On this general eighteenth-century problem, see J. G. A. Pocock, *The Machiavellian Moment* (Princeton: Princeton University Press, 1975), chap. 14. On Montesquieu, Steuart, and Ferguson in relation to it, see Albert Hirschman, *The Passions and the Interests* (Princeton: Princeton University Press, 1977), 70–87, 119–22. On Ferguson, see Gellner, *Conditions of Liberty,* chap. 8.

26. See also *EPS,* §395A, pp. 51–52.

27. Schmidt, "A *Paideia* for the *'Bürger als Bourgeois,'"* 492.

28. Nietzsche, *Uber die Zukunft unserer Bildungsanstalten,* in *Werke in drei Banden,* ed. Karl Schlechta (Munich: Carl Hanser, 1969) 3:899.

29. Neuhouser, review of *Hegel's Ethical Thought,* 320.

30. Marx, *Communist Manifesto,* in *Karl Marx: Selected Writings,* ed. Lawrence Simon (Indianapolis: Hackett, 1994), 161–62.

31. Burke, *Reflections on the Revolution in France,* 141.

32. See also *LNR,* §104R.

33. Again, vs. Neuhouser, review of *Hegel's Ethical Thought,* 320; also Hardimon, *Hegel's Social Philosophy,* 187–89.

34. See also *EL,* §80A.

35. On the difference between Hegel's conception of law as "posited" and Hobbes's "positive" conception of law as command, see Foster, *The Political Philosophies of Plato and Hegel,* 110–21.

36. Compare Kant, *Foundations,* 29.

37. See also *EPS,* §529R; *PH,* 453–55/536–38; "ERB," 310–11.

38. See Foster, *The Political Philosophies of Plato and Hegel,* 117–18.

39. See also *VPR₁₉,* 190; *VPR*4:617; *DFS,* 147/84–85. For Fichte's "police state," see *Foundations of Natural Right,* 378–79, 386; *SW* 3:295–96, 302.

40. Compare Tocqueville, *Democracy in America,* 241–44.

41. See also *DFS,* 147–49/187. Compare *PR,* §290A.

42. Kant and Fichte also recognize a duty to provide for the poor, though, unlike Hegel, they derive it from the contractual basis of society; see Kant, *Metaphysics of Morals,* 136; Fichte, *Foundations of Natural Right,* 292–95 (*SW* 3:213–15).

43. Avineri, *Hegel's Theory of the Modern State,* 154.

44. See A. S. Walton, "Economy, Utility and Community in Hegel's Theory of Civil Society," in *The State and Civil Society,* 245, 253–55, 261; Waszek, *The Scottish Enlightenment and Hegel's Account of 'Civil Society,'* 224.

45. For various reasons and to varying degrees, the following commentators claim that the problem of poverty does pose such a challenge: Richard Teichgraeber, "Hegel on Property and Poverty," *Journal of the History of Ideas* 38 (1977), 57–64; Wood, *Hegel's Ethical Thought,* 247–55, 259; Hardimon, *Hegel's Social Philosophy,* 236–50.

46. See Henrich's introduction to *VPR₁₉,* 18–23; John McCumber, "Contradictions and Resolution in the State: Hegel's Covert View," *Clio* 15 (1986): 379–90.

47. Again, see Henrich's introduction to *VPR₁₉;* McCumber, "Contradiction and Resolution in the State." For the view that Hegel's earlier lectures on the philosophy of right contain a sharper critique of civil society than that found in *PR,* see Avineri, "The Discovery of Hegel's Early Lectures on the Philosophy of Right," 201, 204. The translators of the Heidelberg lectures of 1817–18 follow Avineri in this view; see 209n.48.

48. See Oakeshott, *On Human Conduct,* 304n.3.

49. See also *LNR,* §§118R, 120R; *HHS,* 139–40/244; *FPS,* 248/324.

50. Compare Montesquieu's treatment of the problem of poverty in *The Spirit of the Laws,* XXIII, 29, which in many respects parallels Hegel's analysis. Like Hegel, Montesquieu sees poverty as an inevitable byproduct of modern industrial conditions. To ameliorate

this problem he proposes poorhouses, but, again like Hegel, he worries about the "spirit of laziness that poorhouses inspire."

51. See Henrich's introduction to VPR_{19}, 19–20; McCumber, "Contradiction and Resolution in the State," 380, 381–82.

52. Henrich, introduction to VPR_{19}, 20.

53. Here I largely agree with Tunick's reservations about Henrich's argument; see *Hegel's Political Philosophy*, 117–19.

54. Again, compare Montesquieu, *Spirit of the Laws*, XXIII, 29.

55. See also VPR_{19}, 198–99. Note, however, Hegel's reservations about this method of dealing with excess population in *IPH*, 89–90/113–14.

56. In the lectures of 1817–18, Hegel does not yet restrict the corporations to the estate of trade and industry, stating that "the classes in general, and also their various particular branches, should be formed into *corporations*" (*LNR*, §121).

57. See Teichgraeber, "Hegel on Property and Poverty," 61.

58. Teichgraeber, "Hegel on Property and Poverty," 60–63, denies that they do.

59. Avineri, *Hegel's Theory of the Modern State*, 165; Smith, *Hegel's Critique of Liberalism*, 143.

60. On the atomistic spirit of modern civil society, see especially *LNR*, §121R: "The atomistic principle—that each individual fends merely for himself and does not bother about a communal [end] . . . abandons the individual to contingency. The reflective standpoint of our time, this atomistic spirit, the spirit that consists in taking pride in one's individual interest and not in what is communal, is harmful and has brought about the decay of the corporations."

CHAPTER 8 THE RATIONAL STATE

1. Klaus Hartmann, "Towards a New Systematic Reading of Hegel's Philosophy of Right," in *State and Civil Society*, ed. Pelczynski, 119. See also Foster, *The Political Philosophies of Plato and Hegel*, 151–64; Kolb, *The Critique of Pure Modernity: Hegel, Heidegger, and After* (Chicago: University of Chicago Press, 1986), 109–17.

2. See also *VPR* 4:635, where Hegel defines the state as "the universal having the universal as such as its end."

3. See also *VPR* 1:322: "The several branches of civil society must . . . be embodied in corporations, whose conflicting interests, as well as their general interconnections, in turn require overall supervision."

4. See Kolb, *The Critique of Pure Modernity*, 112.

5. Hardimon, *Hegel's Social Philosophy*, 218–27, has a good discussion of this tension in Hegel's doctrine of the state.

6. See also VPR_{19}, 208.

7. The most exaggerated emphasis on the self-conscious or reflective rationality of the members of Hegel's state is to be found in Steinberger, *Logic and Politics;* see especially 152–59, 168, 184, 188, 208–9, 235, 237–41, 248. See also Harry Brod, *Hegel's Philosophy of Politics: Idealism, Identity, and Modernity* (Boulder: Westview Press, 1992), 3–7, chaps. 4–7. Robert Pippin, in "Hegel's Political Argument and the Problem of *Verwirklichung*," *Political Theory* 9 (1981), 521–30, also sees Hegel as making some rather large claims

about the self-conscious or reflective rationality of individual citizens, though he also argues that Hegel's position on this score is highly ambiguous, not to say problematic.

8. See also *PR,* §93R.

9. *HP,* III, 401–2/306–7.

10. On Fichte, see *HP,* III, 503–5/412–13.

11. Rousseau, *Social Contract,* I, 6; III, 12–15.

12. Avineri, *Hegel's Theory of the Modern State,* 176–77.

13. Robert M. Berdahl, *The Politics of the Prussian Nobility: The Development of a Conservative Ideology, 1770–1848* (Princeton: Princeton University Press, 1988), 236; in general, see 232–46.

14. See also *LNR,* §132R.

15. Tocqueville, *Democracy in America,* 235–37.

16. See Kolb, *The Critique of Pure Modernity,* 114; Steinberger, *Logic and Politics,* 237.

17. Kelly, *Hegel's Retreat from Eleusis,* 120. Kelly's essay "Hegel and the Neutral State" in this volume is one of the few sustained discussions of the topic of the relation between religion and the state in Hegel's political thought; see also Dallmayr, *Modernity and Politics,* 140–45.

18. Ilting, "Hegel on the State and Marx's Early Critique," 104.

19. I take this reference to Rabelais's Abbaye de Thélème from Oakeshott, *On Human Conduct,* 78.

20. See Locke, *A Letter Concerning Toleration* (Indianapolis: Hackett, 1983), 51. For the American Founders and Tocqueville, see Galston's discussion in *Liberal Purposes,* 263–67.

21. On this point, see Smith, *Spinoza, Liberalism, and the Question of Jewish Identity,* 195–96.

22. Hegel occasionally expressed his hostility toward Catholicism quite intemperately; see his letter to Altenstein of 3 April 1826 (*L,* 531–32) and Victor Cousin's recollection of an anti-Catholic outburst before the Cathedral in Cologne in October of 1827 (*L,* 663–64).

23. See Smith, *Spinoza, Liberalism, and the Question of Jewish Identity,* 193–96.

24. See also *PH,* 449/531.

25. See Kolb, *The Critique of Pure Modernity,* 114.

26. In *Democracy in America,* see especially 287–301; also 433–36, 442–49, 542–46.

27. See Sheehan, *German History, 1770–1866,* chaps. 5, 7.

28. See also *PR,* §273R and A.

29. See also *PH,* 369/444, 452–53/535.

30. See also *PR,* §274.

31. See Montesquieu, *The Spirit of the Laws,* 36.

32. See Montesquieu *The Spirit of the Laws,* 25.

33. Montesquieu, *The Spirit of the Laws,* 155; see XI, 6 in general.

34. *Federalist Papers,* #51.

35. See Rousseau, *Social Contract,* III, 1.

36. See Kant, *Metaphysics of Morals,* §§45–49.

37. See also $VPR_{19},$ 234; *PR,* §273R.

38. Steinberger, *Logic and Politics,* 234–49.

39. See also *PR,* §§267, 269.

40. Compare Machiavelli, *The Prince,* chap. 15.

41. Nisbet translates *die fürstliche Gewalt* as "the sovereign," but this creates some confusion with Hegel's somewhat different notion of "sovereignty" (*die Souveränität*). Knox's translation of the term as "the crown" is less confusing. I have simply adopted the most literal translation.

42. Ilting, "The Structure of Hegel's *Philosophy of Right,*" 105–9; see also Hartmann, "Towards a New Systematic Reading of Hegel's Philosophy of Right," 121–22.

43. Though Foster, in *The Political Philosophies of Plato and Hegel,* 188–95, sharply distinguishes the Hegelian notion of sovereignty from the Hobbesian notion.

44. Interestingly, Hegel identifies Montesquieu's conception of monarchy with feudal monarchy (see *PR,* §273R).

45. These are the terms Sheehan uses in his *German History: 1770–1866* to organize the broad sweep of German history in the eighteenth and nineteenth centuries. *Herrschaft* refers to the dispersed, patrimonial authority that characterized German social and political reality up to the eighteenth century, while *Verwaltung* refers to centralized authority of the state which came more and more to dominate German social and political reality in the eighteenth and nineteenth centuries.

46. Avineri, *Hegel's Theory of the Modern State,* 187–88, tends to see Hegel's monarch as merely symbolic.

47. Michael Oakeshott, *Rationalism in Politics and Other Essays,* new and expanded edition (Indianapolis: Liberty Press, 1991), 456.

48. See also *PH,* 456/539.

49. See also "ERB," 330/128.

50. See also *PR,* §284.

51. See also *PR,* §315A.

52. Sheehan, *German History, 1770–1866,* 298–99.

53. On Stein's reforms, see editorial note to *PR,* §284; also Sheehan, *German History, 1770–1866,* 298–99.

54. Earlier in his career, in a letter to Niethammer from November 1807, Hegel offers a different assessment of the degree of governmental centralization in France, though his main point about the dangers of excessive centralization remains the same: "So far we have seen that in all imitations of the French only half the example is ever taken up. The other half, the noblest part, is left aside: liberty of the people; popular participation in elections; government decisions taken in full view of the people; or at least public exposition, for the insight of the people, of all the reason behind such measures. . . . For in Germany no official has his own [defined] sphere of activity. Instead, the higher authorities take it as their duty to do what should be the business of their underlings, so that there is nothing present or known of that sacrifice by which higher authorities leave something to be done at the lower echelons. Nor is anything known of the state having sufficient trust in itself not to interfere with its parts—which is the essence of liberty" (*L,* 151/1:197–98).

55. See Max Weber, "Bureaucracy," in *From Max Weber: Essays in Sociology,* ed. Gerth and Mills (New York: Oxford University Press, 1946), 198–204.

56. This safeguard against arbitrary dismissal is more fully developed in *LNR,* §144R.

57. See Karl Marx, *Critique of Hegel's 'Philosophy of Right'*, ed. Joseph O'Malley (Cambridge: Cambridge University Press, 1970), 41–54.

58. On this point, see Foster, *The Political Philosophies of Plato and Hegel*, 193.

59. See Rousseau, *Social Contract*, II, 6; III, 1.

60. Hegel uses the same word, *Stände*, to refer to the legislative body, the Estates, and the social estates (agricultural, business, and universal). Following Nisbet, I have capitalized the former, political use of the term to distinguish it from the social estates.

61. Rousseau himself seems to have been eminently aware of the limitations of democratic populaces; see especially his remarks on the need for a legislator in the *Social Contract*, II, 6; also III, 4.

62. See also *EPS*, §544R.

63. Burke, *Reflections on the Revolution in France*, 141.

64. See also "PEAW," 264/483–84; "ERB," 317–18/110–11.

65. See Burke's famous speech to the electors of Bristol of 3 November 1774, where he declares: "Parliament is not a *Congress* of Ambassadors from different and hostile interests . . . but Parliament is a *deliberative* Assembly of *one* Nation, with *one* Interest, that of the whole; where, not local Purposes, not local Prejudices ought to guide, but the general Good, resulting from the general Reason of the whole. You chuse a Member indeed; but when you have chosen him, he is not a member of Bristol, but he is a member of *Parliament*" (*The Writings and Speeches of Edmund Burke*, vol. 3, ed. W. M. Elofson with J. A. Woods [Oxford: Clarendon Press, 1996], 69).

66. See Hanna Pitkin, *The Concept of Representation* (Berkeley: University of California Press, 1967), chap. 8.

67. See Kant, "Theory and Practice," 77–78; *Metaphysics of Morals*, §46.

68. See Kant, "What Is Enlightenment?" in *Political Writings*, 55. For a historical examination of the concept of public opinion in the eighteenth and nineteenth centuries, with substantial discussions of Kant and Hegel, see Jürgen Habermas, *The Structural Transformation of the Public Sphere: An Inquiry into a Category of Bourgeois Society*, trans. Thomas Burger (Cambridge, Mass.: MIT Press, 1989).

69. Kant, "Theory and Practice," in *Political Writings*, 85.

70. See Fichte, *Science of Ethics*, 258–66 (*SW* 4:245–53); *Vocation of the Scholar*, 156–61, 170–76.

71. Hegel's reservations about freedom of the press are not confined to his mature and allegedly more conservative outlook but go all the way back to the time when he himself was editor of the *Bamberger Zeitung*; see his letter to Niethammer of 22 January 1808 (*L*, 156–57/1:208–10).

72. Foster, *The Political Philosophies of Plato and Hegel*, 178–79.

73. Once again, the *locus classicus* is Popper, *The Open Society and its Enemies*, II, 62–71.

74. See Errol E. Harris, "Hegel's Theory of Sovereignty, International Relations, and War," in *Hegel's Social and Political Thought*, ed. D. Verene (Atlantic Highlands, N.J.: Humanities Press, 1980), 146; also Smith, *Hegel's Critique of Liberalism*, 160.

75. Kant, *Critique of Judgment*, trans. W. Pluhar (Indianapolis: Hackett, 1987), §28.

76. See also *HHS*, 171/275.

77. See Avineri, *Hegel's Theory of the Modern State,* 205–6; Harris, "Hegel's Theory of Sovereignty, International Relations, and War," 147.

78. Kojève attributes to Hegel the view that there will be no more wars at the end of history; see *Introduction to the Reading of Hegel,* 158–9n.6. Smith, *Hegel's Critique of Liberalism,* 164, follows Kojève in attributing to Hegel the notion of an end of history in which humanity is homogenized and occasions for large-scale conflict are removed, but he recognizes that this notion is in tension with what Hegel says about the continuing need for war.

79. Adriaan Peperzak raises this point, accusing Hegel of a "logical mistake" in his view of international relations, in "Hegel Contra Hegel in His Philosophy of Right: The Contradictions of International Politics," *Journal of the History of Philosophy* 32 (1994), 257–63.

80. Kant, "Theory and Practice," 90; "Perpetual Peace," 113.

81. For Kant's view of the relationship between morality and politics, see "Perpetual Peace," 116–25.

82. Kant, "Perpetual Peace," 96.

83. See also *IPH,* 92–98/133–41.

84. See Kojève, *Introduction to the Reading of Hegel.*

85. See Fukuyama's original article, "The End of History?" *The National Interest* (Summer 1989): 3–18, later expanded into a book, *The End of History and the Last Man* (New York: Free Press, 1992).

86. Kojève sometimes adopts such a pragmatic and historicist view of the rationality of history; see what he says about the "method of historical verification" in *On Tyranny,* 152–76, especially 167–68. Similarly, Smith argues that "presumably the only way we have of knowing whether a social institution or belief is fully in accord with reason is its ability to adapt and survive over time," though he also tries to distinguish this view from a doctrine of *Machtpolitik* (*Hegel's Critique of Liberalism,* 225). Finally, Fukuyama offers an example of this way of viewing the end of history in *The End of History and the Last Man,* 136–37. Though his original article "The End of History?" largely reflects the empirical and historicist understanding of the end of history described here, in the book-sequel he no longer seems to subscribe to it entirely (see 137–39).

87. Nietzsche, "The Advantages and Disadvantages of History for Life," 105, 114.

88. See the denials by Gans, Weisse, and Daub that Hegel's philosophy represents a closed system which forecloses the possibility of future discoveries and developments (*L,* 522–23, 539–41).

89. Plant makes a similar point in *Hegel,* 236–37, 239–40.

EPILOGUE

1. See Charles Larmore, *Patterns of Morality* (Cambridge: Cambridge University Press, 1987), 91–107.

2. See Oakeshott, *On Human Conduct,* 256–63. While Oakeshott's reconstruction of the argument of the *Philosophy of Right* here is extremely interesting and serves as a good corrective to excessively communitarian and teleological readings of Hegel, it is ulti-

mately too formalistic and reduces Hegel's argument to the dimensions of Oakeshott's nonpurposive conception of civil association.

3. This quote is from Oakeshott's *Morality and Politics in Modern Europe,* 85, though Oakeshott speaks of the historic disposition to individuality in a number of places, notably, in the essays "On Being Conservative" and "The Masses in Representative Democracy" (both published in *Rationalism in Politics*), and in the third essay of *On Human Conduct.*

4. Oakeshott, *Morality and Politics in Modern Europe,* 83–85. Compare Rawls, "Justice as Fairness: Political Not Metaphysical," *Philosophy and Public Affairs* 14 (1985): 223–51.

5. Again, see Rawls's article, "Justice as Fairness: Political Not Metaphysical"; also *Political Liberalism* (New York: Columbia University Press, 1993). For Rorty, see "The Priority of Democracy to Philosophy," in *The Virginia Statute for Religious Freedom,* ed. Merrill Peterson and Robert Vaughan (Cambridge: Cambridge University Press, 1988); also *Contingency, Irony, and Solidarity* (Cambridge: Cambridge University Press, 1989). In the latter book, Rorty invokes Oakeshott's notion of civil association to support his postmodern version of liberalism, characterizing it as "a society conceived as a band of eccentrics collaborating for purposes of mutual protection rather than as a band of fellow spirits united by a common goal" (59).

6. This seems to be the view that Wood takes in *Hegel's Ethical Thought,* 256–60.

Index